I0125865

Equality for Women

Equality

for

Women

Where Do We Stand on Millennium Development Goal 3?

Mayra Buvinić
Andrew R. Morrison
A. Waafas Ofosu-Amaah
and Mirja Sjöblom
Editors

© 2008 The International Bank for Reconstruction and Development / The World Bank
1818 H Street NW
Washington DC 20433
Telephone: 202-473-1000
Internet: www.worldbank.org
E-mail: feedback@worldbank.org

All rights reserved

1 2 3 4 5 11 10 09 08

This volume is a product of the staff of the International Bank for Reconstruction and Development / The World Bank. The findings, interpretations, and conclusions expressed in this volume do not necessarily reflect the views of the Executive Directors of The World Bank or the governments they represent.

The World Bank does not guarantee the accuracy of the data included in this work. The boundaries, colors, denominations, and other information shown on any map in this work do not imply any judgement on the part of The World Bank concerning the legal status of any territory or the endorsement or acceptance of such boundaries.

Rights and Permissions

The material in this publication is copyrighted. Copying and/or transmitting portions or all of this work without permission may be a violation of applicable law. The International Bank for Reconstruction and Development / The World Bank encourages dissemination of its work and will normally grant permission to reproduce portions of the work promptly.

For permission to photocopy or reprint any part of this work, please send a request with complete information to the Copyright Clearance Center Inc., 222 Rosewood Drive, Danvers, MA 01923, USA; telephone: 978-750-8400; fax: 978-750-4470; Internet: www.copyright.com.

All other queries on rights and licenses, including subsidiary rights, should be addressed to the Office of the Publisher, The World Bank, 1818 H Street NW, Washington, DC 20433, USA; fax: 202-522-2422; e-mail: pubrights@worldbank.org.

ISBN: 978-0-8213-7446-7
eISBN: 978-0-8213-7447-4
DOI: 10.1596/978-0-8213-7446-7

Library of Congress Cataloging-in-Publication Data

Equality for women : where do we stand on millennium development goal 3? / editors, Mayra Buvinić ... [et al.].
    p. cm.
 Includes bibliographical references and index.
 ISBN 978-0-8213-7446-7—ISBN 978-0-8213-7447-4 (electronic)
 1. Women's rights. 2. Sex discrimination against women. 3. Equality. I. Buvinić, Mayra.

HQ1237.E68 2008
323.3'4091724—dc22

2008021327

Cover image by Quang Minh Nguyen, untitled.
Cover design: Naylor Design.

Contents

Boxes

Figures

Tables

Acknowledgments

Many people deserve recognition for taking part in the production of this book.

The genesis of the volume was the February 2006 High-Level Consultation "Promoting the Gender Equality Millennium Development Goal: The Implementation Challenge." We would like to acknowledge the support for this event from the government of Norway, the government of the United Kingdom, the Organisation for Economic Co-operation and Development Development Assistance Committee (DAC) Network on Gender Equality, and UN system colleagues (including United Nations Development Fund for Women, the UN Division for the Advancement of Women, and the UN Millennium Project). We acknowledge the dedication of the task team for the consultation, consisting of staff from the Gender and Development Group at the World Bank, who worked tirelessly on the consultation and its follow-up.

We are deeply grateful to the chapter authors for their intellectual contributions and for sharing our commitment to gender equality. We are thankful to Blanca Moreno-Dodson and Maria-Beatriz Orlando, who reviewed each chapter and provided thoughtful comments and suggestions that greatly enhanced the overall quality of this publication. Shwetlena Sabarwal deserves special thanks for help beyond the call of duty in revising the volume and for providing constructive comments and support. We also express our gratitude to Dorthea Damkjær and Patti O'Neill of the OECD-DAC Network on Gender Equality for providing support to the editors. We are most appreciative of the help from the World Bank Office of the Publisher (Denise Bergeron, Stephen McGroarty, and Dina Towbin) who supported us throughout the production process and contributed to successfully turning the manuscript into a book. The government of Norway funded this project through the Norwegian Trust Fund for Gender Mainstreaming (GENFUND). Without their generous support this book would not have seen the light of day.

Contributors

Chandrika Bahadur, UN Millennium Project
Mayra Buvinić, Gender and Development, World Bank
Maitreyi Bordia Das, South Asia Sustainable Development, World Bank
Diane Elson, Department of Sociology, Essex University, U.K.
Caren Grown, Department of Economics, American University, Washington, DC
Geeta Rao Gupta, International Center for Research on Women (ICRW)
Jessie Handbury, UN Millennium Project
Rekha Mehra, ICRW
Andrew R. Morrison, Gender and Development, World Bank
Shwetlena Sabarwal, Gender and Development, World Bank
Miguel Székely, Undersecretary for Middle Education, Ministry of Public Education, Mexico
Mirja Sjöblom, Development Economic Research Group, World Bank
P. Zafiris Tzannatos, World Bank Institute, Human Development, World Bank

Foreword

There is compelling evidence of the importance of gender equality for poverty reduction and sustainable growth. So it should come as no surprise that most development actors—international agencies, bilateral donors, and most developing countries—have an official policy for promoting gender equality. Millennium Development Goal 3 (MDG3) on gender equality and women's empowerment is our shared global commitment.

With only seven years remaining until the end date for the MDGs, it is an opportune time to take stock of where the world stands in terms of progress toward gender equality. This volume documents trends both on the official MDG3 indicators and on an expanded set of indicators that provide a more complete measure of gender equality—especially in the area of women's economic empowerment. The message that emerges is both hopeful and sobering: progress toward equality in capabilities (for example, education) has been considerable, but progress toward equality of opportunities for women's economic livelihoods leaves much to be desired.

Beyond tracking trends toward gender equality, the volume reviews different measures of gender equality and estimates the financial resources required to achieve this objective. While necessarily imprecise, such estimates can provide a rough guide as to whether the level of effort devoted by international donors and developing countries is adequate in the area of women's economic empowerment.

Equality for Women also makes clear that adequate funding is necessary, but not sufficient: policies must also be appropriate, and execution of these policies must be reasonably efficient—both at the national level and within international agencies charged with supporting national governments. Only when these three elements—funding, policy, and execution—are aligned will progress toward gender equality be rapid.

The collaboration between the World Bank and the Development Assistance Committee of the Organisation for Economic Co-operation and Development (OECD/DAC) on this subject began in 2006, when we jointly cosponsored, with the governments of Norway and the United Kingdom and UN-system colleagues, a high-level consultation on the implementation challenges facing MDG3. Awareness at this consultation that the Bank and its partners could do significantly more to promote gender equality resulted in the Bank's announced commitment to produce a gender action plan in 100 days.[1] Our collaboration deepened during the plan's preparation. The OECD/DAC Network on Gender Equality provided a venue for useful deliberations on successive drafts, and we have continued our joint efforts in the first phases of the plan's implementation.

The World Bank and the OECD/DAC are pleased to publish this volume as a contribution to the debate on how to most effectively promote gender equality, poverty reduction, and growth. We are grateful to the government of Norway for their generous support of this volume and the high-level consultation.

Danny Leipziger	Eckhard Deutscher
Vice President	Chairperson
Poverty Reduction and Economic	Development Assistance
Management	Committee
World Bank	OECD

---

[1] World Bank and International Finance Corporation, September 2006, "Gender Equality as Smart Economics: A World Bank Group Gender Action Plan," World Bank, Washington, DC.

Abbreviations

AfDB	African Development Bank
ADB	Asian Development Bank
ASFR	age-specific fertility rate
CCT	conditional cash transfer
DAC	Development Assistance Committee
DHS	Demographic and Health Survey
EAP	East Asia and Pacific
ECA	Europe and Central Asia
GAP	Gender Action Plan
GDI	Gender-related Development Index
GDP	gross domestic product
GE	gender equality
GEM	Gender Empowerment Measure
GER	gross enrollment rate
GMR	*Global Monitoring Report*
GNP	gross national product
GPI	gender parity index
HDI	Human Development Index
HIV/AIDS	human immunodeficiency virus/acquired immune deficiency syndrome
ICOR	incremental capital ouput ratio
IDB	Inter-American Development Bank
ILO	International Labour Organization
ISCED	International Standard Classification of Education
ISCO	International Standard Classification of Occupations
ISIC	International Standard Industrial Classification
IT	information technology
LAC	Latin America and the Caribbean
MDG	Millennium Development Goal
MDG3	Millennium Development Goal Number 3
MENA	Middle East and North Africa
NER	net enrollment rate

NGO	nongovernmental organization
NTGE	nontargeted gender equality
ODA	official development assistance
OECD	Organisation for Economic Co-operation and Development
SAR	South Asia Region
SIGE	Standardized Index of Gender Equality
SSA	Sub-Saharan Africa
UAE	United Arab Emirates
UIS	UNESCO Institute of Statistics
UN	United Nations
UNDP	United Nations Development Programme
UNESCO	United Nations Educational, Scientific and Cultural Organization
UNIFEM	United Nations Development Fund for Women
UNRISD	United Nations Research Institute for Social Development

All dollar amounts are U.S. dollars.

1

Introduction, Overview, and Future Policy Agenda

Mayra Buvinić and Andrew R. Morrison

The international community, upon signing the Millennium Declaration in 2000, committed itself to eight development goals with time-bound targets and measurable indicators. This definition of goals raised the bar for measuring countries' performance on ambitious development objectives, including goal 3 to "promote gender equality and empower women."

The target for goal 3 was defined as "eliminate gender disparity in primary and secondary education, preferably by 2005, and at all levels of education no later than 2015." This target was operationalized as the ratio of girls' to boys' enrollment in primary, secondary, and tertiary education. Three other indicators were added to Millennium Development Goal 3 (MDG3): the ratio of literate females to males among 15- to 25-year-olds, the share of women in wage employment in the nonagricultural sector, and the proportion of seats held by women in national parliaments.

This definition of gender equality and women's empowerment has been criticized as overly narrow. Some even felt that gender-equality issues lost ground with the Millennium Declaration—that the declaration displaced the importance given to gender equality for development at the Beijing UN World Women's Conference (1995) with a narrower definition of gender equality in the formulation of its goals.

The inclusion of MDG3 in the Millennium Declaration, however, has spurred useful national and international efforts to improve measurement of gender equality and women's empowerment and, as logical follow up, to identify what is needed to speed countries' progress toward MDG3. The work on metrics has expanded the number of indicators used to assess MDG3 and measure countries' performance (UNDP 2005; World Bank 2007a). The work on what it takes to implement MDG3 has focused on reviewing donor agencies' and client countries' experience with mainstreaming gender issues and on quantifying the resources needed to scale up MDG3 implementation at the country level.

This volume brings together these efforts and updates them. It assesses countries' progress at the midpoint between the Millennium Declaration and 2015—the end date for attaining the goals—using an expanded set of indicators that better capture gender equality and women's empowerment.

To set the stage for this midpoint review of progress toward MDG3, this chapter first summarizes the volume's main messages. The book also discusses various implementation constraints to achieving MDG3 as well as what is required in terms of financing and changes in policies to achieve MDG3 by 2015. Chapter 2 takes stock of the world's progress to date in achieving MDG3 using the expanded set of indicators. It charts countries' progress over time and, where possible, benchmarks country performance against regional trends. Chapter 3 reviews methodological issues with available indicators and composite indexes of gender equality and chapter 4 provides an in-depth analysis of how to measure gender equality in labor markets—a critical indicator for MDG3, especially for middle-income countries. Chapter 5 estimates, for the first time, the minimum financial resources required to achieve MDG3 by identifying the costs of interventions aimed at promoting gender equality and women's empowerment across sectors. To emphasize that adequate funding is a necessary but not sufficient precondition for achieving MDG3, chapter 6 turns the focus to institutional and implementation-related impediments to achieving MDG3, drawing on several countries in South Asia. Chapter 7 underscores how cultural norms and traditions shape behavior and stand in the way of attaining gender equality in Mexico. The final chapter focuses on the main tool international agencies and national governments have used to promote gender equality since the World UN Women's Conference in Beijing in 1995—*gender mainstreaming*. Chapter 8 reviews progress in gender mainstreaming and highlights challenges and implementation constraints.

The chapter begins with an overview of the main messages of the volume. Then, the efficiency rationale for MDG3 is presented, including the pathways through which gender equality leads to poverty reduction and economic growth. The following sections give a brief introduction to ways to measure gender equality and women's empowerment along with a summary of the current status of official and new MDG3 indicators. The subsequent section turns to public policy to promote gender equality and discusses laws, institutions, and policies. The final sections provide a summary of the financial requirements to achieve MDG3.

Main Messages

The good news is that 82 of 122 countries for which data are available achieved the official MDG3 target of gender parity in primary and secondary enrollment by 2005. However, 19 countries are seriously off track to meet this target, even by 2015. In general, progress in expanding women's opportunities has lagged behind progress in expanding women's capabilities. Efforts are needed to "level the playing field" for women so they can use their increased capabilities in the economy and society.

Better indicators are needed to measure progress toward gender equality, especially in economic participation. Numerous attempts have been made to develop indexes of gender equality. While indexes are useful in focusing public opinion on an issue and in galvanizing political will to take action, policy is best informed by a set of individual indicators. An analysis of country performance on gender equality and empowerment using an expanded set of indicators reveals few high-performing countries and many low-performing ones.

Gender equality requires changing underlying social norms in addition to observable outcomes. One particularly promising approach to changing social norms is to use financial incentives to change the behavior of families toward girls and women, provided that the incentives are adequate and sustained.

Gender-specific and gender-mainstreaming actions—as well as gender-neutral or nontargeted MDG interventions—are needed to achieve MDG3.[1] Estimates of the costs associated with these interventions show that the largest share of costs is accounted for by gender-neutral interventions, while the lowest share is accounted for by gender-specific interventions. Gender-specific interventions, however, may incur additional political and economic costs associated with targeting interventions to girls and women.

It is premature to judge the success or failure of gender-mainstreaming efforts by international financial institutions or by bilateral donors, largely because mainstreaming has not been fully implemented in country operations. Two important lessons learned from attempts to mainstream gender are (i) gender mainstreaming should be more narrowly targeted to sectors where change is needed and (ii) it is much easier to build a business case for mainstreaming by building a project record than by broad-brush organizational mandates.

Changes in laws, institutions, and policies all matter for scaling up gender-equality objectives. Most of these changes come with a price tag.

Sometimes the funding to implement these changes is available in domestic budgets but is not fully used because of institutional bottlenecks. Many other times, domestic budgets do not cover expenditures for MDG3, even in cases where the changes were included in planned budgets.

Both domestic and donor resources need to be mobilized to finance MDG3 interventions. Given desirable domestic commitment of resources to gender-specific and gender-mainstreaming interventions, the remaining financing gap—estimated at about $13 billion yearly using UN Millennium Project calculations—could be met if donors, private foundations, and other nontraditional sources of funding increased spending on MDG3.

The Efficiency Rationale

Why might gender equality matter? The first possible answer is that gender equality is desirable in and of itself—it has intrinsic value. MDG3 is evidence of the international community's commitment to the intrinsic value of gender equality.

Many would argue that inequalities based solely on one's biological makeup are inherently unfair and unjust. But to delve any further into the issue requires that a distinction be made between inequalities of opportunity and inequalities in outcome. Rawls' version of "fairness" refers to a world in which outcomes may be unequal, but where one does not know whether one will end up with a relatively favorable or unfavorable outcome (Rawls 1971).

Roemer (1993, 2002) has argued that social welfare cannot be maximized if outcomes differ because of individuals' differential circumstances, where circumstances refer to factors that individuals cannot control. Differential outcomes that reflect differential effort or individual choice, however, are consistent with maximization of social welfare.

Clearly, educational gaps or earnings gaps that are ordained at birth for women would not be "fair" in a Rawlsian or Roemerian sense; conversely, wage gaps that reflect only differences in skills and productivity could be labeled a fair outcome.

Beyond any notion of fairness, however, gender inequalities in capabilities and opportunities are inefficient. The World Bank's 2007 Global Monitoring Report (World Bank 2007a), summarizing a large body of research, outlined several pathways by which gender inequalities in rights, resources, and voice lead to increases in poverty and potentially—although the evidence is significantly less strong on this score—to lower growth.[2] One important pathway goes from equality of opportunity through participation in labor, land, financial, and product markets, while the other pathway links equality of opportunity for women to improved children's well-being. Both pathways end in accelerated poverty reduction, increased productivity, and potentially more rapid growth (see figure 1.1).

Women's ability to participate productively in the labor market is constrained in many regions, both by women's lower educational levels relative to men's and by social norms. Wage gaps that do not reflect underlying productivity differentials, in turn, may be a disincentive for women to seek employment and for parents to invest in the education of girls, which would allow them to successfully compete in labor markets in the future. (There is extremely limited empirical evidence to support these disincentive effects; however, see Anderson, King, and Wang [2003].)

As noted in the World Development Report 2008 (World Bank 2007b), land is the most important productive asset for households engaged in

FIGURE 1.1

Women's Earnings, Children's Well-Being, and Aggregate Poverty Reduction and Economic Growth: The Pathways

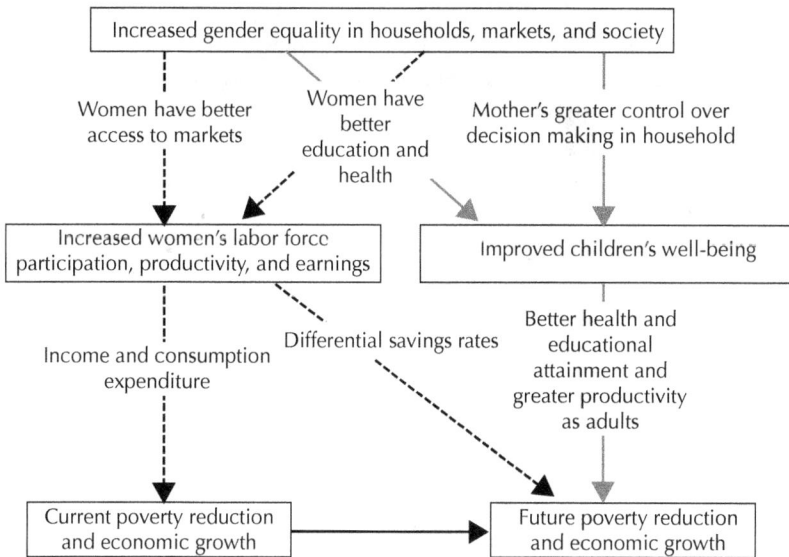

Source: World Bank 2007a, 109.

agricultural production. Yet, the distribution of land ownership is heavily skewed toward men. In a set of Latin American countries, 70–90 percent of titles to farmland are held exclusively by men (Deere and Leon 2003); land holding is similarly skewed toward men in Sub-Saharan Africa (Doss 2005; Udry 1996; Quisumbing, Estudillo, and Otsuka 2004). While land titling programs in some countries and regions are beginning to emphasize joint titling, much work on that issue remains to be done.

Access to credit is an important determinant of productivity and earnings for firms and for the self-employed. Although unexpected, there is little evidence from developing countries that women face differential treatment in financial markets after controlling for observable factors—at least, as measured by higher loan rejection rates or higher interest rates; rather, the limited evidence suggests that women are less likely to seek credit than are men (Baydas, Meyer, and Aguilera-Alfred 1994; Buvinić and Berger 1990; Storey 2004; Ratusi and Swamy 1999).

Women appear to have lower rates of adoption of technological innovations that determine farmers' access to agricultural product markets. Most of the evidence suggests that many of women's barriers to adoption are not related to the characteristics of the technology but originate in other markets relevant to the adoption decision, such as land, labor, credit, and information. For example, Croppenstedt, Demeke, and Meschi (2003) find that female-headed households in Ethiopia have significantly lower endowments of land, and that land size is a significant positive determinant of fertilizer use.

Agricultural extension services also often fail to reach female farmers, in particular, female-headed farming households, even though female farmers often indicate a strong demand for such services (Saito, Mekonnen, and Spurling 1994). Summarizing evidence from six studies in Sub-Saharan Africa in the 1980s, Quisumbing (1994) reported that male-headed households were roughly 30–220 percent more likely to have ever had contact with an extension agent than female-headed households.

The second channel by which gender equality affects poverty and productivity is through children's well-being. Abundant empirical evidence supports the notion that increased control over resources by women leads to better child development outcomes, including educational attainment and nutrition. Thus, contemporaneous, nonmonetary measures of poverty may register improvements as a result of women's increased control over resources—and future monetary and nonmonetary measures of poverty will be affected by the higher human capital and earnings potential of children with better nutrition, health, and educational outcomes.

Early studies in this vein from the 1980s and early 1990s measured women's control over resources using data on individual earnings and asset ownership, but current earnings and asset ownership are clearly endogenous: they both affect and are affected by women's ability to influence household decision making. A second generation of studies attempted to deal with this endogeneity by proxying for control over resources or bargaining power with measures of resources brought to marriage. The argument is that resources brought to marriage are exogenous to decision making after marriage, but this assertion has also been questioned.

Most recently, studies have employed a "natural experiment" approach, examining the effect on intrahousehold resource allocation of receiving old-age pension benefits, conditional cash transfers, and loans from micro-credit programs targeted at women. Pitt and Khandker (1998) find that female borrowing from micro-credit institutions has had a larger impact on children's enrollment in school than does borrowing by males. Rubalcava, Teruel, and Thomas (2004) demonstrate that conditional cash transfers in Mexico received by women increase the share of household budgets spent on education, children's clothing, and meat, while the share of expenditures spent on male clothing, transport, and other types of food declined. In an evaluation of a pension program in South Africa, Duflo (2003) finds that pensions received by grandmothers result in weight gains for young girls in the household, while pensions received by grandfathers have no such effect. Natural experiments or randomized designs offer the strongest evidence on the causal links between women's control over resources and subsequent household decisions about resource allocation (Morrison, Raju, and Sinha 2007).

One particularly important realm of household decision making is fertility choice. To the extent that greater gender equality allows women to exercise more control over their fertility, one would expect better child development outcomes because of lower dependency ratios and standard quantity-quality tradeoffs in children.

Measuring Gender Equality and Women's Empowerment

Gender equality and women's empowerment are not synonymous and, therefore, cannot be tracked using a single indicator. Equality indicators measure women's status relative to men's status and are expressed as ratios, while empowerment indicators measure changes in absolute levels of women's well-being.

Care must be used in interpreting measures of equality because perfect equality (a ratio of one) may indicate equality of deprivation rather than equality of opportunity. The most obvious example is the case of some countries (Haiti and Zimbabwe, for example) that show parity between the sexes in secondary school enrollment—but at very low levels of enrollment for both boys and girls (World Bank 2007a).

Empowerment indicators often are conflated with indicators of gender equality, but should not be. Measures of women's empowerment include indicators that are specific to women and that measure changes in absolute values for women rather than in comparison with men. These indicators include, notably, reproductive health measures and incidence and prevalence data on violence against women. The former are widely available and comparable, while indicators of violence against women have only recently begun to be collected systematically. Comparable violence indicators are available for only a handful of countries (see WHO [2002]). Another class of indicators of women's empowerment includes those that measure women's decision-making power in both private (household) and public (governance) life. Again, these indicators are not widely available.

Perhaps the most important distinction between measures of gender equality is between index approaches and individual indicators.

While an index can be useful for creating a summary statistic that captures media and policy attention, associated problems (such as the choice of weights and methods of aggregation) complicate its interpretation and, therefore, make it less useful for informing policy makers.

The Millennium Declaration defined a set of four associated indicators (as reviewed above), rather than an index, to measure MDG3. These indicators provide important but incomplete measures of achievements (since 1990) in gender equality.

To address the shortcomings of the official MDG3 indicators—and in particular to do a better job of measuring health status and economic empowerment—this volume argues for the use of an "MDG3 plus" approach—using official MDG3 indicators, but supplementing them with additional indicators where feasible and appropriate.[3]

Progress on MDG3 at the Midpoint

Using the MDG3 plus approach, the World Bank (2007a) and Morrison, Sabarwal, and Sjöblom (chapter 2) provide the most up-to-date snapshot on the status of countries' progress at midpoint (2007) in meeting the third Millennium Development Goal.

Progress on the Official MDG3 Target

First, 82 out of 122 countries achieved the official MDG3 midterm target of parity in primary and secondary schooling by 2005.[4] Only one country that did not achieve parity in 2005 is on track to achieve it by 2015. Some 19 countries are off track or unlikely to achieve the target by 2015. Of these 19 countries, 13 are in Sub-Saharan Africa. So unless these countries significantly intensify actions to increase girls' school enrollment, the official MDG3 goal will not be attained.

The substantial gains in enrollment and parity rates in primary and secondary schooling in the years since 1990, even in countries that started with low enrollment levels, show that scaling up concerted policies to increase and equalize enrollment rates between the genders can make a difference (World Bank 2007a).

The official MDG3 indicators concern themselves only with the ratio of girls to boys in enrollment but are silent on the absolute levels of enrollment. This comes with the obvious hazard of attributing "good" performance to countries where there is not much gender disparity in school enrollment even though overall enrollment rates (primary, secondary, or both) are not high. Clearly, policy should be informed not just by gender-equality concerns but also by the overall levels of education attainment.

A first challenge is to scale up educational interventions in the countries that currently are projected not to meet the target for gender equality in primary and secondary schooling. A second challenge is to increase the education level of girls in secondary school in Sub-Saharan Africa and South Asia and the education level of girls and boys in tertiary schooling in all regions, except Europe and Central Asia, where levels are already high. Without rising educational levels, the goal of women's empowerment will be difficult to achieve. And these rising levels need to be realized in excluded groups, especially girls who are doubly disadvantaged by being female and by belonging to racial, ethnic, or other excluded groups (Lewis and Lockheed 2007).

A third challenge is to increase the completion rate of education for all, along with a specific focus on keeping girls in school. The latter objective is particularly a challenge for countries such as Malawi, Mauritania, Oman, and Rwanda, which have very high female-to-male primary enrollment ratios (70 and above), but where fewer than 50 percent of girls complete primary schooling. There are 21 countries in the World Bank data set where this phenomenon is observed (Morrison, Sabarwal, and Sjöblom). These countries need to implement and scale up gender-specific policies to eliminate discriminatory policies and behaviors of teachers in schools as well as to target stipends and other incentives to parents and communities to keep girls in school.

The last challenge addresses the gap in opportunities, which was first underscored by the late Mahbub el Haq in 1995 (UNDP 1995). When comparing indicators of capabilities (education and health) with those of opportunities (employment and political participation), it is clear that progress in expanding women's opportunities in the economy and in society has lagged behind progress in expanding their capabilities. Figure 1.2 shows this uneven progress using the official MDG3 indicators. The share of girls enrolled in primary and secondary schooling has improved substantially since 1990. At the same time, however, the share of women in nonagricultural employment and in parliaments has grown only modestly. Gender-equality policy needs to seek ways to level the playing field for women so they can use their increased capabilities in the economy and in society. Not to do so is not only unfair; it is inefficient.

Progress on the MDG3 Plus Approach

Information on the state of progress is much richer when the official MDG3 indicators are complemented by the additional six indicators described above. The additional indicators recommended in our MDG3 plus approach are: i) primary completion rates disaggregated by gender; ii) under-five mortality rates disaggregated by gender; iii) percentage of reproductive-age women and their partners using modern contraception; iv) percentage of 15- to 19-year old girls who are mothers or pregnant with their first child; v) labor force participation rates for 20- to 24- and 25- to 49-year olds, disaggregated by gender; and vi) average hourly wages, also disaggregated by gender.

The numbers presented in chapter 2 clearly show that no one country or region has achieved gender equality in all the areas covered by this expanded set of indicators. Most countries have varying scores across indicators, showing that progress is sector or area specific.

The comparison of school attendance with labor force participation rates signals the need for targeted investments to adolescent girls to expand their economic opportunities so they will not be left behind in the transition from schooling to the labor market (see Buvinić, Guzmán, and Lloyd [2007]; Morrison, Sabarwal, and Sjöblom [chapter 2]). These policies are especially relevant for regions that have achieved parity or close to parity in school enrollment but exhibit wide gender gaps in labor force participation, such as Latin America and the Caribbean and Europe and Central Asia. Sub-Saharan

FIGURE 1.2
Progress in Official Indicators of Gender Equality and Women's
Empowerment, by Region, 1990–2005

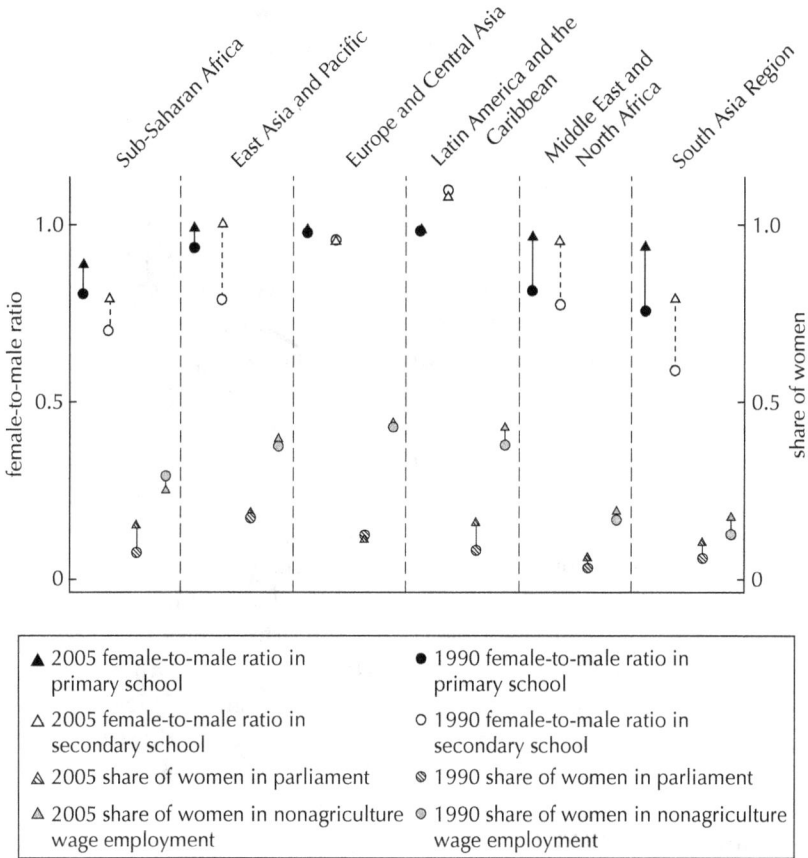

Source: World Bank 2007, 11.

Note: The regional averages are calculated using the earliest value between 1990 and 1995 and the latest value between 2000 and 2005. The averages are weighted by the country population size in 2005.

Africa is the only region for which the data suggest that the emphasis (to date, at least) should be in closing the gender gaps in schooling rather than on promoting labor force participation.

The health indicators single out the comparatively high mortality rates of girls under age 5 in East Asia and Pacific and South Asia, as well as the high adolescent fertility rates in 36 countries, with a majority of those countries being in Sub-Saharan Africa. These data suggest the need to implement policies to deter infanticide and neglect of girl children, in the former instance, and to provide access to reproductive health services to adolescents, in the latter case. Policies to deter infanticide and the neglect of girl infants through prohibition of sex selection technology have not worked well (Das Gupta, 2007). Similarly, the recent use of cash incentives to mothers to influence sex ratios at birth seem to have worked only in the very short term in one program, partly perhaps because payouts were not maintained over time (Holla, Jensen, and Oster 2007). The one intervention that appears to have reduced son preference in rural India was the availability of cable television, suggesting the potential effect of the media in changing norms (Jensen and Oster 2007). There are, however, well-known, cost-effective interventions to prevent teen pregnancies that countries with high teenage pregnancy rates can adopt.

The two added economic indicators—labor force participation data and the ratio of female to male hourly wages—give a more nuanced picture of progress in equality of economic opportunities for women and men. The labor force participation indicator makes the important point that much of women's work in all world regions is in wage employment in agriculture and in self-employment, dimensions that are not captured in the official MDG indicator. Especially useful are the wage data that add information on the quality of women's work in the marketplace. Such countries as Cambodia, Latvia, Macedonia, Mongolia, Panama, and Thailand, with high participation of women in wage employment in the nonagricultural sector, also have relatively high female-to-male wage rates (0.80 or higher). Other countries, however, have high female participation with comparatively low wages for women. Brazil, Mexico, Paraguay, and Tajikistan fall into this latter group and might consider implementing policies to reduce gender wage gaps (see chapter 2).

However, without data on levels, data on gender wage gaps can be misleading. Women in the Middle East and North Africa have higher female relative wages than women in high-income European or East Asian economies, but this is likely an indication of selectivity (mostly women with high returns to market labor work as part of a small female labor force in Middle East and North African countries, and their wages are compared with male wages based on all male workers—those with high and those with low wages) rather than greater gender equality (Tzannatos 2007).

In addition to wage data, indexes of occupational segregation can be used to gauge progress in gender equality in the economy, especially in middle-income countries for which data are more readily available. Again, however, reductions in segregation do not necessarily imply improvement in women's labor market position; the feminization of previously male-dominated jobs can be associated with depressed wages for both genders (Tzannatos 2007).

The set of MDG3 plus indicators is perhaps most usefully applied to assess the performance of individual countries when compared with or benchmarked against a standard. Comparing a suite of indicators for a country with a benchmark identifies areas of policy priority and can also be used to evaluate the progress of countries through the use of scorecards that can garner public attention similar to that attracted by indexes.

Comparatively few countries are high performers and very few countries are repeat high performers in different dimensions of gender equality. The highest performers compared to regional averages across indicators (one standard deviation above the regional average) are Argentina, Lithuania, Maldives, and Tunisia. Many more countries are repeat low performers in one or more dimensions of gender equality. Chad, Guatemala, Niger, and Turkey are low performers (one standard deviation below the regional average) across the range of indicators, even though in Chad, education and employment indicators improved significantly in the last decade (chapter 2).

Country variability in rankings across indicators suggests that progress in gender equality is sector or dimension specific. Correspondingly, policies need to be specific. It cannot be assumed, for instance, that meeting the MDG3 official target of parity in schooling, even along with high levels of schooling, will necessarily translate into gender equality in other dimensions.

The MDG3 plus indicators, however, still fall short in capturing important dimensions of gender equality and women's empowerment for which data are unavailable, including indicators of voice, participation and citizenship, and security. At the national level, however, some countries have customized the official MDG3 indicators to add country-specific ones to sharpen the government's focus on specific gender inequalities. One example is Cambodia, which added a new target to reduce all forms of violence against women and children, and expanded the list of indicators to include, for instance, literacy rates for 25- to 44-year-olds, to cover women in prime childbearing and working ages (Phavi and Urashima 2006). Similarly, the Dominican Republic expanded its official measures to include indicators of reproductive and sexual health, property rights, and gender-based violence, as well as of institutional performance (Sikoska 2006).

Public Policy to Promote Gender Equality

Székely (chapter 7) singles out the need to change cultural norms, traditions, and day-to-day practices, normally regarded as "private matters," as a main challenge to the implementation of MDG3.[5] Consensus on the desirability of achieving MDG3 is often hampered by mores, traditions, and perceptions of zero-sum games (in public and private life). As result, he makes the point that gender equality policy needs to focus not only on changing observed outcomes but also on changing underlying laws, mechanisms, and cultural patterns. Policy that only focuses on outcomes, he argues, "will swim against the tide," and will not be efficient in addressing gender disparities.

The policy framework for promoting gender equality, therefore, calls for changes in laws that define the rules of the game for society, in the behavior of social institutions (including, of great importance, the family) that embody and transmit norms and traditions, and in policies and programs that affect outcomes. Such changes define the scope for government action, as well as underscore the complexity of the task. These "private matters" also help to explain the overall slow progress made to date.

Laws

There is significant scope for changing laws to promote and protect women's rights, deter and punish transgression of rights, and level the playing field of opportunities for women and men. Considerable work has been done in this area, both nationally and internationally. Examples of legislation range from international conventions on women's rights (Committee on the Elimination of Discrimination against Women), to regional conventions to eliminate violence against women (Belem do Para Convention for Latin American and the Caribbean), to national legislation on equal rights (on ownership of land, property, labor, and so forth), to antidiscrimination legislation, and to reform of regulatory frameworks for financial transactions, business ownership, and the like.

Lessons learned from the experience with legal reform include, first, the importance of enforcement mechanisms to the success of legislation in reducing gender inequalities. Without enforcement, gender-equality legislation remains only a statement of good intentions. Second is the observation that while equality legislation per se may make little difference, the existence of laws condoning inequality acts to perpetuate inequality. Third, changes in laws are more often than not the reflection, rather than the cause, of social change (World Bank 2007a). See box 1.1 for a discussion of legal reforms to promote gender equality.

Box 1.1
Legal Reforms to Promote Gender Equality

Legal frameworks for women's status and rights are derived from several sources: international laws, constitutional and statutory provisions, and customary law. Many legal frameworks embody human rights principles of equality and nondiscrimination, but they also reflect gendered systems and social norms that often define females' rights only through family relationships. This is true of customary laws that govern domestic relations, such as marriage, divorce, and custody (Chirayath, Sage, and Woolcock 2005). These laws perceive women as individuals to be protected in the private sphere in their roles as wives, mothers, daughters, or sisters. Similar protective attitudes spill over to the public sphere as well.

One legal provision with important consequences for women's rights and opportunities is the legal age of marriage. Early marriage can lead to early pregnancy or school dropout, stifling girls' aspirations for secondary or higher education. International human rights standards encourage countries to establish a minimum legal age of 18 for marriage for both sexes.[a] In several countries, however, the legal age of marriage is determined by customary provisions, family codes, or personal status laws. Some of these laws diverge from international norms because they sanction a lower legal age for girls than for boys. In a landmark reform resulting from the work of a Royal Commission, the Moroccan Personal Status Code (*moudawana*) was revised to raise the legal age of marriage for girls to 18 years old from 15 (World Bank 2005b).

Legal systems regulating land ownership can either enable or impede women's rights of access to land. In many developing societies, customary laws determine women's individual rights to own or inherit property, bring property into marriage, have joint title, or take property out of marriage upon dissolution (World Bank 2005a). Customary norms also determine which land rights a woman, as opposed to a man, may freely exercise. For example, while customary norms may grant women a right to cultivate communal land, only their male relatives have the right to dispose of the land (Kevane and Gray 1999). Statutory provisions can be enacted to override customary provisions with unequal outcomes. However, reforms often must overcome deeply rooted cultural norms and attitudes toward land and incorporate detailed regulations to ensure that women can officially register title to that land, for example, through the provision of space on land deeds to record multiple names (Lastarria-Cornheil 2003). Cambodia and the Lao People's Democratic Republic have enacted progressive legislative and regulatory reforms to mandate and facilitate joint land titling.

(continued)

Box 1.1 (*continued*)

A third set of reforms relates to labor laws and regulations. Well-intentioned laws to protect women from dangerous jobs or long hours can have pernicious effects on the demand for female labor. So, too, can maternity leave and child care; legal provisions that prohibit women from working in certain occupations, industries, or at night; and laws with different retirement ages for men and women (World Bank 2006). In Jordan, for example, labor code provisions for long maternity leaves and firm-provided child care seem to have limited female employment in export-processing zones (Razzaz 2007).

Legal reforms are important mechanisms for enforcing constitutional guarantees of gender equality. They can provide legally binding provisions contravening discriminatory practices that undermine women's rights in the name of customary or religious norms. Reforms can provide the enabling legal environment to meet MDG commitments to promote gender equality. Legal reforms to promote women's rights do not occur easily, though; such reforms often challenge established norms and therefore face strong resistance. Even when enacted, they are often plagued by significant enforcement gaps in many countries. Enforcement weaknesses can be addressed by linking legal reform with leadership at high levels, public awareness campaigns, strong institutions, and financial resources for implementation. This is the approach adopted by Vietnam in support of new gender equity legislation, where a public education and dissemination program was put in place during the 2003–07 seminars and workshops on gender equality and women's rights organized and funded by different government agencies (UN 2005a).

Source: Authors' compilation.

a. Article 1 of the Convention on the Rights of the Child and Article 16, para 2 of the Convention on the Elimination of All Forms of Discrimination against Women.

Institutions

Székely in chapter 7 cogently expresses a widely shared view of the important role of social institutions, especially the family, in perpetuating gender inequalities. Equally, Das in chapter 6 underscores the role of institutional constraints affecting demand and the ability to use or spend budgets that have been allocated to gender-equality interventions. The experience of South Asia, Das argues, stresses the importance of women's political voice (through self-help groups, solidarity groups, and elected members in local government) in increasing demand for government investments in gender equality and government accountability.

Conditional cash transfer programs, such as Oportunidades in Mexico (see chapter 7), are perhaps one of the most interesting recent developments in demand-side programs to promote better educational and health outcomes. The results have been impressive. Two features, in particular, of these programs are promising for promoting gender equality. First, these programs function by using financial incentives to change the behavior of families toward their (girl) children—and behavioral change often precedes and determines attitudinal or cultural change. These programs, therefore, should be especially well-suited for promoting cultural changes regarding gender equality, provided that program incentives are adequate and sustained. Second, the evidence to date shows that the effects of these programs on outcomes seem to be larger for groups that had the lowest probability of enrollment at baseline, including females when compared with males, suggesting that conditional cash transfers may be efficient tools to reduce inequality of opportunities between the genders (Schady 2007).

More generally, the use of financial incentives to bring about changes in the behavior of organizations and institutions, both formal and informal, is comparatively new in the promotion of gender equality. The government of Chile has an innovative program of good governance and public sector management, wherein public sector staff are rewarded with yearly bonuses for achieving government program targets (Raczynski 2007). Mainstreaming gender-equality concerns into government programs is one of these targets (see chapter 8 on gender mainstreaming). Results are not yet in, but it should prove interesting to see if concrete incentives, rather than broad mandates without "teeth," have an effect on gender-equality programming.

Despite general agreement on the importance of institutions in perpetuating gender inequalities, little rigorous study of institutional constraints has been undertaken, partly because of the difficulty in measuring such constraints. A recent advancement is an institutional database set up by the Development Assistance Committee (DAC) of the Organisation for Economic Co-operation and Development (OECD), which provides social institution indicators grouped into four categories—family code, physical integrity, civil liberties, and ownership rights—for 161 countries (Jütting and Morrisson 2005).

Policies

While institutions are critical, well-conceived policies also matter, both universal policies and policies designed specifically to address gender disparities. The overall success in raising girls' primary school enrollment rates in developing countries was the result of concerted will and resources to ensure education for all, rather than education for girls only. In this case, a universal program was able to both increase the level of enrollment for girls and reduce the gender gap in enrollment (World Bank 2007a). Similarly, implementation of a national scholarship program for secondary schools led to Bangladesh's success in increasing female secondary school enrollments (Das in chapter 6).

However, as this review has shown, additional or incremental targeted efforts are often needed to close gender gaps in capabilities and level the playing field of opportunities for girls and women. Increasing girls' completion rates in primary schooling in countries with good levels of girls' enrollment in school, helping ease the transition between schooling and work for adolescent girls, and expanding women's access to formal financial services, among others, all require policies specifically designed to address gender disparities by focusing on girls and women. Targeting girls and women does not necessarily mean separate programming but it does mean additional or incremental resources going to girls or women only, along with associated political and economic costs.

One example is microfinance programs that have reduced many of the costs associated with targeting by self-targeting financial services to poor women. By offering very small loans with low transaction costs to the borrower (through increased access to loan services and immediacy of loan disbursement), flexible repayments, and minimal and flexible collateral requirements, these programs have been successful in reaching women clients without targeting services to them (Lycette and White 1989). It is a well-established fact that women are the majority of clients of microfinance programs. Similarly, public works programs have successfully reached poor women when they have offered very low wages, allowed flexible working hours, reduced transportation costs, and allowed women to bring their children to work (Buvinić 1996).

However, self-targeting is not always possible or desirable. Gender-specific and gender-mainstreaming actions, as well as gender-neutral or nontargeted MDG interventions, are also needed to achieve MDG3. (The next section, based on chapter 5, quantifies unit costs for these different interventions.)

The review of MDG3 indicators in this book also shows that gender equality is multidimensional and that progress in equality in one area (education) does not automatically translate into progress in other areas (labor force participation). A set of interventions in different sectors is required;

but this is easier said than done. Ambitious objectives and complex designs often result in inaction or failure. Gupta and Mehra (chapter 8) attribute the perceived failure of mainstreaming gender in development agencies to objectives too ambitiously defined. They rightly argue that the scope of gender mainstreaming should be more narrowly defined and should give priority to building up a mainstreaming record through operations rather than organizational directives. Gupta and Mehra suggest that it is premature to pass judgment on the success or failure of gender mainstreaming because it has not been fully implemented in country-level operations— where it matters most. They make the case for both selectivity in goals and dedicated financial resources for mainstreaming.

Financing for Gender Equality

Substantial administrative, economic, and political costs can be associated with initiatives to promote gender equality. Unfortunately, there are no reliable estimates for these costs. While gender-mainstreaming interventions may, in fact, entail only minor change in the design of projects, identifying this change will often require significant investments (chapter 8).

Grown et al. (chapter 5) and Ebbeler (2007) estimate costs of actions to achieve MDG3 in selected countries, allowing for costs for gender-specific actions, gender-mainstreaming interventions, and gender-neutral or non-targeted MDG interventions. Their efforts expand on a first costing attempt made by the Millennium Project and follow the Millennium Project's methodology of basing costing on needs assessments (Grown, Gupta, and Pande 2005). Chapter 5 estimates costs for five countries. Using the same method, Ebbeler goes beyond estimates and obtains planned expenditures for 10 countries and planned as well as actual expenditures for 3 countries.

Method

At the outset, the difficulty of calculating the financial costs of reducing gender inequality must be underscored because this inequality is both multidimensional and multisectoral. In addition, an inherent problem underlies any assessment of the resources associated with actions that are mainstreamed—the more fully gender issues are mainstreamed into a program or project, the more financial resources are mingled and the more difficult it is to track budget resources assigned specifically to gender issues.

Each of the different approaches for costing the MDGs has its own set of advantages and limitations. (In chapter 5, box 5.2 briefly reviews these approaches.) The UN Millennium Project developed a list of interventions for each MDG sector (education, health, rural development, urban development and slum upgrading, water and sanitation, and energy) and estimated the per unit capital and recurrent costs of implementing them. The proportion of the cost of each intervention that could be attributed to promoting gender equality was identified and added across interventions to obtain total costs attributable to promoting gender equality.

Interventions that promoted gender equality were divided into MDG3-specific interventions and gender-mainstreaming interventions. In practice, gender-specific interventions were defined as interventions that fell outside the various MDG sectors and were implemented by a Ministry of Women's Affairs or a non-MDG sector ministry (for instance, labor). Examples of these interventions include funds: to increase telephone support lines for victims of domestic violence in Niger; to alleviate the burdens of female-headed households in Ethiopia; to set a minimum age of marriage in Mauritania; and to provide credit to encourage women's off-farm work in the Republic of Yemen. Interventions directed at helping to achieve gender equality and empower women in all other MDG sectors and that were implemented by an MDG sector ministry were defined as gender-mainstreaming interventions. Examples include increases in health budget allocations for free prenatal care in Tajikistan, as well as resources to educate men about safe motherhood in Kenya through the Health Ministry, increase land access for women in Senegal through the Ministry of Agriculture, and improve female literacy rates in Ethiopia through the Education Ministry. Annex 1A to this chapter provides a list of gender-specific and gender-mainstreaming interventions by country and their estimated total and per capita annual costs (Ebbeler 2007).

This usage of gender-equality interventions is different from the generally accepted definition in which "gender-specific" refers to a stand-alone intervention and "gender-mainstreamed" to an action integrated into a larger project, independent of the nature of the executing agency. In addition, the costs of other MDG interventions that were neither gender specific nor gender mainstreamed but could indirectly promote gender equality, such as monies for new wells or rural roads, were also estimated (these are termed "gender neutral").

Estimates

Table 1.1 presents projected average annual per capita financial requirements to achieve gender equality by 2015 (that is, over the 2006–15 period)

TABLE 1.1
**Projected Average Annual per Capita Financial Requirements to Achieve Gender Equality, 2006–15
(2007 $)**

Country	Gender-specific interventions ($)	Gender-mainstreaming interventions ($)	Gender-neutral interventions ($)	Total cost of promoting gender equality[a] ($)	Total MDG costs ($)	Specific and mainstream costs as % of total MDG costs	Total gender costs as % of total MDG costs
Dominican Republic	2.09	7.52	120.31	129.92	296.21	3.24	43.86
Ethiopia[b]	0.13	0.26	35.24	35.63	115.07	0.34	30.96
Gabon	6.38	14.90	71.48	92.76	173.62	12.26	53.43
Kenya	4.64	4.06	41.08	49.78	141.95	6.13	35.07
Mauritania	2.38	9.78	38.61	50.77	114.21	10.65	44.45
Niger	2.24	3.36	43.19	48.80	105.44	5.31	46.28
Senegal	0	2.87	8.60	11.47	83.25	3.45	13.78
Tajikistan[c]	1.50	43.38	61.27	106.15	170.49	26.33	62.26
Togo	2.70	7.05	85.52	95.27	204.40	4.77	46.61
Yemen, Rep. of	0.06	5.82	79.73	85.61	195.94	3.00	43.69

Source: Ebbeler 2007; UN 2005b.

a. All costs are based on average projected costs for 2006–15 provided by individual country needs assessments listed, and per capita costs are based on the UN 2004 population projections.

b. The mainstream interventions for Ethiopia are underreported for the health sector (because the MDG needs assessment results are not disaggregated for goals 4 and 5 on child and maternal health).

c. The mainstreaming interventions for Tajikistan are overreported to the extent that they include interventions to strengthen the primary health-care system under the costs for goals 4 and 5.

for 10 countries that were involved in the UN Millennium planning exercise and provided the data on planned expenditures (Ebbeler 2007).

The variation in costs between individual countries may be partly a function of underestimating or overestimating costs because of reduced capacity to account for and disaggregate costs by gender. Nevertheless, excluding outlier values, overall planned costs for gender-specific and gender-mainstreaming interventions vary annually between $5.6 and $21 per capita (in 2007 US dollars) and between 3 percent and 12.3 percent of total MDG costs. When the share of MDG interventions indirectly benefiting women is added, annual costs increase to between $36 and $106 per capita and to between 31 percent and 53.4 percent of all MDG costs.

Using the same method, estimates for five countries (Bangladesh, Cambodia, Ghana, Tanzania, and Uganda) in chapter 5 show roughly comparable percentages of all MDG costs associated with increased gender equality. At the same time, however, the authors of that chapter attribute a larger share of costs to gender-specific and gender-mainstreaming interventions (presumably because the desk exercise included a larger range of possible interventions) and a smaller share to gender-neutral interventions. Grown et al. found that the share of MDG interventions directly benefiting women varied between 23 percent and 30 percent of all MDG costs, and when interventions indirectly benefiting women were added, the share of all gender costs was between 35 percent and 52 percent of all MDG costs (and between $37 and $57 per capita per year).

The authors of chapter 5 also estimated the additional financing low-income countries would need to implement gender-specific and gender-mainstreaming interventions for 2006–15, based on the Millennium Project method for estimating MDG financing needs. For 2006, this value varied between $8.6 billion (assuming that governments commit domestic resources to gender-equality interventions in the same proportion as their contribution to overall MDG interventions) and $29.7 billion (if no domestic resources are used to finance these interventions). For 2015, these values rise to $23.8 billion and $83.2 billion.

These costing exercises make the obvious but often overlooked point that achieving MDG3 costs money. The exercises also result in a useful listing of planned gender-specific and gender-mainstreaming interventions with comparative unit costs and show that the portion of total MDG costs devoted to gender equality is comparatively small. Costs increase to between 31 percent and 53 percent of all MDG costs when interventions indirectly benefiting women are added. These interventions constitute the largest component of the MDG gender costs and highlight the critical importance of cross-sector investments to achieve gender-equality goals.

In addition to the national cost estimates based on planned expenditures, Ebbeler (2007) collects information for three countries (the Dominican Republic, Kenya, and the Republic of Yemen) on actual expenditures for gender interventions (see table 1.2). Despite progress in incorporating gender needs into the budget process in these countries, only a small proportion of planned expenditures for gender-specific action had translated into actual identified disbursements (on average, less than 15 percent). This low proportion is partly the result of the inability of national systems to disaggregate budget resources by gender. It is also the result of countries' slow progress in implementing the gender-equality agenda. Countries are making progress, but in small, incremental steps; the challenge of MDG3 is one of intensifying and scaling up gender-equality actions.

Ebbeler (2007) also collects information on official development assistance (ODA) received from international donors to promote gender equality (both gender-specific and gender-mainstreaming interventions). For the three countries (Dominican Republic, Kenya, and the Republic of Yemen) analyzed in detail (see table 1.3), the 2001–05 period saw an increase in the absolute amount of funding but no linear year-by-year trend in percentage devoted to gender equality—although the percentage of gross disbursements spent on gender-specific and gender-mainstreaming interventions was higher in 2005 than in 2001 for all three countries.

TABLE 1.2

Planned per Capita MDG Expenditures for Gender Interventions Versus Actual Reported National Budget Allocations Disaggregated by Gender, FY2006

($)

Country	Gender specific (Women's Ministry)		Gender mainstreaming (All other sectors)	
	Planned	*Actual*	*Planned*	*Actual*
Dominican Republic	2.09	0.73	7.52	—
Kenya	4.64	0.14	4.06	—
Yemen, Rep. of	0.06	—	5.82	0.13

Source: Ebbeler 2007.

Note: — = Not available. Planned expenditures are based on estimates from individual 2005 MDG needs assessments and actual expenditures are based on actual reported national budget allocations.

TABLE 1.3
Donor Disbursements for Gender-Specific and Gender-Mainstreaming Interventions: Percentage of Total Gross Disbursements and per Capita Amounts
(2007 $)

	2001		2002		2003		2004		2005	
	%	$ per capita	%	$ per capita	%	$ per capita	%	$ per capita	%	$ per capita
Dominican Republic	7.1	5.4	3.6	4.9	11.4	16.2	9.9	14.4	7.2	9.7
Kenya	11.7	33.0	11.8	37.9	9.1	42.1	10.4	65.5	19.4	133.0
Yemen, Rep. of	6.0	5.7	7.5	14.5	9.9	13.9	18.1	32.5	13.0	35.0

Source: Ebbeler 2007.

Development Resources

Where should the financing for scaling up gender-equality work come from? Given that investing in gender equality is "smart economics"—these investments yield tangible development returns, especially for poverty reduction—countries, in theory, should finance this work through domestic resource mobilization. While in the long term this is the most desirable option, in the short term, grants or loans are needed to jump start, complement, and scale up this work. Grants and loans are justified, too, because many of these investments yield benefits only in the long term, given that there are large public externalities, and that knowledge about the solutions to gender inequality is an international public good.

Development financing has grown substantially in recent years, although it still falls significantly short of the commitments made at the 2000 Monterrey Conference (World Bank 2007a). In addition, non-traditional sources of development financing have multiplied. Unfortunately, tracking resources assigned to gender equality is difficult, partly because of the problem inherent in disaggregating resources that are mainstreamed and partly because many funding sources do not track gender-equality allocations.

An exception is the effort of the OECD-DAC gender marker to measure official development resources devoted to gender equality. The gender marker uses a somewhat (but not wholly) comparable definition to that of Grown et al. (chapter 5) to derive estimates of the amount of ODA that is allocated to promote gender equality. OECD-DAC applies the gender marker to all funding where gender equality is the principal or a significant objective of aid. Examples of aid classified as "principal" include funding for legal literacy for women and for male networks against gender violence. An example of aid coded as "significant" includes funding potable water connections while ensuring women's access to this water. This gender marker categorization, therefore, is somewhat more restrictive than that of the Millennium Project because it does not fully count the category (in chapter 5) of aid that only indirectly benefits women.

Given the desirable domestic commitment of resources for gender-specific and gender-mainstreaming interventions, the remaining financing gap to implement MDG3 in low-income countries—estimated starting at $8.6 billion in the first year and averaging $13 billion yearly, using UN Millennium Project calculations—is large but could be met if donors, private foundations, and other nontraditional sources of funding increased their spending on MDG3.

The OECD-DAC gender marker has shown that during the 2001–05 period, 16 of 23 donors reported on the gender marker, and this reporting yielded annual amounts of $5 billion. This amount represents 25 percent of total ODA allocated by sector. In the 2005–06 period, this figure increased to $8.5 billion, revealing donors' renewed commitment to gender equality.[6] The table in box 1.2 reports, by donor country, the share of ODA that is designed to promote gender equality (OECD 2007, 2008).

The $100 million gap between this latest figure and the lowest estimate of $8.6 billion may have been partly met already because not all donors reported to the gender marker. A moderate increase in ODA funding, tapping private foundations and other nontraditional funding sources, and most important, domestic resource mobilization—crucial for ensuring aid effectiveness—should go a long way toward overcoming financial constraints to promoting gender equality.

However, the funding gap is not necessarily the main or only constraint to scaling up MDG3 implementation. This overview has mentioned that changes in laws, institutions, and policies all matter for scaling up gender-equality objectives. While most of these changes come with a price tag, funding for them sometimes is available in domestic budgets, as Das (chapter 6) shows for Bangladesh and India for education and health—but this funding is not fully used for benefiting women or the poor because of institutional bottlenecks. Ultimately, specific country circumstances will define the main constraints to attaining MDG3 and the reforms needed to accelerate progress.

Box 1.2
Sources of ODA to Promote Gender Equality

Investment in gender equality and women's empowerment is vital for the achievement of MDG3. Ideally, domestic resource mobilization should be the main source of financing; however, external aid can play an important role in supporting this development.

To date, the best available measurement of the proportions of ODA focused on gender equality and women's empowerment are made available by OECD, to which countries report on the gender marker. In the context of cross-country comparisons of ODA, the proportion of aid being screened (coverage ratios) varies between countries and those countries that do not report to the gender marker, or for which the marker coverage is too low, are not included.

The table below illustrates that commitment to gender equality varies significantly among donors. Some of the largest donors, such as Japan and the Netherlands, have relatively low shares of aid focused on gender equality. The countries with the highest percentage of gender equality–focused aid are Sweden (86 percent), New Zealand (66 percent), and Germany (59 percent).

Total Sector-Allocable ODA, 2006

Country	Total sector allocable ODA (million $)	Gender equality–focused ODA (percent)
European Commission	9,185	40
Japan	8,106	6
Netherlands	5,011	29
United Kingdom	4,832	45
Germany	4,777	59
Sweden	1,920	86
Norway	1,702	26
Canada	1,323	57
Australia	1,317	45
Belgium	844	48
Denmark	742	39
Finland	394	44
New Zealand	204	66
Austria	197	34
Portugal	160	1
Greece	139	36

Source: OECD 2008.

ANNEX 1A

Country Examples of Proposed Budget Allocations for Scaling Up Gender-Specific and Mainstreaming Interventions

Intervention	Country	Average annual cost, 2006–15 (million 2007 $)	Average annual cost per capita, 2006–15 (2007 $)
Gender specific			
Eliminate gender-based violence through raising awareness, abuse hotlines, temporary housing for victims, and sensitivity training for police and military	Dominican Republic	12.98	1.36
Strengthen institutions to mainstream gender, defend equal rights to property and inheritance, and promote equal employment opportunities	Dominican Republic	4.29	0.45
Fight HIV/AIDS among female sex workers	Gabon	1.60	1.04
Strengthen ministries and government agencies to handle gender issues and implement international agreements on ending gender discrimination	Kenya	52.30	1.32
Build coalitions and mobilize communities to ensure women's participation in political and economic affairs and raise awareness of reproductive rights and violence	Kenya	62.50	1.58
Support setup of data systems and increase data collection of sex-disaggregated information to monitor progress toward the gender-equality goal	Kenya	26.10	0.66
Promote awareness of women's rights to legal redress and state services and improve state responsiveness to incidences of violence and victim rehabilitation	Kenya	24.10	0.61
Transition of secondary-school girl graduates to vocational training and the workplace	Niger	35.70	2.13
Gender mainstreaming			
Construct 30 new and rehabilitate 43 child day care centers and construct emergency and community care shelters	Dominican Republic	1.56	0.16

(continued)

Country Examples of Proposed Budget Allocations for Scaling Up Gender-Specific and Mainstreaming Interventions (continued)

Intervention	Country	Average annual cost, 2006–15 (million 2007 $)	Average annual cost per capita, 2006–15 (2007 $)
Provide subsidies to mothers with children in preprimary, primary, and secondary school	Dominican Republic	17.05	1.78
Provide emergency obstetric care, capacity building for public health staff, and antenatal and newborn care to reduce maternal mortality by 75 percent	Dominican Republic	10.06	1.05
Provide energy subsidies to female-headed households to facilitate income generation through biomass and renewable energy, petroleum, and electricity	Kenya	95.42	2.41
Decrease maternal mortality through family planning for women and teens, management of malaria and anemia in pregnancy, and emergency obstetrics	Senegal	9.85	0.74
Increase microcredit programs for small farmers, targeted specifically at women	Tajikistan	5.65	0.81
Free school lunch targeted to girls of poor families in primary grades 1–4	Tajikistan	14.55	2.08
Re-enroll in primary and secondary education mothers who could not previously continue their educations because of marriage or birth	Togo	10.30	1.45
Increase female medical staff recruitment, upgrade clinics with comprehensive obstetric care, increase medical coverage of deliveries, and provide family planning	Yemen, Rep. of	75.50	3.03

Source: Ebbeler 2007.

Notes

1. Gender-specific interventions refer to actions with the explicit objective to target gender equality (e.g., a law reform that gives women and men equal rights to own property). Gender-mainstreaming interventions are those that specifically target women but do not necessarily have as the main objective increasing gender equality (e.g., a micro credit program for small farmers that specifically targets women). A gender-neutral intervention is an action that promotes gender equality but was not specifically targeted to do so. An example is the construction of a dwelling that in a community allows the community women to work instead of spending time fetching water.
2. The following discussion draws on World Bank (2007a) and Morrison, Raju, and Sinha (2007).
3. This is the same strategy that was used in the *2007 Global Monitoring Report* (World Bank 2007a).
4. Out of 131 countries with data available, 67 have met the official MDG3 target of parity in primary education and 77 out of 124 countries with data available have met the target in secondary education. The primary reason for differences between performance in meeting MDG3 goals for primary and secondary education separately and primary and secondary education combined is the wide discrepancy found in primary education gender ratio and secondary education gender ratio for some countries.
5. This section is based on a number of background papers that were commissioned in preparation for the 2007 Global Monitoring Report (World Bank 2007a).
6. It might also be caused by exchange rate effects, that is, the appreciation of currencies from countries that have relatively high allocations to gender.

References and Other Resources

Anderson, J. R., and G. Feder. 2003. "Rural Extension Services." Policy Research Working Paper No. 2976, World Bank, Washington, D.C.

Anderson, K., E. M. King, and Y. Wang. 2003. "Market Returns, Transfers and Demand for Schooling In Malaysia, 1976 89." *Journal of Development Studies* 39 (3): 1–28.

Baydas, M. M., R. L. Meyer, and N. Aguilera-Alfred. 1994. "Discrimination against Women in Formal Credit Markets: Reality or Rhetoric?" *World Development* 22 (7): 1073–82.

Bruns, B., A. Mingat, and R. Rakotomalala. 2003. "Achieving Universal Primary Education by 2015: A Chance for Every Child." World Bank, Washington, D.C.

Buvinić, M. 1996. "Promoting Employment among the Urban Poor in Latin America and the Caribbean: A Gender Analysis." Discussion Paper 12, Issues in Development, International Labour Organization, Geneva.

Buvinić, M., and M. Berger. 1990. "Sex Differences in Access to a Small Enterprise Development Fund in Peru." *World Development* 18 (5): 695–705.

Buvinić, M., J. C. Guzmán, and C. B. Lloyd. 2007. "Gender Shapes Adolescence." *Development Outreach*, Nov. 2007, World Bank Institute, Washington, D.C.

Chirayath, L., C. Sage, and M. Woolcock. 2005. "Customary Law and Policy Reform: Engaging with the Plurality of Justice System." Background Paper for *World Development Report 2006: Equity and Development*. World Bank, Washington, D.C.

Croppenstedt, A., M. Demeke, and M. M. Meschi. 2003. "Technology Adoption in the Presence of Constraints: The Case of Fertilizer Demand in Ethiopia." *Review of Development Economics* 7 (1): 58–70.

Das Gupta. November 2007. Personal communication. Senior Social Scientist with the Development Research Group.

Deere, C. D., and M. Leon. 2001. *Empowering Women: Land and Property Rights in Latin America*. Pittsburgh: University of Pittsburgh Press.

Delamonica, E., S. Malhotra, and J. Vandemoortele. 2001. "Is EFA Affordable? Estimating the Global Minimum Cost of 'Education for All.'" Division of Evaluation, Policy and Planning, Staff Working Paper No. 01-01, UNICEF, New York.

Devarajan, S., M. J. Miller, and E. V. Swanson. 2002. "Goals for Development: History, Prospects and Costs." Policy Research Working Paper No. 2819, World Bank, Washington, D.C.

Doss, C. 2005. "The Effects of Intrahousehold Property Ownership on Expenditure Patterns in Ghana." *Journal of African Economies* 15: 149–80.

Duflo, E. 2003. "Grandmothers and Granddaughters: Old Age Pension and Intra-Household Allocation in South Africa." *World Bank Economic Review* 17 (1): 1–25.

Ebbeler, J. L. 2007. "Financial Requirement to Achieve Millennium Development Goals on Gender Equality and Women's Empowerment: A Review of Country Experiences." World Bank, Washington, D.C.

Grown, C., G. Gupta, and R. Pande. 2005. *Taking Action: Achieving Gender Equality and Empowering Women*. London: Earthscan and the Millennium Project.

Holla, A., R. Jensen, and E. Oster. 2007. "Daughters as Wealth? The Effects of Cash Incentives on Sex Ratios." Working Paper, Department of Economics, Brown University.

Jensen, R., and E. Oster. 2007. "The Power of TV: Cable Television and Women's Status in India." NBER Working Paper No. 13305, National Bureau of Economic Research, Cambridge, MA.

Jütting, J. P., and C. Morrisson. 2005. "Changing Social Institutions to Improve the Status of Women in Developing Countries." OECD Development Centre Policy Briefs No. 27, OECD, Paris.

Kevane, M., and L. C. Gray. 1999. "A Woman's Field Is Made at Night: Gendered Land Rights and Norms in Burkina Faso." *Feminist Economics* 5 (3): 1–26.

Klasen, S. 2006. "UNDP's Gender-Related Measures: Some Conceptual Problems and Possible Solutions." *Journal of Human Development* 7 (2): 243–74.

Lastarria-Cornhiel, S., S. Agurto, J. Brown, and S. Rosales. 2003. "Joint Titling in Nicaragua, Indonesia, and Honduras: Rapid Appraisal Synthesis." Land Tenure Center Report, University of Wisconsin, Madison, WI.

Lewis, M., and M. Lockheed. 2006. *Inexcusable Absence: Why 60 Million Girls Still Aren't in School and What to Do about It*. Washington, DC: Center for Global Development.

Lycette, M., and K. White. 1989. "Improving Women's Access to Credit in Latin America and the Caribbean: Policy and Project Recommendations." In *Women's Futures: Assistance to the Informal Sector in Latin America*, eds. Marguerite Berger and Mayra Buvinić. West Hartford, CT: Kumarian Press.

Morrison, A., D. Raju, and N. Sinha. 2007. "Gender Equality, Poverty, and Economic Growth." Background paper for *Global Monitoring Report 2007*. World Bank, Washington, D.C.

OECD (Organisation for Economic Co-operation and Development). 2007. "Aid in Support of Gender Equality and Women's Empowerment." OECD, Paris.

———. 2008. "Aid in Support of Gender Equality and Women's Empowerment." OECD, Paris.

Phavi, I. K., and C. Urashima. 2006. "Policies to Promote Women's Economic Opportunities in Cambodia." Presented at the High-Level Consultation: Promoting the Gender Equality MDG—The Implementation Challenge. World Bank, Washington, DC, February 16.

Pitt, M. M., and S. R. Khandker. 1998. "The Impact of Group-Based Credit Programs on Poor Households in Bangladesh: Does the Gender of Participants Matter?" *Journal of Political Economy* 106: 958–96.

Quisumbing, A. R. 1994. "Gender Differences in Agricultural Productivity: A Survey of Empirical Evidence." Education and Social Policy Discussion Paper No. 36, World Bank, Washington, D.C.

Quisumbing, A. R., J. P. Estudillo, and K. Otsuka. 2004. *Land and Schooling: Transferring Wealth Across Generations*. Baltimore, MD: Johns Hopkins University Press.

Raczynski, D. 2007. "Tranversalización del enfoque de genero en el proceso presupuestario del Estado: Estudio de case en Chile." Asesorias para el Desarrollo, Santiago.

Ratusi, M., and A. V. Swamy. 1999. "Explaining Ethnic Differentials in Credit Market Outcomes in Zimbabwe." *Economic Development and Cultural Change* 47: 585–604.

Rawls, J. 1971. *A Theory of Social Justice*. Cambridge, MA: Harvard University Press.

Razzaz, S. 2007. "Resolving Jordan's Labor Market Paradox of Concurrent Economic Growth and High Unemployment." Report No. 39201-JO, World Bank, Washington, D.C.

Roemer, J. E. 1993. "A Pragmatic Theory of Responsibility for the Egalitarian Planner." *Philosophy and Public Affairs* 22: 146–66.

———. 2002. "Equality of Opportunity: A Progress Report." *Social Choice and Welfare* 19: 455–71.

Rubalcava, L., G. Teruel, and D. Thomas. 2004. "Spending, Saving and Public Transfers Paid to Women." Working Paper 024-04, California Center for Population Research, University of California, Los Angeles.

Saito, K., H. Mekonnen, and D. Spurling. 1994. *Raising the Productivity of Women Farmers in Sub-Saharan Africa*. Washington, D.C: World Bank.

Schady, N. 2007. "How Much Do Girls Benefit from Conditional Cash Transfers?" PowerPoint presentation to the Gender and Development Board, World Bank, Washington, D.C.

Sikoska, T. 2006. "Policy Interventions to Meet MDG3 in Middle Income Countries: The Case of the Dominican Republic." Presented at the High-Level Consultation: Promoting the Gender Equality MDG—The Implementation Challenge. World Bank, Washington, D.C, February 16.

Storey, D. J. 2004. "Racial and Gender Discrimination in the Micro Firms Credit Market? Evidence from Trinidad and Tobago." *Small Business Economics* 23 (5): 401–22.

Tzannatos, Z. 2007. "Monitoring Progress in Gender Equality in the Labor Market." Presented at the High-Level Consultation: Promoting the Gender Equality MDG—The Implementation Challenge. World Bank, Washington, DC, February 16.

Udry, C. 1996. "Gender, Agricultural Production, and the Theory of the Household." *Journal of Political Economy* 104: 1010–46.

United Nations. 2005a. United Nations Document CEDAW C/VNM/5–6. 22 June 2005, Combined 5th and 6th Report, Vietnam.

———. 2005b. *World Population Prospects: The 2004 Revision*. New York: United Nations, Economic and Social Affairs.

UNDP (United Nations Development Programme). 1995. *Human Development Report 1995: Gender and Human Development*. New York: UNDP.

———. 2005. *Investing in Development: A Practical Plan to Achieve the Millennium Development Goals. UN Millennium Project*. New York: UNDP.

WEF (World Economic Forum). 2007. "The Global Gender Gap Report 2007." Geneva.

WHO (World Health Organization). 2002. *World Report on Violence and Health*. Geneva: WHO.

World Bank. 2005a. "Gender Issues and Best Practices in Land Administration Projects." Agriculture and Rural Development Department, World Bank Report No. 32571-GLB, Washington, D.C.

———. 2005b. "The Status and Progress of Women in the Middle East and North Africa Region." World Bank, Washington, D.C.

———. 2006. "Investment Climate Survey Online." http://iresearch.worldbank. org/InvestmentClimate/.

———. 2007a. *Global Monitoring Report 2007: Millennium Development Goals: Confronting the Challenges of Gender Equality and Fragile States*. Washington, DC: World Bank.

———. 2007b. *World Development Report 2008: Agriculture for Development*. Washington, DC: World Bank.

2

The State of World Progress, 1990–2007

Andrew R. Morrison, Shwetlena Sabarwal,
and Mirja Sjöblom

The Millennium Development Goal on gender equality and women's economic empowerment (MDG3) promotes inclusion of gender equality in the broader development agenda; it also has been a catalyst for improving the measurement of gender equality across countries. This chapter summarizes the state of progress toward gender equality in the world using the official MDG3 indicators and a select set of supplementary indicators. Emphasis is placed on the value added by the supplementary indicators and on country performance relative to regional benchmarks.

The chapter is structured as follows: The first section discusses how to measure gender equality and provides arguments for using individual indicators and indexes of gender equality. The second section provides a snapshot of country and regional progress toward gender equality in capabilities (education and health) and access to resources and opportunities (employment and political participation). This section measures performance using the official MDG3 indicators as well as a limited number of supplementary indicators (an "MDG3 plus" approach). The third section examines the additionality—or value added—of the proposed supplementary indicators. The fourth section focuses on country performance with respect to gender equality relative to regional benchmarks. The fifth section provides conclusions.

Measuring Gender Equality: Indexes Versus Indicators

There are many existing measures of gender equality, but no consensus about any single best measure. Perhaps the most important distinction between measures of gender equality is between index approaches and individual indicators. While this distinction is analyzed in more detail in chapter 3, a brief discussion is offered here.

The two best-known indexes of gender equality are the Gender Empowerment Measure (GEM) and the Gender-related Development Index (GDI), both introduced by the United Nations Development Programme (UNDP) in 1995. The GEM is principally a measure of female empowerment in earned incomes, the economy, and political decision making, while the GDI is an adjusted Human Development Index, with scores adjusted down for gender gaps in income, life expectancy, and educational attainment (Grown 2006). Both measures have been subject to well-known withering criticisms that will not be summarized here; for details, see Grown (2006) and a special issue of the *Journal of Human Development* devoted to the measurement of gender equality (*Journal of Human Development* 2006).

Three different responses have emerged as a result of the criticisms of the GEM and the GDI. First, recommendations have been made for fixing these indexes (Klasen 2006). Second, new composite indexes have been developed, such as the Standardized Index of Gender Equality (SIGE), the Gender Equality Index, the Relative Status of Women Index, and the World Economic Forum's Gender Gap Index (for details on these and other new composite measures, see Grown [2006]).

The third response to the shortcomings of existing indexes of gender equality has been to argue for the use of a set of indicators instead of an index. While an index can be useful for creating a summary statistic that can capture media and policy attention, it is less useful for policy formulation (Grown 2006).

The progress toward the Millennium Development Goals (MDGs) is measured through indicators. MDG3 has four official indicators: ratio of girls' to boys' enrollment in primary, secondary, and tertiary education; ratio of literate females to literate males among 15- to 24-year-olds; share of women in nonagricultural wage employment; and the proportion of parliamentary seats held by women.

These indicators, while useful, have been subject to strong criticism. The Millennium Project Task Force on Gender Equity, for example, has noted the following:

- Enrollment ratios capture neither the proportion of boys and girls enrolled as a share of school-age population nor learning outcomes.
- Literacy does not have a universally accepted definition and is consequently measured differently across countries.
- The share of women in nonagricultural wage employment does not capture barriers to remunerative employment or the quality of jobs; it

also excludes the agricultural sector, which frequently employs a large share of the female labor force.

- Representation in parliament does not measure women's decision-making power in the parliament; nor does it capture women's political participation at local or regional levels (Grown, Gupta, and Pande 2005).

The Millennium Project Task Force recommended the use of 12 indicators to replace the official MDG3 indicators, including measures of (i) education, (ii) sexual and reproductive health and rights, (iii) infrastructure, (iv) property rights, (v) employment, (vi) participation in national parliaments and local government bodies, and (vii) violence against women (Grown, Gupta, and Pande 2005). Unfortunately, many of the recommended indicators do not have widely available data (for example, hours per day women and men spend fetching water and collecting fuel or prevalence of domestic violence).

The World Bank's 2007 Global Monitoring Report (GMR) suggested a more modest list of indicators that would complement the official MDG3 indicators. The new indicators proposed by the GMR meet three criteria: (i) data are available on them for a relatively large number of developing countries (or are likely to be available in the near future), (ii) evidence links these indicators to progress in reducing poverty or spurring growth, and (iii) the indicators can be affected by policy interventions in the short to medium term. Finally, indicators that passed these three screens but were highly correlated with the official MDG3 indicators were not included because they would not add enough new information compared with the official indicators—they would not provide "additionality."

We call this approach an "MDG3 plus" approach—using the official indicators for MDG3, but supplementing them with additional indicators where feasible and appropriate. The GMR made a first attempt at using this approach; this chapter updates and expands the information provided in the GMR. Specifically, for all the official and supplementary indicators, information is updated by including additional years. For such indicators as ratio of females to males in primary, secondary, and tertiary education and under-five mortality rates, data have been updated for all countries. Also, increased data availability has allowed information on many countries to be added. In the GMR, data on all official MDG indicators were available for 54 countries; this chapter presents this information for 67 countries. For certain indicators (official and new), such as ratio of literate females to males among 15- to 24-year-olds, share of females in the nonagricultural wage sector, adolescent motherhood, and modern contraceptive use, information on approximately 15 to 24 more countries has been included.

In addition, this chapter substantially expands GMR data on gender disparities in access to resources and opportunities. A major contribution of this chapter is to provide an estimate of gender-based wage disparities by reporting the ratio of female to male hourly earnings in primary, secondary, and tertiary sectors. The labor force participation data presented in the GMR have been revised and expanded. The labor force participation rates for countries in Europe and Central Asia have been revised, new countries from all regions have been included, and where possible, existing data have been updated.

This chapter also provides a detailed analysis of relative country performance. For all indicators (official and new), individual country performance is compared with regional performance; this enables the identification of high and low performers in different parts of the world.

Progress on Gender Equality in Education, Health, Employment, and Political Participation

Table 2.1 presents the official and new indicators, grouped by different dimensions of gender equality (capabilities, access to resources and opportunities) and level of aggregation (household, economy and markets, society).[1]

In the realm of capabilities, four new indicators have been added. The inclusion of primary completion rates for girls and boys is motivated by the fact that the official indicator for education does not indicate whether enrolled students go on to complete primary school. The remaining new capabilities indicators are related to health and reflect the fact that health is one of the elements of gender equality currently not adequately covered by the official MDG3 indicators.[2] For measuring access to resources, two new indicators related to employment are proposed to strengthen the official MDG indicator in this area (i.e., share of women in wage employment in the nonagricultural sector). The first, women's labor market participation rate, is an indication of women's potential economic empowerment (World Bank 2007).[3] The second, the ratio of female to male hourly earnings, captures differences in how female and male labor is rewarded in the labor market; it includes differences generated by observable differentials in human capital, unobservable factors (talent, motivation, and so forth), and, in the case of wage employment, gender-based discrimination.[4]

TABLE 2.1
Official MDG3 Indicators and Recommended Additional Indicators

Domain	Household	Economy and markets	Society
Capabilities: Education	Ratio of girls' to boys' enrollment in primary, secondary, and tertiary education		
	Ratio of literate females to males among 15- to 24-year-olds		
	Primary completion rate of girls and boys[a]		
Capabilities: Health	*Under-five mortality for girls and boys*[b]		
	Percentage of reproductive-age women and their sexual partners using modern contraception[c]		
	Percentage of 15- to 19-year-olds who are mothers or pregnant with their first child		
Access to resources: Employment		Share of women in wage employment in the nonagricultural sector	
		Labor force participation rates among women and men ages 20–24 and 25–59	
		Ratio of female to male hourly earnings in primary, secondary, and tertiary sectors[d]	
Access to resources: Political participation			Proportion of seats held by women in national parliaments

Source: Authors.

Note: Text in italics signifies recommended additional indicators by the Millennium Project Task Force.

a. This indicator is a gender-disaggregated version of the MDG2 indicator.

b. This is a gender-disaggregated version of the MDG4 indicator.

c. This is a modified version of MDG6.

d. This indicator was not recommended in the 2007 Global Monitoring Report. Since that report was published, additional data have become available making this indicator feasible.

From a policy perspective, any indicator that provides reliable and actionable information on relative outcomes for men and women is inherently useful. From an empirical standpoint, however, the additionality of new indicators has to be assessed by the value added in overall information. The key question is how much the relative performance of countries changes when the official MDG indicators are augmented with the new indicators. The value added by new indicators can then be assessed by measuring to what extent they alter the conception of the relative performance of countries on gender equality.

The effect of the addition of the new indicators is measured by comparing country performance on one official MDG indicator with country performance for a close and complementary new indicator, where possible. Later, the issue of additional indicators will be examined by comparing scores on a set of official indicators with scores on several new indicators. The chapter now turns to country and regional performance for each indicator, grouped by domain.

Capabilities: Education

Since the 1980s, both macro- and microeconomists have, stressed the importance of education for economic growth and development (Lucas 1988; Barro 1991; Mankiw, Romer, and Weil 1992; Psacharopoulous 1985; Duflo 2001). Some of the benefits of education include increased earnings potential, better health, higher probability of adopting new technologies, and reductions in fertility. Countries may particularly benefit from investing in girls' education because diminishing returns to education imply that the marginal return of investing in women's education is higher than of investing in men's education, given that ability is evenly distributed between men and women and that women are less educated in most countries of the world. In addition, there is a closer relationship between mothers' education—as opposed to fathers' education—and health and schooling of children (Schultz 2002).

Figure 2.1 shows population-weighted girls' enrollment rates and girls-to-boys enrollment ratios for 1990 and 2006 by world region. Great progress has been made in most regions, especially in primary and secondary enrollment. Girls' enrollment in primary education has increased substantially worldwide. Gains in primary education are particularly large in the regions that started at a relatively low level (Sub-Saharan Africa, the Middle East and North Africa, and South Asia), while there has been little growth in enrollment rates (or even negative growth in East Asia and Pacific) in the regions that started at levels above or close to 100 percent.[5]

FIGURE 2.1
Population-Weighted Girls' Enrollment Rates and Girls'-to-Boys' Enrollment Ratios by Region, 1990 and 2006

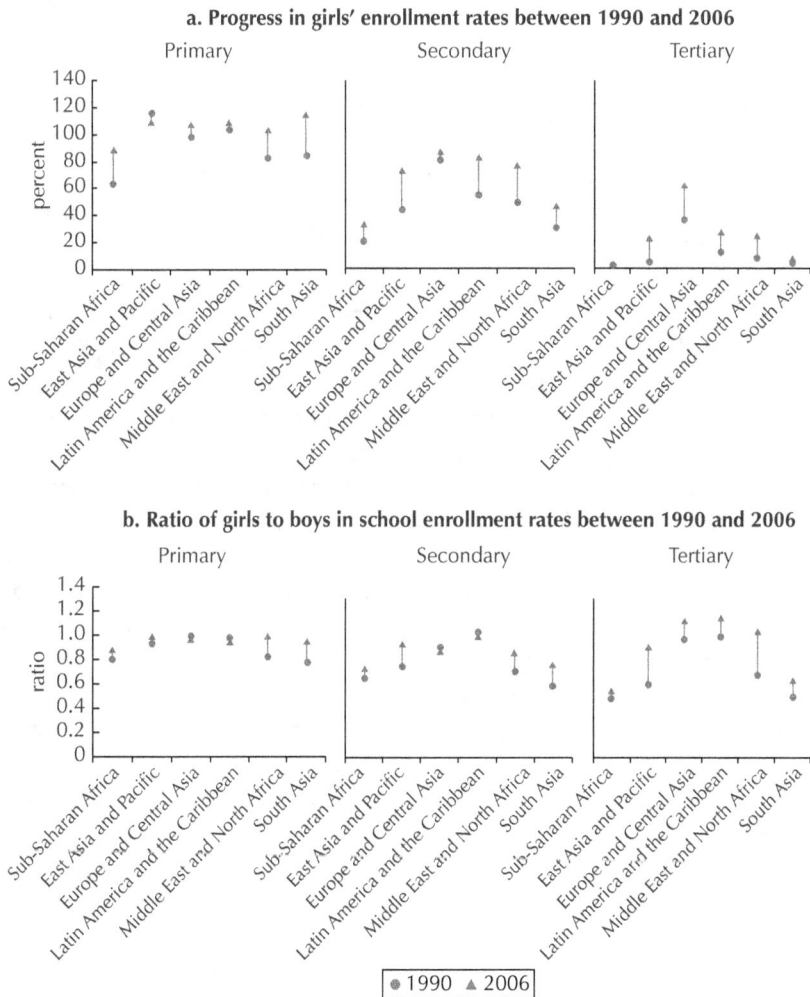

a. Progress in girls' enrollment rates between 1990 and 2006

b. Ratio of girls to boys in school enrollment rates between 1990 and 2006

● 1990 ▲ 2006

Source: World Development Indicators 2007.

Note: The regional averages are calculated by using the earliest value between 1990 and 1995 and the latest value between 2000 and 2006 for each country. The averages are weighted by country population in 2006.

All regions except Sub-Saharan Africa show gender parity in primary enrollment rates at the end of the period.

East Asia and Pacific, Latin America and the Caribbean, and the Middle East and North Africa have made impressive strides in increasing the percentage of girls enrolled in secondary education. South Asia and Sub-Saharan Africa have also made some progress, but in these regions, gender gaps in education are still large and only modest progress toward parity has been made. Parity in secondary education has been achieved in East Asia and Pacific and in Europe and Central Asia. In Latin America and the Caribbean, there are more girls than boys enrolled—indicating that the gender issue for this region is how to enroll boys and keep them in school.

The overall levels of girls' participation in tertiary education are low across all regions except Europe and Central Asia; nonetheless, girls' enrollment exceeds boys' in Latin America and the Caribbean, the Middle East and North Africa, and in Europe and Central Asia. The progress in girls' enrollment rates for tertiary education in Sub-Saharan Africa and South Asia has been slower than for other regions; as a result, only very modest movement toward gender parity is observed for South Asia and no progress is seen for Africa.

The second official indicator for MDG3 is the population-weighted ratio of literate females to males among 15- to 24-year-olds, which is plotted by region in figure 2.2 for 1990 and 2006. The literacy ratios follow a similar pattern to the ratios of girls to boys in school enrollment, with one exception. Regarding the two lagging regions, observe that for literacy ratios, South Asia underperforms Sub-Saharan Africa, while Sub-Saharan Africa underperforms South Asia for enrollment ratios. East Asia and Pacific, Europe and Central Asia, and Latin America and the Caribbean have achieved or are close to achieving parity in literacy rates, while the Middle East and North Africa still has more literate men than women.

Additional MDG3 Indicators: Education

There has been a tendency to interpret gender gaps in education only in the narrow terms of enrollment. In reality, differences in education enrollment are only crude proxies for a multidimensional gender gap in education. Outcome variables, such as completion rates or measures of skills[6] (literacy, for instance), are arguably more important for economic development.

The population-weighted regional rates of primary school completion for girls are given in figure 2.3 for 1990 and 2006. Primary completion rates are measured as the number of students in the last primary grade minus repeaters in this grade as a proportion of the number of children at

FIGURE 2.2
Population-Weighted Ratio of Literate Females to Males among 15- to 24-Year-Olds by Region, 1990 and 2006

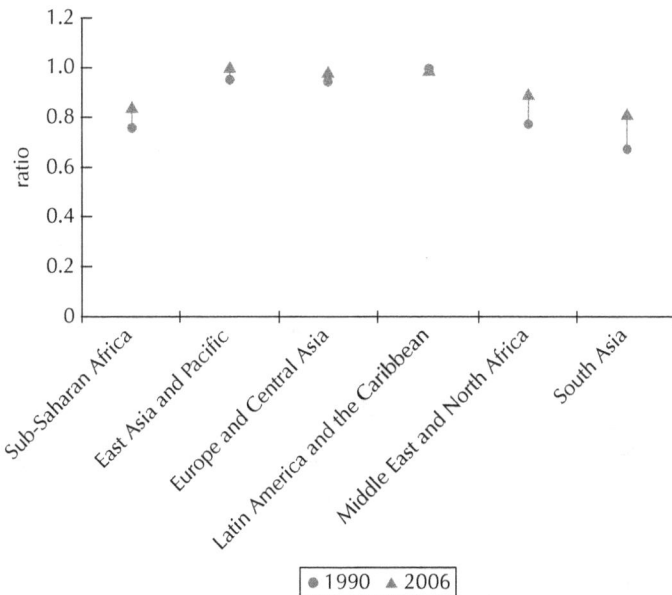

Source: World Development Indicators 2007.

Note: The regional averages are calculated by using the earliest value between 1990 and 2000 and the latest value between 2000 and 2006 for each country. The averages are weighted by country population in 2006.

expected graduation age. The figure reveals that primary completion rates for girls mirror trends in primary enrollment ratios: rapid increases in completion rates take place in the same regions (South Asia—at least in India and Nepal[7]—Middle East and North Africa, and Sub-Saharan Africa) that showed rapid progress in primary school enrollment ratios.

Additionality: Completion Rates Versus Enrollment Rates
One way to capture the extent to which this new indicator adds value is by comparing female-to-male ratios in primary enrollment with female-to-male ratios in primary completion. To compare relative country performance in these indicators, the analysis reviews the entire sample of 82 countries for which gender-disaggregated rates for both primary enrollment and primary completion are available. These 82 countries are ranked for each of the two indicators, from low to high (rank 1 reflecting the

FIGURE 2.3
Populated-Weighted Rates of Primary School Completion for Girls by Region, 1990 and 2006

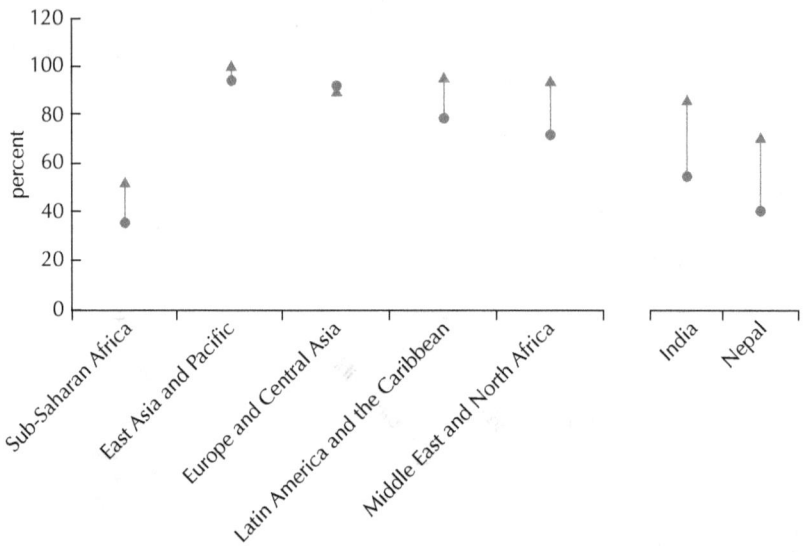

Source: World Development Indicators 2007.

Note: The regional averages are calculated by using the earliest value between 1990 and 1995 and the latest value between 2000 and 2006 for each country. The averages are weighted by country population in 2006. As a result of the lack of data for most countries in the South Asia Region, rates for India and Nepal are shown separately.

worst value and rank 82 reflecting the best). Figure 2.4 plots country rank in primary enrollment ratio against country rank in primary completion ratio. Countries above the 45 degree line have higher rank for primary completion ratio than primary enrollment ratio, while the opposite is true for countries below the line.

Countries such as Malawi, Mauritania, Oman, and Rwanda rank very high (70 and above) for female-to-male ratio in primary enrollment but fairly low (50 and below) for female-to-male ratio in primary completion. However, Cape Verde, Nicaragua, Swaziland, and Trinidad and Tobago rank high (70 and above) in primary completion ratio but low (50 and below) on primary enrollment ratio. These "outliers" drive home the point that performance on enrollment and completion do not necessarily go hand in hand.

Figure 2.5 plots the primary enrollment ratios and completion ratios in 2006, or the most recent year, for countries in which the completion ratio is substantially lower than the enrollment ratio (the difference in

FIGURE 2.4
Country Rank in Primary Enrollment Ratio against Country Rank in Primary Completion Ratio

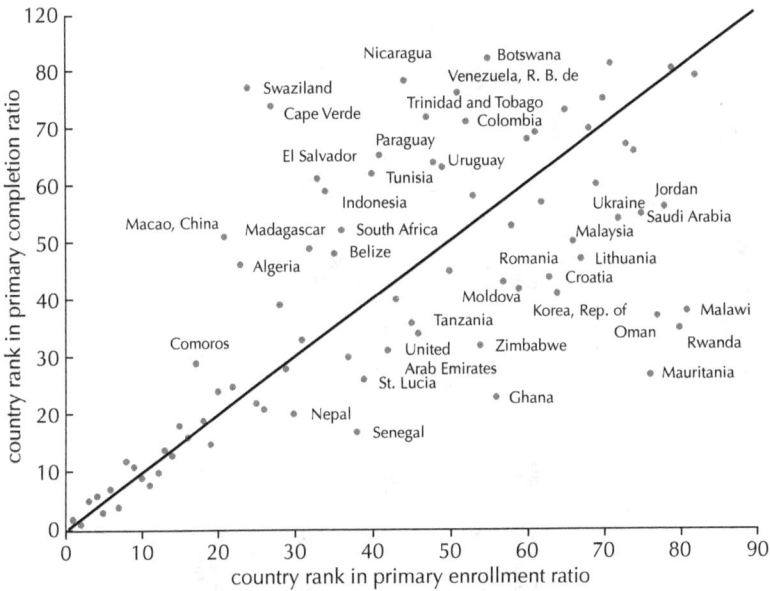

Source: World Development Indicators 2007.
Note: For clarity in exposition only certain data points are labeled.

the two ratios is at least 0.7). Without exception, these countries are in South Asia or the Middle East and North Africa. Low retention of females in primary school could be a reflection of parental biases favoring the education of boys over girls, which translates into higher dropout rates for girls if families prefer to pull girls from school first in times of financial or other resource constraints, or for domestic chores if a family member falls ill or a new baby is born. Alternatively, lower retention of girls may result from push factors in educational institutions. Haddad et al. (1990) note that available evidence indicates that family economic conditions are more important in explaining the gender gap in human capital accumulation than school-related variables.

Education of marginalized groups. One of the main obstacles to universal education is inequality in access and attainment linked to ethnicity, gender, poverty, and geography. New research on this topic accentuates the interaction effect between gender and culture as a key determinant of

FIGURE 2.5

Girls'-to-Boys' Primary Completion Ratio Versus Primary Enrollment, 2006 or Most Recent Year

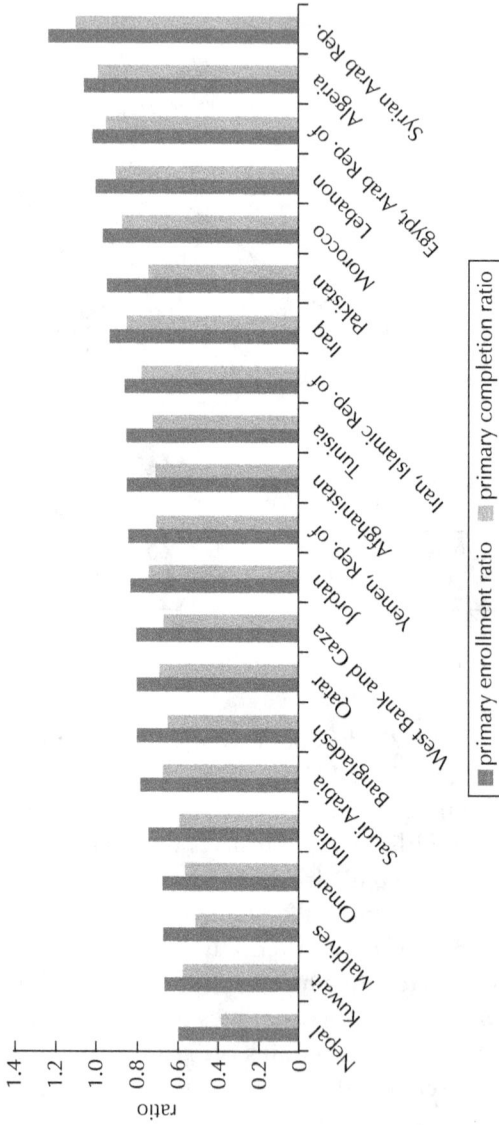

Source: World Development Indicators 2007.

Note: The figure shows countries where girls'-to-boys' ratio in primary completion is substantially (i.e., the difference in the two ratios is at least 0.7) lower than ratio in primary enrollment.

educational disadvantage. Lewis and Lockheed (2006, 2007) note that girls in marginalized groups are at higher risk of being excluded from education because they suffer as members of the excluded group, but also as girls. The Lewis and Lockheed (2007) case studies show that girls from impoverished households or from tribal, ethnic, or linguistic "minority" communities have a clear educational disadvantage—as do girls from the lowest social class and girls living in remote rural areas.

Transition from school to work. The transition between school and work is a critical period for sustaining the achievements made toward gender equality in education to later stages in life (Buvinić, Guzmán, and Lloyd 2007). As boys become teenagers they tend to increase their labor supply in the labor market outside the home, while girls typically split their time between household chores and economic activities in the labor market. Figure 2.6 plots sex-disaggregated school attendance in relation to labor force participation by

FIGURE 2.6
School-to-Work Transition, 1995–2004

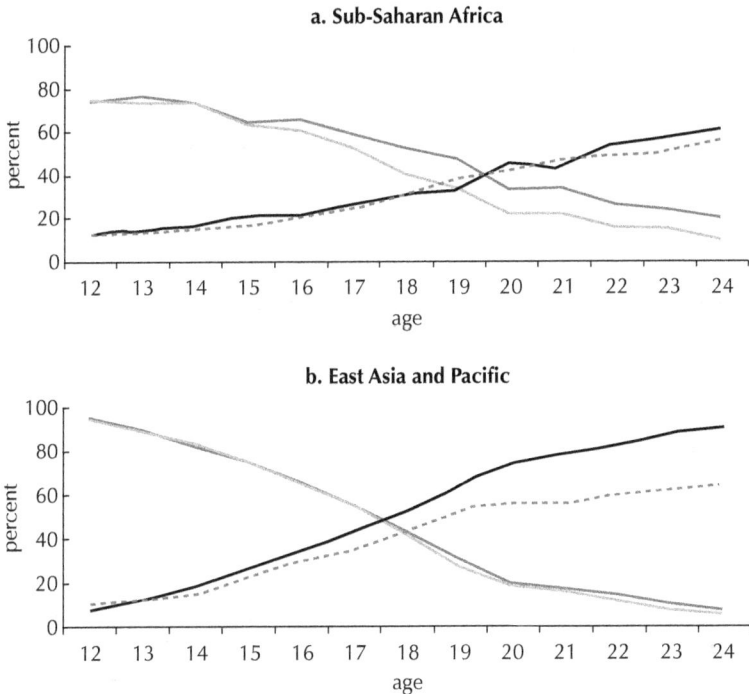

a. Sub-Saharan Africa

b. East Asia and Pacific

(continued)

FIGURE 2.6
School-to-Work Transition, 1995–2004 *(continued)*

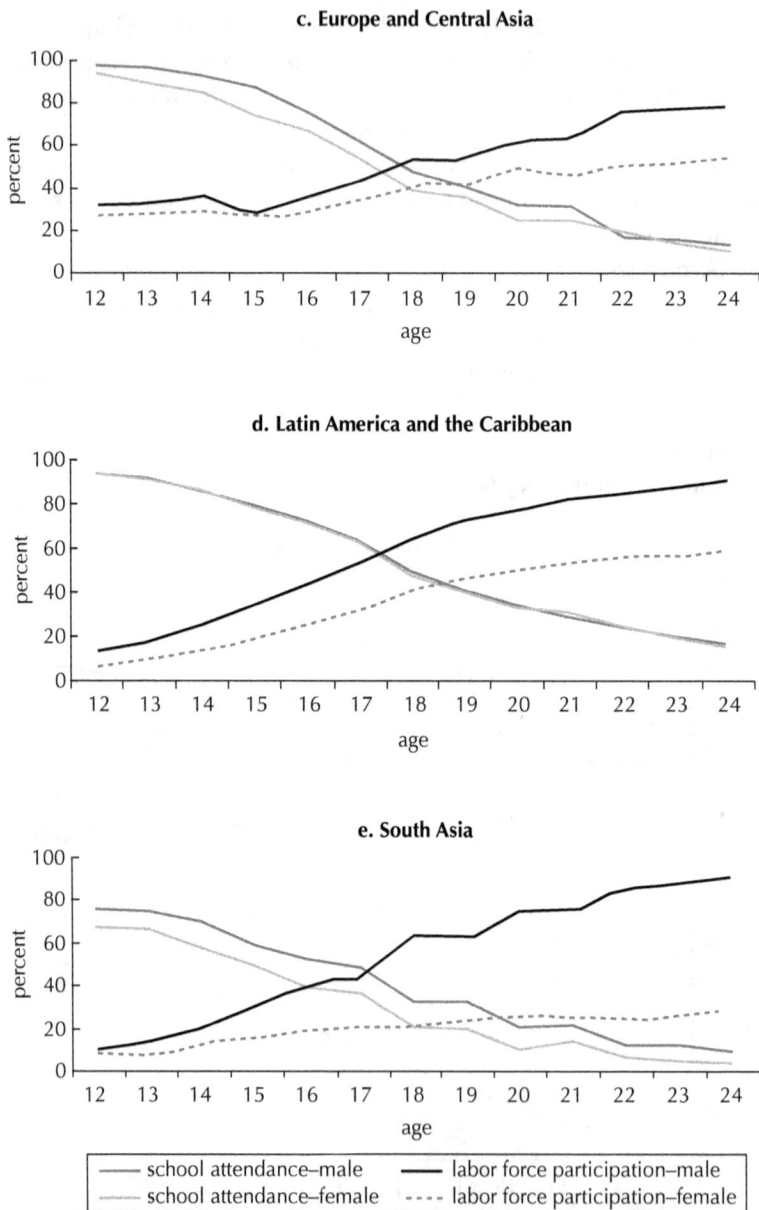

c. Europe and Central Asia

d. Latin America and the Caribbean

e. South Asia

school attendance–male ——— labor force participation–male
school attendance–female ----- labor force participation–female

Source: Buvinić, Guzmán, and Lloyd 2007.

region.[8] This indicator captures the extent to which boys and girls are able to make the transition from education to work.[9] The figure indicates that in all regions except South Asia, there is parity or close to parity in school attendance at age 12; by age 24, however, women lag far behind men in labor force participation in all regions except Sub-Saharan Africa. In Europe and Central Asia, East Asia and Pacific, and Latin America and the Caribbean, with almost universal access to primary education, the gender gaps in labor force participation at age 24 are surprisingly high—between 25 and 32 percent. The gender gap in labor force participation is even higher in South Asia, where only 28 percent of women are active in the labor market at age 24 in comparison with 90 percent of men. These figures plainly illustrate the difficulty for girls in making the transition from school to the labor market. Clearly, the obstacles to labor force participation transcend human capital constraints. In many developing countries and traditional societies, early marriage, motherhood, and cultural norms about women's roles in society impede women's participation in the labor market.

Capabilities: Health

None of the official MDG3 indicators measure progress in women's and girls' health status or their access to sexual and reproductive health services, even though these variables are key to women's ability to build their human capital, take advantage of economic and political opportunities, and control their lives. This section discusses trends in three additional indicators measuring progress in gender equality and empowerment of women in health status.

Sex-disaggregated under-five mortality rates provide a measure of gender equality in nutrition and health care during early childhood. (Countries with a high degree of gender equality are characterized by higher under-five mortality rates for boys than for girls; this differential is a function of health and nutritional inputs' differences between the sexes.)

Two key messages emerge from the data in figure 2.7, which plots under-five mortality rates by sex.[10] First, urgent action is clearly warranted for both boys and girls in Sub-Saharan Africa and South Central Asia. Second, there are only two regions in which girls' under-five mortality rates exceed boys'—East Asia and South and Central Asia. This pattern can potentially be explained by female infanticide and discrimination against girls in nutrition and health care (World Bank 2007).

The decline in under-five mortality has been modest since about 1980. After a period of sharp decline in child mortality rates throughout the world

FIGURE 2.7
Under-Five Mortality Rate for Boys and Girls, 2000–05

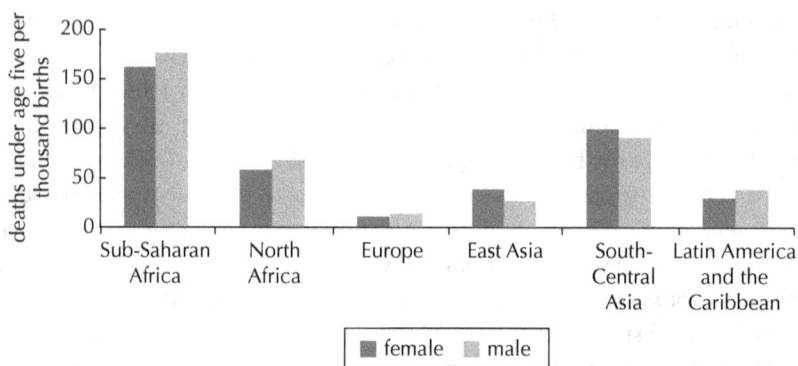

Source: World Population Prospects 2006.
Note: UN regional definitions are used in the figure.

during the early 1980s, the rate of decline began to taper off in the late 1980s and 1990s (Ahmad, Lopez, and Inoue 2000). In the years since 2000, the only regions that have been able to decrease female and male under-five mortality rates by about 20 percent are North Africa and Latin America and the Caribbean. The remaining regions, and in particular Sub-Saharan Africa, have made only marginal progress since 2000.

The second health indicator considered is adolescent fertility. This indicator is of special interest for three reasons. First, births to teenagers have a higher probability of being unplanned and untimely, and carry a higher risk for both mother and child of delivery complications and mortality (Grown 2006). Second, early motherhood is a threat to women's empowerment because it frequently precipitates early departure from school, lower human capital accumulation, lower earnings, and higher probability of living in poverty (World Bank 2007). Finally, adolescent motherhood is associated with poorer development outcomes for children—including low educational attainment and future adult poverty—thus perpetuating the vicious circle of poverty.

Figure 2.8 shows data by region for the percentage of young women (15–19 years old) who were pregnant or had children at the time of the survey. Overall, figure 2.8 indicates that adolescent motherhood and pregnancy is most common in Sub-Saharan Africa. Certain countries in other regions—such as Bangladesh, Nepal, and Nicaragua—also have high rates of adolescent motherhood and pregnancy.

FIGURE 2.8
**Percentage of 15- to 19-Year-Old Girls Who Are Mothers or Pregnant,
1990–2000 and 2001–06**

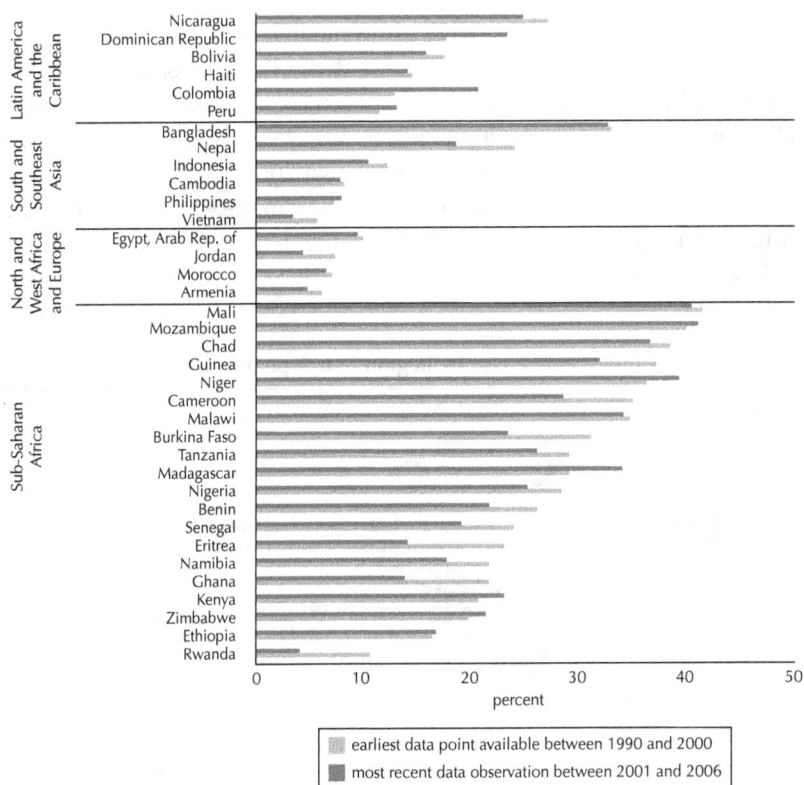

Source: DHS data.

Of the 36 countries with available data, 73 percent had decreasing adolescent motherhood rates during the period. Ghana and Burkina Faso, for instance, managed to reduce adolescent pregnancy and motherhood from 21.5 percent and 31.1 percent, respectively, to 13.8 percent and 23.2 percent during the period 1993 to 2003. Ten countries, however, showed the reverse trend of increasing rates—Colombia, the Dominican Republic, Ethiopia, Kenya, Madagascar, Mozambique, Niger, Peru, the Philippines, and Zimbabwe. In Colombia and the Dominican Republic, adolescent motherhood rates increased from 17.6 percent (1991) and 12.8 percent (1990), respectively, to 23.3 percent (2003) and 20.5 percent (2002).

The third health indicator is contraceptive use, that is, the percentage of women ages 15–49 in marital or consensual unions who report that they are using (or whose sexual partners are using) contraception (plotted in figure 2.9).

The left-most segment indicates use of modern contraception, while the right-most segment captures use of nonmodern birth control methods (e.g., safe period early withdrawal). Modern contraceptive use is an important additional indicator because it captures a woman's ability to space pregnancies and obtain the desired family size (Grown 2006). Research also shows that contraceptive prevalence is the most important proximate determinant of total fertility, which, in turn, affects female labor market participation

FIGURE 2.9
Percentage of Contraceptive Use by Region and Type of Contraceptive

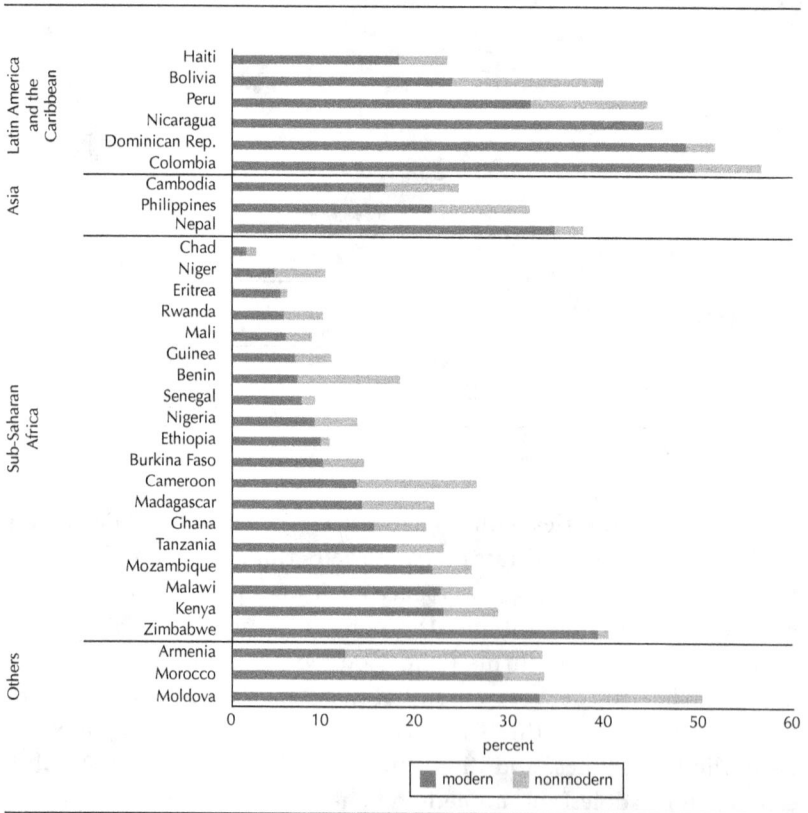

Source: DHS data, most recent year.

and women's empowerment. Fertility may also be closely related to ability to move out of poverty; Eastwood and Lipton (1998), for instance, find a causal link between lower fertility rates and overall poverty rates at the macro level. In addition, the use of one form of modern contraception (e.g., condoms) also prevents HIV/AIDS transmission.

As shown in figure 2.9, the prevalence of use of modern contraception varies enormously from region to region and even from country to country within a region. The highest rates of modern contraceptive use are registered in Latin America and the Caribbean, where 49, 48, and 44 percent of couples used modern contraception in Colombia, the Dominican Republic, and Nicaragua, respectively. At the same time, prevalence rates of use in some countries in the region were only 24 percent and 18 percent in Bolivia and Haiti, respectively—substantially lower than the 39 percent registered in Zimbabwe, the country with the highest percentage rate in the African region. The lowest rates of use of modern contraception are in some of the poorest countries in the sample, including Chad (1.5 percent), Niger (4.5 percent), Eritrea (5.2 percent), Rwanda (5.6 percent), and Mali (5.8 percent).

Also interesting is the large variance in the relative importance of traditional methods of contraception. In some countries (Eritrea, Ethiopia, Nicaragua, and Zimbabwe), nonmodern contraception is a minuscule percentage of total contraceptive use. In other countries (Benin, Bolivia, Cameroon, and Moldova), traditional methods represent a significant share of total contraceptive use.

Fragile states face enormous challenges in achieving their development targets; their health indicators—as well as labor force indicators—are therefore reported on separately in box. 2.1.

Access to Resources: Employment

In the literature relating to female empowerment and agency, themes of female labor force participation have received a great deal of attention. From a macroeconomic perspective, increased participation of women in the labor force can be an important pathway to poverty reduction. Among the poor, female economic activity is instrumental in increasing consumption and savings. It can also lead to future poverty reduction through increases in human capital of children.

Economic activity for women is also a means of enhancing their autonomy and participation in household decision making (Horton 1996).

Box 2.1
Fragile States and MDG3

Fragile states face particularly difficult development challenges, including weak institutions, poor governance, political instability, and ongoing violence. Women and men are likely to be affected differently by state fragility, and gender roles may be important factors affecting the likelihood that state-building takes place. For all these reasons it is crucial to monitor with particular care these countries' progress in achieving MDG3.

The figure below shows the progress on three of the proposed indicators—female labor force participation, adolescent motherhood, and contraceptive use—for fragile and nonfragile International Development Association (IDA) states.[a] The figure indicates that female labor force participation in fragile states is substantially higher than in nonfragile states, although it has decreased slightly during the period. This shows the ambiguity in the interpretation of this indicator because it probably reflects that females take on greater work burdens when basic services are limited and when men are drafted into war, rather than being a sign of more favorable conditions for women's entry into the labor force. It is possible, however, that the high labor force participation rates observed for women may be sustained beyond the conflict. Because conflict inherently causes social change, it may create a window of opportunity for the adoption of new values that permit women to participate more fully in labor markets.

For the two health-related indicators (adolescent motherhood and contraceptive use), it is clear that fragile states are lagging behind other IDA countries. Compared with nonfragile IDA states, fragile states have adolescent motherhood rates about 8 percentage points higher in the first period and about 7 percentage points higher in the second. Even if there appears to be a downward-sloping trend in adolescent motherhood for both fragile and nonfragile states, still one out of four young women in fragile states are mothers or pregnant. The poor performance of fragile states in adolescent motherhood is likely to be related to the fact that women are often vulnerable to rape and other forms of gender-based violence in the context of conflict. Extreme poverty may also force women to marry early and have children at a young age. In addition, social services, such as primary education and health, are weaker in fragile states. This implies low access to contraceptive use and knowledge about how to plan pregnancies. Turning to contraceptive use, the figure indicates that only 16 percent of women (or their partners) in fragile states use any form of contraceptive, while the equivalent figure is 22 percent in nonfragile states. The low access to contraceptives is most likely related to inadequate provision of health services.

Population-Weighted Female Labor Force Participation, Adolescent Motherhood, and Contraceptive Use in Fragile and Nonfragile States

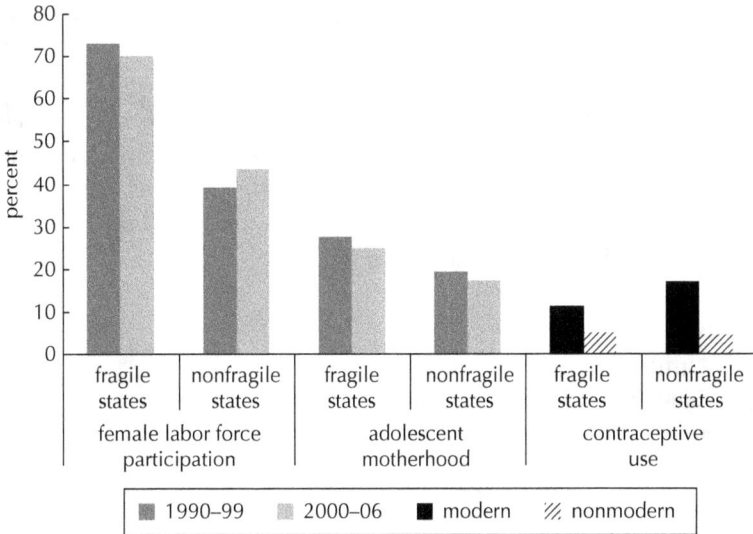

Source: Labor surveys for female labor force participation and Demographic Health Surveys for adolescent motherhood and contraceptive use.

Note: The data for contraceptive use represent the latest year available during the period 2000–06.

a. Fragile states are defined as those countries scoring 3.2 or below on the Country Policy and Institutional Assessment (CPIA). This is similar to the bottom two quintiles of the CPIA, which the OECD–Development Assistance Committee has used for research purposes on fragile states, but has the advantage of being an absolute rather than a relative threshold, allowing the total number of countries covered to vary from year to year depending on changes in performance. This classification—previously referred to as "Low Income Countries Under Stress" (LICUS)—has been in use in the World Bank since 2003; CPIA scores over the years 1998 to 2005 are used to determine what states were fragile over this period. For years before 1998, cutoff values were determined by comparing the distribution of the CPIA in each year with that for 1998–2001. Because it is determined for each year, fragility is a status, not a permanent classification. Countries may thus be intermittently fragile (World Bank 2007).

Furthermore, it is widely recognized that increasing female participation in the labor force can positively impact women's freedom and attainment in other areas, such as education and health, and have a favorable impact on education and health outcomes for their children (Kanbur and Haddad 1994).

In view of these effects, the official MDG3 indicators include share of women in nonagricultural wage employment. Figure 2.10 shows that between the periods 1990–95 and 2000–06, the relative share of women in nonagricultural wage employment rose in almost all regions; the sole exception is the Middle East and North Africa region, where the share has remained almost constant at 18 percent. Women in Europe and Central Asia have the highest share in nonagricultural wage employment (45 percent), with Latin America and the Caribbean showing only slightly lower numbers (43 percent). The share of women in nonagricultural wage employment has increased considerably in the South Asia region but remains low (17 percent) compared with the rest of the world.

FIGURE 2.10
Population-Weighted Share of Women in Nonagricultural Wage Employment by Region, 1990 and 2006

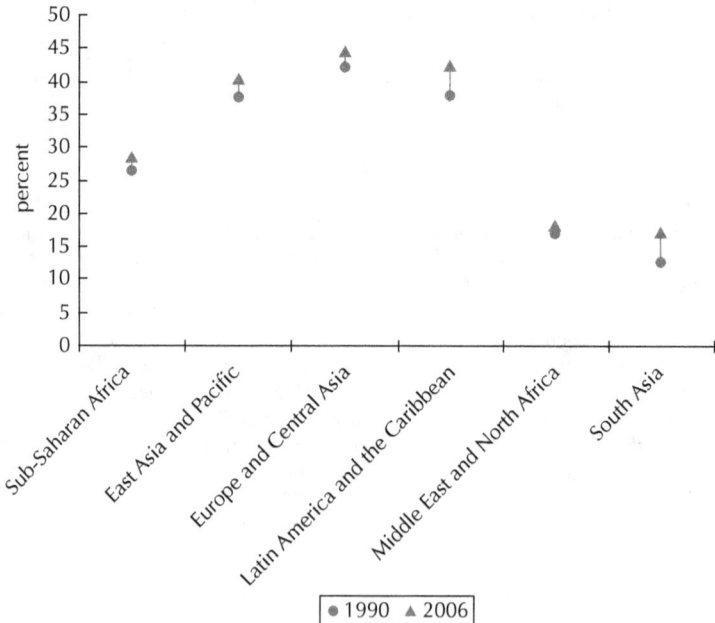

Source: World Development Indicators 2007.

Note: The regional averages are calculated by using the earliest value between 1990 and 1995 and the latest value between 2000 and 2006 for each country. The averages are weighted by country population in 2006.

Countries that have achieved close to a 50 percent share of women in nonagricultural wage employment include The Bahamas, Belarus, Bulgaria, the Cayman Islands, Estonia, Georgia, Latvia, Lithuania, Macao, China, Moldova, Mongolia, the Russian Federation, Tajikistan, and Ukraine. Most of these countries are in the Europe and Central Asia region. Countries that show the sharpest increases in this indicator (greater than 10 percent) include Albania, Argentina, Azerbaijan, Kenya, Papua New Guinea, and Tajikistan.

Countries with very low values for this indicator (lower than 15 percent) are Bahrain, Burkina Faso, Chad, the Islamic Republic of Iran, Malawi, Niger, Pakistan, Saudi Arabia, and the United Arab Emirates. Most of these countries are either in Sub-Saharan Africa or the Middle East and North Africa. In the Middle East and North Africa region, patterns of low female participation in nonagricultural wage employment can be explained by norms of female seclusion. Cultural norms in this region place restrictions on female mobility, and women's wage work is often associated with loss of status for the household. Some African countries are also characterized by relatively low rates of female wage employment outside of agriculture; evidence suggests that there are few cultural restrictions on female labor market participation in Africa and that these patterns may be driven by a gendered division of labor in which much female labor is concentrated in the agricultural sector (Kabeer 2003).

In fact, one of the major drawbacks of this official MDG indicator is that it ignores female work in agriculture, the preponderant sector in many developing economies. Several rationales underpin the exclusion of female work in agriculture for MDG3s. First, this work is frequently unpaid or underpaid. Beyond low or zero earnings, it is also frequently poor-quality employment (low opportunities for advancement, no social benefits, and so forth). However, it must be emphasized that the agricultural sector employs a large proportion of female workers in many developing countries. While the percentage of men and women employed in agriculture is expected to fall as economies develop, the rate and pattern of this shift can be of considerable interest to researchers and policy makers. At least in Sub-Saharan Africa, men appear to be moving into the off-farm sector at a faster rate than women (Kabeer 2003).

The share of women in nonagricultural wage employment does not capture the full range of issues relating to women's economic participation. The impact of women's workforce participation on gender equality depends heavily on the returns accruing to men's and women's paid work.

It is therefore imperative to supplement female labor force participation rates with information on women's wages compared with those of men.

Additional MDG3 Indicators for Employment

To overcome some of the deficiencies in the official MDG3 indicator relating to economic participation of women, two additional indicators are proposed in this area: female labor force participation rates and the ratio of female to male hourly earnings in primary, secondary, and tertiary sectors.

The female labor force participation rate is considered a powerful source of information on the status of women in society. It provides a more complete picture of the relative economic participation of women by looking at all sectors of the economy, including agriculture. The measurement of women's labor force participation is complicated, however, by measurement difficulties (Tzannatos 2006; Grown 2006; Grown in chapter 3). Women's employment, particularly in the primary sector, has been notoriously difficult to capture. Women's roles in subsistence agriculture and in home-based activities are often treated as extensions of their domestic duties and are frequently not captured in household or labor market surveys. In some countries, female employment is concentrated in the informal sector, presenting other challenges for data collection. In response to these issues, efforts have been made to broaden and standardize the definitions of female economic activity.

Figure 2.11 plots female labor force participation rates by region for two age groups: ages 20–24 and ages 25–49. The labor force participation rate for the younger age group indicates young women's success in transitioning from school to work and to what extent they have acquired marketable skills that can be translated into employment. The greatest differences in male and female labor market participation rates are usually observed when women reach the older age group (ages 25–49) because this is the age range when women tend to make a greater contribution to care giving (for children, the sick, and the elderly), while men increase their labor supply outside the home.

Female labor force participation rates vary significantly by world region (female labor force participation in fragile states is reported upon separately in box 2.1). Labor force participation rates for 20- to 24-year-old women are highest in East Asia and Pacific (60 percent) and Sub-Saharan Africa (59 percent), followed closely by Latin America (56 percent) and Europe and Central Asia (53 percent). Female labor force participation rates are lowest in the Middle East and North Africa (47 percent) and in South Asia (21 percent). Participation rates are uniformly higher for women ages

FIGURE 2.11

Population-Weighted Female Labor Force Participation by Region for Ages 20–24 and 25–49, 1991 and 2007

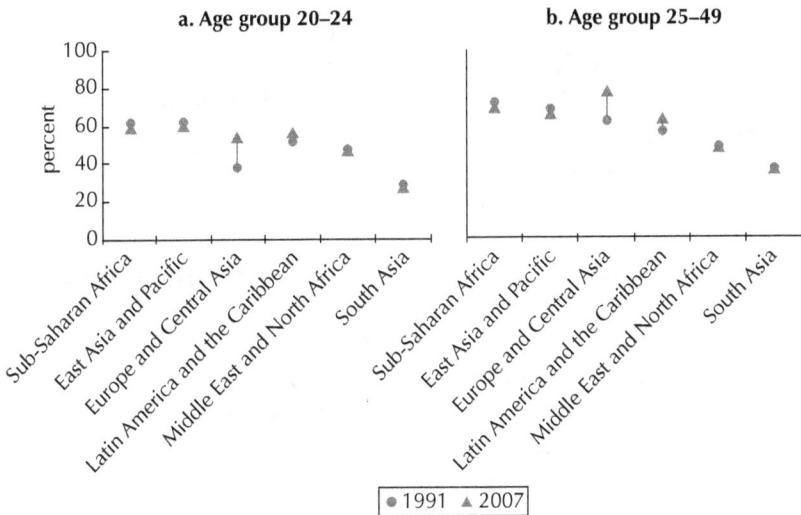

a. Age group 20–24   b. Age group 25–49

● 1991 ▲ 2007

Source: Household and Labor Force Surveys, various years.

Note: The regional averages are calculated using the earliest year between 1991 and 1998 and the latest year between 2000 and 2007. Regional averages are weighted by country populations in 2006.

25–49 than for women ages 20–24 (although, as mentioned above, the gap between men's and women's participation rates is also higher for the older age cohort). For women in the older age cohort, labor force participation rates in Europe and Central Asia (74 percent) surpass other regions. Aside from this, the overall pattern remains the same, with Sub-Saharan Africa (69 percent) and East Asia and Pacific (67 percent) showing much higher rates compared with the Middle East and North Africa (47 percent) and South Asia (36 percent).

Evidence from figure 2.11 also shows that, with the exception of Europe and Central Asia (and Latin America and the Caribbean to some extent in the older age group), labor force participation rates have not increased over the period; in fact, female participation rates declined slightly in Sub-Saharan Africa, East Asia and Pacific, the Middle East and North Africa, and South Asia for the age 20–24 cohort.

Turning from regional to country-level analysis, what appears as lack of progress at the aggregate level in fact conceals great variation at the country level (see figure 2.12). Countries in which female labor force participation has decreased cancel out countries in which participation has increased. Substantial declines in women's labor force participation were registered in several African countries (Madagascar, Mali, Niger, Swaziland, and Tanzania), which were offset in the aggregate regional trends by more modest percentage increases in more populous South Africa. The same pattern occurs in East Asia and Pacific, where Vietnam and Thailand show increases in participation, while female participation in Indonesia fell by almost 10 percentage points. The Europe and Central Asia region shows significant increases in participation in five countries: Azerbaijan, Hungary, the Kyrgyz Republic, Poland, and Ukraine. At the same time, there are several countries in the region in which female labor force participation rates have dropped—Albania, Armenia, Bulgaria, and Moldova. In Latin America, female participation rates have increased substantially in Argentina, Chile, Colombia, Costa Rica, Mexico, and Peru, while the trend in Jamaica and Paraguay goes in the opposite direction. Nepal and Pakistan showed substantial declines in female labor force participation, which were offset in aggregate for South Asia by more modest percentage increases in more populous India. It is not possible to distinguish any trend in the Middle East and North Africa because the region lacks data for the two periods.

The sharp increase in participation in the Eastern European countries deserves particular mention. Many countries in this region, most notably the Kyrgyz Republic and Poland, have witnessed very sharp increases in female labor force participation rates. This may be a return to more long-run equilibrium levels following the collapse in female participation that accompanied the disintegration of the Soviet Union. One explanation for the rapid increases in Poland and Hungary could be the accession of these countries to the European Union during this period. Recall that the share of women in nonagricultural wage employment is also the highest for this region. Seen in combination, these statistics might be reflecting structural differences in the labor markets of Europe and Central Asia compared with other developing regions. Other factors could include market reforms and other changes in the labor market institutions of Eastern European countries. Most Eastern European countries initiated major reforms in 1990 or 1991 and have made progress in creating institutions for a market economy (Brainerd 2000). Many of these countries saw wage liberalization and tax and other legal reforms. For instance, in Ukraine the government allowed the minimum wage to fall considerably by 1995 (Brainerd 2000). Alternatively, these statistics could be capturing a shift of female employment

FIGURE 2.12

Population-Weighted Female Labor Force Participation Rates for Age Group 25–49 by Country, 1991 and 2007

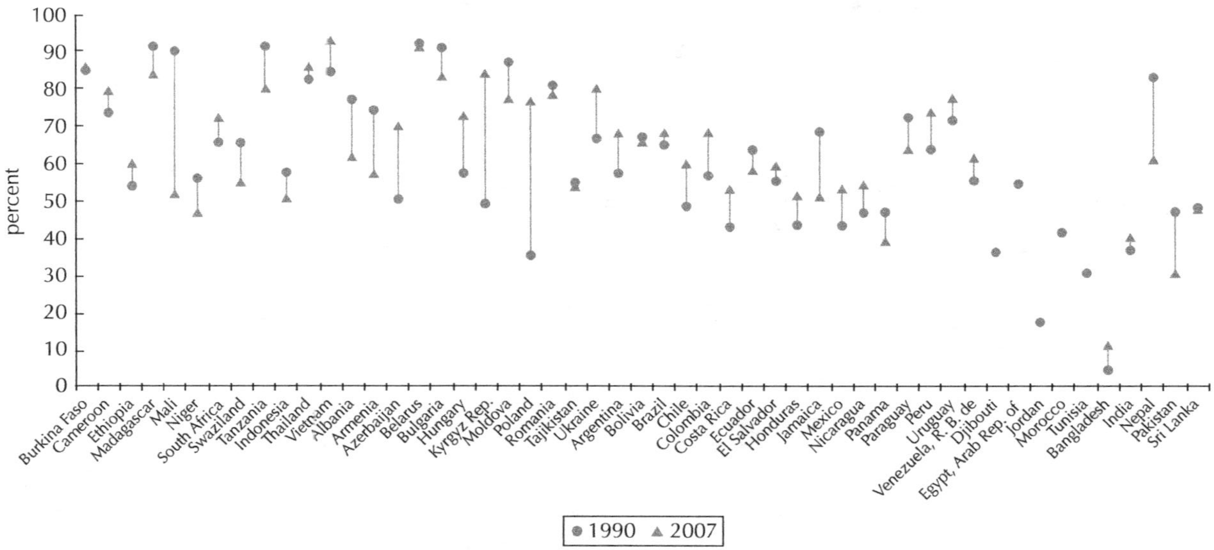

● 1990   ▲ 2007

Source: Household and Labor Force Surveys, various years.

Note: Regional averages are calculated using the earliest year between 1991 and 1998 and the latest year between 2000 and 2007. Regional averages are weighted by country populations in 2006.

from invisible home-based activities to formal market work. Whatever the underlying cause, the female labor market experience in Eastern Europe requires closer analysis.

How can we explain sharp differences in labor force participation rates of women across the world? Following Ester Boserup's (1970) groundbreaking work on this issue, Mammen and Paxson (2000) argue that there is a u-shaped relationship between female labor force participation rates and economic development. In very poor countries, female participation is high and women are concentrated in farm employment or family enterprises. Increases in incomes move women out of the labor force, both because of income effects and because of social barriers to women working for pay. At high levels of development, women begin to move into white-collar employment as their education levels rise (Mammen and Paxson 2000).

Beyond level of development and human capital, labor market institutions and cultural norms also seem to be important in shaping female labor force participation rates across countries. Clearly, these factors are interrelated: cultural factors (for example, norms relating to female mobility) could influence female labor force participation via their impact on other variables, such as female education and fertility choices.

Increased access of women to paid work is, by itself, an inadequate measure of their economic and social advancement. An important contribution of this chapter is the introduction of an additional indicator that measures women's empowerment—the ratio of female to male hourly earnings. Hourly earnings ratios were used rather than hourly wage ratios because the share of the population in wage employment is very small for many countries.[11] It is important to note that differences in hourly earnings between men and women may be driven by (i) differences in observable human capital characteristics; (ii) differences in unobservable characteristics, such as talent; (iii) discrimination (only in the case of wage employment); or (iv) differences in the sectoral or occupational distributions of women and men.

Figure 2.13 shows the ratio of female to male hourly earnings by region and by sector.[12] To control for differences between men and women in number of hours worked, hourly earnings were used rather than total earnings. For the four regions for which hourly earnings data are available, there is significant variation in women's relative earnings across sectors.[13] Women's hourly earnings relative to men's are highest in the tertiary sector (ranging from 70 percent in Sub-Saharan Africa to 85 percent in Europe and

FIGURE 2.13
Population-Weighted Ratio of Female-to-Male Hourly Wages by Region and Sector, 2006

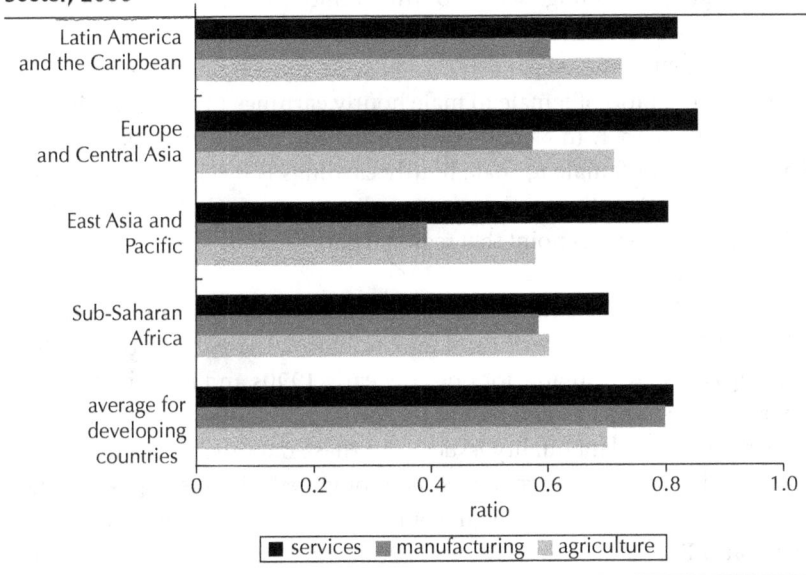

Source: Household surveys, various years.

Note: Latest year between 1997 and 2006. Based on 41 countries; the Middle East and North Africa region and the South Asia region not represented because of lack of data.

Central Asia) and lowest in manufacturing (ranging from 39 percent in East Asia and Pacific to 61 percent in Latin America and the Caribbean). One explanation for the smaller relative wage gaps in the tertiary sector is that in many countries a significant proportion of tertiary sector jobs are in the public sector, where the gender wage gap is typically lower (Weichselbaumer and Winter-Ebmer 2005).

Within sectors, the interregional variation in hourly earnings ratios among regions is relatively modest. The manufacturing sector in East Asia and Pacific is a notable exception (where women's hourly earnings are only 39 percent of men's) compared with secondary sector hourly earnings ratios in other regions.[14]

While there is an insufficient number of countries with earnings data in the Middle East and North Africa and South Asia regions to compute regional averages, household surveys from individual countries can be illustrative. Household survey data from the Arab Republic of Egypt (1998) show negligible gender disparity in hourly earnings, with a ratio of female to male hourly earnings of 1.32, 0.93, and 0.98 in the primary, secondary, and tertiary sectors, respectively. However, the proportion of females in the nonagricultural wage sector for this country, at only 21 percent, is still very low. In South Asia, survey data from two very different countries—Maldives (1998) and Nepal (2003)—provide some interesting insights. In Maldives, the ratio of female to male hourly earnings in all sectors is equal to or higher than 1. In Nepal, however, the situation is remarkably different: the ratio of female to male hourly earnings is 0.47, 0.32, and 0.54 in the primary, secondary, and tertiary sectors, respectively. These disparities underline the obvious point that regional data can hide significant country-level variations.

Figure 2.14 shows the evolution of female-to-male earnings ratios for 14 countries in Latin America and the Caribbean, the only region for which earnings data are available for both the early 1990s and more recent years. Sharp changes and extreme values for earnings data shown by some countries may reflect data quality issues, and these data should be interpreted with caution. Relative wages for women compared with men appear to have risen in the primary sector for all countries except Honduras, Jamaica, and República Bolivariana de Venezuela. In the secondary sector, all countries except Bolivia, Ecuador, and Peru have shown at least a small increase in the ratio of female to male hourly earnings. In the tertiary sector, Ecuador, Honduras, and Paraguay show significant increases in the female-to-male wage ratio, while this ratio falls substantially in Bolivia and El Salvador. Other countries of the region show little change.

On the whole, data from Latin America and the Caribbean appear to indicate an overall decline in gender earnings gaps and, hence, an improvement in the relative position of women in the labor market. This is consistent with more rigorous research on gender wage gaps that suggests that there has been a fall over time in the raw wage differentials between men and women, mostly because of better human capital endowments of women (Weichselbaumer and Winter-Ebmer 2005; Duryea, Cox Edwards, and Ureta 2001).

*Additionality: New Indicators Versus Share in
Nonagricultural Wage Employment*
This section evaluates the information added by the new indicators to the official MDG3 indicator of share of women in nonagricultural wage employment. First, the analysis compares country performance in share of women in nonagricultural wage employment with performance in female labor

FIGURE 2.14

Female-to-Male Hourly Wage Ratios in Latin America and the Caribbean over Time and by Sector, 1991 and 2006

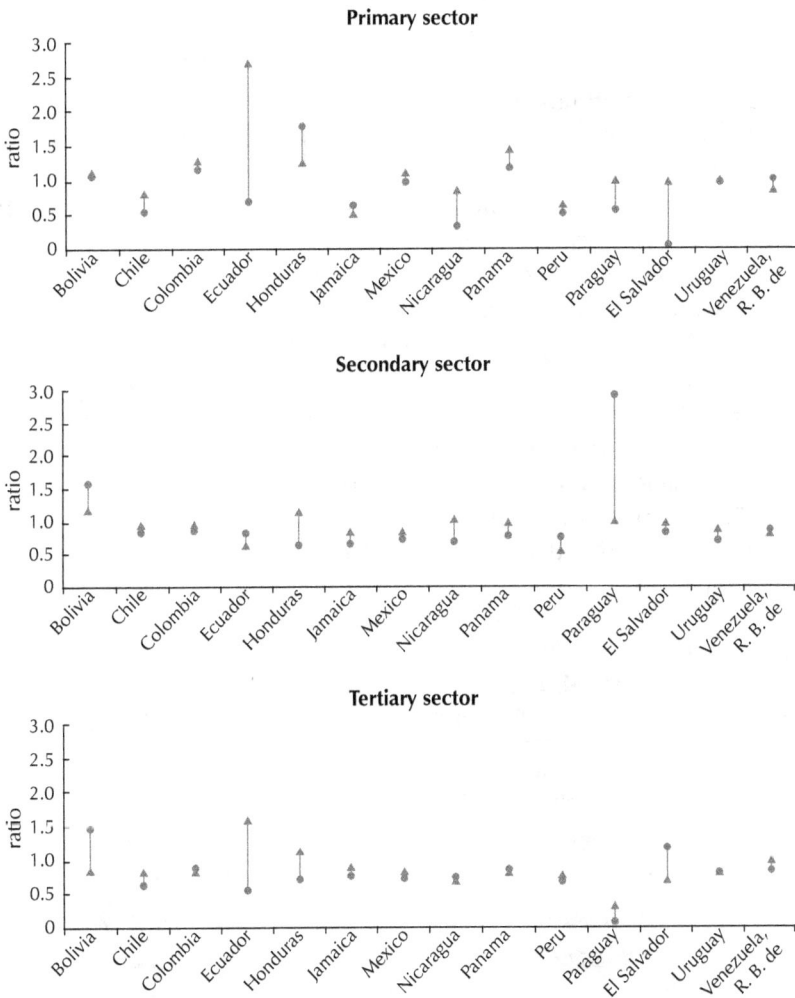

Primary sector

Secondary sector

Tertiary sector

Source: Household surveys.

Note: Earliest year between 1991 and 1996 and latest year between 2001 and 2006.

force participation rates (figure 2.15). The two indicators capture the relative economic participation of women in very different ways. Share of women in nonagricultural wage employment leaves out information on labor force participation of women in the agricultural sector. Also, share of women in nonagricultural wage employment is relative to males (a gender-equality measure) while the female labor force participation rate is an absolute value for women alone (an empowerment measure).

Figure 2.15 makes clear that agricultural employment and self-employment are important sources of employment for women in some regions. East Asia and Pacific, for example, has the highest female labor force participation rate of any developing region, despite the fact that women represent less than 40 percent of workers in nonagricultural wage employment.

If only nonprimary employment is included, Europe and Central Asia emerges with the highest regional female labor force participation rate. It is not surprising that the female labor force participation rates for Sub-Saharan Africa rise dramatically when agricultural employment is included.

Because marked differences arise at the regional level between the two indicators, it is expected that for some countries the differences are even more significant. The differences between female labor force participation rates and share of women in nonagricultural wage employment are particularly noticeable for Burkina Faso, Cameroon, Lithuania, Maldives, Nepal, and Vietnam (not shown in figure 2.15). The fact that these countries belong to different regions underscores the need to consider female labor force participation in addition to nonagricultural wage employment.

FIGURE 2.15
Population-Weighted Share of Women in Nonagricultural Wage Employment Versus Female Labor Force Participation

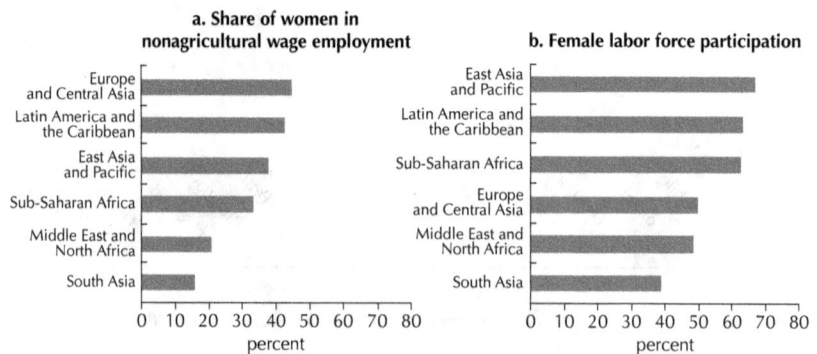

Source: World Development Indicators (2007) for share of women in nonagricultural wage employment; Household Surveys for female labor force participation.

Note: Regional averages calculated by weighting country values by country population for 2006.

Figure 2.16 compares the share of women in nonagricultural wage employment with the ratio of female to male hourly earnings in nonagricultural wage employment. For the sample of 45 countries for which data are available for both indicators, country performance is compared by calculating z scores on each of the two indicators. In figure 2.16, country z score for share of women in nonagricultural wage employment is compared with country z score for average ratio of female to male hourly earnings in secondary and tertiary sectors.

In Bulgaria, Paraguay, Russia, South Africa, and Vietnam, women have a relatively high share in nonagricultural wage employment (40 percent and

FIGURE 2.16

Share of Women in Nonagricultural Wage Employment Versus Ratio of Female to Male Hourly Earnings in Secondary and Tertiary Sectors

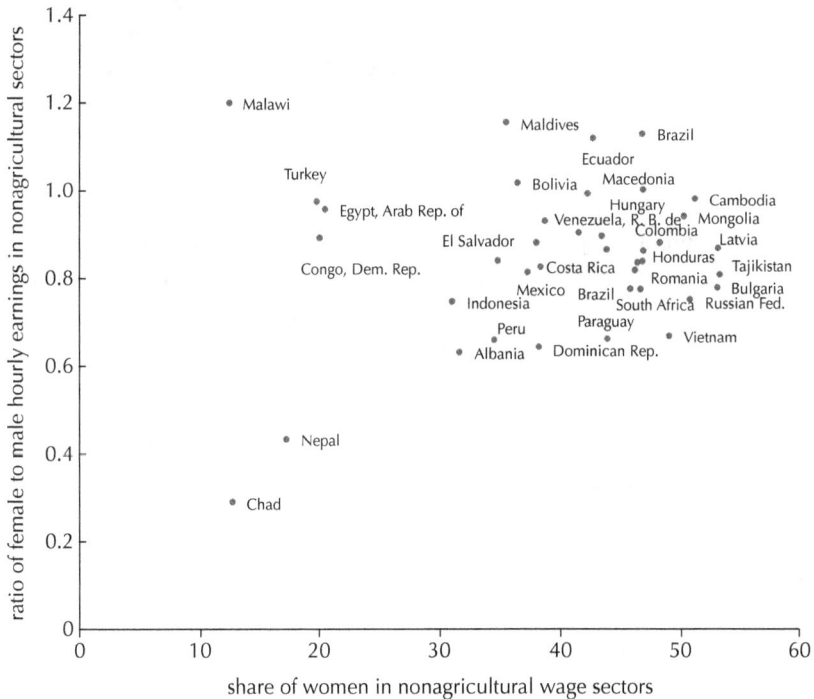

Source: World Development Indicators (2007) for share of women in nonagricultural wage employment; Household Surveys for earnings data.

Note: Ratio of female to male earnings calculated as an average of ratios in secondary and tertiary sectors. For clarity of exposition, only certain data points labeled.

above) but receive considerably lower hourly earnings compared with men (ratio of female to male hourly earnings less than 0.8). In direct contrast, Egypt, Malawi, and Turkey show relatively equitable earnings for males and females (ratio of female to male hourly earnings 0.9 or above) despite women having a low share in the nonagricultural wage sector (25 percent or less). This suggests that relative gains from economic participation of women can vary considerably from their overall level of participation. The impact of female labor force participation on welfare cannot be judged by participation rates alone. Furthermore, differences in hourly earnings coupled with lower hours worked because of housekeeping and child-rearing activities could combine to significantly lower returns to women despite participation in formal labor markets.

Female Labor Force Participation and Empowerment

The relationship between female labor force participation and women's welfare or empowerment is mediated by several other variables. First is the issue of relative wages compared with men, as discussed above. Another issue relates to the patterns of time use for women who are in the labor force.

The extent to which increasing female employment is likely to increase gender equality depends in part on the extent to which increased labor force participation by women is offset by decreased work at the household level. Evidence from around the world suggests that women have to shoulder a disproportionate share of household duties in addition to their work in the labor force. Hence, despite high rates of labor force participation, the burden of nonmarket work remains high for women. This means that women in the labor force typically endure longer working days than their male counterparts (UNDP 1995). And access to paying jobs is not likely to have a perceptible impact on female welfare if these jobs are invisible or if earnings are appropriated by male heads of household. Finally, occupational segregation of women into low-paying jobs may mean that gains in female welfare from increased participation could be low.

Increased opportunities for women in the labor force can improve their relative position both directly and indirectly. In many contexts, increased participation in the labor force by women can be linked directly to increased empowerment, access to resources, and welfare. It can also lessen women's disadvantages in other areas by increasing their access to education, health care, and reproductive freedom. However, the relationship between female labor force participation and welfare is neither clear nor straightforward

(Tzannatos 2006). The general strategy of advocating increasing female participation in the formal labor market needs to be constructed with care and modified in a context-specific way. Nonetheless, there is growing consensus that increased economic participation of women can be a powerful weapon in the global fight against poverty and inequality.

Access to Resources: Political Participation

Increasing women's representation in political office is one of four official indicators for tracking progress toward achieving MDG3. In the absence of additional indicators, progress in this dimension is tracked solely by the official indicator of percentage of seats held by women in national parliaments, which is plotted by region in figure 2.17 for 1990 and 2006.

As indicated in the figure, all regions except Europe and Central Asia increased the number of women in national parliaments during the period. The greatest progress was observed in Sub-Saharan Africa

FIGURE 2.17
Population-Weighted Percentage of Seats Held by Women in National Parliaments, 1990 and 2006

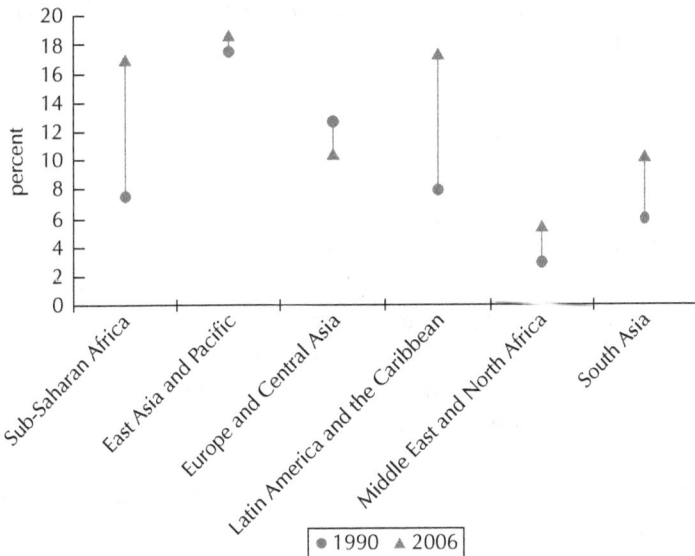

Source: World Development Indicators 2007.

Note: The reigonal averages are calculated by using the earliest value between 1990 and 1995 and the latest value between 2000 and 2006 for each country. The averages are weighted by country population in 2006.

and Latin America and the Caribbean, with increases of approximately 10 percentage points (in both cases, an increase of more than 100 percent). While the trend is toward increased women's representation in national parliaments, no region has yet reached the goal of 25 percent women in parliament as set out in the Beijing Declaration and Platform for Action. The Middle East and North Africa and South Asia lag furthest behind in female political representation.

The increase in the share of women in national parliaments can be attributed to a large extent to the increasing global pressure for the inclusion of women in international politics (Paxton and Kunovich 2003). To accomplish the goal of increasing the share of women in parliament, more than 100 countries, including developing countries, such as Argentina, Bangladesh, Eritrea, India, Tanzania, and Uganda, have adopted (or considered adopting) quotas for the selection of female candidates. While this strategy is useful in improving women's representation, it is not clear that it translates into increases in women's actual decision-making power (Grown 2006). Dahlerup and Freidenvall (2005) conducted a worldwide analysis of the implementation process of quotas; their results indicate that unless the quota system is accompanied by rules about the rank-order of candidates and sanctions for noncompliance, quota provisions may be merely symbolic.

The Usefulness of the Extended Indicators: Global Measures

The preceding section presented, by domain of gender equality, the official MDG3 indicators and the proposed additional indicators. Domain by domain, the analysis attempted to give a sense of the additionality of the proposed indicators—that is, to what extent did the new indicators add information above and beyond that contained in the official indicators. This section continues with the analysis of additionality, but for the official and proposed indicators as a whole, rather than indicator by indicator and domain by domain.

This analysis of additionality is undertaken by focusing on regional performance rather than country ranking.[15] The analysis first computes z scores for all countries for all four official MDG3 indicators and two of the new indicators (female under-five mortality rates and female labor force participation rates). It then averages z scores for the official MDG3 indicators. Country z scores on average official MDG3 indicators, female under-five mortality rates, and female labor force participation rates are then averaged by region. This method allows us to compare performance on a region-by-region basis, as well as to evaluate intraregional performance on different dimensions.[16] Because education is overrepresented in the official MDG indicators, comparing regional z scores on these indicators with regional z scores on under-five mortality and female labor force participation allows the evaluation of regional performance in education relative to performance in health and the economy.

Figure 2.18 shows that for some regions—notably Sub-Saharan Africa and the Middle East and North Africa—performance on the new indicators relative to the rest of the world is substantially different from that on the official indicators. Africa's mean z score on the official MDG3 indicators is nearly a full standard deviation below the world average. It fares even worse on female under-five mortality, at nearly two standard deviations below the world average. With regard to female labor force participation, however, Sub-Saharan Africa scores quite close to the world average. In the Middle East and North Africa, female labor force participation rates are nearly 1.5 standard deviations below the world mean—at the same time, the region's overall score on the official MDG3 indicators is quite close to the world mean and its female under-five mortality is nearly 0.5 standard deviations above the world mean.

For East Asia and Pacific, Europe and Central Asia, and South Asia, the relative performance on the new indicators mirrors quite closely the relative performance on the official indicators. In this sense, the new indicators add little information at the regional level. Latin America and the Caribbean is an intermediate case: the region does slightly better on female under-five mortality and has slightly lower female labor force participation relative to the rest of the world, compared with its z scores on the official MDG3 indicators.

Country Performance

The first section of this chapter discussed the relative merits of indexes and individual indicators as measures of gender equality. Indexes provide a quick and easy way to rank countries' performance on gender equality; given the various problems associated with indexes, however, this chapter eschews their use.[17]

What option, then, is available for reviewing country performance in gender equality?

FIGURE 2.18
Comparison of Relative Country Performance on Official MDG3 Indicators with Selected New Indicators

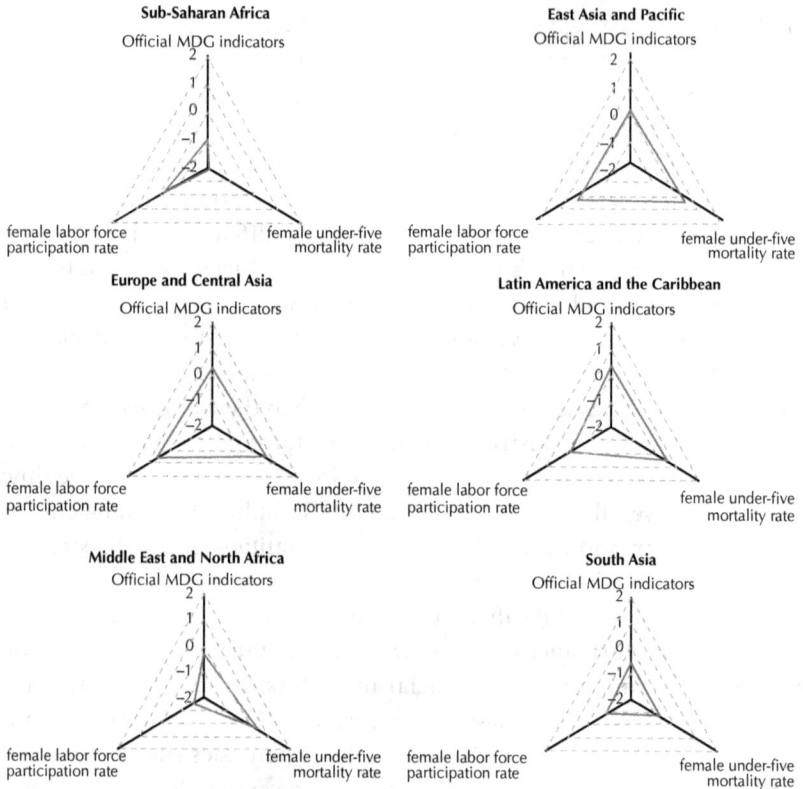

Sub-Saharan Africa
Official MDG indicators
female labor force participation rate
female under-five mortality rate

East Asia and Pacific
Official MDG indicators
female labor force participation rate
female under-five mortality rate

Europe and Central Asia
Official MDG indicators
female labor force participation rate
female under-five mortality rate

Latin America and the Caribbean
Official MDG indicators
female labor force participation rate
female under-five mortality rate

Middle East and North Africa
Official MDG indicators
female labor force participation rate
female under-five mortality rate

South Asia
Official MDG indicators
female labor force participation rate
female under-five mortality rate

Source: Authors' calculations based on World Development Indicators 2007 and household survey data.

Note: Average z scores on official MDG indicators compared with z scores on female under-five mortality rate and female labor force participation rate (new indicators); z scores for each indicator calculated on the basis of data for total of 55 countries and then averaged by region.

We start by considering individual country performance on the official MDG3 indicators relative to other countries in the same region. We then do the same for a set of the new indicators for which data are widely available. We next examine performance on individual indicators grouped into the four domains of gender equality (education, labor, health, and political participation) discussed above.

To calculate relative performance, the analysis calculates standardized z scores for each country on each gender equality indicator (using regional means). For the comparisons that span several indicators (for example, performance on the official MDG3 indicators as a whole or on the new indicators as a whole), the z scores for the various indicators are simply added to get a country-specific composite score. For performance on individual indicators, countries with scores of more than two standard deviations above the regional mean score for that indicator are labeled "high performers," while those with more than two standard deviations below the regional mean are labeled "low performers." Regional means are used rather than global means to better compare countries at similar levels of economic development and to (presumably) focus more on country-specific actions or conditions that may influence the level of an indicator by controlling for regional commonalities.[18]

Overall Performance: Official MDG3 Indicators

Figure 2.19 shows countries' relative performance on the official MDG3 indicators when benchmarked against other countries within a region. The average performance across all official MDG3 indicators is measured as the mean z score (sum of z scores for all indicators divided by the number of indicators).

Looking only at the Sub-Saharan African experience, it would be tempting to attribute low performance to low levels of per capita income (and perhaps with associated institutional weaknesses in very poor countries). But the experience in Latin America and the Caribbean belies this facile explanation: Honduras performs much better than Nicaragua, despite similar levels of development (in fact, Honduras has a purchasing power parity gross national income about 25 percent lower than Nicaragua's).[19] Of interest in Latin America, Chile—the region's economic superstar for sustained growth rates—has a mean aggregate z score (−0.61) that almost qualifies it for low-performer status. In East Asia and Pacific, Mongolia (a high performer) has a purchasing power parity gross national income that is 22 percent lower than Cambodia's (a low performer).[20]

Almost all countries in Europe and Central Asia are clustered between the mean and 0.4 standard deviations above it, which indicates balanced progress in this region. There are, however, two countries classified as low performers: Turkey and Tajikistan. Finally, Maldives is a high performer in the South Asia region; Pakistan, with a mean aggregate z score of -0.62, approaches low-performer status.

FIGURE 2.19
Countries' Relative Performance on the Official MDG3 Indicators Compared with Other Countries in the Same Region

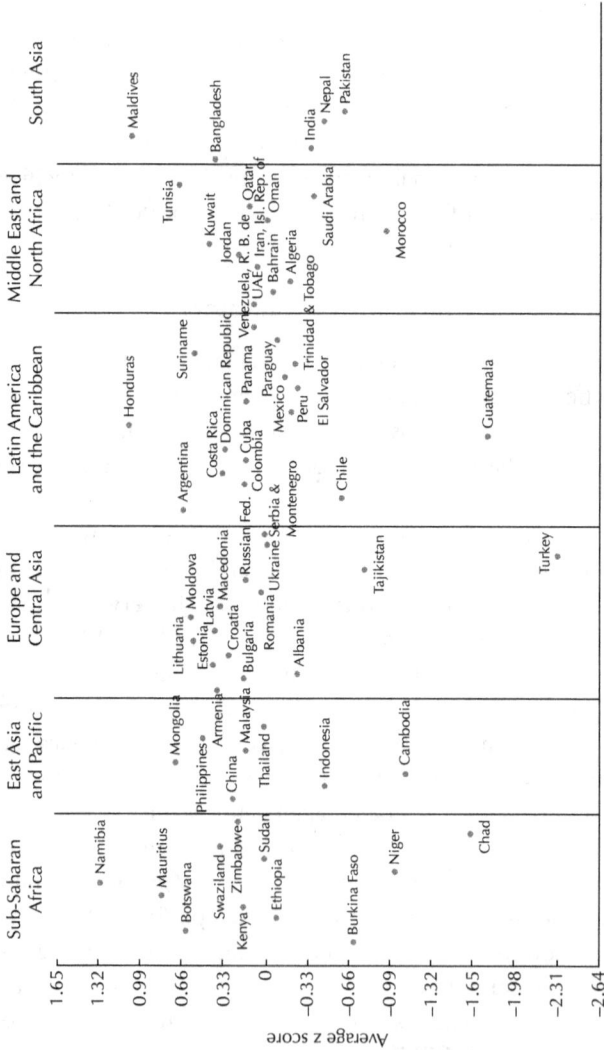

Source: Authors' calculations based on World Development Indicators, 2007.

Note: Countries are compared only with other countries within the same region. Regions include Sub-Saharan Africa (11 countries), East Asia and Pacific (7 countries), Europe and Central Asia (26 countries), Latin America and the Caribbean (17 countries), the Middle East and North Africa (11 countries), South Asia (5 countries). Z score = country value minus region average, divided by region standard deviation. Values are for the latest year between 2000 and 2005.

Overall Performance: New Indicators

Figure 2.20 reports country performance for three of the new indicators: female-to-male primary completion ratio, female labor force participation rate, and under-five female-to-male mortality ratio. Once again, high (low) performers are defined as countries with an average z score per indicator greater than 0.66 (less than –0.66).

It is difficult to compare this figure to the earlier figure for performance on the official indicators because the sample for the two figures is not identical. Two high performers (Namibia and Mauritius) and one low performer (Guatemala) on the official MDG3 indicators, for example, are not included in figure 2.20 because of lack of data.

With this caveat, the same general picture emerges for heterogeneous performance within regions. On the new indicators, Sub-Saharan Africa has five high performers (Cape Verde, Ghana, Lesotho, Madagascar, and South Africa) and six low performers (Chad, Côte d'Ivoire, Malawi, Mali, Niger, and Nigeria). Chad and Niger were also low performers on the official MDG3 indicators.

Europe and Central Asia has only one high performer (Lithuania) and three low performers (Azerbaijan, Tajikistan, and Turkey—the latter two were also low performers on the official MDG3 indicators). In Latin America and the Caribbean, Argentina and Uruguay score as high performers, while Bolivia and Guatemala are low performers. Finally, South Asia has both a high performer in Maldives (as it was with the official indicators), and a low performer (Afghanistan).

Countries with poor scores for the set of new indicators and the official MDG3 indicators have a broad range of issues requiring attention. Those that score low on just one set of indicators have a narrower range of issues. Formulating policy responses to address these issues requires detailed information on exactly what forms of gender inequality are present. The chapter now turns to that topic by examining performance on individual indicators grouped into the domains of education, health, labor markets, and political participation.

Country Performance on Individual Indicators

For all individual indicators, the discussion is limited to those with a z score with an absolute value greater than 2. As with the sets of indicators examined above, the z scores are calculated using regional mean values rather than world means. A normal distribution of z scores is equivalent

FIGURE 2.20

Intraregional Comparison of High and Low Performers for New Indicators

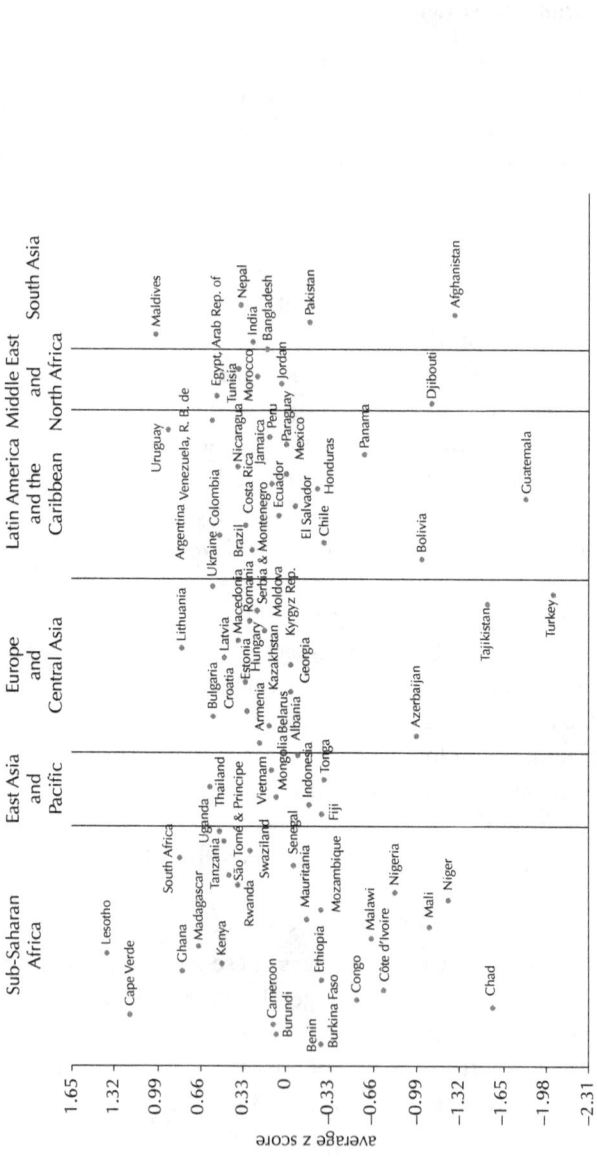

Source: Authors' calculations based on World Development Indicators, 2007 and household survey data.

Note: Countries are compared only with other countries within the same region for selected new indicators for which most data are available. Regions include Sub-Saharan Africa (27 countries), East Asia and Pacific (6 countries), Europe and Central Asia (20 countries), Latin America and the Caribbean (18 countries), the Middle East and North Africa (5 countries), and South Asia (6 countries). Z score = country value minus region average, divided by region standard deviation. Values are for the latest year between 2000 and 2005. New indicators include girls-to-boys ratio in primary completion, female under-five mortality rate, female labor force participation rate. Z scores for under-five mortality rates adjusted so that low rates reflect high scores.

to focusing on the 4.56 percent of the observations with the most extreme values. This approach keeps manageable the number of countries identified as outliers.

Table 2.2 summarizes these high and low performers for official and new indicators across the four domains of gender equality. The scatter plots for each indicator are presented in annex 2A to this chapter. Table 2.2 also includes information regarding countries that showed significant change in the period 1990 to 2006. For each indicator, the annual rate of change for each country is calculated using the earliest available data point between 1990 and 1997 and the latest available data point between 2000 and 2007. Z scores are then calculated for each country. In this case, however, z scores are calculated at the global level (not the regional). Countries with z scores greater than 0.66 are identified as countries showing rapid progress and countries with z scores less than –0.66 are identified as countries showing slow progress or deterioration.

Two observations immediately stand out in table 2.2. The first is that several countries are repeat entrants in the "low performers" category. Turkey is a low performer relative to its regional peers in primary enrollment, secondary enrollment, female participation in nonagricultural wage employment, and female labor force participation rate.[21] Chad is a low performer in primary and secondary enrollment ratios. Guatemala, Malawi, and Russia are low performers in the two labor market measures: female participation in nonagricultural wage employment and female labor force participation rate. Djibouti is a low performer in female under-five mortality and the secondary enrollment ratio. Tajikistan is a low performer in both tertiary enrollment ratio and female under-five mortality. Only two countries are repeat high performers: the Islamic Republic of Iran (on both primary enrollment and primary completion ratios) and Lesotho (on both primary completion and secondary enrollment ratios).

The second salient observation is that there are far fewer high performers than low performers. It seems that performance is not normally distributed; rather, it is skewed to the left toward low performance. A final observation is that no country appears as a high performer on one indicator and a low performer on another.

Conclusions

This chapter examines progress toward MDG3 using the official indicators and an expanded set of indicators that more completely measures

TABLE 2.2
High and Low Performers for Official and New Indicators

Domain	Indicator	High performers within region	Low performers within region	Rapid progress (annual % change)	Slow progress or deterioration (annual % change)
Official indicators					
Capabilities: Education	Primary enrollment ratio	Armenia Iran, Islamic Rep. of St. Kitts and Nevis	Cayman Islands Central African Republic Chad Guinea-Bissau Lao PDR Papua New Guinea Turkey St. Vincent and the Grenadines Yemen, Rep. of	Iran, Islamic Rep. of Mauritania Nepal Chad Benin The Gambia Guinea Yemen, Rep. of	Eritrea
	Secondary enrollment ratio	Lesotho Suriname	Chad Cambodia Djibouti Turkey	Chad The Gambia Malawi Mauritania Nepal	Ethiopia
	Tertiary enrollment ratio		Tajikistan	Mali Guinea Jamaica Equatorial Guinea	Tajikistan Congo, Dem. Rep. of

Access to resources and opportunities: Employment	Literacy ratio	Nicaragua	Turkey Guatemala Yemen, Rep. of Chad Niger Cambodia Afghanistan Morocco Lao PDR Benin	Yemen, Rep. of Nepal	Ethiopia
	Female participation in nonagricultural wage employment	—	Guatemala Malawi Russian Fed. Turkey	Azerbaijan Bahrain Albania Papua New Guinea West Bank and Gaza Chad	Niger Sudan Swaziland
Access to resources and opportunities: Political representation	Female representation in parliament	Costa Rica Tunisia	—	Kenya Samoa Antigua and Barbuda Djibouti Morocco South Africa	Yemen, Rep. of St. Kitts and Nevis Armenia Albania Mongolia Romania
New indicators					
Capabilities: Education	Primary completion ratio	Iran, Islamic Rep. of Lesotho	St. Lucia Turkey	Mauritania Nepal Chad Guinea	—

(continued)

TABLE 2.2 (continued)
High and Low Performers for Official and New Indicators

Domain	Indicator	High performers within region	Low performers within region	Rapid progress (annual % change)	Slow progress or deterioration (annual % change)
Capabilities: Health	Female under-five mortality	Cape Verde Mauritius	Afghanistan Azerbaijan Bolivia Djibouti Haiti Iraq Sierra Leone Tajikistan Turkmenistan	Congo, Rep. of Belize Kazakhstan Hong Kong, China Lao PDR Mauritania Moldova	Solomon Islands Congo, Dem. Rep. Hungary Grenada
	Percentage of reproductive-age women and their sexual partners using modern contraception	*	*	*	*
	Percentage of 15- to 19-year-olds who are mothers or pregnant with their first child	*	*	*	*
Access to resources and opportunities: Employment	Female labor force participation rate among women ages 20–24 and 25–59	—	Guatemala Malawi Russian Fed. Turkey	*	*

Source: Authors' calculations based on World Development Indicators, 2007, and Household Survey data.

Note: High and low performers identified at the regional level, rapidly and slowly progressing countries identified at the global level.

* insufficient data.

— = no countries in this category.

capabilities and access to resources. A new approach is used to evaluate country performance on gender equality by comparing performance on the official and new indicators with regional means for these indicators.

Several conclusions emerge from the analysis. First, the expanded set of indicators seems to add information (and value) to the four official MDG3 indicators. Of particular interest is the addition of indicators—labor force participation rate and the ratio of hourly earnings—that capture opportunities in labor markets.

A second important conclusion is the need to focus on individual indicators rather than on broader indexes of gender equality. This conclusion is supported by the heterogeneous progress registered within domains of gender equality. With respect to capabilities, rapid and sustained progress has been made on enrollment ratios, completion rates, and—in those countries starting from positions of female disadvantage—literacy. However, much less progress has been made on reducing female disadvantage in under-five mortality in East Asia and Pacific and South Asia. And the picture is decidedly mixed for reducing adolescent pregnancy and births to adolescent girls.

A similar mixed picture emerges for access to resources. There has been slow progress on women's share in nonagricultural wage employment, little change in female labor force participation rates, and quite heterogeneous trends in the hourly earnings ratio among those Latin American countries for which data are available. In sum, policy making requires focusing on individual indicators that have strong links to women's welfare and to poverty reduction.

A third conclusion that emerges from the chapter is that it is possible to analyze country performance on gender equality against regional benchmarks. When this exercise is undertaken, there are far more low performers than high performers, suggesting that the distribution of performance is skewed to the left. Several countries emerge as repeat low performers across several indicators, while only two countries emerge as high performers on more than one indictor. Finally, no country that is a high performer on any indicator appears as a low performer on another indicator; good performance on even one indicator seems to be associated with at least adequate performance on other indicators.

Annex 2A: Scatter Plots for Country Scores on Individual Indicators

Capabilities: Education

FIGURE 2A.1
High and Low Performers for Ratio of Girls to Boys in Primary Enrollment

Country performance relative to region

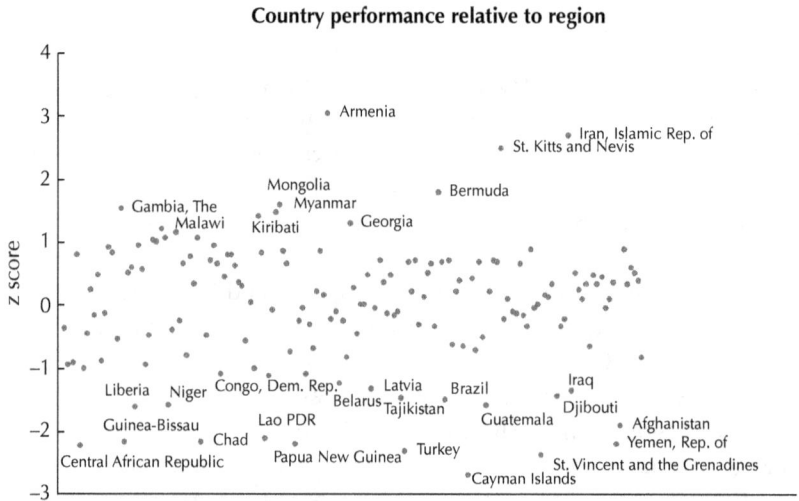

Source: Authors' calculations.

Note: Countries are compared only with other countries within the same region. Regions are Sub-Saharan Africa (45 countries), East Asia and Pacific (25 countries), Europe and Central Asia (26 countries), Latin America and the Caribbean (35 countries), Middle East and North Africa (11 countries), and South Asia (7 countries).

Values used are for the most recent year between 1995 and 2005. Only outliers (those one-half of a standard deviation above or below the mean) are labeled.

FIGURE 2A.2

High and Low Performers for Ratio of Girls to Boys in Secondary Enrollment

Country performance relative to region

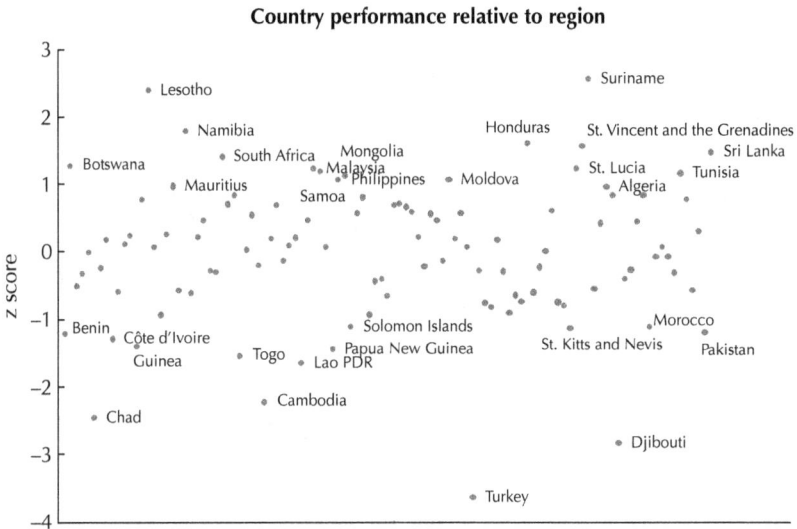

Source: Authors' calculations.

Note: Countries are compared only with other countries within the same region. Regions are Sub-Saharan Africa (32 countries), East Asia and Pacific (19 countries), Europe and Central Asia (18 countries), Latin America and the Caribbean (20 countries), Middle East and North Africa (14 countries), and South Asia (4 countries).

Z score = country value minus region average, divided by region standard deviation. Values used are for the most recent year between 2000 and 2005. Only outliers (those one standard deviation above or below the mean) are labeled.

FIGURE 2A.3
High and Low Performers for Ratio of Girls to Boys in Tertiary Enrollment

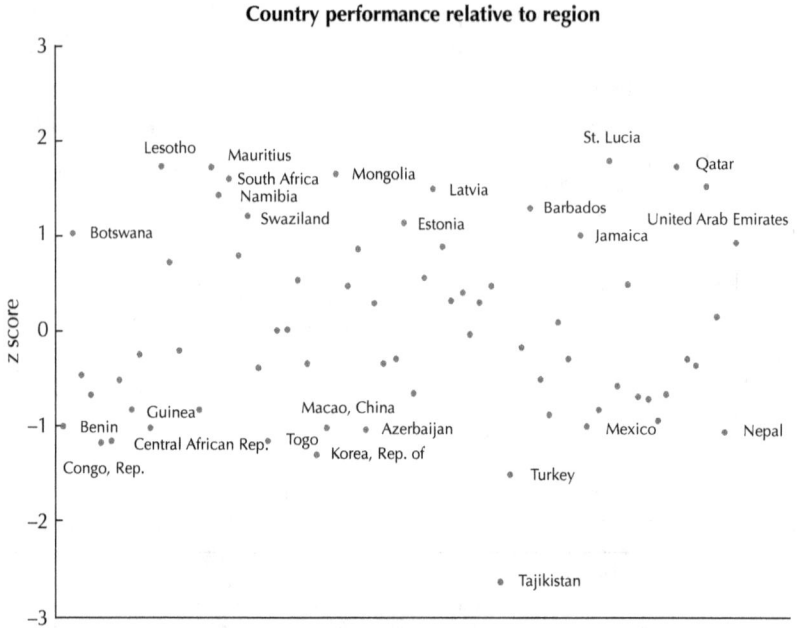

Country performance relative to region

Source: Authors' calculations.

Note: Countries are compared only with other countries within the same region. Regions include Sub-Saharan Africa (24 countries), East Asia and Pacific (6 countries), Europe and Central Asia (18 countries),Latin America and the Caribbean (10 countries), Middle East and North Africa (9 countries), and South Asia (3 countries).

Z score = country value minus region average, divided by region standard deviation. Values used are for the most recent year between 2000 and 2005. Only outliers (those one standard deviation above or below the mean) are labeled.

FIGURE 2A.4
High and Low Performers for Ratio of Girls to Boys in Primary School Completion

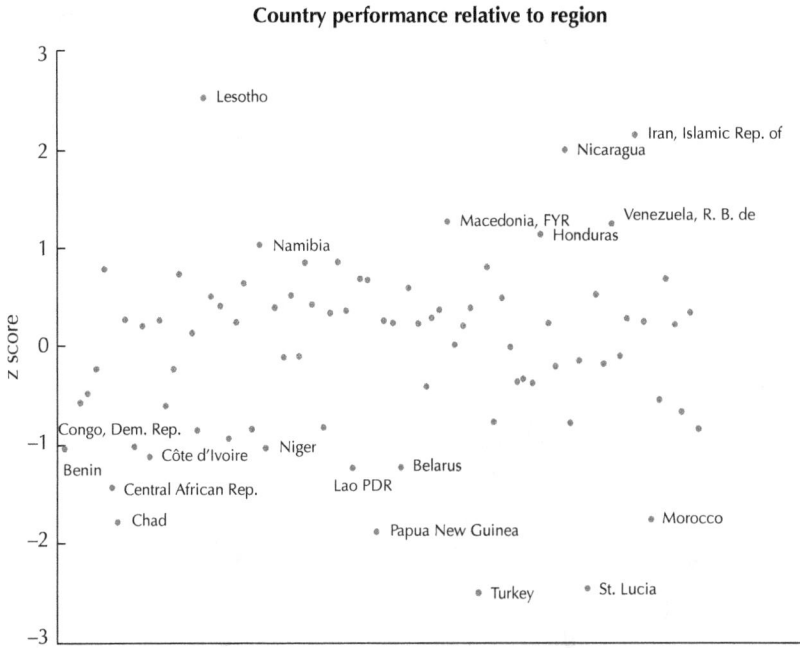

Country performance relative to region

Source: Authors' calculations.

Note: Countries are compared only with other countries within the same region. Regions include Sub-Saharan Africa (35 countries), East Asia and Pacific (8 countries), Europe and Central Asia (12 countries), Latin America and the Caribbean (29 countries), Middle East and North Africa (11 countries). South Asia is not presented because of lack of data.

Z score = country value minus region average, divided by region standard deviation. Values used are for the most recent year between 2000 and 2005. Only outliers (those one standard deviation above or below the mean) are labeled.

Capabilities: Health

FIGURE 2A.5
High and Low Performers for Female Under-Five Mortality (per 1,000 live births)

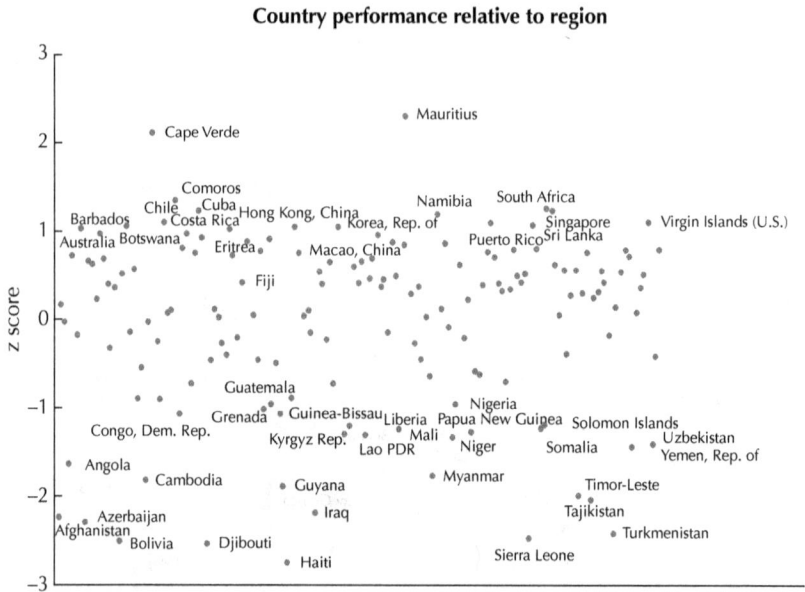

Country performance relative to region

Source: World Population Prospects: 2006 Revision (UN 2007).

Note: Countries are compared only with other countries within the same region. Regions include Sub-Saharan Africa (46 countries), East Asia and Pacific (26 countries), Europe and Central Asia (27 countries), Latin America and the Caribbean (33 countries), Middle East and North Africa (18 countries), and South Asia (8 countries).

Z score = country value minus region average, divided by region standard deviation. Values adjusted so that low under-five mortality values have high z scores. Only outliers (those one standard deviation above or below the mean) are labeled.

Access to Resources and Opportunities: Employment

FIGURE 2A.6
High and Low Performers for Share of Women in Nonagricultural Wage Employment

Country performance relative to region

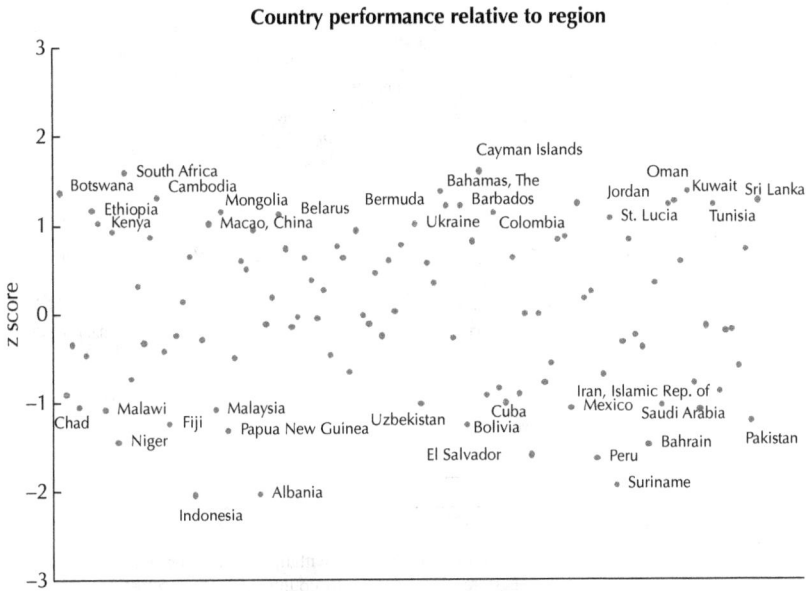

Source: Authors' calculations.

Note: Countries are compared only with other countries within the same region. Regions include Sub-Saharan Africa (14 countries), East Asia and Pacific (17 countries), Europe and Central Asia (26 countries), Latin America and the Caribbean (33 countries), Middle East and North Africa (14 countries), and South Asia (5 countries).

Z score = country value minus region average, divided by region standard deviation. Values used are for the most recent year between 2000 and 2005. Only outliers (those one standard deviation above or below the mean) are labeled.

FIGURE 2A.7
High and Low Performers for Female Labor Force Participation among 25- to 49-Year-Olds

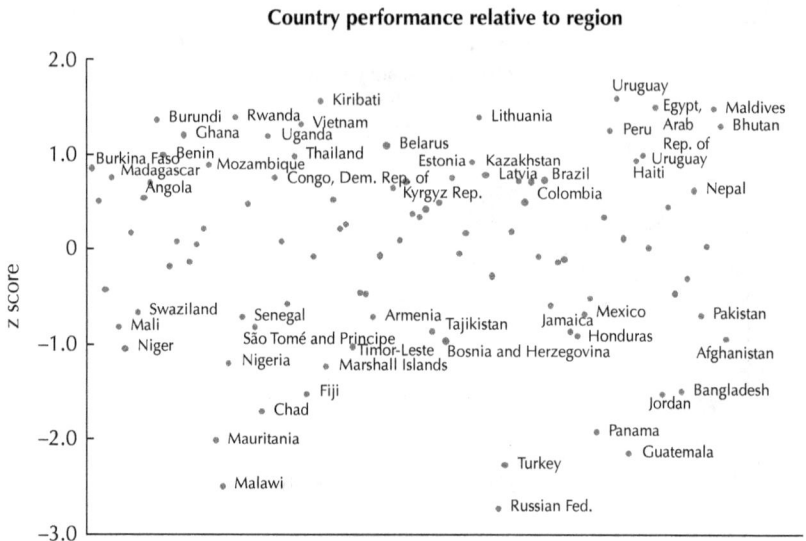

Country performance relative to region

Source: Authors' calculations.

Note: Countries are compared only with other countries within the same region. Regions include Sub-Saharan Africa (30 countries), East Asia and Pacific (8 countries), Europe and Central Asia (26 countries), Latin America and the Caribbean (20 countries), Middle East and North Africa (5 countries), and South Asia (8 countries).

Z score = country value minus region average, divided by region standard deviation. Values used are for the most recent year between 2000 and 2005.

Access to Resources and Opportunities: Political Participation

FIGURE 2A.8
High and Low Performers for Percentage of Seats Occupied by Women in National Parliaments

Country performance relative to region

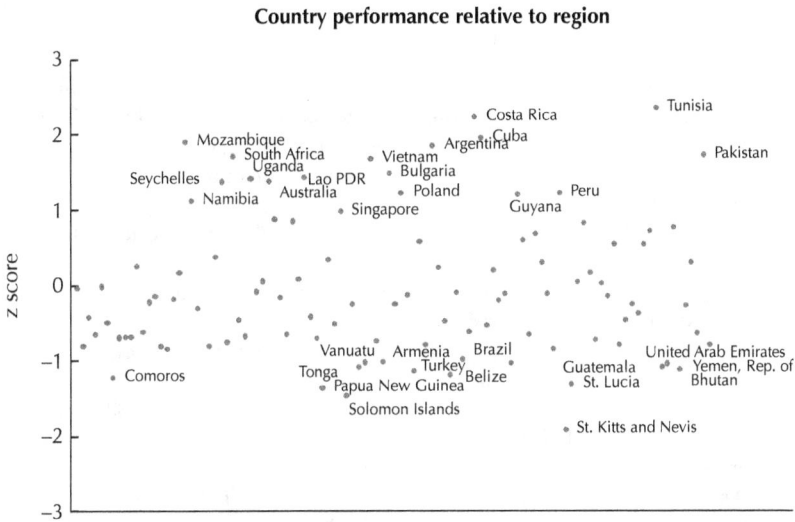

Source: Authors' calculations.

Note: Countries are compared only with other countries within the same region. Regions include Sub-Saharan Africa (32 countries), East Asia and Pacific (18 countries), Europe and Central Asia (8 countries), Latin America and the Caribbean (30 Countries), Middle East and North Africa (11 countries), and South Asia (7 countries).

Z score = country value minus region average, divided by region standard deviation. Values used are for the most recent year between 2000 and 2005. Only outliers (those one standard deviation above or below the mean) are labeled.

Notes

1. These domains of gender equality were developed by the Millennium Task Force (Grown, Gupta, and Pande 2005). The third domain that was proposed was security: it is important to note that this chapter does not propose any indicators for this domain because of the simple fact that there is no source for data on violence against women that offers comparable cross-country data for a significant number of countries. The World Health Organization's multicentric survey offers comparable data for 12 countries on intimate partner violence (Garcia Moreno et al. 2005). Demographic and Health Surveys collect data on intimate partner violence, but differences among countries in the way in which Demographic and Health Surveys elicit information about violence limits comparability across countries (Kishor and Johnson 2005).

2. For additional information on why each indicator was selected, please see World Bank (2007).

3. This indicator is a far-from-perfect measure of empowerment. See the discussion later in the chapter for details.

4. See the discussion later in the chapter for an explanation of why a narrower measure of labor discrimination was not used.

5. Gross enrollment rates above 100 percent do not mean that all school-age children are enrolled in school. It could reflect high repetition rates or over-reporting of the number of enrolled students (Glewwe and Kremer 2006).

6. Test scores and other measures of skills obtained are not available for a broad enough set of countries to be viable as indicators.

7. There are insufficient data points to produce a regional average for the SAR, so India and Nepal are reported individually.

8. Figure 2.6 updates original work by Buvinić, Guzmán, and Lloyd (2007). The Middle East and North Africa region is not included in this analysis because of a lack of data.

9. It has been shown that the quality and quantity of education, training, and experience also matter for women's labor force participation. For example, girls exposed to teaching methods favoring boys may be disadvantaged when entering the labor market, regardless of whether they have the equivalent number of years in school as their male classmates. Thus, parity in the number of years of schooling between girls and boys may not be a complete measure of human capital gender equity.

10. Please note that the UN regional definitions are used in this section.

11. Given that wage earners and the self-employed are both included in this calculation, one cannot estimate a wage equation and use the Oaxaca-Blinder decomposition to isolate the part of the wage gap that is unexplained by human capital characteristics and thus presumably a result of discrimination.

12. Primary sector refers to that portion of a country's economy devoted to the extraction of basic materials (mining, lumbering, agriculture); secondary sector refers to industries that process material extracted from the primary sector

(manufacturing); and tertiary encompasses the administrative and services sectors of the economy.

13. Regional averages could not be computed for the Middle East and North Africa or South Asia regions because of lack of data.

14. Seguino (2000) argues that low wages for women workers in East Asian export sectors have been an important source of competitive advantage for these countries.

15. Another way of gauging the additionality of the new indicators is by looking at relative country ranking (global) on all official MDG3 indicators and comparing it with the country ranking in two of the new indicators. This methodology was used in the 2007 GMR; countries were ranked from low to high depending on their indicator values, then these ranks were summed for official MDG indicators and new indicators. This method, however, has several weaknesses. Country ranking is highly sensitive to the number of indicators included (and the consequent sample size). Also, this method ignores the overall variation in data.

16. This is, in essence, the Standardized Index of Gender Equality (SIGE), which measures female achievement relative to male achievement in education, health, labor markets, and political representation. In the SIGE, scores on each of the five indicators are computed as the number of standard deviations from the world mean; the index score is the sum of all five standardized scores.

17. Problems mentioned above associated with gender equality indexes include the use and choice of weights, the choice of dimensions to be covered, and difficulty in linking index scores to concrete policy responses.

18. Clearly, we would like a more precise measure of performance on gender equality than that obtained via z scores. Economists typically measure relative efficiency of firms by estimating stochastic frontier production functions or by using data envelopment analysis (DEA). It would be very attractive to use these types of techniques to examine the relative efficiency of countries in attaining gender equality, but these techniques require specifying production functions (in the case of stochastic frontiers) or at least some type of input-output relationship (in the case of DEA). Unfortunately, we cannot specify a relationship for the "production" of gender equality and consequently cannot generate these types of efficiency measures.

19. 2006 data. World Bank Country-at-a-Glance tables.

20. *Ibid.*

21. Turkey is classified by the World Bank as a member of the Europe and Central Asia region. Relative to these peers, it is a negative outlier on many indicators of gender equality. Compared with the countries in the Middle East and North Africa region, Turkey's relative performance is far better. Given Turkish ambitions to join the European Union, the comparison with other ECA countries is appropriate.

References and Other Resources

Ahmad, O. B., A. D. Lopez, and Mie Inoue. 2000. "The Decline in Child Mortality: A Reappraisal." *Bulletin of the World Health Organization* 78: 1175–91.

Anderson, K. H., E. M. King, and Y. Wang. 2003. "Market Returns, Transfers and the Demand for Schooling in Malaysia, 1976–1989." *Journal of Development Studies* 39 (3): 407–43.

Barro, R. 1991. "Economic Growth in a Cross-Section of Countries." *Quarterly Journal of Economics* 106 (2): 407–43.

Boserup, Ester. 1970. *Women's Role in Economic Development.* New York: St. Martin's Press.

Brainerd, Elizabeth. 2000. "Women in Transition: Changes in Gender Wage Differentials in Eastern Europe and the Former Soviet Union." *Industrial and Labor Relations Review* 54 (1): 138–62.

Buvinić, M., J. C. Guzmán, and C. B. Lloyd. 2007. "Gender Shapes Adolescence." *Development Outreach* Nov. 2007, World Bank Institute.

Dahlerup, D., and L. Freidenvall. 2005. "Quotas as a 'Fast Track' to Equal Representation for Women." *International Feminist Journal of Politics* 7 (1): 26–48.

Duflo, E. 2001. "Schooling and Labor Market Consequences of School Construction in Indonesia: Evidence from an Unusual Policy Experiment." *American Economic Review* 91 (4): 795–814.

Duryea, S., A. Cox Edwards, and M. Ureta. 2001. "Women in the Latin American Labor Market: The Remarkable 1990s." William Davidson Working Paper No. 500, The William Davidson Institute, University of Michigan Business School.

Eastwood, R., and M. Lipton. 1998. "Impacts of Changes in Human Fertility on Poverty." *Journal of Development Studies* 36 (1): 1–30.

Garcia Moreno, C., H. A. Jansen, M. Ellsberg, and C. H. Watts. 2005. *WHO Multicountry Study on Women's Health and Domestic Violence against Women.* Geneva: World Health Organization.

Glewwe, P., and M. Kremer. 2006. "Schools, Teachers, and Education Outcomes in Developing Countries." In *Handbook of the Economics of Education*, volume 2, eds. E. A. Hanushek and F. Welch, chapter 16. Amsterdam: North-Holland.

Grown, C. 2006. "Indicators and Indices of Gender Equality: What Do They Measure and What Do They Miss?" Background paper for Global Monitoring Report 2007. World Bank, Washington, DC.

Grown, C., G. Gupta, and A. Kes. 2005. *Taking Action: Achieving Gender Equality and Empowering Women.* London: Earthscan and the Millennium Project.

Haddad, W. D., M. Carnoy, R. Rinaldi, and O. Regel. 1990. "Education and Development: Evidence for New Priorities." Discussion Paper No. 95, World Bank, Washington, DC.

Hallman, K., S. Peracca, J. Catino, and M. J. Ruiz. 2007. "Indigenous Girls in Guatemala: Poverty and Location." In *Exclusion, Gender and Schooling: Case Studies from the Developing World*, eds. M. A. Lewis and M. E. Lockheed, chapter 16. Washington, DC: Center for Global Development.

Horton, S. 1996. "Women and Industrialization in Asia: An Overview." In *Women and Industrialization in Asia*, ed. Susan Horton. London: Routledge.

Journal of Human Development. 2006. "Special Issue: Revisiting the Gender-related Development Index (GDI) and Gender Empowerment Measure (GEM)." *Journal of Human Development* 7 (2).

Kabeer, N. 2003. *Gender Mainstreaming in Poverty Eradication and the Millennium Development Goals: A Handbook for Policy Makers and Other Stakeholders.* London and Ottawa: Commonwealth Secretariat.

Kanbur, R., and L. Haddad. 1994. "Are Better Off Households More Equal or Less Equal?" *Oxford Economic Papers* 46 (3): 445–58.

Kishor, S., and K. Johnson. 2005. "Women at the Nexus of Poverty and Violence: How Unique Is Their Disadvantage?" In "A Focus on Gender: Collected Papers on Gender Using DHS Data," ed. S. Kishor, OCR Macro, Calverton, MD. http://pdf.dec.org/pdf_docs/Pnade016.pdf.

Klasen, S. 2006. "UNDP's Gender-Related Measures: Some Conceptual Problems and Possible Solutions." *Journal of Human Development* 7 (2): 243–74.

Lewis, M. A., and M. E. Lockheed, eds. 2006. *Inexcusable Absence: Why 60 Million Girls Still Aren't in School and What to Do about It.* Washington, DC: Center for Global Development.

———. 2007. Exclusion, Gender and Schooling: Case Studies from the Developing World. Washington, DC: Center for Global Development.

Lucas, R. 1988. "On the Mechanics of Economic Development." *Journal of Monetary Economics* 22 (1): 3–42.

Mammen, K., and C. Paxson. 2000. "Women's Work and Economic Development." *Journal of Economic Perspectives* 14 (4): 141–64.

Mankiw, N. G., D. Romer, and D. Weil. 1992. "A Contribution to the Empirics of Economic Growth." *Quarterly Journal of Economics* 107 (2): 407–37.

Paxton, P. M., and S. Kunovich. 2003. "Women's Political Representation: The Importance of Ideology." *Social Forces* 82 (1): 87–113.

Psacharopoulous, G. 1985. "Returns to Education: A Further International Update and Implications." *Journal of Human Resources* 20 (4): 583–604.

Rawls, J. 1971. *A Theory of Social Justice.* Cambridge, MA: Harvard University Press.

Roemer, J. E. 1993. "A Pragmatic Theory of Responsibility for the Egalitarian Planner." *Philosophy and Public Affairs* 22: 146–66.

———. 1995. "Equality and Responsibility." *Boston Review* 20 (2): 3–7.

———. 1996. *Theories of Distributive Justice.* Cambridge, MA: Harvard University Press.

———. 1998. *Equality of Opportunity.* Cambridge, MA: Harvard University Press.

———. 2002. "Equality of Opportunity: A Progress Report." *Social Choice and Welfare* 19: 455–71.

Schultz, T. P. 2002. "Why Government Should Invest More to Educate Girls." *World Development* 30: 207–25.

Seguino, S. 2000. "Gender Inequality and Economic Growth: A Cross-Country Analysis." *World Development* 28 (7): 1211–30.

Tzannatos, Z. 2006. "Monitoring Progress in Gender Equality in the Labor Market." Background paper for the High-Level Consultation: Promoting the Gender Equality MDG—The Implementation Challenge. World Bank, Washington, DC, February 16.

UN (United Nations). 2007. "World Population Prospects: 2006 Revision." Population Division of the Department of Economic and Social Affairs, United Nations, New York.

UNDP (United Nations Development Programme). 1995. *Human Development Report 1995.* New York: Oxford University Press.

Weichselbaumer, D., and R. Winter-Ebmer. 2005. "A Meta-Analysis of the International Gender Wage Gap." *Journal of Economic Surveys* 19 (3): 479–511.

World Bank. 2007. *Global Monitoring Report 2007: Confronting the Challenges of Gender Equality and Fragile States.* Washington, DC: World Bank.

3

Indicators and Indexes of Gender Inequality: What Do They Measure and What Do They Miss?

Caren Grown

In 2008, more than 13 years after ratification of the Beijing Platform for Action, availability and quality of gender-disaggregated indicators of well-being remain poor. Data are not collected, and indicators do not exist, for many domains of well-being important for both males and females. Country coverage is woefully incomplete, stymieing cross-country comparisons. Given the universal commitments to the Millennium Development Goals (MDGs)—especially to eliminating gender inequality and promoting women's empowerment—remedying this situation should be a priority for national statistical agencies and international data collection institutions.

It is true that numerous conceptual and technical issues need to be addressed, although none are insurmountable. As Klasen (2004, 1) notes,

> [w]hen it comes to constructing appropriate measures of well-being that take into account these gender differentials, numerous problems emerge. Among the many difficult conceptual issues to be considered are the space in which gender inequality in well-being is to be measured, whether the indicators should track well-being of males and females separately or adjust overall measures of well-being by the gender inequality in well-being, whether gender equality in every indicator is necessarily the goal... and what role indicators of empowerment should play in gender-related indicators of well-being.

This chapter discusses various options for resolving these issues. It begins with an overview of the various measures currently used to capture gender inequality and women's empowerment, focusing first on discrete or individual indicators and then on composite, aggregate indexes. The chapter concludes with recommendations for government agencies and international institutions interested in improving data coverage and development of indicators for tracking progress toward the achievement of Millennium Development Goal 3 (MDG3).

Conceptual and Measurement Issues Related to Gender Equality and Women's Empowerment

MDG3 refers to the promotion of both gender equality and women's empowerment. These concepts are distinct, but related, and the indicators that measure them are also distinct and related. Gender equality is concerned with women's status relative to men's status, while empowerment is concerned with whether women have the ability to exercise—in an absolute sense—control, power, options, and choice over practical and strategic decisions.[1] As discussed below, indicators of gender equality far outnumber those of women's empowerment.

Domains of Measurement

This chapter uses the operational framework developed by the Millennium Project Task Force on Education and Gender Equality (UN Millennium Project 2005) for understanding gender equality:

- The *capabilities domain* refers to basic human abilities, such as knowledge and health, that are fundamental to individual well-being. These are typically measured by various education, health, and nutrition indicators.
- The *access to resources and opportunities domain* refers primarily to equality in the opportunity to use or apply basic capabilities through access to economic assets and resources as well as political decision making. Land, housing, other property, and infrastructure are all measures of economic assets. Income and employment are used as measures of access to economic resources. Political opportunity is often gauged by representation in parliaments and other political bodies.
- The *security domain* refers to reduced vulnerability to violence and conflict. Violence and conflict result in physical and psychological harm and lessen the ability of individuals, households, and communities to fulfill their potential. Security can be measured by various indicators, such as the prevalence of intimate partner violence, rape, female trafficking, or sexual harassment.

Ideally, indicators should be available to measure all domains of capability, resources, opportunity, and security. The four United Nations (UN)–recommended indicators for MDG3 cover only two of these domains. The two education indicators (the ratio of girls to boys in primary, secondary, and tertiary education and the ratio of literate females to males among those 15 to 24 years old) are imperfect measures of gender equality in capabilities, while the share of women in wage employment in the nonagricultural sector and the proportion of seats held by women in national parliaments are imperfect measures of gender equality in opportunities. The UN did not recommend an indicator for the security domain. By contrast, Task Force 3 of the UN Millennium Project proposed 12 potential indicators for capturing gender equality and empowerment in these three domains. However, not all indicators are operational yet; lack of data restricts measurement in certain key domains. The capability domain contains the largest number of cross-country, comparable, gender-equality indicators, followed by the opportunity domain. The security domain contains the fewest indicators, which will be discussed further in the next section of this chapter.

As noted above, issues of power and control are at the core of the concept of women's empowerment. Malhotra, Schuler, and Boender (2002) and Kabeer (1999) define female empowerment as the ability of women to control their own destiny, that is, to make decisions and affect outcomes of importance to themselves and their families. It can be argued that to be empowered, women must not only have equality in the domains identified above—equal capabilities (such as education and health), equal access to resources and opportunities (such as land and employment), and freedom from violence—but they must also have the agency to use those capabilities, resources, and opportunities to make strategic choices and decisions (UN Millennium Project 2005). Women themselves must be significant actors in the process of the change that is being described or measured.

Yet there are several difficulties with measuring women's empowerment. The first is identifying which domains of empowerment are relevant in different countries and socioeconomic contexts. As Malhotra, Schuler, and Boender (2002, 18) note, "a shift in women's ability to visit a health center without getting permission from a male household member may be a sign of empowerment in rural Bangladesh but not in urban Peru." A second issue is the difficulty of measuring a multidimensional process that takes place over time. For instance, women may become empowered in some aspects of their lives in a relatively short period (say, one to three years) while other changes may evolve over decades (Malhotra, Schuler, and Boender 2002). Specifying the aspects of women's empowerment that are expected to change as well as the "acceptable" time period for change is critical for identifying appropriate policy and programmatic indicators.

Despite these difficulties, several empirical studies have developed proxies for measuring women's empowerment. According to Malhotra, Schuler, and Boender (2002), the most frequently used individual-level indicators of empowerment are (i) decision making over expenditures and resource allocation, social and domestic matters (for example, cooking), and child-related issues (for example, well-being, schooling, health); (ii) control over resources (income, assets, unearned income, welfare receipts, household budget, participation in paid employment); and (iii) mobility or freedom of movement. Measures of the process of female empowerment are more difficult; most available indicators tend to measure the enabling factors or conditions for empowerment, such as labor force participation, female literacy or school enrollment, and political representation by women (Malhotra, Schuler, and Boender 2002). Only one of these—the share of seats in national parliaments held by females—is included among the official indicators for monitoring progress toward MDG3.

Data Issues

The paucity of data automatically restricts the development of critical indicators of inequality and empowerment, including those that the research community has identified as being especially appropriate. The lack of standardization across countries also limits a complete and accurate measurement of gender equality and empowerment. There are data gaps across all domains—capabilities, opportunity, and security—but gaps are particularly prevalent in the domain of economic opportunity.[2] For example, most countries of Sub-Saharan Africa and South Asia are missing data on the share of women in wage employment in the nonagricultural sector. Even fewer have information on women's relative earnings.[3] Lack of time-series data is an additional hindrance. Finally, data are often missing for countries that experience violent conflict.

Relative Versus Absolute Measures

Relative Measures
As noted, gender inequality is a measure of women's status relative to men's status. There are at least three ways to represent gender disparities, each

of which presents a different view of the same numbers. One approach is to construct a ratio of female to male achievement (which can be termed the "gender parity index" or GPI). In education, gender parity indexes can be computed for enrollment rates, completion rates, and literacy rates. For instance, the GPI of gross enrollment rates is calculated by dividing the female gross enrollment rate by the male gross enrollment rate for a given level of education. A GPI of 1 indicates parity between the sexes. A GPI that varies between 0 and 1 typically means a disparity in favor of males, whereas a GPI greater than 1 indicates a disparity in favor of females.

A second approach is the absolute gap or the difference between the absolute number of males and females enrolled in school or able to read and write. This would be calculated by subtracting females from males. A third approach is the relative gap, which is given by the formula (F − M)/F × 100. For instance, with respect to literacy rates, the relative gap indicates the proportion of females that should be enrolled or made literate to achieve parity with males.

Of the three measures discussed above, international and national institutions seem to prefer ratios to capture gender disparities. Ratios and other relative statistics use the group represented in the denominator (males) as the benchmark against which to judge outcomes. Yet, several caveats apply to the use of ratios.

First, access to the underlying data is necessary to interpret changes in ratios. Consider the example of changes in the ratio of female-to-male enrollment rates. Increases in female-to-male ratios can result from a fall in male rates with female rates remaining constant, from a decline in both female and male rates with male rates declining faster, or from female rates increasing faster than male rates. Without additional information, the GPI says little about whether improvements in the ratio reflect increases in girls' school enrollment (desirable) or decreases in boys' enrollment (undesirable). It also does not show whether the overall level of participation in education is low or high. Thus, for interpretation, information on the data used to construct the difference measures must be presented.

Seguino (2004) proposed a ratio that can be used to identify changes in well-being that result from improvements in women's position, rather than declines in men's. Her proposal can be illustrated with a measure of the gender wage gap:

$$R_{t+n} = \frac{W_{F(t+n)}}{W_{M(t+n)}} \times \frac{W_{M(t+n)}}{W_{M(t)}} = \frac{W_{F(t+n)}}{W_{M(t)}},$$

where R_{t+n} is the female-to-male ratio of wages in year $t + n$ (t is the base year), W_F is female wages, W_M is male wages, and $W_{M(t)}$ is male wages in the benchmark year against which the change in female wages is evaluated.

Seguino (2004) illustrates how her ratio compares with the standard (unadjusted) ratio using data from the Republic of Korea. In 2001, average female wages in manufacturing were 350,000 won per month as compared with 650,000 won for men; in 2002, female wages did not change but men's wages fell to 600,000 won per month. By the unadjusted measure, the gender wage ratio increased from 54 percent to 58 percent. Using the revised formula, Seguino shows the female-to-male wage ratio remains unchanged from 2001 to 2002, indicating no improvement in women's relative well-being relative to the benchmark male wage. It shows the rise in the relative wage was entirely due to downward harmonization. Although no global report on gender equality has yet made this adjustment to gender-equality ratios, such an adjustment can be easily done and would be a useful exercise where the data permit.

A second problem with unadjusted ratios is that there may be some domains where a ratio of one, indicating gender parity, is misleading. For instance, it is well known that females enjoy a biological survival advantage over males in both infancy and old age. A ratio of one, or equal infant mortality rates, is actually an example of gender bias favoring males rather than equality of survival (Klasen 2004).

Absolute Measures

As opposed to relative measures, absolute measures use a constant or fixed threshold against which to measure outcomes. For example, a female literacy rate of 65 percent (an absolute measure) is measured against a benchmark of 100 percent. Yet it is important to keep in mind that there are some domains where the benchmark of adequacy is not 100 percent. This is the case, for instance, for maternal mortality. The benchmark or reference should be maximum achievement, that is, the country or region with the lowest maternal mortality rate.

Review of Indicators of Gender Equality and Women's Empowerment

Good indicators are concise and intuitively meaningful to the public and decision makers and meet statistical standards of rigor and validity. Excellent indicators are those in which factors causing changes in the indicator are known and for which impact can be modeled. Unfortunately, it is hard to find any excellent indicators of gender inequality and women's empowerment. Several good indicators exist, but even these can use improvement.[4] International data-compiling institutions, such as the World Bank, the United Nations Educational, Scientific and Cultural Organization (UNESCO) Institute of Statistics, and the International Labor Organization, among others, can actively contribute to this field by investing in country-level data collection and working with sister international institutions on better indicator development.

Annex 3A describes all the indicators that have been used by the UN, its specialized agencies, and the World Bank for monitoring gender equality on a global basis. The list is long and not all of the indicators are suitable for global monitoring of MDG3. This section will focus only on indicators that already or can potentially meet the following criteria:

- *Analytically rigorous and publicly available.* The indicators should be robust and statistically validated and recognized as meaningful by different users. They should also be grounded in data that are accessible to interested parties regardless of location or position.
- *Broad country coverage and comparability.* Indicators for which many potential countries do not have data or for which the methods for assessing the indicator vary widely are unacceptable because there is no ability to compare the countries.
- *Fluidity over the short-term.* The indicators should be able to reflect changes over two to three years. This means that data must be collected and reported in a timely manner.
- *Related to government policy.* An indicator should change when relevant government policy changes.
- *Comprehensible and transparent.* Government officials and civil society can interpret changes.

Finally, to reflect gender inequality and women's empowerment fully, the portfolio of indicators should be balanced across the different domains discussed above.

Capability Indicators

Education
As shown in annex 3A, several indicators measure gender equality in education. The most widely available education indicators are enrollment rates. Net enrollment rates, which take into consideration the appropriate age for each grade, are good indicators of access to education, but are not available

for many countries. Gross enrollment rates are more widely available, but include repeat students in the calculation and thus will be higher than net enrollment rates. Literacy rates and completion rates are also used to measure gender equality in education.

As noted in Grown, Rao Gupta, and Khan (2003), these education indicators have both substantive and technical limitations. Enrollment rates reflect only the input side of education, which is where most policy efforts have been directed. Getting girls and boys to school is clearly an important first step, but as Bruns, Mingat, and Rakotomalala (2004) argue, the more important policy issue is school completion and student learning outcomes. The completion of five to six years of school is necessary for mastery of basic competencies, such as literacy and numeracy. School enrollment ratios, whether on a gross or net basis, are poorly correlated with the rate of primary school completion, and enrollment ratios are consistent with many different patterns of dropout and retention.

Moreover, enrollment data are a flow variable, reflecting outcomes at a specific time. Stock data are needed to measure how women and men fare beyond school age. Educational attainment—a stock variable reflecting years of schooling completed in a population—can be used to complement enrollment data.[5] Although the data are available, very few international agencies use it (the World Bank is an exception).[6]

Another commonly used education indicator is literacy, which is supposed to reflect the performance of the national education system, as well as the quality of the human resources within a country in relation to those resources' potential for growth, contribution to development, and quality of life. Yet, this indicator also has problems. First, the quality of the literacy data is suspect. Some countries collect literacy information using sophisticated and comprehensive techniques, yet others are not able to provide the most basic information on learning outcomes. In addition, because literacy is not a simple concept with a single, universally accepted meaning, different countries measure literacy differently. The UNESCO definition ("a person is literate if s/he has completed five or more years of schooling") has been widely criticized, partly because it assumes that people can be easily categorized as "literate" or "illiterate," or because adults with five or more years of schooling may still be functionally illiterate, while those with fewer than four years of schooling may have acquired literacy skills by nonformal means.[7]

Because of limitations with the literacy indicator, the UN Millennium Project (2005) recommended replacing it in the short term with a measure of school completion: the ratio of girls' to boys' completion rates at the primary and secondary levels. The completion rate captures the total number of students successfully completing, or graduating from, the last year of a given education cycle in a given year, expressed as a proportion of the total number of children of graduation age in the population (UNESCO 2004). The UNESCO and the World Bank's Human Development Network have consolidated data on sex-disaggregated completion rates in primary school (reported in chapter 2).[8] However, secondary completion rates are not being regularly tracked or reported by countries, so there are no comprehensive cross-country data for this indicator. The data that are available for secondary completion rates come primarily from developed countries and a few middle-income developing countries.[9] The UN Millennium Project (2005) recommended a concerted effort among countries and international agencies to collect data on secondary school completion in developing countries, using UNESCO's International Standard Classification of Education 1997 (ISCED–97) for education cycles.

In the longer term, it may be possible to reincorporate a literacy indicator into global monitoring as more reliable literacy data become available. The UNESCO Institute of Statistics (UIS) has already developed an alternative literacy assessment method, the Literacy Assessment and Monitoring Programme (LAMP), which uses assessments of individuals' skills to measure literacy across a range of levels. LAMP is now being piloted in several countries. International donors should provide additional resources to the UIS to consolidate improvements in the LAMP survey and implement it in a larger number of countries. Once available, the absolute levels of this indicator could be used as a measure of empowerment while the ratio of female to male achievement could serve as an indicator of gender disparity.

Health

International agencies use a wide range of health indicators to track gender equality and women's empowerment. The most common, life expectancy, is not particularly revealing as a measure of gender equality because there is no benchmark ratio of female-to-male life expectancy against which to measure country-level outcomes. Moreover, life expectancy data are based on model life tables rather than real data. As Saith and Harriss-White (1998) point out, improvements in overall life expectancy can be misleading because they often mask important age-specific differentials in mortality.

In contrast, the ratio of females to males in the population (FMRs) is likely to more clearly reflect gender inequality (Saith and Harriss-White 1998; Seguino 2004). This measure captures society's valuation of women as well as women's ability to protect female children in vulnerable years. Benchmark ratios for countries at varying levels of development are provided in numerous studies, against which to compare actual ratios (Saith and Harriss-White 1998). As Seguino (2004) argues, the FMR may be a proxy for a variety of other mechanisms by which women are empowered or disempowered.

The examples of China, Jamaica, Korea, and Singapore illustrate why female-to-male population ratios may be a superior measure of gender disparity than the ratio of female-to-male life expectancy. All these countries have rising female-to-male life expectancy ratios but declining female-to-male population ratios (Seguino 2002, 2003; Klasen and Wink 2003); they also rank well in female educational attainment and labor force participation. In Korea, sex-selective abortions (favoring males) are a likely explanation for the declining FMR (Goodkind 1996). In Jamaica, the explanation for a declining FMR is likely female emigration in response to high female unemployment. However, for FMR to become an indicator for global monitoring, more research is needed to understand its determinants and its relationship to other indicators.

As described in annex 3A, additional important health indicators to assess women's empowerment are maternal mortality and measures of reproductive health. The maternal mortality ratio, the proportion of births attended by skilled health personnel, HIV prevalence among 15- to 24-year-old pregnant women, and the contraceptive prevalence rate are all useful indicators, but they do not assess women's and adolescents' ability to act on their reproductive preferences. Nor are the data on maternal mortality sufficient to recommend its use for global monitoring. The UN Millennium Project (2005), therefore, recommended using two other sexual and reproductive health and rights indicators. One, the proportion of contraceptive demand satisfied, captures the central connection between women's control over their reproductive preferences and their decision-making ability and is thus a good proxy for women's empowerment.

The proportion of contraceptive demand satisfied combines two commonly used indicators: the contraceptive prevalence rate and the unmet need for family planning. The contraceptive prevalence rate is the percentage of women between 15 and 49 years old who are practicing, or whose sexual partners are practicing, any form of contraception (including condoms, female and male sterilization, injectable and oral hormones, intrauterine devices, diaphragms, spermicides, and natural family planning). Unmet need for family planning is defined as the number of women of child-bearing age (who are married or in consensual union) who desire either to terminate childbearing or to postpone their next birth for a specified time (usually two years or longer) and who are not using a contraceptive method (WHO 2005).

The proportion of contraceptive demand satisfied is the contraceptive prevalence rate as a proportion of the sum of the contraceptive prevalence rate and the unmet need for family planning. It measures the proportion of all women of reproductive age whose demand for contraception is actually satisfied (which the more common unmet need measure does not capture). The United Nations Population Division (UNPD) and ORC-Macro's Demographic and Health Surveys include the data needed to compute this indicator for 75 developing countries and for two time periods, 1990–95 and 1996–2002. Bernstein (2004) has established the usefulness of this indicator; however, further work is needed to synchronize UNPD and ORC-Macro surveys to produce data for a larger sample of countries and to popularize the use of this indicator.

The age-specific fertility rate (ASFR) for 15- to 19-year-olds is another indicator of female empowerment recommended by the UN Millennium Project (2005) for global monitoring of MDG3 and MDG4. Adolescent fertility rates give insight into the reproductive behavior of an important target population for meeting the sexual and reproductive health and rights strategic priority. Childbearing among girls ages 15–19 is of special concern because births to teenagers are more likely to be unintended and premature and are associated with greater risks of complications during delivery and higher levels of maternal and child mortality. It is a good measure of empowerment; young women who bear children are less likely to complete school, more likely to be in low-wage positions, and more likely to be poor (World Bank 2006).

A large number of countries (173) collect data for this indicator and these data have been compiled by the United Nations Population Division. A disadvantage of ASFR is that the indicator does not provide a straightforward interpretation and is difficult to present in a user-friendly way to a nontechnical audience. Also, the ASFR 15–19 covers a wide age range, including ages 18 and 19, when reproduction does not pose particular health risks and women are considered to have reached adulthood. However, single year age-specific rates are not available, and ASFR 15–19 has been shown to be a good proxy for ASFR 15–17.

An alternative to ASFR for capturing both gender equality and empowerment is the average age of females and males at first marriage. The data indicate women's average age is below men's, with age at first marriage inversely correlated to educational attainment. Early marriage for women often forecloses opportunities for education. Furthermore, when childbearing starts at a young age, women are relatively disempowered with regard to their male partners, and less able to escape possible abuse. Data on age at marriage can be obtained from a database compiled by the UNPD, from population censuses, and from the Demographic and Health Surveys.

Indicators of Access to Resources and Opportunities

Economic Opportunity

A number of indicators can be used to capture gender inequality and empowerment in the opportunity domain, including paid employment, income, and assets. For paid employment, such indicators include labor force participation, female share of paid nonagricultural employment, and unemployment. For unpaid work, indicators include the female share of nonmarket time devoted to care. A number of indicators capture conditions of and returns from work, including female-to-male earnings and occupational segregation. Other important indicators of access to economic opportunity include women's ownership and control over productive assets, such as land or housing. These are discussed below.

Paid employment. Labor force participation rates, which measure the number of persons in the workforce as a percentage of the working population, and which can be disaggregated by age and sex, are common indicators of gender inequality in paid work as well as of female empowerment. Labor force participation data are generally available, so the indicator is widely used. However, for a number of reasons, it may be more suitable as a measure of gender equality than as a measure of empowerment.

First, an upward trend in female labor participation rates does not necessarily signify increased labor force participation in reality. Much of the increase in female labor participation rates in the 1980s and 1990s may be a statistical artifact resulting from improvements in labor force surveys attempting to capture the full extent of women's economic activity (Beneria 1992). Second, labor force participation may not be a good proxy for female empowerment because it includes all types of employment, including that which is more precarious, insecure, and less well remunerated, such as unpaid family work, own-account work, and self-employment. National data on labor force participation may not be comparable because of differences in concepts and methodologies. And, finally, few countries can report labor force statistics frequently; according to the UN (2006), only 59 countries reported data for five years in the period 1995–2003.

A better proxy for empowerment may be the female share of paid nonagricultural employment because it at least excludes unpaid family workers who do not directly enter the market. This indicator, calculated as the number of women in nonagricultural paid employment divided by the total number of persons in paid employment in the nonagricultural sector, is used for monitoring MDG3.[10] Although this measure is superior to labor force participation as an indicator of both labor market inequality and female empowerment, it has several limitations. First, being paid does not necessarily entail retaining control over income (Elson 1999). Second, the indicator measures only the presence or absence of work and not the quality of work. Third, it is difficult to interpret unless additional information is available on the share of women in total employment, which would allow assessment of whether women are under or overrepresented in nonagricultural wage employment. In many countries, nonagricultural wage employment represents only a small portion of total employment. Finally, it does not reveal that there are different types of nonagricultural wage employment, some better than others in earnings and legal and social protection (UNIFEM 2005).

Despite these difficulties, there is a consensus in the international community to continue to use this indicator for global monitoring exercises but to continue to develop an additional indicator on the percentage distribution of employment by type for women and men (see box 3.1). This indicator, Gender Differences in the Structure of Employment, is based on a cross-classification of formal and informal employment, agricultural and nonagricultural employment, and status in employment, and combines several indicators into a matrix. It shows women in different types of employment (agricultural employment, nonagricultural formal and informal wage employment, and nonagricultural formal and informal self-employment) as a percentage of total employment. The indicator can also be disaggregated by age.

Some of the data required for this new indicator are available in International Labour Organization (ILO) databases, and the remainder can be obtained as part of regular ILO data collection exercises. In addition, some special data collection will be necessary to consolidate data currently available at the national level but not at the international level. In fact, more data

Box 3.1
Gender Differences in the Structure of Employment

Row		Women	Men
0	Share in total employment (Both sexes = 100%)	%	%
1	Total Employment	100%	100%
2	Agricultural Employment	%	%
2.1	Own-account workers, employers, and members of producers' cooperatives	%	%
2.2	Contributing family workers (informal)	%	%
2.3	Employees	%	%
	2.3.1 Formal	%	%
	2.3.2 Informal	%	%
3	Nonagricultural Employment	%	%
3.1	Own-account workers, employers, and members of producers' cooperatives	%	%
	3.1.1 Formal	%	%
	3.1.2 Informal	%	%
3.2	Contributing family workers (informal)	%	%
3.3	Nondomestic employees	%	%
	3.3.1 Formal	%	%
	3.3.2 Informal	%	%
3.4	Domestic employees	%	%
	3.4.1 Formal	%	%
	3.4.2 Informal	%	%
3.I	Formal Nonagricultural Employment (3.1.1 + 3.3.1 + 3.4.1)	%	%
3.II	Informal Nonagricultural Employment (3.1.2 + 3.2 + 3.3.2 + 3.4.2)	%	%

Source: UN 2005.

are generally available at the national level and used in national reports than those presented in the UN Statistics Division or ILO databases. The ILO has initiated work to collect data from countries for this expanded indicator, but major technical cooperation efforts are needed to obtain data for more countries. Lack of resources is a major barrier preventing development of data for this indicator; this is a good opportunity for international donors to hasten progress.

Because of data problems and other issues, it is difficult to recommend any other global indicator to measure progress toward eliminating gender inequalities in access to paid employment beyond "Gender Differences in the Structure of Employment." However, a number of other indicators can be adapted for use in specific countries or regions. These indicators may proxy for equality in access to and fair treatment in employment; they include the ratio of female-to-male unemployment rates, the female-to-male wages or earnings ratio (divided by years of school, which controls for human capital), and occupational segregation by sex (the percentage of nonagricultural employment in male-dominated and female-dominated occupations and the index of dissimilarity),[11] among others.

Unemployment rates. Unemployment rates are an important indicator of labor market performance in industrial countries, but are much less useful in low-income economies in which the majority of the population engages in informal or self-employment. Unemployment data can reflect the degree of exclusion from work or the extent to which women are placed at the back of the job queue in job-scarce countries (Seguino 2004). Many countries rely on unemployment rates as a key economic indicator.

At the same time, this indicator has to be viewed with caution. Ambiguities over who is in the labor force and who is not make the official unemployment rate a somewhat questionable indicator of employment opportunities, especially if taken by itself. For example, the unemployment rate will fall when the number of discouraged workers (those who have stopped looking for employment) increases.

The number of countries reporting statistics on unemployment is lower than the number reporting on the economically active population (115 versus 127; UN 2006). Of these 115, all but 1 provide data by sex, but only 96 provide statistics by sex and age. Moreover, unemployment data are not regularly available. For instance, of the 115 countries with data, only 72 could provide the data disaggregated by sex and age for at least five out of nine years in the period 1995–2003.

Occupational segregation. Another indicator of equality in work is occupational segregation by sex, which is measured in two ways: (i) women in male occupations as a percentage of total working in those occupations; and (ii) men in female occupations as a percentage of total working in those occupations. The goal of equality is achieved when each indicator matches the percentage of women (men) in the whole workforce. An index of variation can be calculated for these percentages; comparisons are made with the same percentages calculated for the base year (see annex 3A for details).[12]

Data on *occupational distribution* can reflect opportunities available to women and have been used to assess the degree of discrimination in the labor market. Data for occupational segregation are available in ILO's SEGREGAT data set, which contains statistics for more than 80 developed and developing countries and for years near to 1970, 1980, 1990, and 2000. The statistics are not always comparable across countries or across points in time, given differences regarding the sources of data collection, worker coverage, and national classifications used. However, it may be possible to compare specific and well-defined occupational groups, such as teachers, doctors, and taxi drivers.[13] One drawback is that occupational segregation indicators may not cover informal employment, and in some countries, they may not be correlated with other indicators of labor market disadvantage.

Although we may want to know whether the jobs women obtain have job ladders and permit decision making, and whether their jobs are "good"—secure, safe, and provide for training and advancement—such information is not currently available. The one available proxy indicator that may be more revealing than others is female share of administrators and managers. An upward trend in this indicator could proxy how societies value women and the degree to which a gender hierarchy continues to be socially imposed. One problem with using female share of administrators and managers, however, is that different countries define these categories in different ways, so comparisons need to be made carefully.

Earnings. Earnings are probably one of the most important direct and indirect indicators of equality in economic opportunity, as well as of empowerment. Earnings are a broad measure that includes gross remuneration from all work activities.[14] Most statistics on earnings are obtained from payroll data collected mainly from labor force establishment censuses or surveys. Unfortunately, data on the gender earnings gap—in both paid and self-employment—are currently not available for many countries, although there is greater availability than is represented in global reports.

There are different ways to measure gender wage differentials. A straightforward approach is to calculate average remuneration per female wage earner, divide by average remuneration per male wage earner, and multiply by 100. A result of 100 denotes equality between women and men who are active in the labor force. The indicator can be corrected for hours worked (calculated by measuring the hourly wage) and educational level (calculated using different levels of education).

The education-adjusted wage gap measure, which is a wage gap corrected for educational attainment, is a good candidate for global monitoring. It is expressed as

$$WGAP = \log\left(\frac{W_m}{E_m}\right) - \log\left(\frac{W_f}{E_f}\right),$$

where W_m and W_f are wages or earnings data, corrected for hours worked if possible, for males and females, and E_m and E_f are average number of years of secondary education per male and female ages 15 and above. In the same spirit, another alternative is to present the unadjusted gender wage gap (again corrected for hours worked) by quintiles of educational attainment.

Another approach to defining gender pay gaps is the Oaxaca-Blinder decomposition. It begins with the observation that the unadjusted pay gap (noted above) does not compare "like with like." Therefore, the data are adjusted to distinguish what proportion of the overall pay gap is due to differences in individual characteristics and what proportion is due to sex discrimination. This approach is seen to have three benefits: it identifies the pay differential between male and female workers that remains after controlling for differences in individual characteristics; it identifies what fraction of the gap is due to differences in productivity and what fraction is due to labor market discrimination; and it isolates the issue of labor market discrimination and facilitates a clear policy focus (Grimshaw and Rubery 2002).

However, Grimshaw and Rubery (2002) point out several problems with using the adjusted measure having to do with simplifying assumptions about the way labor markets operate to disentangle the independent effects of various factors on the wage structure. "Despite its apparent simplicity and policy focus, the Oaxaca-Blinder decomposition relies on a number of assumptions and in the way particular statistical techniques are deployed, this adds a certain ambiguity to the results generated and lends complexity rather than simplicity to the interpretation of these results" (Grimshaw and Rubery 2002, 25).[15] One challenge is to identify all individual characteristics that can be said to have an impact on productivity and to develop a technique that separates out the independent effects of productivity and discrimination on gender differential in pay. Another challenge is the specification of appropriate control variables. Finally, where decomposition techniques have been applied to cross-national comparisons of the gender pay gap, it is assumed that the degree of statistical error is of a similar type for each country when, in fact, diversity in the way labor markets operate exposes severe limitations to a statistical approach to decomposing the gender pay gap (Grimshaw and Rubery 2002). Thus, it may not be a good indicator to use in global monitoring.

Data problems currently hamper development of an earnings gap indicator. First, as noted above, earnings data disaggregated by sex are not widely available. Most frequently, they are available for nonagricultural work, often only for the manufacturing sector. Wage data that are collected from establishment surveys do not provide information on remuneration of informal employment, where gender gaps in earnings are wider than in formal employment (UNIFEM 2005). Furthermore, data on formal employment are for monthly wages in many cases, and data on hours of work may be unavailable.

Second, comparability of earnings data across countries is affected by the type of workers covered in the survey and the inclusion or exclusion of overtime pay, incentive pay, bonuses, payments in kind, and other allowances, as well as the unit of time used (per hour, per day, per week, or per month). Some sources use average earnings whereas others use wage rates. International comparability is additionally hampered by differences across countries in the size criterion of the enterprises or establishments in the surveys.

Other problems of interpretation can also arise if the data are not used with broader measures of employment. In the Arab Republic of Egypt, for instance, women's average earnings in wage employment are higher than men's (Assad 2002). Yet employment data reveal that among economically active women, unpaid workers in family enterprises predominate, although only a very small fraction are in paid wage employment. Those in paid employment tend to be much better educated, on average, than men who work in wage employment (who, by and large, work as wage laborers).

To the extent that data are available, earnings data can potentially be used to reflect women's empowerment. One possible indicator would be female household income as a share of total household income, or female earnings as a share of total household earnings. The indicator can be presented as an average or by income quintile.

The development of sex-disaggregated data on earnings needs to be accelerated if such data are to be used in global monitoring.[16] Work is required to develop and test questions in countries and prepare methodological guidelines before any large-scale data collection effort can be undertaken. International agencies could work together to support countries' efforts to collect and standardize statistics on sex differences in earnings from employment. It would also be useful to compile an earnings data set from all available household surveys that collect sex-disaggregated information.

Unpaid work. Unpaid work is classified by the 1993 UN System of National Accounts (SNA) in three categories: (i) housework, child care, and other family-related services not recognized by SNA as economic activity; (ii) subsistence and nonmarket activities, such as agricultural production for household consumption and imputed rent of owner-occupied dwellings, which are treated by SNA as economic output valued on the basis of the market value of similar services that are sold; and (iii) household enterprises producing for the market for which more than one household member provides unpaid labor. An indicator for gender gaps in unpaid work could be the ratio of female hours per day or week spent on unpaid work to male hours per day or week spent on unpaid work. A ratio greater than one would mean that women do more of such work than men do.

Time use surveys are essential for the construction of an indicator of gender gaps in unpaid work. The Multinational Time Use Study, maintained by the University of Oxford, comprises a cross-nationally harmonized set of time use surveys composed of identically recoded variables from 29 countries. Time diary studies have been conducted in more than 60 countries since the 1990s, although not all are harmonized.[17] More work is needed to standardize classification of activities in time accounts for useful cross-country comparisons. For broader coverage, new questions on time use would have to be incorporated into regularly repeated household surveys or small area surveys. Several countries and institutions, such as the World Bank, sponsor national or subnational surveys that include time use modules to capture the division of labor within households. For instance, the World Bank's Living Standards Measurement Study surveys include time use questions in selected country surveys. The UN Millennium Project (2005) recommended expanding the collection of time use data, with periodic updates, in a representative sample of developing countries where infrastructure deficits are large, and this recommendation is echoed here.

Assets. As Agarwal (1995) and others have pointed out, in agricultural societies, access to assets, such as land and credit, may be more salient as indicators of gender equality and empowerment than wages and employment. Yet sex-disaggregated indicators of assets are almost nonexistent. Sex-disaggregated data on the distribution of land and housing ownership are patchy. Very few agricultural censuses ask for the legal landowner in the household or keep records on ownership of land by sex.[18] In Africa and Asia, most of the information on the distribution of land ownership by sex comes from scattered household surveys. Some of the Living Standards Measurement Study surveys have included questions on individual ownership of land, but the frequency is low and the questions have been included in surveys for only a few countries in Sub-Saharan Africa.

National agricultural surveys in some Latin American countries also collect information that can be used to calculate the distribution of landowners by sex (Deere and Leon 2003).

Some data are available on female share of credit, based on reports by lending institutions, but they are very small in coverage, and there is no possibility of using them to evaluate trends over time. Data on housing titles are also scarce. UN-Habitat's Global Campaign for Secure Tenure emphasizes the importance of women's rights to tenure security. It recommends collecting data on the percentage of female- and male-headed households in different tenure categories (owned, rental, communal property, government-owned).

Although legal data will provide some information on women's access to resources, even if women have access to land or house titles, or to credit, social pressures might militate against their control over such resources (Goetz and Sengupta 1996; Tinker and Summerfield 2000). The absence of data on behavior and use of title implies that assessment of gender equality and women's empowerment in agricultural societies is challenging.

Political Opportunity

The most commonly used indicator of empowerment and equality in the political arena is the female share of seats in parliament and in ministerial bodies. Currently, this is the only indicator that can be tracked on a global scale, yet it is an imperfect proxy for tracking aggregate levels of female empowerment because it says nothing about whether women have power in parliament to make decisions or whether they are sensitive to gender issues and can promote a gender-equality legislative agenda. Data for this indicator are collected for 182 countries by the Inter-Parliamentary Union.

Some have suggested that empowerment is better measured in municipal bodies, as well as by women's representation in professional bodies, trade unions, and other civic institutions. Efforts to collect global data on these indicators would improve the knowledge base but, in the interim, proxies must be relied upon. Trade union data are a possibility and are available for a number of countries through the ILO and the International Confederation of Free Trade Unions. Recently, United Cities and Local Governments (UCLG), an organization supported by the Ministry of Foreign Affairs of the Netherlands, has begun to collect data on the proportions of female local elected representatives, councilors, and mayors in 54 countries. The UCLG plans to construct a global database on women in local government. However, diversity in local government structures makes construction of this database a challenging task. At present, no other alternative data exist for developing an indicator on women's participation in local-level decision making.

Indicators of Security and Empowerment

Violence against Women

One barrier that stands in the way of women being able to use their capabilities, exploit economic and political opportunities, and exercise agency is violence.[19] Worldwide, it has been estimated that violence against women is as serious a cause of death and incapacity among women of reproductive age as cancer and is a greater cause of ill-health than traffic accidents and malaria combined. The prevalence of physical intimate partner violence in the past year is an indicator of both gender inequality and empowerment (albeit in a negative way). The prevalence rate is expressed as a percentage of women ages 15–49 who report experiencing physical violence in the past year at the hands of an intimate partner.

There is fairly broad consensus in the research community on how to measure physical intimate partner violence, and it is currently included in most surveys on violence against women. For instance, the Demographic and Health Survey now includes a module on physical intimate partner violence that has been used in 12 nationally representative household surveys. The World Health Organization has worked with partners in eight countries to collect data on the dimensions, health consequences, and the risk and protective factors of violence against women.[20] It is currently collaborating with the Economic Commission of Latin America and the Caribbean, the European Women's Lobby, and the U.S. Centers for Disease Control and Prevention to strengthen data collection on this issue.

Interpreting the data may be difficult initially. One issue is that domestic violence reporting rises with female empowerment and more gender-aware police training. In addition, domestic violence may be triggered by female defiance of male partners or family members and the attempts to exit from the household. Thus, disentangling the sources of change in this indicator will need to be done on a country-by-country basis.

Composite Indexes of Gender Inequality and Women's Empowerment

An alternative to the analysis of discrete indicators of gender equality and women's empowerment is the construction of a composite index that combines discrete variables into one framework. This section discusses the strengths and weaknesses of various aggregate indexes for monitoring and tracking progress toward gender equality and women's empowerment.

The Gender-Related Development Index and the Gender Empowerment Measure

In 1995 the United Nations Development Programme introduced two composite gender-related indexes in the Human Development Report: the Gender-related Development Index (GDI) and the Gender Empowerment Measure (GEM).[21] The GDI adjusts the Human Development Index (HDI) by imposing a welfare penalty for gender inequality in the HDI's three components. The HDI is calculated as an unweighted average of the values of three variables: life expectancy, educational attainment, and per capita gross domestic product (GDP). To obtain the GDI, a downward adjustment is made to the HDI according to the degree of aversion to inequality and gender gaps in income, life expectancy, and educational attainment. The idea behind the GDI is to "penalize" the HDI if gender inequality exists in any of the three dimensions of the HDI. The larger the gap between men and women in achievements, the more the GDI differs from the HDI. The GEM is mostly a measure of female empowerment in political decision making, the economy, and in earned incomes.

A large literature evaluates these two composite indexes, including, a special issue of the *Journal of Human Development* (2006), which analyzed the impact the measures have had on policy. Several contributions suggest constructive refinements and modifications to the measures, and in some cases, propose new composite indexes. Two critiques of the GDI and GEM bear mention here: problems of use and interpretation, and conceptual and measurement issues.

First, in a comprehensive review of the academic and policy literature as well as media reports, Schuler (2006) finds substantial problems in using and interpreting both the GDI and the GEM. She notes that the correct use of the GDI is to compare it with the HDI, either using the difference or the ratio of the two. The GDI is not interpretable in itself if conclusions about the welfare loss from gender inequality are to be drawn. Yet countries, and even the UN Human Development Reports, have interpreted the GDI as a measure of gender inequality. From her review, Schuler (2006, 173) concludes that "the formula of computation of the GDI is not understood very well" while at the same time there is great demand and need for a direct gender inequality measure.

Second, some of the problems may be traced to both conceptual and empirical issues in measuring the GDI and the GEM, summarized by Klasen (2006). The GDI does not meet the need for a measure of gender inequality, has serious conceptual and empirical problems associated with both the life-expectancy and earned-income components, and is difficult to interpret in a situation in which gender gaps in the three components favor one sex in one component and another in the other components. This last problem applies as well to the GEM, which also suffers from poor country coverage and elite bias in the first two components of the index (Cueva Beteta 2006).

The GEM, moreover, simultaneously measures inequality between men and women and between women across countries. Dijkstra (2002, 312) points out that "in indexing average incomes on a scale from 0 to 100, unadjusted income per capita is used," which means that "the absolute income level weighs even more heavily in the core for the income component of the GEM than in the GDI," and rich countries score more highly than do poor countries. As a result, women in rich countries appear relatively more empowered than women in poor countries with otherwise equal relative shares of economic and political power. Finally, combining absolute levels of human development with relative female well-being makes it difficult to sort out which is changing over time—women's relative status or levels of development (Dijkstra 2006; Klasen 2006).

As this discussion suggests, more work needs to be done to arrive at a composite index that measures gendered well-being, for gender equality in capabilities, empowerment, and some combination of the two. Sensitivity analyses are required to test various combinations of indicators. Further agreement is needed also on the appropriate indicators.[22]

The *Journal of Human Development* (2006) articles make a number of suggestions for improving the GDI and the GEM, and it is hoped that the Human Development Report will respond favorably. Some recommendations are easily implemented in the short term, while others will take more time. In the short term, agencies that report the GDI should rank countries according to the welfare penalty of gender inequality. Klasen (2006) suggests using either the ratio of the GDI to the HDI or the difference, but using the ratio would be consistent with current global monitoring efforts. In the longer term, some authors suggest replacing the GDI and the GEM with new composite measures of gender inequality and women's empowerment. Dijkstra (2006), for example, prefers using the three current components of the GDI to create a new composite index using a different aggregation methodology.[23] Klasen (2006) argues for a new index of gender gaps in human development, which would be loosely related to the HDI by continuing to focus on gender gaps in longevity and education, but replacing gender gaps in earned income with gender gaps in labor force participation. However, the value added of a new index is questionable given the plethora of composite indicators that have been developed in the past few years. Ample alternatives already exist, some of which are good candidates as alternatives to the GDI. The chapter turns to those next.

New Composite Measures

The GDI and the GEM have inspired a number of new composite gender-equality indexes. Some of these measures incorporate dimensions not included in the GDI or the GEM and are tailored to reflect circumstances specific to particular regions of the world. Others have been motivated by an aspiration to create a genuine measure of gender inequality.

Dijkstra (2002) uses five indicators that reflect eight dimensions of gender equality, outlined in a workshop in The Hague, to develop the Standardized Index of Gender Equality (SIGE).[24] SIGE seeks to avoid the methodological limitations of the GDI and the GEM. The five indicators cover education, health, and labor market participation, defined as the relative achievement of females to males, as well as the female share of higher labor market occupations or positions and female share in parliament. For each country and indicator, the resulting score is standardized by expressing the score as the number of deviations from the mean of scores from all countries. The index is the simple arithmetic average of the standardized scores.

Social Watch (2006) developed a similar index, the Gender Equity Index (GEI), that includes three composite indicators representing the economic, social, and political dimensions of gender equality. The social dimension though includes only education (as in the GDI) with enrollment and literacy used to measure it; the economic dimension uses income and share in total paid jobs to detect inequity; and the political dimension includes both the share in parliament and the share in higher labor market positions. In comparison with SIGE, the Gender Equity Index does not include the health indicator (life expectancy), thus avoiding the problem of adjusting for biological differences between men and women. The Gender Equity Indicator is the simple average of the indicators for the three dimensions. The scores of the Gender Equity Indicator are not standardized, which means that the indicator with the widest variation in scores among countries dominates the overall index (Dijkstra 2006). Indeed, Dijkstra avoids this problem with the SIGE, which expresses the component scores as deviations from the arithmetic mean.

One drawback of both the SIGE and the GEI is that they mix dimensions of empowerment and capability. As Schuler (2006) notes, it is possible for a country to have achieved high levels of gender equality in basic capabilities while women remain disempowered.

Yet another composite index was introduced in 2004 by the Economic Commission for Africa. The Africa Gender and Development Index has two parts: the Gender Status Index and the African Women's Progress Scoreboard. The former uses several indicators representing basic capabilities, economic power, and political power: enrollment rates, dropout rates, and literacy rates; child health indicators, life expectancy at birth, new HIV infection, time spent out of work on health; wages in formal, agricultural, and informal employment; income from formal, agricultural, and informal enterprises; remittances; time use for market, nonmarket, and leisure activities; access to resources; and political participation, measured by position held in public sector and civil society institutions. For every variable, the female-to-male ratio is calculated. The Gender Status Index is a weighted average of these indicators.

The African Women's Progress Scoreboard measures government policy performance regarding women's advancement and empowerment in four areas: women's rights, capabilities, economic opportunities, and political power. It tracks government progress in ratifying conventions such as the Committee on the Elimination of Discrimination against Women and the African Protocol, and the implementation of policies to harmonize domestic laws with international obligations. The Africa Gender and Development Index combines both indexes (the Gender Status Index and the African Women's Progress Scoreboard) into one by averaging over both.

There are a number of concerns about this index, including the difficulty of interpreting it, understanding how to judge country performance, and lack of data on several of the specific indicators. There are also concerns about the weighting process for each indicator. These conceptual and empirical problems presently render this index unsuitable for use.

Finally, Dijstkra (2002, 2006) proposes an index of gender inequality that abstracts from absolute levels of human development and is a true measure of gender inequality, called the Relative Status of Women (RSW) Index, which reveals the extent of inequality between female and male achievements in human development. The RSW index uses the HDI indicators and constructs an index of gender equality that abstracts from absolute levels of well-being. It is defined as

$$RSW = \frac{1}{3}\left(\frac{E_f}{E_m} + \frac{L_f}{L_m} + \frac{w_f}{w_m}\right),$$

where E_m and E_f is the male and female educational attainment index, L_m and L_f is the male and female life expectancy index, and w_m and w_f are the average rates of return to male and female labor time. When $RSW = 1$, there is equality between men and women; when $RSW < 1$, there is inequality for women; and when $RSW > 1$, there is bias against men.

Dijkstra (2002, 2006) argues that the RSW is the most promising improvement on the GDI. But the RSW also suffers from the shortcoming that the variable with the highest variation—the income variable—has the highest actual weight in the overall score. This can be resolved by standardizing the three different scores or by applying data envelopment analysis.[25]

In summary, there is no perfect composite indicator. Given data problems, there is little value added in developing yet another composite indicator at this time. The existing composite indexes all have some advantages as well as some shortcomings. In considering the present alternatives to the GDI, the SIGE might have a slight advantage because it encompasses more domains of gender equality and avoids the conceptual and empirical problems of the GDI. At the same time, it is difficult to make comparisons of the SIGE over time because the weights are different every year. In the longer term, if the GDI and the GEM can be improved, as suggested above, they may be better candidates as composite indicators of equality and empowerment.

Indicators or Composite Indexes?

Which is preferable in global monitoring of progress toward gender equality and women's empowerment—a composite index or a suite of indicators? This section reflects on this question.

The benefits to a composite index are well known and include the creation of a summary statistic or measure that captures media and policy attention. In Sharpe's (2004, 10) words, "The benefits of a composite index based on the aggregation of indicators relative to a social welfare function include simplicity and transparency even at the cost of less theoretical purity." Saith and Harriss-White (1998, 38) note that composite indexes have an advantage over individual indicators in that they draw attention to the existence of gender inequality on a broad plane, thus "promoting policies with multiple prongs to tackle gender inequality rather than concentrating on single functionings."

Detractors of composite indexes point to conceptual and methodological issues about what weights are used and how they are assigned. They voice concerns about different methods of aggregation. Value judgments also have to be made about the dimensions that are most important to include in an index. The logic and mathematical challenges associated with combining indicators into a credible index are also considerable. Changes in various dimensions of an index may not move in the same direction, making interpretation more complicated, and composite indexes have been criticized for obscuring more than they reveal.

While indexes may be useful in synthesizing information into a simple message for a lay audience, they may not provide enough information for policy makers who need to make judgments about policies, programs, and resource allocations. A suite of indicators, by contrast, can make it easier to interpret changes in direction and magnitude in each indicator individually and to isolate the types of policies or programs that should be brought to bear for improvements in the indicator. With an appropriate media strategy, changes in various indicators can garner as much attention as a composite indicator. Finally, it is still possible to present scorecards of various indicators without combining them into an aggregate index, for instance, by tallying indicators that trend upward or downward or using the top performers as benchmarks against which other countries are evaluated (Sharpe 2004).

Conclusion

This chapter reviews existing indicators and indexes of gender equality and women's empowerment. Unfortunately, lack of data constrains global monitoring to a small number of indicators. Yet global monitoring requires a range of new indicators that can be used in the longer run. As noted above, work to prepare some of these new indicators on gender equality and women's empowerment is well under way. Such efforts are supported by key recommendations of international conferences on women, as well as by other international mandates of the past two decades. Improving countries' capacity to enhance the coverage, quality, and frequency of collection of sex-disaggregated data remains a priority.

The development of new statistical series requires a lengthy process of discussion between producers and users of statistics, pilot work and testing, and review of this experience. Country statistical agencies need resources to strengthen their capacity and efforts to do all that is necessary to collect and prepare sex-disaggregated data. Work at the country level also requires technical support from key international statistical agencies to develop methodological guidelines and undertake new data collection efforts. Substantial funding is required to coordinate these activities within the appropriate international and regional organizations. If donors and countries are serious about their commitments to MDG3, such investments cannot wait.

Annex 3A: Indicators for Monitoring Gender Equality

Education

Ratio of Female to Male Net Enrollment Rate in Primary or Secondary Education (Gender Parity Index of Net Enrollment Rates)

Definition. The *net enrollment rate* (NER) is the number of pupils of the official school-age group for a given level of education, expressed as a percentage of the total population in that age group.[26]

    Method of computation. To obtain the net enrollment rate, divide the number of pupils enrolled in primary education who are of the official school age by the population for the same age group and multiply the result by 100. This method requires information on the structure of education, enrollment by single years of age, and population of the age group corresponding to the given level of education. The equation is

$$NER_h^t = \frac{E_{h,a}^t}{P_{h,a}^t} \times 100 \, ,$$

where

NER_h^t = net enrollment ratio at level of education h in school year t,

$E_{h,a}^t$ = enrollment of the population of age group a at level of education h in school year t,

$P_{h,a}^t$ = population in age group a that officially corresponds to level of education h in school year t.

    Example: If the entrance age for primary education is 7 years old, and the duration of primary school is 6 years, then a comprises all those 7 to 12 years old.

Compute the rate separately for boys and for girls, and then take the ratio of the female to male rate for the Gender Parity Index (GPI).

Interpretation. A high NER denotes a high degree of participation of the official school-age population. The maximum value is 100 percent. Increasing trends can be considered as reflecting improving participation at the specified level of education.

When the NER is compared with the gross enrollment rate (GER), the difference between the two ratios highlights the incidence of under-age and over-age enrollment. If the NER is below 100 percent, the difference (between the value and 100 percent) provides a measure of the proportion of children not enrolled at the specified level of education.

A GPI of 1 signals parity, a GPI < 1 signals disparity in favor of males, and a GPI > 1 signals disparity in favor of females.

Limitations. NERs have more limited country coverage than GERs. For tertiary education, this indicator is not pertinent because of the difficulties of determining an appropriate age group resulting from the wide variations in the duration of tertiary programs.

Data collection for global monitoring. The UNESCO Institute for Statistics (UIS) produces time series based on enrollment data reported by education ministries or national statistical offices and UN population estimates. These data are gathered through questionnaires sent annually to countries. These questionnaires are typically completed by ministries of education or national statistical offices. Countries are asked to report data according to the levels of education defined in the International Standard Classification of Education, 1997 version (ISCED–97) to ensure international comparability of resulting indicators.

The UIS will, if necessary, adjust nationally reported data to take account either of underreporting (that is, data gaps) or overreporting (inclusion of education programs not covered by its surveys) before calculating indicators. In such cases, the results, if published, will normally be designated as UIS estimates (denoted by ** in UIS publications).

NERs produced by the UIS are available on an annual basis. The primary NER is available for about 140 countries. Data are published for most countries approximately two years after the reference year.

Treatment of missing values. The UIS estimates certain key items of data that may be missing or incomplete. If data for a country are entirely missing or an estimate is not based on evidence from or about the country directly, the UIS does not publish the resulting country-level estimates.

*Ratio of Female to Male Gross Enrollment Rate in
Primary, Secondary, and Tertiary Education
(GPI of Gross Enrollment Rates)*

Definition. The gross enrollment rate (GER) is the number of pupils enrolled in a given level of education, regardless of age, expressed as a percentage of the population in the official age group for the same level of education. For the tertiary level, the population used is the five-year age group following the secondary school-leaving age.

Method of computation. To obtain the GER, divide the number of pupils or students enrolled in each level of education by the population of the official school age for that level of education and multiply the result by 100. The equation is

$$GER_h^t = \frac{E_h^t}{P_h^t} \times 100,$$

where

GER_h^t = gross enrollment rate at level of education h in school year t,

E_h^t = enrollment of the level of education h in school year t, and

P_h^t = population in age group a that officially corresponds to level of education h in year t.

Compute the rate separately for boys and for girls, and then take the ratio of the female to male rate for the GPI.

This method requires information on the structure of education (that is, theoretical entrance age and duration of ISCED97 Level 1 and Levels 2 and 3), enrollment in each level of education, and the populations of the age groups corresponding to the given levels of education.

Interpretation. A high GER generally indicates a high degree of participation, regardless of whether the pupils belong to the official age group. A GER of 100 percent indicates that a country is, in principle, able to accommodate all of its school-age population, but it does not indicate the proportion already enrolled. The achievement of a GER of 100 percent is therefore a necessary but not sufficient condition for enrolling all eligible children in school. When the GER exceeds 90 percent for a particular level of education, the aggregate number of places for pupils is approaching the number required for universal access of the official age group. However, this is a meaningful interpretation only if one can expect the under-age and over-age enrollments to decline in the future to free up places for pupils from the expected age group.

A GPI of 1 signals parity, a GPI < 1 signals disparity in favor of males, and a GPI > 1 signals disparity in favor of females.

Limitations. Gross enrollment rates can be higher than 100 percent because of the inclusion of overage and underage students resulting from early or late entrance and grade repetition. In this case a rigorous interpretation of the GER needs additional information to assess the extent of repetition, late entrants, and so forth.

Data collection for global monitoring. The UIS produces time series based on enrollments. GERs are available for about 180 countries in primary education, 160 in secondary education, and 135 in tertiary education. No tertiary education is provided in about 20 countries worldwide and hence no tertiary GER. Data are published two years after the reference year.

Ratio of Proportion of Males Starting Grade 1 Who Reach Grade 5 to Proportion of Females Starting Grade 1 Who Reach Grade 5 (GPI of the Survival Rate to Grade 5)

Definition. The *survival rate to grade 5* is the percentage of a cohort of pupils enrolled in grade 1 of the primary level of education in a given school year who are expected to reach grade 5, regardless of repetition.

Method of computation. The survival rate to grade 5 is typically estimated from data on enrollment and repetition by grade for two consecutive years, in a procedure called the reconstructed cohort method. This method makes three assumptions: dropouts never return to school; the promotion, repetition, and dropout rates observed in the last two years remain constant over the entire period in which the cohort is enrolled in school; and the same rates apply to all pupils enrolled in a given grade, regardless of whether they previously repeated a grade.

This method requires data on enrollment and the number of repeaters in each grade of primary education in two consecutive school years. The equation is

$$SR^k_{g,i} = \frac{\sum\limits_{t-1}^{m} P^t_{g,i}}{E^k_g} \times 100 \, ,$$

where

$P^t_{g,i} = E^{t+1}_{g,i+1} - R^{t+1}_{g,i+1};$

i = grade (1, 2, 3, ..., n); t = year (1, 2, 3, ..., m); g = pupil-cohort;

$SR^k_{g,i}$ = survival rate of pupil-cohort g at grade i for reference year k;

E^k_g = total number of pupils belonging to cohort g at reference year k;

$P^t_{g,i}$ = promotees from E^k_g who would join successive grades i throughout successive years t; and

R^t_i = number of pupils repeating grade i in school year t.

Compute the rate separately for boys and for girls, then take the ratio of the female to male rate for the GPI.

Interpretation. A survival rate approaching 100 percent indicates a high level of retention and low incidence of dropout. The survival rate may vary from grade to grade, giving indications of grades with relatively more or fewer dropouts. The distinction between the survival rate with and without repetition is necessary to compare the extent of dropout and repetition. The survival rate to grade 5 of primary education is of particular interest because this is commonly considered a prerequisite for sustainable literacy.

Limitations. The survival rate is a percentage of a cohort of pupils (that is, children who have already entered school) and not a percentage of children of school age. Various factors account for poor performance on this indicator, including low quality of schooling, high levels of grade repetition, and the direct and indirect costs of schooling.

Because the calculation of this indicator is based on pupil-flow rates, the reliability of the survival rate depends on the consistency of data on enrollment and repeaters in coverage over time and across grades.

Data collection for global monitoring. The UIS produces time series on school enrollment and repeaters based on data reported by education ministries or national statistical offices.

Survival rates produced by the UIS are available on an annual basis but refer to the earlier of the two years on which the reconstructed cohort method is based. The survival rate to grade 5 is available for about 110 countries. For 34 countries the indicator is not applicable because their education systems have fewer than five grades in primary education. Data are published three years after the reference year.

Ratio of Male to Female Literacy Rates of the 15- to 24-Year-Old Population (GPI of Youth Literacy Rate)

Definition. The *youth literacy rate* is the percentage of the population ages 15–24 who can both read and write and can understand a short simple statement on everyday life.

Method of computation. To obtain the youth literacy rate, divide the number of people ages 15–24 who are literate by the total population in the same age group and multiply that total by 100. The equation is

$$LIT^t_{15-24} = \frac{I^t_{15-24}}{P^t_{15-24}} \times 100,$$

where

LIT^t_{15-24} = literacy rate of persons ages 15–24 in year t,

L^t_{15-24} = literate population ages 15–24 in year t, and

P^t_{15-24} = population ages 15–24 in year t.

Compute the rate separately for boys and for girls; then take the ratio of the female to male rate for the GPI.

Interpretation. Low values of youth literacy indicate poor-quality schooling or high dropout rates.

Limitations. Measurements of literacy can vary from simply asking "Are you literate or not?" to testing, to assessing literacy skills. In some cases literacy is measured crudely in population censuses, either through self-declaration or by assuming that people with no schooling are illiterate. This causes difficulty for international comparisons. Comparability over time, even for the same survey, may also be a problem because definitions of literacy used in the surveys are not standardized.

The literacy rate is not a measure of the quality and adequacy of the literacy level needed for individuals to function in a society. The Millennium Project Task Force does not recommend the use of literacy data for global monitoring until the quality of the data can be improved.

Data collection for global monitoring. The UIS collects global literacy data on an annual basis and updates its statistics twice a year, in April and September. These data are based on observed data reported by countries and territories. Youth literacy rates are available for about 117 countries. Published data reflect the most recent year available.

Health

Maternal Mortality Ratio

Definition. Annual number of deaths of women from pregnancy-related causes, when pregnant or within 42 days of termination of pregnancy, for a specified year (expressed per 100,000).[27]

Methods of computation. The maternal mortality ratio can be calculated by dividing recorded (or estimated) maternal deaths by the total recorded (or estimated) live births in the same period and multiplying by 100,000.

Interpretation. The maternal mortality ratio is useful as a measure of health status. It also reflects the status of poor women and the low-priority given to investments in the health sector because access to emergency obstetric care as part of a well-functioning primary-level health system is the single most important determinant of maternal mortality.

Limitations. Maternal mortality is difficult to measure. Vital registration and health information systems in most developing countries are weak, and thus do not provide an accurate assessment of maternal mortality. Even estimates derived from complete vital registration systems, such as those in developed countries, suffer from misclassification and underreporting of maternal deaths.

Because maternal mortality is a relatively rare event, large sample sizes are needed if household surveys are used. Large sample sizes result in high costs and may still yield estimates with large confidence intervals. To reduce sample size requirements, the sisterhood method measures maternal mortality by asking respondents about the survivorship of sisters. While this method reduces sample size requirements, it produces estimates covering some 6–12 years before the survey, which renders the data not as useful for monitoring progress or observing the impact of interventions. The direct sisterhood method asks respondents to provide date of death, which permits the calculation of more recent estimates, but even then the reference period tends to center on 0–6 years before the survey.

In addition, because of the very large confidence limits around these estimates, they are not suitable for assessing trends over time or for making comparisons between countries.

Data collection for global monitoring. The maternal mortality ratio can be calculated directly from data collected through vital registration systems, household surveys, reproductive age mortality studies, and national population censuses. However, those sources all have data quality problems, particularly related to the underreporting and misclassification of maternal deaths. WHO, UNICEF, and UNFPA have developed a method to adjust existing data for quality issues. The method involves a dual approach whereby existing data are adjusted for underreporting and misclassification of deaths, and model-based estimates are made for countries with no reliable national level data.

Adjusted estimates of maternal mortality ratio are calculated every five to seven years.

Proportion of Births Attended by Skilled Health Personnel

Definition. Percentage of births attended by skilled health personnel (doctors, nurses, or midwives).

Method of computation. The number of births attended by skilled health personnel (doctors, nurses, or midwives) is expressed as a percentage of live births in the same period. Skilled health personnel include those who are trained in providing life-saving obstetric care, including giving the necessary supervision, care, and advice to women during pregnancy, labor, and the postpartum period; to conduct deliveries on their own; and to care for newborns. Traditional birth attendants, even if they receive a short training course, are not included.

Interpretation. Higher numbers indicate progress toward universal access of women to prenatal care. The indicator is a measure of a health system's ability to provide adequate care for pregnant women.

Limitation. Concerns have been expressed that the term "skilled attendant" may not adequately capture women's access to good quality care, particularly when complications arise. In addition, standardization of the definition of "skilled" health personnel is sometimes difficult because of differences in training of health personnel in different countries.

The lack of regular data collection presents a problem for the use of this indicator and hinders the ability of this indicator to show change in the short term. Should the measurement problems be resolved, this indicator should be able to change in the relatively short term because the outcome reflected in this indicator is directly tied to an input measure that is reflected at the time of delivery (Becker, Pickett, and Levine 2006).

Data collection for global monitoring. Data are collected through national-level household surveys, including Multi-Indicator Cluster Surveys and Demographic and Health Surveys (DHS). These surveys are generally conducted every three to five years.

Contraceptive Prevalence

Definition. Percentage of women ages 15–49 who are using or whose partners are using a contraceptive method at a particular time.

Method of computation. The number of women ages 15–49 in marital or consensual unions who report that they are practicing (or whose sexual partners are practicing) contraception is divided by the total number of women ages 15–49 (and same marital status, if applicable) in the survey.

Interpretation. This indicator measures voluntary use of contraception to space pregnancies or avoid additional pregnancies after the desired family size has been reached, and is regarded by many as the highest quality reproductive health indicator (Becker, Pickett, and Levine 2006). The impact of increased contraceptive prevalence includes lower total fertility rates (Shah 2006) and reduced maternal and child mortality (UNFPA 2004), making it a strong overall measure of maternal and child health. The behavioral motivation behind it is unambiguous, unlike either unwanted fertility or unmet need, which both require cognitive changes in women's perception of their ability to manage their fertility; it also reflects maternal protection of infant health against compromise from an ensuing closely spaced pregnancy (Becker, Pickett, and Levine 2006).

Existing literature shows that contraceptive prevalence is the single most important proximate determinant of total fertility (Shah 2006). Eastwood and Lipton (1998) find a causal link between lower fertility rates and overall poverty rates at the macro level, and as Becker, Pickett, and Levine (2006) note, one can hypothesize that increases in contraceptive prevalence will contribute to poverty reduction in the long term. Other poverty-reduction effects may occur because some forms of contraception also prevent HIV/AIDS and other sexually transmitted diseases that help contribute to poverty incidence in developing countries.

Limitations. Provides no information on the context or appropriateness of the method of contraception and is seen by some as a weak proxy of reproductive health. Interpretation is enhanced when supplemented by data on unmet need.

Data collection for global monitoring. Data for this indicator are collected in all DHSs and include all methods in the definition of contraception: modern, traditional, and folkloric. It is usually tabulated for currently married women, ages 15–49, but in most countries it can be tabulated for sexually active, nonpregnant women of childbearing age.

Unmet Need for Family Planning

Definition. The number of women of childbearing age, either married or in consensual union, who desire either to terminate childbearing or to postpone their next birth for a specified time (usually two years or longer).

Method of computation. The indicator is calculated as

$$U = U_L + U_S,$$

where U is the number or percentage of women with unmet need for family planning; U_L is the number or percentage of women with an unmet need for limiting births; and U_S is the number or percentage of women with an unmet need for spacing.

Interpretation. High levels of unmet need indicate that family planning programs and policies either do not exist or are inadequate. This can mean that programs are failing to fully inform women of the options available to them, or that the mechanisms for delivering those options are inadequate for the demand in a country. Governments can respond to these failings by adopting policies aimed at strengthening and expanding family planning programs within their health systems.

From a conceptual standpoint, this measure is useful in measuring the overall responsiveness of the health system to women's needs and gender-equity issues (Becker, Pickett, and Levine 2006). However, one limitation is that it is not always clear why women decide to use or not use contraception. The reasons could vary from lack of information and access to services to having access but deciding not to act on it. Another issue is that the indicator does not decrease linearly when family planning programs improve and desired fertility decreases (Becker, Pickett, and Levine 2006). Initial improvements in family planning programs will first increase demand for contraception, causing demand to exceed existing supply, so that unmet need will rise until supply catches up with demand (Bongaarts 1991).

Contraceptive prevalence rate and unmet need, taken together, provide a good picture of desired levels of fertility and the effectiveness of programmatic responses to helping to realize stated preferences.

Limitations. The lack of regular data collection presents a problem for the use of this indicator and hinders the ability of this indicator to show change in the short term. If the measurement problems are resolved, this indicator should be able to reflect recent policies and practices because it is directly linked to an input measure that is reflected at the time of delivery.

Data collection for global monitoring. Unmet need is routinely collected in DHSs.

Adolescent Fertility Rate

Definition. The annual number of live births among girls ages 15–19 divided by the number of girls in that age group. It is expressed per 1,000 population.

Method of computation. This indicator is calculated as

$$AFR = \frac{N}{D} \times 1,000,$$

where
N = number of live births to females ages 15–19, in one year, and
D = total number of females ages 15–19 in same year.

Estimates of age-specific fertility rates and births by age of mother are available from the UN Population Division. Raw data are obtained from vital registration records, census data, and survey data collected by countries. Where data on births by age of mother are of good quality, or adjustments for incomplete or incorrect age can be made, the fertility of females ages 15–19 is directly calculated as the number of births by females ages 15–19 divided by the total number of females ages 15–19. When data on births by age of mother are unavailable from registration systems, the rate is calculated through indirect methods based on special questions asked in censuses or demographic surveys.

Interpretation. The adolescent fertility rate gives insight into the reproductive behavior of an important target population for meeting the sexual and reproductive health and rights strategic priority.

Higher numbers reflect higher fertility. Childbearing among females ages 15–19 is of special concern because births to teenagers are more likely to be unintended and premature and are associated with greater risks of complications during delivery and higher levels of maternal and child mortality.

Limitations. The adolescent fertility rate counts only live births; stillbirths and spontaneous or induced abortions are not reflected in the calculations (UN Population Fund 2003).

Many developing countries lack reliable registration systems and obtain data on fertility based on indirect estimates. In cases in which no empirical information on age-specific fertility rates is available, a model is used to estimate the share of births to adolescents.

Data collection for global monitoring. Most countries now report fertility statistics by age. This enables regular monitoring of this indicator for a large number of countries. The adolescent fertility rate, as reported by countries, is available for 1970, 1980, 1990, and the most recent year. In some countries, data on the adolescent fertility rate have been collected separately for urban and rural areas. In 2000 the UN database included adolescent fertility statistics for 107 countries.

The UN Statistics Division collects data on live births by age of mother through an annual questionnaire sent to all countries. These data are published regularly in the *Demographic Yearbook.*

Age at First Marriage

Definition. Age at first marriage.

Method of computation. A simple numerical value taken from a questionnaire survey.

Interpretation. Early marriage is more prevalent for girls than for boys. It is associated with negative consequences for girls and the societies in which they live. Young married girls are at greater risk of reproductive morbidity and mortality. Early marriage can limit the education and economic opportunities of females. Young married women often lack power in relation to their husbands and in-laws and are vulnerable to violence, abuse, divorce, and abandonment.

Limitations. The definition of marriage used in censuses may differ from that used in standardized surveys, although research suggests that data are largely comparable across countries (Mensch, Singh, and Casterline 2005). For some countries, marriage is not a well-defined event, and age at marriage may be difficult to establish (Van de Walle 1993).

Data collection for global monitoring. Data on age at marriage can be obtained from a database compiled by the UN Population Division from population censuses and from the DHSs. The UN database presents the proportion of the population that is married in five-year age groups for most developing countries. The DHS asks questions about age and date of first union in all countries where the survey is conducted.

Work

Ratio of Male to Female Labor Force Participation Rate (GPI of Labor Force Participation)

Definition. The *labor force participation rate* is the number of persons in the labor force as a percentage of the working-age population. It can be broken down by sex and by age group.[28]

Method of computation. The labor force participation rate is calculated by expressing the number of persons in the labor force as a percentage of the working-age population. The labor force is the sum of the number of persons employed and the number unemployed. The working-age population is the population within a certain age range prescribed for the measurement of economic characteristics. Labor force participation rates can be constructed for males and females and for specific age categories (15–24, 25–49, 50 and above). The ratio of the female to male labor force participation rate is GPI.

Interpretation. The female labor force participation rate indicates the size of the economically active female population within a country. An upward trend suggests that more women are working for pay or looking for paid work.

Limitations. Labor force participation may not be a good proxy for female empowerment because it includes all types of employment status, including underemployment and unemployment. Unless specific questions are incorporated into the survey, labor force participation rates may underestimate certain groups of workers, such as those who work for only a few hours in the reference period, are in unpaid employment, or work in or near their homes. Because females more than males are found in these types of employment, labor force participation statistics will underestimate their participation.

A second limitation is that national data on labor force participation may not be comparable because of differences in concepts and methodologies.

Data collection for global monitoring. Labor force participation rates can be estimated from a combination of sources. The International Labour Organization (ILO) estimates and projections are derived from establishment censuses and establishment sample surveys, as well as from various types of administrative records, such as employment exchange registers, unemployment insurance records, social security files, public sector payrolls, and personnel lists.

National labor force surveys are likely to be more comparable than data obtained from other sources or from a combination of different sources. Nevertheless, despite their strength, labor force survey data may contain noncomparable elements of scope and coverage, mainly because of differences in the inclusion or exclusion of rural areas and the incorporation or nonincorporation of conscripts. Also, there are variations in national definitions of the labor force concept, particularly with respect to the statistical treatment of "contributing family workers" and "unemployed not looking for work," which lead to underestimation of the female workforce.

The *ILO Key Indicators of the Labor Market*, 4th edition, contains labor force participation rates, by age and sex, for 191 countries over the years 1980–2004.

Ratio of Male to Female Unemployment Rate (Unemployment GPI)

Definition. The unemployment rate is the proportion of the labor force that does not have a job and is actively looking for work.

Method of computation. The unemployment rate consists of all persons above a specified age who, during a defined reference period, were without work, currently available for work, and seeking work. Youth unemployment covers persons ages 15–24. The rate can be computed separately for boys and for girls; the ratio of the female to male unemployment rate is the GPI.

Interpretation. High unemployment rates signal inadequate employment opportunities for a country's population.

Limitations. Differences in operational definitions have implications for comparability across countries. People living in regions or countries where there is little or no formal employment would not be captured in unemployment rates even if they were jobless or seeking work.

Data collection for global monitoring. The ILO collects unemployment data from four main national sources: labor force sample surveys and general household sample surveys; social insurance statistics; employment office statistics; and official national estimates based on some combination of the above. Currently, the ILO has data from 114 countries on unemployment disaggregated by sex.

Share of Women in Wage Employment in the Nonagricultural Sector

Definition. The *share of women in wage employment in the nonagricultural sector* is the share of female workers in wage employment in the nonagricultural sector expressed as a percentage of total wage employment in that same sector.

The nonagricultural sector includes industry and services. "Industry" includes mining and quarrying (including oil production), manufacturing, construction, electricity, gas, and water, corresponding to divisions 2–5 in the International Standard Industrial Classification of All Economic Activities (ISIC-Rev.2) and to tabulation categories C–F in ISIC-Rev.3 (http://laborsta.ilo.org/). "Services" include wholesale and retail trade and restaurants and hotels; transport, storage, and communications; financing, insurance, real estate, and business services; and community, social, and personal services, corresponding to divisions 6–9 in ISIC-Rev.2, and to tabulation categories G–Q in ISIC-Rev.3.

Employment refers to people above a certain age who worked or held a job during a specified reference period (according to the ILO resolution concerning statistics of the economically active population, employment, unemployment, and underemployment,[29] adopted by the Thirteenth International Conference of Labour Statisticians [ICLS], October 1982).

Wage employment refers only to wage earners and salaried employees, or "persons in paid employment jobs." Employees are typically remunerated by wages and salaries, but may be paid by commission from sales, piece rates, bonuses, or payments in kind, such as food, housing, training, and the like. These persons are in wage employment as opposed to self-employment— employers, own-account workers, members of producers' cooperatives, or contributing family workers.

Method of computation. The indicator is calculated as the number of women in nonagricultural paid employment divided by the total number of persons in paid employment in the nonagricultural sector. This is the proportion of women in "paid employment jobs" (in other words "women employees") in the nonagricultural sector.

Interpretation. Higher values of this indicator are supposed to represent progress toward improved gender equality. Yet it is difficult to judge if participation in nonagricultural wage employment constitutes empowerment. An increase in women's share of nonagricultural employment is often accompanied by an increase in women's total workload (because they do not reduce their time in domestic work) and is often not matched by an equivalent increase in women's share of national income because women are paid less than men (UNIFEM 2000).

Limitations. Technical limitations include (i) national statistical offices do not necessarily follow the same definitions or classifications, and the coverage of paid employment may differ from one country to another and over time; and (ii) only about half of countries provide the data necessary for estimating the indicator with regular frequency.

In addition, the indicator has a number of substantive limitations, including the following:

- In many countries (especially developing countries), nonagricultural wage employment represents only a small portion of total employment. As a result, the contribution of women to the national economy is underestimated and therefore misrepresented.
- The indicator is difficult to interpret unless additional information is available on the share of women in total employment, which would allow an assessment to be made of whether women are under- or over-represented in nonagricultural wage employment.
- The indicator does not reveal any differences in the quality of the different types of nonagricultural wage employment (differences that apply to all jobs) regarding earnings, conditions of work, or the legal and social protections the jobs offer. The indicator also cannot reflect whether women are able to reap the economic benefits of such employment.

Data collection for global monitoring. Statistics on paid employment disaggregated by sex, branch of economic activity, occupation, and status in employment are collected annually through a specialized questionnaire for the *Yearbook of Labour Statistics* sent directly to the official national sources in various countries and territories. Statistics are also gleaned from national publications and Web sites. These statistics are published in the ILO *Yearbook of Labour Statistics* and *The Bulletin of Labour Statistics*, and are also available online in LABORSTA (http://laborsta.ilo.org/). LABORSTA has statistics for 196 countries and territories.

Not all available data perfectly match the indicator as defined above. Where paid employment data do not exist, a proxy series (total employment rather than paid employment) has been used, with the expectation that the share of women in total employment is not much different from that in paid employment.

Treatment of missing values. To impute the missing values for the indicator, various multilevel modeling techniques (five basic models and their variants) have been developed and tested. The model adopted was selected on the basis of its goodness-of-fit to the existing data as well as its predictive power, as determined through a jackknife procedure. The model is fitted separately for each region and takes into account the variation over time within and between countries. The missing values are predicted on the assumption that the data that are available for a given country are representative of that country's deviation from the average trend across time, which is estimated based on the whole sample in the region.

Occupational Segregation

Definition. The separation of women and men into different occupations.

Method of computation. There are various ways to measure occupational discrimination, including

- percent of nonagricultural employment in female-dominated and in male-dominated occupations; and
- *index of dissimilarity,* which is an inequality statistic whose value is between 0 (no segregation) and 1 (complete segregation).

The index of dissimilarity measures the sum of the absolute difference in women's and men's distribution over occupations. It is calculated as

$$\text{ID} = \frac{1}{2} \sum_i \left| \frac{M_i}{M} - \frac{F_i}{F} \right|,$$

where F_i is the proportion of females in the ith occupation and F is the number of females in the workforce and M_i is the proportion of males in the ith occupation and M is the number of males in the workforce (Blackburn et al. 1993).

This can be rewritten more simply as

$$ID = \frac{F_f}{F} - \frac{M_f}{M},$$

where F_f is the number of women in "female" occupations and M_f is the number of men in "female" occupations.

Interpretation. The index of dissimilarity has values that range between 0 (no segregation, implying an equal percentage of women in each occupation) and 1 (complete segregation, implying that all female workers are in occupations where there are no male workers). The higher an index value, the greater is segregation.

The index of dissimilarity does not measure discrimination itself, but the tendency of labor markets to be segmented along gender lines.

Limitations. The index of dissimilarity is sensitive to the level of disaggregation and changes in the occupational classification on which it is based.

Emerek et al. (2003) are concerned about the use of a single measure for a complex process. They recommend that if the index of dissimilarity is used, the trends be interpreted through use of decomposition techniques and with attention to their shortcomings, especially for comparisons across countries. They also argue that the index should not be used as an indicator of short-term trends in gender equality.

Data collection for global monitoring. The ILO maintains a database, SEGREGAT, that contains data on employment by sex and detailed occupational groups for more than 80 developed and developing countries and for years 1970, 1980, 1990, and 2000. Data are drawn from population censuses and labor force surveys and in some cases from administrative records and establishment-based surveys. Data are not always comparable across countries or points in time because of differences in sources of data, worker coverage, and national classifications.

Ratio of Women's to Men's Hourly Earnings or Average Earnings (Earnings GPI)

Definition. Measures trends or changes in the level of remuneration from paid employment.

Method of computation. Earnings include direct wages and salaries, remuneration for time not worked (excluding severance and termination pay), bonuses and gratuities, and housing and family allowances paid by the employer directly to the employee. Wage rates are defined more narrowly to include basic wages, cost-of-living allowances, and other guaranteed and regularly paid allowances, but exclude overtime payments, bonuses and gratuities, family allowances, and other social security payments made by employers. Payments in kind, supplementary to normal wage rates, are also excluded in calculating wage rates.

Interpretation. The ratio of female to male earnings can be interpreted as the extent to which women have access to economic resources as compared with men. Caution must be used in interpreting the extent to which earnings data translate into women's control over income.

Limitations. Caution must be exercised in interpreting data on earnings differentials. Women's earnings may be lower than men's because of discrimination (job or training), occupational segregation, direct earnings discrimination, or because women are prepared to enter the labor force for less as a result of lower "aspiration earnings." Given the patchiness of data, it is hard to make determinations about the direction of international trends (Standing 1999).

Data collection for global monitoring. "Statistics of wage rates are in most cases based on collective agreements, arbitral awards or other wage-fixing decisions, which generally specify minimum rates for particular occupations or groups of workers. In some countries, rates actually paid correspond closely to these minima. In countries where the fixing of wage rates is widespread, series of average wage rates in particular industries or groups of industries are calculated, using as weights the numerical importance in a given year of the different occupations for which rates are available in the industries covered. Data on wage rates usually refer only to rates for adults working normal hours, and therefore payments for overtime and other supplementary wage elements are not taken into account; cost-of-living allowances, however, are often included, and other allowances fixed in the wage-setting process, such as housing allowances, are sometimes included. Some countries obtain average *rates actually paid* (straight-time earnings) from establishment payrolls in the same way as average earnings are obtained. Rates actually paid usually cover the remuneration on the basis of normal time worked, both for normal and overtime hours, but exclude incentive pay and other bonuses as well as the premium part of overtime pay. Rates actually paid are sometimes also gathered by labor inspectors" (http://laborsta.ilo.org/applv8/data/c5e.html).

The ILO October Inquiry on Statistics on Occupational Wages and Hours of Work have been collected since 1921 and cover 159 occupations in 49 industry groups in more than 70 countries. For 1995–2003, only 52 countries reported data on wages by industry group and sex from any source. As Freeman and Oostendorp (2001) note, the October Inquiry data are incomplete and inconsistent in that national data are reported for different pay periods (hourly, weekly, monthly), pay definitions (actual wages, actual earnings, statutory rates), and sources (labor force or establishment surveys), and cross-country comparisons must be made with extreme caution.

"Data on *average earnings* are mostly obtained from payroll data and derived from national establishment sample surveys or censuses often furnishing at the same time data on hours of work and on employment.

In a few cases, *average earnings* are compiled on the basis of social insurance statistics, collective agreements or other sources" (http://laborsta.ilo.org/applv8/data/c5e.html).

Political Participation

Proportion of Seats Held by Women in National Parliament
Definition. This indicator shows the percentage of women members in single or lower chambers of national parliaments.[30]

National parliaments can be bicameral or unicameral. This indicator covers the single chamber in unicameral parliaments and the lower chamber in bicameral parliaments. It does not cover the upper chamber of bicameral parliaments. Seats are usually won by members in parliamentary elections. Seats may also be filled by nomination, appointment, indirect election, and rotation of members.

Method of computation. The total number of women divided by the total number of seats filled in single or lower chambers of parliament.

Interpretation. Not a good measure of whether women actually have decision-making power. Only indicates extent of representation in political bodies.

Limitations. The number of countries covered varies with suspensions or dissolutions of parliaments. As of January 1, 2006, 188 countries were included.

There can be difficulties in obtaining information on by-election results and replacements resulting from death or resignation. These changes are unexpected events that are difficult to keep track of. By-elections, for instance, are often not announced internationally as gender elections are.

The data exclude the numbers and percentages of women in upper chambers of parliament. This information is available on the Inter-Parliamentary Union Web site at http://www.ipu.org/wmn-e/classif.htm.

Data collection for global monitoring. The data used are official statistics received from parliaments. After each general parliamentary election or renewal a questionnaire is dispatched to parliaments to solicit the latest available data.

Data are collated and updated on a monthly basis, available at http://www.ipu.org/wmn-e/classif.htm.

Notes

1. Measurement of women's empowerment has lagged because many important dimensions are hard to measure: institutional context, decision making, and

social norms, among others. Because the work of developing indicators in these domains remains to be undertaken, they will not be discussed in this chapter.

2. According to the United Nations (2006), between 1995 and 2003, although 125 countries reported the economically active population at least once from either surveys or censuses, only 69 countries reported such data by sex, age, and education level. Some 114 countries reported unemployment data by sex, but only 87 countries disaggregated unemployment rates by both sex and education level.

3. Between 1995 and 2003, 51 countries reported data on wages by major industry group from a labor-related establishment survey, but only 27 of these reported the data by sex. Data on wages from a labor-related establishment census were reported by 23 countries, but only 8 reported the data by sex (UN 2006).

4. An indicator is a numerical value on some scale of measurement, while an index aggregates variables and combines them with weights.

5. In a number of countries in Latin America and the Caribbean, where female enrollment rates exceed male rates at the secondary level, the female *stock* of education is less than men's (World Bank 2001). This suggests that female disadvantage is not overcome in the region, although the problems young females face may have attenuated.

6. Educational attainment is available in Barro and Lee (2000).

7. Additional problems include the fact that literacy rates are often collected by censuses that are usually conducted only once every 10 years. In some cases, countries report data from only one to three censuses. Trends are therefore difficult to detect and more than 30 countries have never published any kind of literacy data. Second, countries mostly use indirect (and problematic) measures of literacy. Third, countries use different criteria to decide whether people are literate. For example, some countries report the percentage of literate citizens based on one type of indirect measure (that is, self-report) while others report literacy levels using school records (some based on over four years of schooling and others on five or eight years). Fourth, UN agencies do not have the same "data points" for all countries.

8. In 2000, UNESCO had primary completion rates for 128 countries, 125 of them gender disaggregated. See chapter 2 for the current status of the collection of these data by the World Bank.

9. The Organisation for Economic Co-operation and Development (OECD) and UNESCO maintain a World Economic Indicators program that tracks gender-disaggregated secondary school completion rates, mostly for OECD countries.

10. The ILO database on this indicator has data for 196 countries and territories. Some 102 countries provide data on paid employment in the nonagricultural sector. Three countries provide data on total paid employment. Data on total employment in the nonagricultural sector is provided by 30 countries. Data on total employment is provided by 26 countries. No data is provided by 35 countries, but the information on the economically active population is used.

11. The index of dissimilarity is an inequality statistic whose value must be between 0 (no segregation) and 1 (complete segregation) although in practice, national values are found to range from about 0.35 to 0.75.

12. This is known as the Duncan index.
13. The countries with data are predominantly European but all regions have some data (UN 2006).
14. According to the ILO, earnings include direct wages and salaries, remuneration for time not worked (excluding severance and termination pay), bonuses and gratuities, and housing and family allowances paid by the employer directly to the employee. By contrast, wage rates include basic wages, cost-of-living allowances, and other guaranteed and regularly paid allowances, but exclude overtime payments, bonuses and gratuities, family allowances, and other social security payments made by employers. Payments in kind, supplementary to normal wage rates, are also excluded.
15. If a decomposition approach is pursued, the Juhn-Murphy-Pierce (1991) decomposition should be considered. Grimshaw and Rubery (2002) claim that it is superior to the Oaxaca-Blinder decomposition because it minimizes the problem of sample selection bias by avoiding the need to make separate estimates of wage equations for female workers. Moreover, in the application to cross-national comparisons, this method allows for changes in the overall wage distribution to affect the gender pay gap.
16. The ILO has sex-disaggregated earnings data for the manufacturing sector for only 43 countries, most in the OECD (ILO 2006).
17. See www.iser.essex.ac.uk for more information on time diary studies.
18. Deere and Leon (2003) use several sources to build a quantitative study of women's property rights in Latin America and the Caribbean.
19. Population-based surveys from around the world show that anywhere from 10 percent to 69 percent of women report being hit or otherwise physically harmed by an intimate male partner at some time in their lives (WHO 2002).
20. The countries are Bangladesh, Brazil, Japan, Namibia, Peru, Tanzania, Thailand, and Samoa. The research has been replicated in seven other countries: Chile, China, Ethiopia, Indonesia, New Zealand, Serbia, and Vietnam.
21. See Klasen (2006) for the technical construction of each index.
22. While many critics do not raise any concerns about the life expectancy component of the GDI, FMR is likely to be a more comprehensive measure. The most important aspect to be addressed is the use of per capita income, with most critics agreeing that the inclusion of unadjusted per capita income leads to a ranking that is strongly influenced by GDP rather than by broader well-being.
23. The index would take an arithmetic average of three relative scores: the ratio of the female and male indexes for education, the ratio of the female and male indexes for life expectancy, and the relative female and male returns to labor.
24. The eight dimensions are gender identity, autonomy of the body, autonomy within the household, political power, access to social resources (education and health), access to material resources (land and credit), access to employment and income, and time use.
25. Dijkstra (2006) suggests that one solution for the weighting problem is the technique of data envelopment analysis, whereby a set of common weights is established in a linear programming model and the ultimate score is optimized for all countries. Although superior methodologically for establishing weights, it still suffers from the problem of comparisons over time.

26. The material in this "Education" section is adapted from UN (2003).
27. The material in this "Health" section is adapted from UN (2003) and Becker, Pickett, and Levine (2006).
28. The material in this "Work" section is adapted from UN (2003); ILO (2005); and Anker, Melkas, and Korten (2003).
29. http://www.ilo.org/public/english/bureau/stat/download/res/ecacpop.pdf and ILO (2000).
30. The material in this section is derived from http://www.ipu.org/wmn-e/ classif.htm.

Reference and Other Resources

AbouZahr, C., and J. P. Vaughan. 2000. "Assessing the Burden of Sexual and Reproductive Ill-Health: Questions Regarding the Use of Disability-Adjusted Life Years." *Bulletin of the World Health Organization* 78 (5): 655–66.

Agarwal, B. 1995. "Women's Legal Rights in Agricultural Land in India." *Economic and Political Weekly* 30 (12): A39–56.

Anand, S., and K. Hanson. 1997. "Disability-Adjusted Life of Years: A Critical Review." *Journal of Health Economics* 16 (6): 685–702.

Anand, S., and A. Sen. 1995. "Gender Inequality in Human Development: Theories and Measurement." Occasional Paper No. 19, UNDP, New York.

Anker, R., H. Melkas, and A. Korten. 2003. "Gender-Based Occupational Segregation in the 1990s." Working Paper No. 16, ILO, Geneva.

Anríquez, G., and M. Buvinic. 1997. "Poverty Alleviation for Male-Headed and Female-Headed Households in a Fast-Growing Economy (1987–1994)." Unpublished, Inter-American Development Bank, Washington, DC.

Arnesen, T., and E. Nord. 1999. "The Value of Daly Life: Problems with Ethics and Validity of Disability Adjusted Life Years." *British Medical Journal* 319 (7222): 1423–25.

Assad, R. 2002. *The Egyptian Labor Market.* Cairo: American University in Cairo Press.

Bardhan, K., and S. Klasen. 2000. "On UNDP's Revision to the Gender-Related Development Index." *Journal of Human Development* 1 (?): 191–5.

———. 1999. "UNDP's Gender-Related Indices: A Critical Review." *World Development* 27 (6): 985–1010.

Barro, R. J., and J. Lee. 2000. "International Data on Educational Attainment: Updates and Implications." Center for International Development (CID) Working Paper No. 42, Harvard University, Cambridge, MA.

Becker, L., J. Pickett, and R. Levine. 2006. *Health Indicators Working Group Report.* Washington, DC: Center for Global Development.

Beneria, L. 1992. "Accounting for Women's Work: The Progress of Two Decades." *World Development* 20 (11): 1547–60.

Bernstein, S. 2004. "A Proposal for Including a Measure of Unmet Need for Contraception and Adolescent Fertility or Early Marriage Levels as Indicators of the Reproductive Health Component of Gender Equality." Paper commissioned for the UN Millennium Project, New York.

Bhatia, R. 2002. "Measuring Gender Disparity Using Time Use Statistics." *Economic and Political Weekly* 37 (33): 3464–69.

Blackburn, R. M., Jarman, J., and Stiltanen, J. 1993. "The Analysis of Occupational Gender Segregation Over Time and Place: Considerations of Measurement and Some New Evidence." *Work, Employment & Society*, 7 (3): 335–62.

Bongaarts, John. "The KAP-Gap and the Unmet Need for Contraception." *Population and Development Review* 17 (2): 293–313.

Brown, G., and J. Micklewright. 2004. "Using International Surveys of Achievement and Literacy: A View from the Outside." UNESCO, Montreal.

Bruns, B., A. Mingat, and R. Rakotomalala. 2003. *Achieving Universal Primary Education by 2015: A Chance for Every Child*. Washington, DC: World Bank.

Charmes, J., and S. Wieringa. 2003. "Measuring Women's Empowerment: An Assessment of the Gender-Related Development Index and the Gender Empowerment Measure." *Journal of Human Development* 4 (3): 419–35.

Cueva Beteta, H. 2006. "What is Missing in Measures of Women's Empowerment?" *Journal of Human Development* 7 (2): 221–41.

Deere, C. D., and M. Leon. 2003. "The Gender Asset Gap: Land in Latin America." *World Development* 31 (6): 925–47.

Dholakia, K. 2005. "Human Development Index and Status of Women." Unpublished, University of Texas at Dallas.

Dijkstra, A. G. 2002. "Revisiting UNDP's GDI and GEM: Towards an Alternative." *Social Indicators Research* 57 (3): 301–38.

———. 2006. "Towards a Fresh Start in Measures: Some Conceptual Problems and Possible Solutions." *Journal of Human Development* 7 (2): 275–83.

Dijkstra, A. G., and L. C. Hanmer. 2000. "Measuring Socio-Economic Gender Inequality: Toward an Alternative to the UNDP Gender-Related Development Index." *Feminist Economics* 6 (2): 41–75.

Eastwood, R., and M. Lipton. 1998. "Impact of Changes in Human Fertility on Poverty." Monograph, Department of Economics, University of Sussex, U.K. http://www.sussex.ac.uk/Units/economics/dp/pap1.pdf.

ECA (Economic Commission for Africa). 2004. *The African Gender and Development Index*. Addis Ababa, Ethiopia: ECA.

Elson, D. 1999. "Labor Markets as Gendered Institutions: Equality, Efficiency and Empowerment Issues." *World Development* 27 (3): 611–27.

Emerek, R., H. Figueiredo, P. González, L. Gonäs, and J. Rubery. 2003. "Indicators on Gender Segregation." CETE Discussion Paper No. 0302, University do Porto, Faculdade de Economica.

Fox-Rushby, J. A., and K. Hanson. 2001. "Calculating and Presenting Disability Adjusted Life Years (DALYs) in Cost-Effectiveness Analysis." *Health Policy and Planning* 16 (3): 326–31.

Freeman, R., and R. Oostendorp. 2001. "The Occupational Wages around the World Data File." *International Labour Review* 140 (4): 379–401.

Goetz, A. M., and R. Sengupta. 1996. "Who Takes the Credit? Gender, Power and Control over Loan Use in Rural Credit Programs in Bangladesh." *World Development* 24 (1): 45–63.

Goodkind, D. 1996. "On Substituting Sex Preference Strategies in East Asia: Does Prenatal Sex Selection Reduce Postnatal Discrimination?" *Population and Development Review* 22 (1): 1–25.

Grimshaw, D., and J. Rubery. 2002. "The Adjusted Gender Pay Gap: A Critical Appraisal of Standard Decomposition Techniques." Manchester School of Management, UMIST.

Grown, C., G. Rao Gupta, and Z. Khan. 2003. "Promises to Keep: Achieving Gender Equality and the Empowerment of Women." Background paper for the UN Millennium Project Task Force on Primary Education and Gender Equality, International Center for Research on Women, Washington, DC.

Gwatkin, D. R., and M. Guillot. 2000. *The Burden of Disease Among the Global Poor, Current Situation, Future Trends and Implications for Strategy.* Washington, DC: World Bank.

Hussmanns, R. 2004. "Measuring the Informal Economy: From Employment in the Informal Sector to Informal Employment." Working Paper No. 53, ILO, Geneva.

ILO (International Labour Organization). 1996. "Uses and Analysis of the ILO October Inquiry Data on Occupational Wages and Hours of Work." ILO, Geneva.

———. 2000. *Current International Recommendations on Labor Statistics.* Geneva: ILO.

———. 2005. KILM 4th Edition: Guide to Understanding the KILM. ILO, Geneva.

———. 2006. Laborsta Internet. http://laborsta.ilo.org/applv8/data/c5e.html.

Journal of Human Development. 2006. "Special Issue: Revisiting the Gender-related Development Index (GDI) and Gender Empowerment Measure (GEM)." *Journal of Human Development* 7 (2).

Juhn, C., K. M. Murphy, and B. Pierce. 1991. "Accounting for the Slowdown in Black-White Wage Convergence." In *Workers and Their Wages: Changing Patterns in the United States,* ed. M. H. Kosters, 107–43. Washington, DC: AEI Press.

Jutting, J. P., C. Morrisson, J. Dayton-Johnson, and D. Drechsler. 2006. "Measuring Gender (In) Equality: Introducing the Gender, Institutions and Development Data Base (GID)." Working Paper No. 247, OECD Development Center.

Kabeer, N. 1999. "The Conditions and Consequences of Choice: Reflections on the Measurement of Women's Empowerment." UNRISD Discussion Paper 108, United Nations Research Institute for Social Development, Geneva.

Klasen, S. 2004. "Gender-Related Indicators of Well-Being." Discussion Paper No. 2004/05, United Nations University, World Institute for Development Economics Research, Helsinki.

Klasen, S. 2006. "UNDP's Gender-Related Measures: Some Conceptual Problems and Possible Solutions." *Journal of Human Development* 7 (2): 243–74.

Klasen, S., and C. Wink. 2003. "Missing Women: Revisiting the Debate." *Feminist Economics* 9 (2,3): 263–300.

Lloyd, C. B., and P. C. Hewett. 2006. "Exploring the Knowledge Component of the Human Development Report's Gender-Related Development Index: Evaluating Alternative Indicators of Educational Progress for the Measurement of Gender Inequalities." United Nations Development Programme Workshop "Revisiting the GDI-GEM," New York, Jan. 20.

Lopez-Claros, A., and S. Zahidi. 2005. "Women's Empowerment: Measuring the Global Gender Gap." World Economic Forum, Geneva.

Malhotra, A., S. R. Schuler, and C. Boender. 2002. "Measuring Women's Empowerment as a Variable in International Development." Background paper prepared for the World Bank workshop "Poverty and Gender: New Perspectives," Washington, DC, May 6–9.

McGillivray, M., and J. R. Pillarisetti. 2002. "International Equality in Human Development, Real Income and Gender-Related Development." Credit Research Paper No. 02/02, Center for Research in Economic Development and International Trade, University of Nottingham.

Mensch, B. S., S. Singh, and J. B. Casterline. 2005. "Trends in the Timing of First Marriage among Men and Women in the Developing World." Policy Research Division Working Paper No. 202, Population Council, New York.

Morrisson, C., and J. P. Jutting. 2005. "Women's Discrimination in Developing Countries: A New Data Set for Better Policies." *World Development* 33 (7): 1065–81.

Murray, C. J., and A. D. Lopez. 1997. "The Utility of DALYs for Public Health Policy and Research: A Reply." *Bulletin of the World Health Organization* 75 (4): 377–81.

Nygaard, E. 2000. "Is It Feasible or Desirable to Measure Burdens of Disease as a Single Number?" *Reproductive Health Matters* 8 (15): 117–25.

PISA Governing Board. 2005. "Longer Term Strategy of the Development of PISA." EDU/PISA/GB (2005) 21, Meeting of the PISA Governing Board, Reykjavik, October 3–5.

Robberstad, B. 2005. "QALYs vs DALYs vs LYs Gained: What are the Differences, and What Difference Do They Make for Health Care Priority Setting?" *Norsk Epidemiologi* 15 (2): 183–91.

Saith, R., and B. Harriss-White. 1998. "Gender Sensitivity of Well-Being Indicators." Discussion Paper No. 95, UNRISD, Geneva.

Sayers, B. M., and T. M. Fliedner. 1997. "The Critique of DALYs: A Counter-Reply." *Bulletin of the World Health Organization* 75 (4): 383–4.

Schuler, D. 2006. "The Uses and Misuses of the Gender-Related Development Index and Gender Empowerment Measure: A Review of the Literature." *Journal of Human Development* 7 (2): 161–81.

Seguino, S. 2002. "Gender, Quality of Life, and Growth in Asia 1970 to 1990." *The Pacific Review* 15 (2): 245–77.

———. 2003. "Is Economic Growth Good For Well-Being? Evidence of Gender Effects in Latin America and the Caribbean." Working Paper, Department of Economics, University of Vermont, Burlington, Vermont.

———. 2004. "Gender, Well-Being, and Equality: Assessing Status, Progress, and the Way Forward." Background paper prepared for UNRISD for Policy Report on Gender and Development, UNRISD, Geneva.

Shah, Iqbal. 2006. "Levels and Trends in Contraceptive Use." World Health Organization, Geneva. http://www.gfmer.ch/Endo/Course2003/PDF/Contraceptive_use.pdf.

Sharpe, A. 2004. "Literature Review of Frameworks for Macro-Indicators." Research Report 2004-03, Center for Study of Living Standards, Ottawa.

Standing, G. 1999. "Global Feminization Revisited." *World Development* 27 (7): 583–602.

Tinker, I., and G. Summerfield. 1999. *Women's Rights to House and Land: China, Laos, Vietnam.* Boulder, CO, and London: Lynne Rienner Publishers.

UN (United Nations). 2003. *Indicators for Monitoring the Millennium Development Goals: Definitions, Rationale, Concepts and Sources.* New York: United Nations.

———. 2005. *Guide to Producing Statistics on Time Use: Measuring Paid and Unpaid Work.* New York: UN.

———. 2006. *The World's Women 2005: Progress in Statistics.* New York: United Nations.

UNDP (United Nations Development Programme). 1995. *Human Development Report 1995.* New York and Oxford, U.K.: Oxford University Press.

UNESCO (United Nations Educational, Scientific, and Cultural Organization). 2004. "EFA Global Monitoring Report 2003/4: Gender and Education for All, the Leap to Equality." Paris.

UNIFEM (United Nations Development Fund for Women). 2000. *Progress of the World's Women 2000.* New York: UNIFEM

———. 2005. *Progress of the World's Women 2005: Women, Work & Poverty.* New York: UNIFEM.

United Nations Millennium Project. 2005. *Taking Action: Achieving Gender Equality and Empowering Women.* Report prepared by the Taskforce on Education and Gender.

UN Population Fund. 2003. *State of World Population 2003.* New York: UNFPA.

———. 2004. "The ICPD and MDGs: Close Linkages." UN Department of Economic and Social Affairs, New York. http://www.un.org/esa/population/publications/PopAspectsMDG/14_UNFPA.pdf.

Van de Walle, E. 1993. "Recent Trends in Marriage Ages." In *Demographic Change in Sub-Saharan Africa,* ed. K. A. Foote, K. H. Hill, and L. G. Martin. Washington, DC: National Academy Press.

World Bank. 2001. *Engendering Development through Gender Equality in Rights, Resources and Voice.* New York: Oxford University Press.

WHO (World Health Organization). 2001. "Executive Summary," in "Report of the Second Interagency Meeting." World Health Organization, Geneva.

———. 2002. "WHO Multi-Country Study on Women's Health and Domestic Violence Against Women." World Health Organization, Geneva.

———. 2005. "Technical Consultation on Reproductive Health Indicators 21–22, September 2005 Meeting Report." WHO Department of Reproductive Health and Research, Geneva.

4

Monitoring Progress in Gender Equality in the Labor Market

Zafiris Tzannatos

Key to achieving the third Millennium Development Goal (MDG3) is the removal of barriers to women's economic participation, including in employment. Working women make substantial contributions to their households but still face many obstacles to their participation in labor markets. This chapter focuses on two issues of key importance in middle-income developing countries: occupational segregation of women into low-paying jobs, and the related topic of male-female wage gaps. The first section examines trends in occupational segregation and wages. The second section formally models and estimates the impact on national output and men's wages if wage parity between men and women were achieved and occupational segregation were eliminated. The final section suggests improvements to indicators to track women's participation in labor markets in developing countries.

Trends in Occupational Segregation and Wage Gaps

Although female labor force participation rates are still lower than men's, they have been increasing rapidly. More than half of women around the world are in the labor force today, and women constitute approximately four out of ten global workers. However, much of the work performed by women is not paid—an outcome of the traditional division of labor within the household or the nature of employment in family farms and enterprises.

When women are in the labor force, they usually perform different tasks and work in different sectors than men. Sex segregation in the labor force implies that female and male workers work in compartmentalized activities that usually lead to different rewards and different career opportunities even though workers may have otherwise comparable labor market characteristics. The conditions of women's employment tend also to

147

be atypical (that is, part-time, temporary, or casual work in the home or in the form of subcontracting). In occupations, for example, nearly two-thirds of women in manufacturing are categorized as laborers, operators, and production workers, with a small percentage in administrative and managerial positions. Women workers are usually employed in a limited number of industrial sectors: more than two-thirds of the global labor force in garment production is female, accounting for almost one-fifth of the total female labor force in manufacturing. With respect to employment status, the majority of family workers are female and often unpaid (Sayed and Tzannatos 1998).

Segregation and the Duncan Index

Sex segregation of employment is a multidimensional concept and concentrating on only one dimension of employment (such as the share of women in nonagricultural wage employment) is bound to leave many other dimensions unexplored. This shortcoming is now widely recognized and additional dimensions of employment indicators are being considered (see table 4A.1 in annex 4A to this chapter). As the layout of the table suggests, however, the presentation of international data of various dimensions of employment can quickly become complex. Furthermore, considering just one dimension of female employment but not the corresponding dimension for men may provide misleading information. For example, a 30 percent share of women in nonagricultural wage employment may be good if the corresponding share of men is also 30 percent, but not so good if the men's share is 6 percent.

An alternative would be to use some summary statistic that would evaluate differences in the whole distribution of women and men across different sectors. This would be closer to measuring gender segregation.

This is the approach taken in this section. Data from the International Labour Organization (ILO) on the employment distribution of women and men by industries and occupations (at the two-digit level) are used to calculate the Duncan index—an index of employment dissimilarity between any two groups of workers (Duncan and Duncan 1955). In the case of women and men, the Duncan index, D, takes the form

$$D = \frac{1}{2} \sum_{i=1}^{N} |f_i - m_i|,$$

where $i = 1,2,...,N$ is the total number of sectors of interest (for example, industries or occupations), f_i and m_i are ratios of female and male employment in sector i to the number of women and men in their respective labor forces, and the summation refers to the absolute differences between women's and men's ratios within each sector. The minimum value of the index is zero; it occurs when women and men have identical employment distributions across sectors (that is, when the percentage of women or men in each sector is the same as their percentage in total employment). The maximum value, unity, occurs when there is complete dissimilarity (no women and men work in the same sector).[1]

The chapter calculates the value of the Duncan index for two periods, from 1950 to the 1980s and early1990s, and from the 1980s to the present, using information derived from national censuses and labor force and establishment surveys. The census information comes primarily in the form of seven comparable-over-time industries and seven occupations, while the survey data use industrial (International Standard Industrial Classification, ISIC) and occupational (International Standard Classification of Occupations, ISCO) classifications as they were revised over time. Examining the behavior of the Duncan index on the basis of different classifications and at different times provides a better understanding of segregation and the role statistics can play in monitoring the changes in segregation over time.

Trends in Sex Segregation: 1950s to 1980s and early 1990s
Census data suggest that industrial sex segregation declined worldwide for all workers as well as for workers in paid employment.[2] The segregation of paid workers declined much faster. For *all workers*, the value of the Duncan index declined from 0.35 in the 1950s and 1960s to 0.31 in the 1970s and 1980s (table 4.1), whereas for paid workers, the decline was from 0.40 in the 1950s and 1960s to 0.31 in the 1970s and 1980s.

Occupational sex segregation among all workers registered practically no change between the two periods under consideration (0.39 and 0.38); however, the employment dissimilarity among paid workers declined from 0.44 to 0.40. One explanation for the more rapid decline in segregation among paid workers compared with all workers may be that market forces discriminate less against women than do noneconomic factors: it may be more difficult for women to break sex stereotypes in self-employment and family work undertaken predominantly in the villages or at the community level.[3]

From a historical perspective, gender segregation in employment has shown a tendency to decline. This, however, understates how much gender employment differentials have narrowed over time because of aggregation

TABLE 4.1
World Value of Duncan Index (Gender Employment Segregation)

	Early period (1950s–1960s)	Late period (1970s–1980s)
Industry		
All workers	0.346	0.306
Paid workers	0.395	0.310
Occupations		
All workers	0.386	0.380
Paid workers	0.442	0.403

Sources: ILO 1990; Tzannatos 1999.

Note: The reported values are unweighted averages of country values of the Duncan index calculated at two times in 61 countries (for industries) and 45 countries (for occupations). The country values are calculated over seven industries (agriculture, mining, manufacturing, construction, utilities, transport, and services) and seven occupations (professional, administrative, clerical, sales, services, farmer, and production). "All workers" refers to wage employment, self-employment, and family work.

biases. The results listed above are based on seven occupations and seven industries (see note to table 4.1), which are too broad. For example, domestic service was the biggest single occupational category for women in Britain from the first census enumeration (1851) until World War II. This "social, community, and personal services" industry continued to be the largest employer of women in the postwar era though domestic servants became a practically extinct group. Thus, changes in the composition of employment within individual sectors go unnoticed in such aggregate statistics.

As will become clearer shortly, the use of a few broad industrial or occupational categories is still too broad for monitoring progress in gender equality (though better than just using, say, the share of women in wage employment or some other simple dimension of the labor market). The next section examines the behavior of the Duncan index since the 1980s because this is more relevant at this time. Use of this period can also shed light on whether the use of more recent and refined sectoral classifications may capture better production realities in the era of globalization.

Trends: 1980s to the Present
This section assesses the value of the index in the more recent period, again for two different groupings of workers (all workers and those in paid employment only) but for six different classifications. First, *all workers* are classified according to two separate industrial classifications (ISIC 1968 and ISIC 1990, referred to as ISIC68 and ISIC90) and two occupational

classifications (ISCO 1968 and ISCO 1988, referred to ISCO68 and ISCO88).[4] These four groups are complemented by two others based on the industrial classification of only *paid workers*. Each group is observed at two times. The sample varies from 41 to 79 countries, depending on the group.

With regard to global trends (irrespective of country income level), the main conclusion from examining the more recent period is that segregation is rather resilient. The data presented in the last column of table 4.2 indicate that the value of the index has changed little since the 1980s (see also table 4A.2 in annex 4A for trends in individual countries).

TABLE 4.2
Value of Duncan Index by Region

	Average early year	Duncan 1	Average late year	Duncan 2	Change in Duncan	
					Total (%)	Annualized (%)
ISIC68, All workers						
MI, 26	1982	0.371	1998	0.368	−0.4	0.0
HI, 23	1976	0.286	1996	0.284	−0.2	0.0
ISIC90, All workers						
MI, 50	1997	0.337	2002	0.343	0.6	0.1
HI, 29	1994	0.314	2003	0.321	0.7	0.1
ISCO68, All workers						
MI, 21	1981	0.389	1997	0.379	−1.0	−0.1
HI, 20	1976	0.353	1995	0.352	0.0	0.0
ISCO88, All workers						
MI, 51	1997	0.348	2003	0.326	−2.2	−0.4
HI, 38	1994	0.360	2004	0.364	0.4	0.0
ISIC68, Employees						
MI, 30	1980	0.244	1996	0.256	1.2	0.1
HI, 24	1977	0.251	1996	0.237	−1.4	−0.1
ISIC90, Employees						
MI, 37	1996	0.342	2003	0.340	−0.1	0.0
HI, 28	1995	0.301	2003	0.319	1.8	0.2

Source: Calculated from annex table 4A.2.

Note: Total = Simple difference between Duncan 1 and Duncan 2; Annualized = Total divided by the time difference between the two values of the index.

MI refers to middle-income countries, followed by number of countries in the sample for each group.

HI refers to high-income countries, followed by number of countries in the sample for each group.

When disaggregated by country income level, the index for all workers seems to have moved about the same way over time for both high- and middle-income countries. When examining paid workers only, the value of the index is again comparable between high- and middle-income countries, though somewhat declining for the high-income countries. The converse is true when the later industrial classification is used, and the value of the index seems to be increasing for high-income countries.

The findings in table 4.2, and the previous ones derived in a more historical context, suggest that aggregate examinations of employment structures in groups of countries fail to capture important differences and trends at the national level. Moreover, the estimates are highly sensitive to the type of industrial classification used.[5] This suggests that there are substantial artificial differences in levels and trends of segregation when different aggregations are used.

One possible explanation for the decline in the value of the Duncan index in the first period but not in the second, is that the newer classifications more accurately reflect the nature of production in the globalization era. As employment and industrial organizations have become more complex—in the wake of the knowledge economy and the emergence of flexible arrangements, including subcontracting and outsourcing—changing classifications are better able to capture the changing economic environment and thus measure gender segregation in more meaningful terms (see box 4.1).

Some evidence points to the fact that an increase in segregation is not necessarily synonymous with poorer opportunities or labor market outcomes for women. In Puerto Rico, segregation patterns have been found to be consistent with median annual earnings for women that are quite close to those of men (Presser and Kishor 1991). An explanation for this is that women are offered more opportunities for upward mobility when production is organized around strictly segregated occupations, rather than when women and men work together. On similar grounds, horizontal desegregation does not unambiguously represent an improvement in the labor market position of women. The feminization of previously male-dominated jobs can be associated with deteriorating employment conditions resulting from the increase in total labor supply that, in turn, depresses wages for both women and men in those jobs.[6] Feminization may also lead to an increase in vertical segregation, if men move up successively to top positions as more women enter the labor market.

Box 4.1
The Mis-Measured Female Worker

Sweden, a country characterized by high levels of gender equality, provides a striking example of the mis-measurement of female work. Women's participation in agricultural activities increased from 8 percent to 52 percent from 1930 to 1965. This was a result of changing definitions for agricultural work. In 1950, for example, agricultural work included workers who spent half of their normal working time on agricultural work, while in 1965 the definition included agricultural activities, such as caring for animals, milking, and so on; these were activities primarily performed by women.

Working Farmers in Sweden, Various Censuses

	1930	1945	1950	1960	1965
Female	751	151	5,217	10,387	58,283
Male	221,777	212,594	195,764	135,263	104,823
% of farmers with working wives	0	0	3	8	56

Source: Tzannatos (1999) adapted from Nyberg (1993).

Similar examples are found in the Dominican Republic, India, and Turkey. According to the Dominican Republic census of 1981, rural female labor force participation was 21 percent, but a study conducted three years later suggested this figure was 84 percent. The difference was caused by the exclusion of such activities as garden cultivation and animal care from the census estimates. In India, narrow and broad definitions of what constitutes work, and by extension who is in or out of the labor force, result in estimates for participation rates that range from 13 to 88 percent, respectively. Finally, according to the Turkish census of 1980, there were 40,000 carpet weavers but estimates based on annual carpet production and number of looms in operation bring the figure of carpet weavers to around half a million, most of them women. Such errors in measuring the labor force have implications for various assessments of the labor market, including segregation along with the measurement of earnings and wages.

Sources: Berik 1987; ILO 1994; Tzannatos 1999.

Wages

In addition to observed gender differences in industry and occupation of employment, pay differences are also significant. As shown in chapter 2, even when it attracts pay, women's work is valued less than men's. Typically, women's earnings average around two-thirds those of men's. Overall, perhaps *no more than one-fifth of the world's wages accrue to women* because fewer women than men work for wages and they are usually engaged in the low-paying sectors; women are usually paid less than men even in the low-paying sectors (Tzannatos 1998).

As a general rule, female wages (relative to male) tend to increase over time. The unweighted worldwide average annual increase in the female relative (to male) wage in our sample[7] comes to 0.5 percent per year. The average female relative wage now stands at around 80 percent of male wages: thus, assuming linear and uniform growth over time, the worldwide average would be around 94 percent one generation (30 years) from now. However, female relative wages can increase faster if increases in female education continue; in fact, in a number of countries, female school enrollment already exceeds male enrollment, even in countries where females have been historically underrepresented in education (see figures 4C.1 and 4C.2 in annex 4C).

The data in table 4.3 show significant cross-country variation in trends in female relative wages (to males). While the trend is mainly positive (middle column in table 4.3), 12 of the 55 countries (including some high-income countries) experienced a decrease in female relative wages—and in six countries (Bahrain, Botswana, Colombia, Netherlands Antilles, Kazakhstan, and Thailand) the decrease was more than 1 percent per year. For three countries with negative trends (Colombia, Netherlands Antilles, and Thailand), the observation period is too short (four years or less), to make reliable inferences. Thus, this negative finding may reflect more of a short-run variation than a consistent trend.[8] In fact, the only two regions that have seen a decline in female relative wages in the recent period are the ones that have the highest relative earnings (the Middle East and North Africa [MENA] and Sub-Saharan Africa [SSA]).

These international comparisons are, however, rather crude and can be misleading. What can one infer about gender equality from the fact that women in the regions usually associated with greatest gender differences (such as MENA, SSA, and the low-income Asian countries) have higher female relative earnings than, say, the high-income European or East Asian economies? Is this an indication of greater equality or just the result of selectivity because in the former countries only the most productive women work for pay? It is likely that in countries with very low female labor force participation rates, female wages are observed mainly for those women with high returns in the labor market while male wages are based on all male workers—those who have high wages and those who have low wages. Also, it is probable that the high relative earnings of women in paid

TABLE 4.3
Relative (Female-to-Male) Wages by Region

1980s and 1990s	Percentage change between the two periods	1990s and 2000s	
Middle East and North Africa	0.95	−2.1	Middle East and North Africa	0.93
Sub-Saharan Africa	0.89	−2.2	Sub-Saharan Africa	0.87
Other Asia	0.88	2.3	Other Asia	0.90
Nordic	0.83	1.2	Nordic	0.84
Latin America and the Caribbean	0.77	1.3	Latin America and the Caribbean	0.78
Europe and Central Asia	0.72	6.9	Europe and Central Asia	0.77
Other Europe	0.71	7.0	Other Europe	0.76
Northern Europe, Australia, New Zealand	0.70	8.6	Northern Europe, Australia, New Zealand	0.76
East Asia, High income	0.60	23.3	East Asia, High income	0.74

Source: Calculated from annex table 4A.9.

Note: The country groups are as follows: Middle East and North Africa = Bahrain, Arab Republic of Egypt, Jordan, West Bank and Gaza; Sub-Saharan Africa = Botswana, Kenya, Swaziland, Tanzania; Other Asia = Mongolia, the Philippines, Sri Lanka, Thailand; Nordic = Finland, Iceland, Norway, Sweden; Latin America and the Caribbean = Brazil, Colombia, Costa Rica, El Salvador, Guadeloupe, Mexico, Netherlands Antilles, Paraguay; Europe and Central Asia = Belarus, Bulgaria, Hungary, Latvia, Lithuania, Turkey, Ukraine, Georgia, Kazakhstan; Other Europe = Gibraltar, Ireland, Malta, Portugal, Cyprus; North Europe, Australia, New Zealand = Australia, New Zealand, Austria, Belgium, Denmark, France, Luxembourg, the Netherlands, Switzerland, United Kingdom; East Asia, High income = Hong Kong, China, Japan, Republic of Korea, Singapore.

employment in developing countries are affected disproportionately by those who are engaged in government jobs.

Impact of Removing Barriers Limiting Female Labor Force Participation

This section uses economic modeling to examine the effects on national output and male wages if occupational segregation were hypothetically eliminated and female wages were equalized to men's wages.[9]

Women's crowding in certain sectors and occupations reduces their wages while men gain in relative terms and possibly in absolute terms. If gender differences in the labor market are the result of discrimination and women are excluded, for example, from some occupations and crowded in others because of regulations, then—by virtue of the distorted relative labor supply across occupations—pay would be higher in male-dominated occupations and lower in female-dominated occupations than it otherwise would be under nondiscriminatory conditions. Another effect of segregation would be a welfare loss (reduction in total output) arising from the misallocation of the labor force: competent female workers are excluded from the most productive activities they can do, which are then undertaken by less able (compared to women) men.

To find out the effects of achieving equality in the labor market, the analysis must first estimate output under current conditions, compare it with the new level of output under equality, and then examine the distributional sequences on employment and wages separately for women and men. The difference between these two output estimates provides an indication of the potential (maximum) welfare gains that could be achieved if women had the same characteristics and preferences as men, as well as the same occupational wages within the same industries as men. This process will not necessarily lead to the same economywide average wages between women and men because the model assumes that differences in the industrial distribution of women and men remain the same.

A caution applies here: a prerequisite for achieving gender equality in the labor market is not just the removal of "labor demand" discrimination, but also the removal of the many other barriers mentioned above. The results of the current exercise are indicative of what can happen in the long run when (i) women and men are equally endowed with human capital, (ii) there is no employer discrimination, (iii) family constraints are no more binding upon women than men, and (iv) the gender-specific effects of social norms and other institutional factors have withered away.

These hypothetical issues are addressed with the aid of the following model. It is assumed that in each industry i (omitted for notational simplicity) output is given by a function

$$Y = f(L_m^m, L_m^f), \qquad (4.1)$$

where Y = output in industry i; L = labor in industry i; and superscripts m and f refer to male and female labor, respectively, that are employed initially in completely segregated occupations.

On the assumption that all factors of production other than male and female are fixed, these other factors are not introduced explicitly into the production function.

Second, it is assumed that in each industry, each occupation is paid its marginal product

$$w^s = \theta Y / \theta L^s, \tag{4.2}$$

where $s = m$ or f.

The problem now is to find the new equilibrium value of labor, levels of wages, and output if reallocation of female labor is allowed from the female occupations to the male occupations, such that

$$Y^* = f(L^{m*}, L^{f*}), \tag{4.3}$$

$$w^{m*} = w^{f*}, \text{ and} \tag{4.4}$$

$$L^{m*} + L^{f*} = L^m + L^f, \tag{4.5}$$

where the asterisk indicates the new equilibrium value of the appropriate variable.

To solve the system of equations (4.3) to (4.5), assume that within each industry the different occupations can be aggregated into a constant elasticity of substitution production function of the form

$$Y = A \left[\sum \alpha L^{m^{-\rho}} + \sum \beta L^{f^{-\rho}} \right]^{-1/\rho}, \tag{4.6}$$

where ρ is a parameter that depends on the elasticity of substitution (σ) of female for male labor (see below), α and β are parameters that depend on the nature of the occupation to which women are restricted (the smaller the value of β the more rigorous the restriction) and A is a constant that takes into account the contribution to output of factors of production other than labor.

Taking into account condition (4.2) and the explicit formulation of the production function (4.6), the system can be solved for the optimal values of labor, wages, and output.

The solution is given by the following formulae[10]:

$$L^{m*} = \left[\alpha^\sigma / (\alpha^\sigma + \beta^\sigma) \right] \left[L^m + L^f \right],$$

$$L^{f*} = L^m + L^f - L^{m*},$$

$$Y^* = \sum w^m \left[(L^m / L^{m*}) / Y \right]^{\rho+1} L^m + \sum w^f \left[(L^f / L^{f*}) / Y \right]^{\rho+1} L^{f*},$$

$$w^{m*} = w \left[L^m / L^{m*} \right]^{\rho+1} \left[Y^* / Y \right]^{\rho+1},$$

$$w^{f*} = w^{m*},$$

where σ is the elasticity of substitution between female and male labor,

$$\sigma = 1 / (1 + \rho),$$

and α and β can be estimated from the formulae

$$\alpha = w^m \left[L^f / Y \right]^{\rho+1} \text{ and}$$

$$\beta = w^f \left[L^f / Y \right]^{\rho+1}.$$

The empirical estimates reported below are based on reported earnings as a proxy for marginal products. It is well known that in a conventional competitive regime, economically fitted production functions, when differentiated, need not give marginal productivity conditions that equal observed earnings. This should not, however, produce unacceptable results in this analysis, if the proportional discrepancy between earnings and their respective marginal products is the same for both sexes.

However, a series of additional qualifications apply. First, at this point, there is no information available on the different educational levels and work experiences attained by men and women in the studied industries. This lack of information precludes a refinement of the estimates that would take into account differences arising from the different human capital levels; thus, the results relate to achieving wage equality under the assumption that women and men are equally productive.

Second, the model itself does not allow for complementarity between nonlabor inputs and different labor categories. This need not adversely affect the results, to the extent that sectoral levels of inputs are being kept constant. However, the lack of complementarity can be important in the longer run, if reallocation of capital were allowed as a response to changes in the returns to capital.

Third, the assumption of a common elasticity of substitution may distort the pattern of optimal industrial allocation of labor although it does not significantly alter the estimate of overall gains. Nevertheless, there is wide agreement that all pair-wise elasticities of substitution are substantially greater than unity, ranging usually between three and nine. *The chapter therefore reports results based on the value of the elasticity of substitution being six.* In general terms, the value of six produces midpoint estimates because simulated effects flatten out asymptotically above six.

Fourth, the assumption of fixed industrial output prices implies an infinitely elastic demand for the product of each industry. This implies, in turn, that the analysis takes place in an open and relatively small economy or that industrial output changes are sufficiently small to leave the relative prices of the final output unchanged.

Finally, the results are based on the assumption that complete equalization of male and female labor is achieved. This is not likely to happen in real life; the economywide structure of the labor market will also depend on decisions made by the suppliers of labor. If households prefer women to work in certain sectors, or restrict the tradeoff between family responsibilities and the market, the optimal allocation of labor would be constrained from an economic perspective. Thus, the estimates provide an upper boundary of possible long-run effects upon a hypothetical society in which production and reproduction are equally shared between men and women.

Overall, the usefulness of the exercise stems from the fact that women have historically improved their position in the labor market, partly through increasing their labor force attachment and also by working in the same sectors as men. If this trend continues, the labor market may asymptotically adjust to the values indicated by the simulations. The fact that the model is based on a simulation implies that the picture emerging from the model and its underlying assumptions should be interpreted cautiously.

The results are presented in table 4.4 by world regions (first and second columns) and by income in table 4.5. The results are based on the ILO data on industrial employment that include information on female and male wages separately for different industries. Each industry is assumed to have two occupations, a low-paid one as proxied by the female employment in the concerned industry, and a high-paid one, as proxied by the male employment. What stands out in the results is that, under the model's assumptions, female wages can increase significantly with little loss in male wages.

In fact, in the process of achieving greater equality, male wages need not decrease at all in the long run. Part of the explanation rests on the fact that there would be output gains (third column in table 4.4). A reduction in segregation is not a purely redistributive issue because the "size of the pie" increases, with women claiming a bigger share. In fact, given that the economy grows over time, men's wages need not decline in absolute terms—a point worth noting because with zero-sum gains, the losers (in this case, men) may devise strategies for forestalling equality. This phenomenon has been emphasized in the political economy literature and is known as "the reversal rest," that is, those losing from economic change can bribe the winners and forestall the move toward a potentially Pareto-efficient outcome.

So, a reduction in inequality can have beneficial effects on both women and men. However, it may take considerable time before equality is achieved (the fourth column of table 4.4 indicates the percentage of the labor force

TABLE 4.4
Effects of Eliminating Gender Differences in Pay and Employment

Region	Increase in female wages	Decrease in male wages	Output (GDP) gains	Percent of labor force to be reallocated
Nordic	9	−4	2	18
Northern Europe, Australia, New Zealand	18	−6	3	26
Southern Europe	28	−5	5	29
East Asia, high income	38	−6	6	32
East Europe	19	−5	4	26
Latin America and the Caribbean	18	−3	3	15
Country average (unweighted)	22	−5	4	25

Source: Annex table 4A.10.

Note: Nordic = Denmark, Finland, Norway, Sweden; Northern Europe, Australia, New Zealand = Australia, Belgium, France, the Netherlands, New Zealand, Switzerland, the United Kingdom; Southern Europe = Cyprus, Gibraltar, Ireland, Portugal; East Asia, High income = Japan, the Republic of Korea, Singapore, Taiwan, China; East Europe = Bulgaria, Croatia, Kazakhstan, Georgia, Latvia, Lithuania, Ukraine; Latin America and the Caribbean = Brazil, Costa Rica, Mexico.

that would have to be reshuffled to achieve the gains estimated in the current exercise). The mere size of labor reallocations (the shift of women to men's jobs and vice versa) is not something that can be achieved in the short run given that the main avenue for changes in existing labor market patterns are through annual *flows* to the labor force, and these are usually only a fraction of the labor force *stock*.[11]

The regional variation of the results suggests that the Nordic countries would benefit the least from gender equalization, which is to be expected because these countries are already closer to equality than others. This is also true, but to a lesser extent, for the most industrial countries in Europe, as well as for Australia and New Zealand. The high-income countries of East Asia (Japan, Singapore, Korea, and Taiwan, China) seem to be affected most by gender differences in the labor market, if the results of the simulation are taken at face value. The results for Latin American and Eastern European countries are not that dissimilar from those of the most industrial countries in Europe, though South European countries come in between them and the East Asian group.

Overall, with the exception of the Nordic countries, gender differences seem to be pervasive across regions. The individual country results reported in annex table 4A.4 and summarized in table 4.5 suggest that,

TABLE 4.5
Three Scenarios of Simulated Changes in Female and Male Wages and GDP under Conditions of Equality

Country income group[d]	Actual data[a] Average percent change			Increase in wage gap[b] Average percent change			Increase in female employment[c] Average percent change		
	Female wages	Male wages	Output	Female wages	Male wages	Output	Female wages	Male wages	Output
Middle income	19	–5	4	28	–6	6	18	–5	4
High income	22	–5	4	33	–6	6	22	–6	4
All countries	21	–5	4	31	–6	6	21	–5	4

Source: Annex table 4A.4.

a. Actual employment and wage data.

b. Wage gap increased by 10 percent, assuming actual employment levels.

c. Female employment increased by 10 percent, assuming actual wage level.

d. Based on 10 middle-income countries and 19 high-income countries; unweighted averages.

though some variation exists, results do not vary by income level. In fact, a sensitivity analysis examining how the results would be affected if the wage difference between women and men were increased by 10 percent, or if female employment were increased by 10 percent, showed that the effects would be broadly similar in all countries studied, irrespective of country income level. The sensitivity analysis additionally showed that decreases in the gender wage gap have a much greater effect than increases in female employment. This suggests that getting the wages right in the labor market (that is, increasing female productivity) may be a more important factor for increasing output than increasing the share of women in the labor force.

Conclusions and Recommendations

Measures to accelerate the process of gender equality on all fronts are now widely accepted in principle, and indicators have been developed to track progress across a wide range of outcomes (see chapter 2). The findings of this chapter suggest that women's status in the labor market has improved in recent decades. However, gender inequality remains pervasive. Moreover, this chapter suggests that this inequality has large costs in forgone output.

While it seems sensible and desirable to have indicators for monitoring progress in the position of women in the labor market, these indicators should be something more than the "share of women in wage employment in the nonagricultural sector." One possible extension could be to use additional distinctions between female and male employment that break down agricultural and nonagricultural employment by type and by formal and informal employment.[12] Such a breakdown could provide more insights about, for example, family workers and domestic employment. Both groups are relevant to gender analysis and often overlooked. In contrast, the presentation of many partial indicators as currently envisaged may not readily lend itself to global monitoring because it is difficult to make cross-country comparisons, given that the indicators apply differently to the wide range of developing countries (see, for example, annex table 4A.1).

Second, new indicators for female employment should ideally take into account the same information for male employment. The value of an indicator only for women can be meaningless, as discussed above. The issue does not rest so much on these gender-relative values but on knowing what is happening in the national labor market at large.

Third, care should be exercised to correctly interpret the implications of a directional change in an indicator for women's labor market status and empowerment. For example, under certain conditions, it may not necessarily be empowering for women to move into nonagricultural wage employment. As mentioned earlier, a reduction in segregation may imply some (at least in the short term) losses for women.[13] In short, it is difficult to qualify a positive trend or make inferences about empowerment by looking at a single employment indicator.

Fourth, focusing only on formal employment may be largely irrelevant for many developing countries, where wage employment in the nonagricultural sector is only a small percentage of total employment. In addition, focusing only on the formality of female employment may miss changes in women's invisible work, including work at home. Even if other forms of women's work remain unchanged, increased formality may imply more rigidity in employment obligations. Finally, care should be exercised not to ignore the burden on women arising from their dual roles as productive family members and disproportional bearers of reproductive costs and care giving.[14]

Fifth, the empowerment of women—a critical dimension of the MDGs—cannot be seen in isolation from agriculture: broad welfare benefits can only be expected to emerge when women are given the opportunity to participate profitably in this sector. In addition to agriculture, the rural nonfarm sector and self-employment are important dimensions of economic development but not monitored under MDG3. During successful rural economic growth, the emergence and rapid expansion of the mainly private nonfarm economy in rural areas and towns can serve as a major source of growth in incomes and employment. The rural nonfarm economy can develop from a relatively minor sector (often largely part-time and subsistence oriented in the early stages of development) to a major driver of economic growth, not only in the countryside, but in the country as a whole. Nonfarm employment has important implications for the welfare of women and poor households, sometimes helping to offset inequities that can arise within the agricultural sector.[15] In much of the developing world, the rural nonfarm sector has been largely ignored by policy makers, at least until recently. The international focus on formal employment indicators may perpetuate this bias.

The rural nonfarm economy is especially important to the rural poor. Landless and near landless households everywhere depend on nonfarm earnings. Low-investment manufacturing and services—including weaving, pottery, gathering, food preparation and processing, domestic and personal services, and unskilled nonfarm wage labor—typically account for a greater share of income for the rural poor than for wealthier rural residents. Although self-employment is often classified as informal, it is not necessarily disadvantageous. For example, in Gujerat, India, the Self-Employed Women's Association program has trained local women, most of them poor, to educate other women on how to use local mobile services for reproductive health. This is an example of the synergies in the MDG areas of employment and health and, ultimately, poverty.

Sixth, with respect to pay differences between female and male workers, wages are easier to measure than employment differences, but the available data frequently do not allow for meaningful comparisons. Among the 55 countries included in this analysis, most report on monthly earnings, 8 report on hourly wages, 4 on daily wages, and another 4 report on weekly wages.[16] None of the 16 countries that reported wages for a shorter period than one month registered a decline in female relative earnings over time. This shows that using a more precise measure of wages can provide a more reliable measure for comparing the "unit price" of female labor to that of men, as also noted in chapter 2.[17]

Ultimately, what matters for the welfare and empowerment of women is not just their wage rate but their labor earnings. For example, the female wage rate can be high but women may be prevented from working as long as they would like or, when they work, other work benefits (such as pensions) may not be accessible to them.[18] Therefore, information on wages and earnings in international statistics should cover more countries, use comparable definitions, be undertaken regularly, and be presented in a way that would enable meaningful tracking of this aspect of MDG3.

This chapter has argued that increases in female wages contribute to greater family welfare and increased national output, thus reducing poverty and inequalities (including gender inequality) in the whole economy. However, one has to examine whether these wage gains come from greater efficiency (such as more female education or less gender discrimination) or from other channels. For example, a positive increase in female relative wages can also be observed by increasing the share of women in the public sector and the efficient functioning of the labor market. The two scenarios can be statistically equivalent but have very different interpretations and policy implications.

Annex 4A: Explanatory Tables

TABLE 4A.1

Share of Women in Employment by Type of Employment

(percent)

Country	Year	Total employment	Agricultural employment	Share of women by type of employment								
				Nonagricultural wage employment			Nonagricultural self-employment					
				Total	Informal	Formal	Total	Informal	Formal			
Albania	2001	37.6	40.2	39.3	—	—	40.2	—	—
Algeria	2004	17.4	18.7	1.6	—	—	19.8	25.5	—
Bahamas, The	2004	48.4	4.9	52.5	—	—	38.6	93.7	—
Brazil	2003	41.5	32.2	46.6	52.9	43.3	37.1	37.7	26.6
Central African Republic	2003	46.8	51.1	15.2	15.2	15.2	42.0	58.9	—
Chile	2004	34.9	15.4	34.1	—	—	43.4	65.6	—
Costa Rica	2004	44.3	12.0	41.7	—	41.7	44.2	66.7	42.4
Ethiopia	2004	43.0	25.2	42.5	—	—	49.7	54.2	24.7
Egypt, Arab Rep. of	2003	15.1[a]	10.0[a]	15.1	20.0	11.2	—	—	—
Georgia	2004	48.1	50.3	50.4	—	—	33.6	54.2	—
Israel	2004	45.8	18.8	48.8	—	—	30.6	75.0	—
Jamaica	2004	41.9	20.6	46.2	—	—	34.8	73.5	—

(continued)

TABLE 4A.1
Share of Women in Employment by Type of Employment (*continued*)
(*percent*)

Country	Year	Total employment	Agricultural employment	Share of women by type of employment					
				Nonagricultural wage employment			Nonagricultural self-employment		
				Total	Informal	Formal	Total	Informal	Formal
Kazakhstan	2004	48.2	46.3	49.3	—	—	48.6	—	—
Korea, Rep. of	2004	41.5	47.4	41.6	—	—	39.5	88.5	—
Kyrgyz Rep.	2003	43.9	43.6	44.6	39.1	46.7	42.1	41.9	53.2
Macao, China	2004	47.3	50.0	49.5	—	—	31.2	14.7	—
Mali	2004	41.6	29.2	38.2	36.6	41.3	55.4	60.5	18.1
Malaysia	2004	35.9	25.9	38.3	—	—	34.9	72.9	—
Mauritius	2004	32.7	26.8	35.4	—	—	24.2	32.2	17.2
Mexico	2005	35.6	11.4	39.1	38.0	40.9	41.5	44.3	32.0
Morocco	2004	27.2	35.8	24.4	—	—	13.2	23.4	—
Pakistan	2003–04	16.9	26.5	10.3	9.8[b]	10.9[c]	8.8	9.0	1.3
Palestine	2004	18.1	38.4	18.0	—	—	6.6	16.8	—
Panama	2004, Aug.	35.3	9.3	38.4	31.1	40.6	36.9	37.4	28.1
Paraguay	2004	39.0	28.6	30.5	—	—	47.2	54.3	—
Philippines	2004	37.5	24.9	40.4	—	—	54.2	65.5	—
Moldova	2004	52.0	51.6	54.5	51.0	55.2	36.1	31.2	42.6
Romania	2004	45.2	45.4	46.6	—	—	25.8	50.0	—

Russian Federation	2004	49.2	38.2	50.9	46.9	51.1	41.0	42.0	34.1
South Africa	2004	43.6	34.9	44.5	50.0	37.9	45.7	53.3	27.3
Sri Lanka	2004	31.7	38.0	29.4	—	—	26.1	56.9	—
Syrian Arab Rep.	2003	17.1 [a]	30.1 [a]	12.4	4.2	14.7	—	—	—
Tonga	2004	40.9	5.9	38.6	29.0	40.0	84.6	93.1	—
Turkey	2004	26.5	44.6	19.9	19.0	20.3	9.6	14.7	4.5
Ukraine	2003	49.1	43.6	51.0	36.2	51.1	37.9	35.1	—
Uruguay	2004	42.7	—	47.0	53.7	44.5	37.2	73.2	—
Venezuela, R. B. de	2004	38.4	7.0	41.8	42.3 [b]	41.6 [c]	42.5	45.2	29.1
Average		38.8	31.2	36.6	33.9	36.3	35.9	49.2	25.7

Source: ILO.

Note: — = Not available.

a. Wage employment only.

b. Wage employment in informal sector enterprises.

c. Wage employment in formal sector enterprises.

TABLE 4A.2
All Workers, Country Duncan Values for Industrial Employment Based on ISIC68

Country	Early year	Duncan	Percentage of women in labor force	Percentage of women to change	Percentage of labor force to change	Late year	Duncan	Percentage of women in labor force	Percentage of women to change	Percentage of labor force to change	Number of industries
OCEANIA											
Australia	1969	0.327	0.316	0.248	0.156	1994	0.277	0.426	0.159	0.135	9
New Zealand	1986	0.277	0.415	0.162	0.134	1998	0.282	0.451	0.155	0.140	10
AMERICAS											
Bolivia	1989	0.358	0.437	0.202	0.176	1992	0.389	0.412	0.228	0.188	10
Brazil	1981	0.358	0.312	0.246	0.154	2001	0.300	0.407	0.178	0.145	8
Canada	1969	0.342	0.323	0.283	0.183	1997	0.280	0.451	0.153	0.138	9
Chile	1980	0.369	0.295	0.260	0.153	2004	0.364	0.349	0.237	0.165	10
Dominican Rep.	1991	0.368	0.286	0.263	0.150	1996	0.332	0.298	0.233	0.139	10
Ecuador	1990	0.308	0.356	0.198	0.141	1998	0.309	0.390	0.188	0.147	10
El Salvador	1975	0.623	0.284	0.284	0.253	1998	0.456	0.396	0.396	0.218	9
Honduras	1985	0.183	0.423	0.106	0.089	1999	0.515	0.360	0.330	0.237	10
Jamaica	1974	0.446	0.389	0.272	0.212	1992	0.362	0.430	0.206	0.178	8
Mexico	1991	0.361	0.304	0.252	0.153	1995	0.344	0.320	0.234	0.150	10
Montserrat	—	—	—	—	—	1991	0.480	0.422	0.277	0.234	10
Panama	1974	0.719	0.409	0.425	0.347	1992	0.671	0.404	0.400	0.323	10

Paraguay	1982	0.941	0.180	0.101	0.893	1996	0.938	0.229	0.134	0.858	10
Trinidad and Tobago	1971	0.324	0.269	0.237	0.127	2002	0.367	0.373	0.230	0.172	10
United States	1969	0.290	0.373	0.215	0.160	2002	0.269	0.466	0.144	0.134	10
Uruguay	1984	0.259	0.389	0.158	0.123	2000	0.314	0.426	0.180	0.153	10
Venezuela, R. B. de	1975	0.375	0.273	0.272	0.149	2002	0.374	0.384	0.230	0.177	10
ASIA											
Bangladesh	1983	0.672	0.087	0.613	0.106	2000	0.294	0.375	0.184	0.138	10
Cyprus	1976	0.230	0.345	0.151	0.104	1995	0.179	0.393	0.109	0.086	10
Hong Kong, China	1978	0.215	0.352	0.139	0.098	2004	0.284	0.450	0.157	0.141	10
Indonesia	1976	0.096	0.386	0.059	0.046	1999	0.144	0.382	0.089	0.068	10
Japan	1969	0.183	0.394	0.122	0.096	2002	0.228	0.410	0.134	0.110	10
Korea, Rep. of	1969	0.103	0.353	0.092	0.065	1994	0.213	0.404	0.127	0.102	8
Malaysia	1980	0.186	0.336	0.123	0.083	2000	0.226	0.347	0.148	0.103	10
Philippines	1971	0.393	0.325	0.265	0.172	2000	0.397	0.379	0.247	0.187	10
Singapore	1974	0.208	0.318	0.142	0.090	1993	0.168	0.402	0.101	0.081	10
Thailand	1971	0.075	0.464	0.040	0.037	2001	0.138	0.448	0.076	0.068	8

(continued)

TABLE 4A.2
All Workers, Country Duncan Values for Industrial Employment Based on ISIC68 (continued)

Country	Early year	Duncan	Percentage of women in labor force	Percentage of women to change	Percentage of labor force to change	Late year	Duncan	Percentage of women in labor force	Percentage of women to change	Percentage of labor force to change	Number of industries
EUROPE											
Belgium	1988	0.317	0.367	0.201	0.147	1992	0.328	0.394	0.199	0.157	10
Denmark	1972	0.343	0.410	0.203	0.166	1993	0.314	0.465	0.168	0.156	10
Finland	1970	0.299	0.446	0.165	0.148	1995	0.351	0.472	0.185	0.175	10
Germany	1991	0.278	0.416	0.162	0.135	1994	0.306	0.418	0.178	0.149	9
Greece	1981	0.236	0.314	0.162	0.102	1992	0.220	0.348	0.143	0.100	10
Ireland	1986	0.332	0.320	0.226	0.145	2004	0.381	0.420	0.221	0.186	18
Italy	1977	0.200	0.305	0.139	0.085	1992	0.202	0.351	0.131	0.092	9
Lithuania	1982	0.340	0.524	0.162	0.169	1991	0.355	0.538	0.164	0.176	8
Luxembourg	1983	0.404	0.329	0.271	0.178	1990	0.388	0.341	0.256	0.174	8
Malta	1969	0.229	0.197	0.203	0.080	1999	0.142	0.289	0.101	0.058	10
Netherlands	1977	0.369	0.275	0.267	0.147	1994	0.296	0.405	0.176	0.143	10
Norway	1972	0.568	0.441	0.223	0.197	1995	0.573	0.403	0.297	0.239	10
Portugal	1974	0.196	0.401	0.118	0.094	1993	0.230	0.442	0.128	0.113	10

San Marino	1978	0.182	0.340	0.120	0.082	1993	0.241	0.395	0.146	0.115	8
Spain	1969	0.261	0.246	0.180	0.088	1993	0.321	0.337	0.213	0.144	10
Sweden	1969	0.428	0.387	0.262	0.203	1994	0.365	0.487	0.187	0.182	10
Turkey	1988	0.443	0.304	0.308	0.188	1999	0.369	0.288	0.263	0.151	10
Ukraine	1999	0.253	0.486	0.130	0.127	2001	0.269	0.487	0.138	0.134	10
United Kingdom	1969	0.304	0.360	0.191	0.137	1993	0.256	0.457	0.139	0.127	10
Grenada	1988	0.339	0.430	0.193	0.166	1998	0.408	0.404	0.243	0.197	10

Source: Annex 4B.

Note: — = Not available.

"Percentage of women in labor force" refers to the share of women in the labor force.

"Percentage of women to change" refers to the percentage of women who should change sector to achieve equality between the sectoral distributions of employment of women and men.

"Percentage of labor force to change" refers to the percentage of labor force that should change sector to achieve equality between the sectoral distributions of employment of women and men.

"Number of industries" refers to the number of available industries for applying the Duncan index.

TABLE 4A.3
All Workers, Country Duncan Values for Industrial Employment Based on ISIC90

Country	Early year	Duncan	Percentage of women in labor force	Percentage of women to change	Percentage of labor force to change	Late year	Duncan	Percentage of women in labor force	Percentage of women to change	Percentage of labor force to change	Number of industries
OCEANIA											
Australia	1994	0.287	0.426	0.165	0.141	2004	0.279	0.446	0.155	0.138	18
New Caledonia	1996	0.351	0.385	0.216	0.166	—	—	—	—	—	16
Samoa	—	—	—	—	—	1976	0.377	0.322	0.256	0.165	9
New Zealand	1998	0.284	0.451	0.156	0.140	2004	0.301	0.457	0.163	0.149	18
AMERICAS											
Anguilla	1999	0.393	0.469	0.209	0.196	2001	0.387	0.459	0.209	0.192	18
Argentina	1991	0.366	0.360	0.234	0.169	2003	0.370	0.430	0.211	0.181	18
Aruba	1994	0.355	0.416	0.208	0.173	1997	0.286	0.434	0.162	0.141	17
Bahamas, The	1991	0.308	0.474	0.162	0.153	2003	0.298	0.489	0.152	0.149	18
Belize	1993	0.440	0.312	0.303	0.189	1999	0.460	0.312	0.316	0.197	15
Bolivia	1992	0.439	0.414	0.257	0.213	2000	0.441	0.441	0.246	0.218	18
Brazil	2002	0.340	0.413	0.199	0.165	2003	0.336	0.414	0.197	0.163	18
Canada	1997	0.292	0.451	0.160	0.145	2004	0.298	0.468	0.159	0.148	17
Dominica	1997	0.396	0.433	0.224	0.194	—	—	—	—	—	15

Ecuador	1999	0.345	0.387	0.212	0.164	2004	0.334	0.407	0.198	0.161	18
El Salvador	1998	0.477	0.396	0.288	0.228	2004	0.484	0.409	0.286	0.234	14
Guyana	1997	0.238	0.331	0.159	0.105	1997	0.238	0.331	0.159	0.105	17
Jamaica	1992	0.363	0.430	0.207	0.178	2004	0.460	0.420	0.267	0.224	10
Mexico	1995	0.348	0.320	0.237	0.152	2004	0.324	0.353	0.209	0.148	18
Netherlands Antilles	1992	0.393	0.425	0.226	0.192	2000	0.338	0.476	0.177	0.169	16
Panama	2001	0.455	0.330	0.305	0.201	2004	0.425	0.352	0.275	0.194	17
Peru	1996	0.375	0.409	0.222	0.181	2004	0.391	0.407	0.232	0.189	16
St. Lucia	1994	0.358	0.442	0.200	0.177	2000	0.353	0.448	0.195	0.175	16
Suriname	1990	0.305	0.385	0.188	0.144	1999	0.347	0.344	0.228	0.157	10
United States	2003	0.281	0.468	0.150	0.140	2004	0.285	0.465	0.152	0.142	10
Uruguay	2000	0.376	0.426	0.216	0.184	2003	0.375	0.429	0.214	0.184	10
ASIA										
Azerbaijan	1999	0.171	0.477	0.090	0.085	2004	0.212	0.476	0.111	0.106	16
Bangladesh	2003	0.336	0.222	0.261	0.116	—	—	—	—	—	14
Cyprus	1999	0.275	0.381	0.170	0.130	2004	0.315	0.435	0.178	0.155	10
Georgia	1998	0.209	0.482	0.108	0.104	2004	0.198	0.480	0.103	0.099	18
Iran, Islamic Rep. of	1996	0.466	0.121	0.410	0.099	—	—	—	—	—	18
Israel	1995	0.349	0.425	0.201	0.170	2003	0.335	0.460	0.181	0.166	16
Japan	2003	0.274	0.411	0.161	0.133	2004	0.276	0.413	0.162	0.134	16

(continued)

TABLE 4A.3
All Workers, Country Duncan Values for Industrial Employment Based on ISIC90 (continued)

Country	Early year	Duncan	Percentage of women in labor force	Percentage of women to change	Percentage of labor force to change	Late year	Duncan	Percentage of women in labor force	Percentage of women to change	Percentage of labor force to change	Number of industries
Kazakhstan	2001	0.244	0.482	0.126	0.122	2004	0.243	0.482	0.126	0.121	16
Korea, Rep. of	1994	0.260	0.404	0.155	0.125	2004	0.294	0.415	0.172	0.143	16
Kyrgyz Rep.	1996	0.159	0.457	0.086	0.079	2001	0.153	0.444	0.085	0.075	16
Macau	1989	0.290	0.411	0.171	0.141	2004	0.272	0.473	0.143	0.135	18
Malaysia	2001	0.265	0.353	0.172	0.121	2003	0.266	0.359	0.170	0.122	16
Maldives	1995	0.573	0.270	0.419	0.226	2000	0.531	0.335	0.353	0.237	12
Mongolia	1993	0.152	0.483	0.079	0.076	2004	0.139	0.509	0.068	0.070	16
Oman	1993	0.522	0.075	0.482	0.073	2000	0.598	0.137	0.516	0.141	18
Philippines	2001	0.404	0.391	0.246	0.192	2004	0.397	0.375	0.248	0.186	16
Qatar	1997	0.722	0.135	0.624	0.168	2001	0.695	0.142	0.597	0.169	16
Saudi Arabia	1999	0.776	0.142	0.666	0.189	2002	0.772	0.135	0.668	0.180	16
Singapore	1985	0.286	0.364	0.182	0.132	2003	0.283	0.449	0.156	0.140	13
Syrian Arab Rep.	2002	0.463	0.184	0.377	0.139	—	—	—	—	—	7
Thailand	2002	0.152	0.449	0.084	0.075	2004	0.158	0.448	0.087	0.078	18
United Arab Emirates	1995	0.601	0.116	0.532	0.123	2000	0.601	0.127	0.525	0.133	18
Uzbekistan	1991	0.087	0.485	0.045	0.043	1995	0.025	0.453	0.014	0.013	2

West Bank and Gaza	1996	0.425	0.149	0.362	0.108	2004	0.503	0.181	0.412	0.149	16
Yemen, Rep. of	1999	0.460	0.246	0.347	0.170	—	—	—	—	—	16
AFRICA											
Algeria	2001	0.474	0.142	0.407	0.115	2004	0.443	0.174	0.366	0.127	18
Botswana	1995	0.321	0.451	0.176	0.159	2001	0.400	0.409	0.366	0.193	17
Egypt, Arab Rep. of	1997	0.327	0.191	0.264	0.101	2003	0.349	0.191	0.278	0.000	17
Ethiopia	—	—	—	—	—	2004	0.340	0.431	0.194	0.167	16
Madagascar	—	—	—	—	—	2002	0.069	0.489	0.035	0.035	14
Mauritius	1995	0.315	0.3.4	0.216	0.136	2004	0.309	0.327	0.208	0.136	22
Morocco	2002	0.309	0.252	0.232	0.117	2003	0.289	0.263	0.213	0.112	12
Namibia	—	—	—	—	—	2000	0.215	0.475	0.113	0.107	18
South Africa	2000	0.282	0.455	0.153	0.140	2003	0.306	0.446	0.169	0.151	12
Tanzania	—	—	—	—	—	2001	0.513	0.506	0.001	0.254	9
EUROPE											
Austria	1994	0.344	0.426	0.198	0.168	2004	0.323	0.449	0.178	0.160	16
Belgium	1994	0.343	0.393	0.208	0.164	2003	0.318	0.431	0.181	0.156	20
Bulgaria	2003	0.256	0.471	0.135	0.127	2004	0.258	0.469	0.137	0.128	14
Croatia	1996	0.244	0.456	0.133	0.121	2004	0.279	0.446	0.154	0.138	16
Czech Rep.	1993	0.265	0.439	0.149	0.131	2004	0.279	0.434	0.158	0.137	16

(continued)

TABLE 4A.3
All Workers, Country Duncan Values for Industrial Employment Based on ISIC90 (*continued*)

Country	Early year	Duncan	Percentage of women in labor force	Percentage of women to change	Percentage of labor force to change	Late year	Duncan	Percentage of women in labor force	Percentage of women to change	Percentage of labor force to change	Number of industries
Denmark	1994	0.339	0.455	0.185	0.168	2004	0.335	0.466	0.179	0.167	18
Estonia	1989	0.311	0.491	0.159	0.156	2004	0.313	0.498	0.157	0.157	16
Finland	1995	0.375	0.471	0.198	0.187	2004	0.375	0.476	0.196	0.187	17
Germany	1995	0.311	0.419	0.180	0.151	2004	0.308	0.448	0.170	0.152	17
Greece	1993	0.225	0.350	0.147	0.102	2003	0.261	0.383	0.161	0.123	17
Iceland	1991	0.335	0.456	0.183	0.166	2002	0.338	0.471	0.179	0.168	17
Ireland	1986	0.332	0.320	0.226	0.145	2004	0.381	0.420	0.221	0.186	18
Italy	1993	0.241	0.341	0.159	0.109	2003	0.256	0.378	0.159	0.120	
Latvia	1996	0.279	0.481	0.145	0.139	2004	0.325	0.488	0.167	0.163	13
Lithuania	1997	0.231	0.472	0.122	0.115	2004	0.287	0.489	0.147	0.143	16
Macedonia, FYR	2002	0.205	0.389	0.125	0.097	2004	0.254	0.387	0.156	0.120	16
Malta	2000	0.260	0.301	0.182	0.110	2004	0.267	0.302	0.186	0.112	17
Moldova	2000	0.172	0.507	0.085	0.086	2004	0.207	0.520	0.099	0.103	17
Netherlands	1995	0.326	0.408	0.193	0.158	2002	0.302	0.436	0.170	0.149	18

Norway	1996	0.607	0.629	0.225	0.283	1996	0.607	0.629	0.225	0.283	17
Portugal	1992	0.276	0.435	0.156	0.136	2003	0.303	0.455	0.165	0.150	16
Romania	1994	0.212	0.462	0.114	0.105	2004	0.194	0.456	0.106	0.096	15
Russian Fed.	1997	0.307	0.474	0.161	0.153	2004	0.329	0.491	0.167	0.164	17
San Marino	1995	0.303	0.383	0.187	0.143	2004	0.289	0.409	0.171	0.140	14
Slovak Rep.	1994	0.291	0.444	0.162	0.144	2004	0.332	0.450	0.182	0.164	17
Slovenia	1993	0.233	0.467	0.124	0.116	2004	0.259	0.459	0.140	0.129	16
Spain	1993	0.328	0.334	0.218	0.146	2004	0.361	0.392	0.220	0.172	17
Sweden	1994	0.400	0.487	0.206	0.200	2004	0.391	0.481	0.203	0.195	16
Switzerland	1991	0.278	0.426	0.159	0.136	2004	0.308	0.451	0.169	0.153	13
Turkey	2000	0.401	0.269	0.293	0.158	2004	0.386	0.265	0.284	0.150	17
Ukraine	1999	0.253	0.486	0.130	0.127	2003	0.276	0.491	0.140	0.138	16
United Kingdom	1993	0.328	0.450	0.181	0.162	2004	0.333	0.463	0.179	0.165	18

Source: Annex 4B.

Note: See note to annex table 4A.2.

TABLE 4A.4
All Workers, Country Duncan Values for Occupation Employment Based on ISCO68

Country	Early year	Duncan	Percentage of women in labor force	Percentage of women to change	Percentage of labor force to change	Late year	Duncan	Percentage of women in labor force	Percentage of women to change	Percentage of labor force to change	Number of industries
OCEANIA											
Australia	1969	0.468	0.316	0.354	0.224	1993	0.398	0.425	0.229	0.195	7
New Zealand	1987	0.403	0.421	0.233	0.196	1991	0.364	0.440	0.204	0.180	8
AMERICAS											
Barbados	1981	0.322	0.427	0.185	0.158	1995	0.270	0.475	0.141	0.134	8
Canada	1973	0.455	0.343	0.299	0.205	1997	0.345	0.451	0.189	0.171	7
Chile	1980	0.471	0.295	0.332	0.196	2004	0.441	0.349	0.287	0.201	8
Colombia	1975	0.419	0.366	0.266	0.194	2000	0.315	0.452	0.172	0.156	8
Costa Rica	1980	0.460	0.243	0.348	0.169	1996	0.411	0.294	0.290	0.171	8
Ecuador	1990	0.375	0.356	0.241	0.172	1994	0.375	0.383	0.231	0.177	7
El Salvador	1980	0.48[9]	0.332	0.326	0.217	1992	0.345	0.456	0.188	0.171	8
Honduras	1985	0.259	0.423	0.149	0.126	1999	0.435	0.360	0.279	0.200	8
Mexico	1991	0.379	0.304	0.264	0.160	1995	0.343	0.320	0.233	0.149	8
Panama	1974	0.592	0.264	0.230	0.230	1999	0.502	0.337	0.224	0.224	8
Paraguay	1982	0.396	0.400	0.238	0.190	1994	0.473	0.413	0.278	0.230	8
Puerto Rico	1975	0.367	0.327	0.247	0.162	1998	0.377	0.412	0.222	0.183	7

Trinidad and Tobago	1973	0.441	0.273	0.321	0.175	1990	0.444	0.323	0.301	0.194	8
United States	1970	0.442	0.378	0.275	0.208	2002	0.321	0.466	0.171	0.160	7
Uruguay	1986	0.371	0.387	0.227	0.176	1999	0.440	0.424	0.253	0.215	8
Venezuela, R. B. de	1976	0.477	0.280	0.343	0.192	2002	0.478	0.384	0.295	0.226	8
ASIA											
Bangladesh	1983	0.617	0.087	0.564	0.098	2000	0.283	0.375	0.177	0.133	8
Hong Kong, China	1978	0.077	0.352	0.050	0.035	1993	0.343	0.369	0.217	0.160	8
Israel	1970	0.339	0.294	0.240	0.141	1994	0.416	0.417	0.242	0.202	8
Japan	1970	0.215	0.393	0.130	0.103	2004	0.260	0.414	0.153	0.126	8
Korea, Rep. of	1970	0.213	0.367	0.135	0.099	1993	0.220	0.402	0.131	0.106	7
Malaysia	1980	0.182	0.335	0.121	0.081	2000	0.249	0.347	0.163	0.113	7
Pakistan	1985	0.300	0.096	0.271	0.052	2000	0.294	0.140	0.253	0.071	8
Philippines	1971	0.340	0.325	0.230	0.149	2000	0.400	0.379	0.248	0.188	8
Saudi Arabia	1999	0.549	0.142	0.471	0.133	2001	0.547	0.134	0.474	0.127	8
Singapore	1974	0.165	0.318	0.112	0.071	—	—	0.401	0.136	0.109	8
Thailand	1971	0.076	0.464	0.041	0.038	2004	0.166	0.448	0.092	0.082	11
EUROPE											
Austria	1984	0.426	0.399	0.256	0.204	1994	0.432	0.426	0.248	0.211	8
Belgium	1983	0.382	0.344	0.251	0.172	1992	0.400	0.394	0.242	0.191	8

(continued)

TABLE 4A.4
All Workers, Country Duncan Values for Occupation Employment Based on ISCO68 (continued)

Country	Early year	Duncan	Percentage of women in labor force	Percentage of women to change	Percentage of labor force to change	Late year	Duncan	Percentage of women in labor force	Percentage of women to change	Percentage of labor force to change	Number of industries
Denmark	1981	0.492	0.476	0.258	0.245	1993	0.420	0.469	0.223	0.209	9
Finland	1977	0.396	0.483	0.205	0.198	1999	0.402	0.471	0.213	0.200	8
Greece	1981	0.258	0.313	0.177	0.111	1992	0.259	0.348	0.169	0.117	8
Ireland	1983	0.440	0.311	0.303	0.189	1991	0.438	0.338	0.290	0.196	8
Netherlands	1977	0.436	0.280	0.314	0.176	1994	0.347	0.409	0.205	0.168	8
Norway	1977	0.486	0.393	0.295	0.232	1995	0.420	0.459	0.228	0.209	8
Portugal	1974	0.217	0.399	0.130	0.104	1992	0.285	0.439	0.160	0.140	8
San Marino	1978	0.288	0.340	0.190	0.129	1993	0.302	0.395	0.183	0.144	7
Spain	1976	0.285	0.286	0.203	0.116	1993	0.402	0.337	0.267	0.180	8
Sweden	1970	0.460	0.394	0.279	0.219	1996	0.346	0.481	0.180	0.173	8
Turkey	1982	0.381	0.121	0.334	0.081	1988	0.448	0.304	0.311	0.189	7

Source: Annex 4B.

Note: See note to annex table 4A.2.

TABLE 4A.5
All Workers, Country Duncan Values for Occupational Employment Based on ISCO88

Country	Early year	Duncan	Percentage of women in labor force	Percentage of women to change	Percentage of labor force to change	Late year	Duncan	Percentage of women in labor force	Percentage of women to change	Percentage of labor force to change	Number of industries
OCEANIA											
Australia	1997	0.389	0.433	0.221	0.191	2004	0.375	0.446	0.208	0.185	10
New Zealand	1992	0.367	0.441	0.205	0.181	2004	0.378	0.457	0.205	0.187	10
AMERICAS											
Argentina	1998	0.351	0.390	0.214	0.167	2003	0.306	0.430	0.175	0.150	11
Aruba	1994	0.387	0.415	0.226	0.188	1997	0.314	0.434	0.178	0.154	10
Bahamas, The	1991	0.412	0.480	0.214	0.205	2003	0.383	0.489	0.196	0.192	10
Barbados	1995	0.292	0.475	0.153	0.146	2004	0.347	0.483	0.179	0.173	10
Belize	1993	0.563	0.320	0.383	0.245	1994	0.505	0.326	0.340	0.222	6
Bolivia	1993	0.398	0.434	0.226	0.196	2000	0.479	0.441	0.267	0.236	9
Brazil	2002	0.340	0.413	0.200	0.165	2002	0.340	0.413	0.200	0.165	11
Canada	1997	0.377	0.451	0.207	0.187	2004	0.378	0.469	0.201	0.188	10
Costa Rica	1997	0.412	0.308	0.285	0.176	2004	0.269	0.339	0.178	0.121	10
Dominica	1997	0.408	0.434	0.231	0.200	—	—	—	—	—	10
Dominican Rep.	1991	0.414	0.286	0.296	0.169	1996	0.433	0.298	0.304	0.181	7
Ecuador	2000	0.311	0.384	0.192	0.147	2004	0.274	0.407	0.162	0.132	10

(continued)

TABLE 4A.5
All Workers, Country Duncan Values for Occupational Employment Based on ISCO88 (continued)

Country	Early year	Duncan	Percentage of women in labor force	Percentage of women to change	Percentage of labor force to change	Late year	Duncan	Percentage of women in labor force	Percentage of women to change	Percentage of labor force to change	Number of industries
El Salvador	1995	0.276	0.378	0.172	0.130	2004	0.252	0.409	0.149	0.122	9
Jamaica	2000	0.446	0.409	0.263	0.216	2004	0.461	0.420	0.267	0.225	8
Mexico	1995	0.364	0.320	0.248	0.159	2004	0.312	0.353	0.202	0.143	11
Netherlands Antilles	1992	0.410	0.425	0.236	0.200	2000	0.366	0.477	0.191	0.183	10
Panama	2001	0.455	0.330	0.305	0.201	2004	0.425	0.352	0.275	0.194	9
Peru	1996	0.316	0.409	0.187	0.153	2004	0.343	0.406	0.204	0.165	10
Puerto Rico	1996	0.355	0.413	0.208	0.172	2004	0.382	0.438	0.215	0.188	9
Saint Lucia	1994	0.324	0.442	0.181	0.160	2000	0.326	0.448	0.180	0.161	10
Trinidad and Tobago	1990	0.314	0.322	0.212	0.137	2002	0.377	0.373	0.236	0.177	10
United States	2003	0.322	0.468	0.172	0.160	2004	0.324	0.465	0.174	0.161	6
Uruguay	2000	0.377	0.425	0.217	0.184	2003	0.354	0.429	0.202	0.174	10
ASIA											
Bangladesh	2003	0.175	0.222	0.136	0.060	—	—	—	—	—	7
Cambodia	2000	0.106	0.519	0.051	0.053	2001	0.111	0.517	0.053	0.055	10
Cyprus	1999	0.417	0.380	0.259	0.197	2004	0.412	0.435	0.233	0.203	10

Georgia	1998	0.215	0.482	0.111	0.107	2004	0.201	0.480	0.105	0.100	11
Hong Kong, China	1994	0.348	0.380	0.216	0.164	2004	0.345	0.450	0.190	0.171	10
Iran, Islamic, Rep. of	1996	0.381	0.121	0.335	0.081	—	—	—	—	—	10
Israel	1995	0.386	0.425	0.222	0.189	2003	0.354	0.460	0.191	0.176	9
Kazakhstan	2001	0.248	0.482	0.128	0.124	2004	0.284	0.482	0.147	0.142	10
Korea, Rep. of	1993	0.249	0.402	0.149	0.120	2004	0.309	0.415	0.181	0.150	9
Kyrgyz Rep.	2002	0.203	0.432	0.115	0.100	—	—	—	—	—	9
Macau	1996	0.293	0.449	0.162	0.145	2004	0.242	0.473	0.128	0.121	9
Malaysia	2001	0.199	0.353	0.129	0.091	2003	0.223	0.359	0.143	0.103	9
Maldives	2000	0.365	0.335	0.243	0.163	—	—	—	—	—	11
Mongolia	2000	0.204	0.460	0.110	0.101	—	—	—	—	—	10
Oman	1993	0.404	0.075	0.374	0.056	2000	0.349	0.137	0.301	0.083	10
Pakistan	2001	0.263	0.140	0.226	0.063	2002	0.240	0.146	0.204	0.060	9
Philippines	2001	0.349	0.391	0.212	0.166	2004	0.345	0.375	0.215	0.162	10
Qatar	1997	0.478	0.135	0.414	0.112	2001	0.494	0.142	0.424	0.120	9
Saudi Arabia	2002	0.497	0.135	0.430	0.116	—	—	—	—	—	7
Singapore	1985	0.311	0.364	0.198	0.144	—	—	0.448	0.197	0.176	10
Sri Lanka	2002	0.151	0.335	0.100	0.067	2003	0.118	0.316	0.081	0.051	10
United Arab Emirates	1995	0.508	0.116	0.449	0.104	2000	0.508	0.127	0.444	0.113	11

(continued)

TABLE 4A.5
All Workers, Country Duncan Values for Occupational Employment Based on ISCO88 (continued)

Country	Early year	Duncan	Percentage of women in labor force	Percentage of women to change	Percentage of labor force to change	Late year	Duncan	Percentage of women in labor force	Percentage of women to change	Percentage of labor force to change	Number of industries
West Bank and Gaza	1996	0.412	0.147	0.352	0.103	2004	0.490	0.181	0.401	0.145	10
Yemen, Rep. of	1999	0.477	0.246	0.359	0.177	—	—	—	—	—	11
AFRICA											
Algeria	2001	0.387	0.142	0.332	0.094	2004	0.333	0.174	0.275	0.096	10
Botswana	1995	0.223	0.452	0.122	0.110	2001	0.292	0.409	0.173	0.141	10
Egypt, Arab Rep. of	1997	0.315	0.191	0.255	0.097	2003	0.334	0.191	0.270	0.103	10
Ethiopia	1999	0.444	0.433	0.252	0.218	2004	0.198	0.431	0.113	0.097	10
Mauritius	1995	0.271	0.314	0.186	0.117	2004	0.221	0.327	0.149	0.097	10
Namibia	—	—	—	—	—	2000	0.220	0.475	0.116	0.110	11
Tanzania	—	—	—	—	—	2001	0.072	0.506	0.036	0.036	9
EUROPE											
Austria	1995	0.387	0.425	0.223	0.189	2004	0.346	0.449	0.191	0.171	10
Belgium	1995	0.339	0.400	0.203	0.163	2003	0.349	0.431	0.199	0.171	11
Bulgaria	2003	0.292	0.471	0.154	0.145	2004	0.296	0.469	0.157	0.147	10
Croatia	1996	0.309	0.456	0.168	0.153	2004	0.317	0.446	0.176	0.157	11

Czech Rep.	1993	0.405	0.439	0.227	0.199	2004	0.384	0.434	0.217	0.189	11
Denmark	1994	0.402	0.455	0.219	0.199	2004	0.387	0.466	0.206	0.192	11
Finland	2000	0.405	0.470	0.215	0.202	2004	0.409	0.476	0.215	0.204	11
France	2003	0.401	0.454	0.219	0.199	2004	0.382	0.456	0.208	0.190	11
Germany	1993	0.425	0.415	0.249	0.206	2004	0.392	0.448	0.216	0.194	11
Greece	1993	0.289	0.350	0.188	0.132	2003	0.329	0.383	0.203	0.156	11
Hungary	1995	0.412	0.443	0.230	0.203	2004	0.394	0.457	0.214	0.195	11
Iceland	1991	0.350	0.457	0.190	0.174	2002	0.399	0.470	0.212	0.199	10
Ireland	1987	0.376	0.333	0.251	0.167	2004	0.414	0.419	0.240	0.202	11
Italy	1993	0.284	0.341	0.187	0.128	2003	0.302	0.378	0.188	0.142	10
Latvia	1996	0.380	0.479	0.198	0.190	2004	0.365	0.488	0.187	0.182	9
Lithuania	1997	0.337	0.472	0.178	0.168	2004	0.335	0.489	0.171	0.168	10
Macedonia, FYR	2002	0.187	0.389	0.114	0.089	2004	0.185	0.387	0.113	0.088	10
Moldova	1999	0.267	0.505	0.132	0.133	2004	0.278	0.520	0.133	0.139	11
Netherlands	1995	0.356	0.408	0.211	0.172	2002	0.345	0.436	0.194	0.170	11
Norway	1996	0.439	0.459	0.237	0.218	2004	0.384	0.472	0.203	0.191	10
Poland	1995	0.352	0.453	0.193	0.174	2004	0.345	0.452	0.189	0.171	10
Portugal	1992	0.270	0.435	0.153	0.133	2003	0.340	0.455	0.186	0.169	11
Romania	1994	0.297	0.462	0.160	0.148	2004	0.240	0.456	0.130	0.119	9
Russian Fed.	1997	0.389	0.474	0.205	0.194	2004	0.369	0.491	0.188	0.185	9
San Marino	1995	0.317	0.383	0.196	0.150	1999	0.354	0.394	0.214	0.169	10

(continued)

TABLE 4A.5
All Workers, Country Duncan Values for Occupational Employment Based on ISCO88 (continued)

Country	Early year	Duncan	Percentage of women in labor force	Percentage of women to change	Percentage of labor force to change	Late year	Duncan	Percentage of women in labor force	Percentage of women to change	Percentage of labor force to change	Number of industries
Slovak Rep.	1994	0.392	0.444	0.218	0.194	2004	0.381	0.450	0.210	0.189	11
Slovenia	1993	0.323	0.467	0.172	0.161	2004	0.311	0.459	0.168	0.154	11
Spain	1994	0.337	0.338	0.223	0.151	2004	0.388	0.392	0.236	0.185	10
Sweden	1997	0.410	0.479	0.214	0.205	2004	0.367	0.481	0.190	0.183	11
Switzerland	1991	0.400	0.419	0.232	0.194	2004	0.375	0.447	0.207	0.185	11
Turkey	2001	0.385	0.277	0.279	0.154	2004	0.334	0.265	0.245	0.130	10
Ukraine	1998	0.304	0.511	0.149	0.152	2004	0.213	0.493	0.108	0.107	9
United Kingdom	1991	0.393	0.436	0.222	0.193	2004	0.376	0.463	0.202	0.187	10

Source: Annex 4B.

Note: See note to annex table 4A.2.

TABLE 4A.6
Employees Only, Country Duncan Values for Industrial Employment Based on ISIC68

Country	Early year	Duncan	Percentage of women in labor force	Percentage of women to change	Percentage of labor force to change	Late year	Duncan	Percentage of women in labor force	Percentage of women to change	Percentage of labor force to change
OCEANIA										
Australia	1969	0.132	0.290	0.160	0.093	1996	0.153	0.423	0.088	0.074
New Zealand	1991	0.292	0.478	0.153	0.146	2000	0.293	0.505	0.145	0.147
Fiji	1980	0.253	0.183	0.207	0.076	1998	0.178	0.336	0.118	0.079
AMERICAS										
Bermuda	1978	0.192	0.419	0.111	0.093	1994	0.196	0.498	0.098	0.098
Brazil	1992	0.244	0.359	0.145	0.118	1999	0.406	0.396	0.236	0.198
Canada	1969	0.184	0.185	0.533	0.198	1997	0.287	0.473	0.151	0.143
Costa Rica	1981	0.125	0.325	0.084	0.055	1996	0.215	0.344	0.141	0.097
El Salvador	1978	0.433	0.229	0.334	0.153	1996	0.216	0.319	0.147	0.094
Mexico	1980	0.096	0.246	0.072	0.035	1986	0.091	0.288	0.065	0.037
Panama	1972	0.176	0.329	0.118	0.078	1991	0.147	0.410	0.087	0.071
Paraguay	1983	0.203	0.349	0.132	0.092	1994	0.223	0.340	0.147	0.100
Trinidad and Tobago	1987	0.184	0.305	0.131	0.075	2002	0.351	0.388	0.211	0.168
United States	1969	0.113	0.364	0.071	0.052	2000	0.108	0.484	0.056	0.054

(continued)

TABLE 4A.6
Employees Only, Country Duncan Values for Industrial Employment Based on ISIC68 (continued)

Country	Early year	Duncan	Percentage of women in labor force	Percentage of women to change	Percentage of labor force to change	Late year	Duncan	Percentage of women in labor force	Percentage of women to change	Percentage of labor force to change
ASIA										
Bahrain	1987	0.499	0.066	0.466	0.061	2004	0.238	0.114	0.211	0.048
China	1987	0.158	0.368	0.100	0.074	1999	0.161	0.392	0.098	0.077
Cyprus	1976	0.423	0.286	0.302	0.172	1991	0.391	0.323	0.265	0.171
Hong Kong, China	1972	0.212	0.447	0.117	0.105	—	—	—	—	—
India	1975	0.265	0.113	0.235	0.053	2003	0.229	0.184	0.187	0.069
Israel	1986	0.161	0.365	0.102	0.075	1994	0.164	0.395	0.099	0.079
Japan	1969	0.235	0.267	0.536	0.286	2002	0.242	0.406	0.144	0.117
Jordan	1973	0.108	0.151	0.092	0.028	1993	0.353	0.227	0.272	0.124
Korea, Rep. of	1980	0.141	0.340	0.100	0.058	1994	0.129	0.312	0.084	0.059
Macau	1988	0.036	0.616	0.014	0.017	1997	0.266	0.508	0.131	0.133
Malaysia	1989	0.398	0.375	0.249	0.187	1993	0.405	0.363	0.258	0.187
Philippines	1977	0.491	0.182	0.402	0.146	2000	0.392	0.376	0.245	0.184
Singapore	1974	0.338	0.336	0.225	0.151	1993	0.223	0.358	0.143	0.102
Sri Lanka	1971	0.344	0.369	0.217	0.160	1994	0.237	0.482	0.123	0.118
Botswana	1976	0.280	0.187	0.228	0.085	1995	0.214	0.382	0.132	0.101

Chad	1986	0.249	0.053	0.236	0.025	1991	0.418	0.058	0.394	0.046
Egypt, Arab Rep. of	1989	0.337	0.165	0.282	0.093	1995	0.358	0.177	0.295	0.105
Kenya	1977	0.200	0.171	0.166	0.057	1997	0.224	0.306	0.155	0.095
Malawi	1970	0.292	0.082	0.268	0.044	1995	0.279	0.208	0.221	0.092
Mauritius	1970	0.221	0.197	0.177	0.070	2000	0.332	0.371	0.209	0.155
Swaziland	1970	0.289	0.173	0.239	0.083	1986	0.293	0.280	0.211	0.118
Zimbabwe	1975	0.264	0.168	0.219	0.074	2002	0.263	0.239	0.200	0.096
EUROPE										
Austria	1975	0.263	0.387	0.161	0.125	1993	0.315	0.411	0.186	0.153
Belgium	1970	0.348	0.049	0.331	0.033	1992	0.293	0.119	0.259	0.061
Croatia	1981	0.279	0.395	0.169	0.133	1996	0.281	0.468	0.150	0.140
Czech Rep.	1987	0.095	0.437	0.054	0.047	1994	0.075	0.402	0.045	0.036
Estonia	1980	0.310	0.502	0.154	0.155	1989	0.325	0.498	0.163	0.163
Finland	1969	0.206	0.276	0.472	0.261	1995	0.191	0.438	0.108	0.094
Gibraltar	1980	0.409	0.239	0.312	0.149	2004	0.245	0.415	0.143	0.119
Greece	1981	0.408	0.196	0.328	0.129	1992	0.358	0.232	0.275	0.128
Ireland	1986	0.314	0.374	0.197	0.147	2004	0.352	0.471	0.186	0.175
Macedonia, FYR	1982	0.305	0.321	0.207	0.133	2001	0.294	0.409	0.174	0.142
Netherlands	1987	0.140	0.151	0.119	0.036	1994	0.155	0.179	0.128	0.046
Norway	1977	0.190	0.198	0.153	0.061	1995	0.162	0.240	0.123	0.059

(continued)

TABLE 4A.6
Employees Only, Country Duncan Values for Industrial Employment Based on ISIC68 (continued)

Country	Early year	Duncan	Percentage of women in labor force	Percentage of women to change	Percentage of labor force to change	Late year	Duncan	Percentage of women in labor force	Percentage of women to change	Percentage of labor force to change
Portugal	1974	0.360	0.287	0.256	0.147	1993	0.323	0.330	0.217	0.143
San Marino	1978	0.093	0.343	0.061	0.042	1993	0.112	0.364	0.071	0.052
Slovak Rep.	1986	0.287	0.456	0.156	0.142	2004	0.331	0.488	0.170	0.166
Spain	1973	0.143	0.231	0.109	0.052	1993	0.178	0.269	0.125	0.074
Sweden	1987	0.401	0.501	0.200	0.201	2004	0.384	0.506	0.190	0.192
Switzerland	1975	0.127	0.279	0.091	0.051	1986	0.108	0.288	0.077	0.044
Ukraine	1988	0.176	0.409	0.104	0.085	2000	0.066	0.352	0.043	0.030
United Kingdom	1971	0.135	0.376	0.088	0.061	1993	0.166	0.429	0.092	0.082

Source: Annex 4B.

Note: See note to annex table 4A.2.

TABLE 4A.7
Employees Only, Country Duncan Values for Industrial Employment Based on ISIC90

Country	Early year	Duncan	Percentage of women in labor force	Percentage of women to change	Percentage of labor force to change	Late year	Duncan	Percentage of women in labor force	Percentage of women to change	Percentage of labor force to change
OCEANIA										
Australia	1993	0.297	0.442	0.165	0.146	2004	0.278	0.463	0.149	0.138
New Zealand	1997	0.296	0.482	0.153	0.148	2004	0.314	0.489	0.160	0.157
AMERICAS										
Argentina	1991	0.386	0.366	0.245	0.179	2003	0.389	0.472	0.205	0.194
Bermuda	1994	0.254	0.498	0.128	0.127	2004	0.268	0.480	0.139	0.134
Brazil	1999	0.303	0.391	0.184	0.144	2003	0.458	0.433	0.260	0.225
Canada	1997	0.299	0.473	0.158	0.149	2004	0.294	0.491	0.149	0.147
Colombia	1992	0.233	0.428	0.133	0.114	2004	0.358	0.422	0.207	0.175
Costa Rica	1996	0.397	0.321	0.270	0.173	2004	0.381	0.348	0.248	0.173
Ecuador	2002	0.389	0.362	0.248	0.180	2004	0.395	0.366	0.251	0.183
Mexico	1991	0.364	0.342	0.240	0.164	2004	0.312	0.351	0.203	0.142
Panama	1992	0.405	0.393	0.246	0.193	2004	0.403	0.400	0.241	0.193
Peru	1996	0.312	0.310	0.215	0.133	2004	0.314	0.345	0.206	0.142
United States	2000	0.243	0.480	0.126	0.121	2004	0.264	0.485	0.136	0.132
Uruguay	2000	0.436	0.453	0.239	0.216	2002	0.443	0.444	0.246	0.219

(continued)

TABLE 4A.7
Employees Only, Country Duncan Values for Industrial Employment Based on ISIC90 (continued)

Country	Early year	Early Duncan	Percentage of women in labor force	Percentage of women to change	Percentage of labor force to change	Late year	Late Duncan	Percentage of women in labor force	Percentage of women to change	Percentage of labor force to change
ASIA										
Cyprus	1995	0.211	0.389	0.129	0.101	2004	0.355	0.479	0.185	0.177
Georgia	1998	0.378	0.485	0.195	0.189	2004	0.419	0.494	0.212	0.209
Iran, Islamic Rep. of	—	—	—	—	—	1996	0.471	0.126	0.411	0.104
Israel	1995	0.355	0.451	0.195	0.176	2003	0.336	0.487	0.172	0.168
Japan	2003	0.290	0.408	0.171	0.140	2004	0.293	0.411	0.172	0.142
Kazakhstan	2001	0.375	0.452	0.206	0.186	2004	0.352	0.467	0.188	0.175
Korea, Rep. of	1994	0.271	0.382	0.167	0.128	2004	0.320	0.419	0.186	0.156
Macau	1998	0.330	0.474	0.174	0.165	2004	0.279	0.531	0.131	0.139
Philippines	2001	0.411	0.382	0.254	0.194	2004	0.403	0.366	0.256	0.187
Singapore	1993	0.235	0.432	0.133	0.115	2003	0.289	0.477	0.151	0.144
Sri Lanka	—	—	—	—	—	—	—	—	—	—
Taiwan, China	1993	0.150	0.425	0.086	0.073	2002	0.179	0.442	0.100	0.088
West Bank and Gaza	1996	0.479	0.153	0.406	0.124	2004	0.512	0.176	0.422	0.149
Yemen, Rep. of	1999	0.460	0.082	0.422	0.069	—	—	—	—	—

Botswana	1995	0.327	0.440	0.183	0.161	2002	0.228	0.420	0.132	0.111
Egypt, Arab Rep. of	1997	0.407	0.177	0.335	0.118	2003	0.403	0.187	0.328	0.123
Mauritius	1999	0.366	0.368	0.231	0.170	2004	0.347	0.359	0.223	0.160
Swaziland	1970	0.289	0.173	0.239	0.083	1986	0.293	0.280	0.211	0.118
EUROPE										
Andorra	2003	0.265	0.454	0.145	0.132	2004	0.268	0.454	0.146	0.133
Austria	1996	0.125	0.318	0.085	0.054	2004	0.336	0.442	0.188	0.166
Belgium	1993	0.391	0.411	0.230	0.189	2003	0.338	0.443	0.189	0.167
Bulgaria	1996	0.265	0.512	0.129	0.133	2003	0.238	0.523	0.114	0.119
Croatia	1996	0.318	0.460	0.172	0.158	2004	0.310	0.454	0.169	0.154
Czech Rep.	1993	0.278	0.458	0.151	0.138	2004	0.289	0.466	0.154	0.144
Denmark	1995	0.341	0.461	0.184	0.170	2004	0.329	0.484	0.169	0.164
Estonia	1989	0.326	0.489	0.166	0.163	2004	0.312	0.516	0.151	0.156
Finland	1989	0.378	0.501	0.189	0.189	2004	0.377	0.503	0.187	0.189
France	1990	0.293	0.436	0.166	0.144	2004	0.289	0.470	0.153	0.144
Germany	1995	0.340	0.429	0.194	0.167	2004	0.337	0.464	0.181	0.168
Greece	1993	0.273	0.361	0.174	0.126	2003	0.331	0.403	0.197	0.159
Iceland	1991	0.347	0.503	0.172	0.173	2002	0.335	0.515	0.163	0.168
Italy	1993	0.286	0.361	0.183	0.132	2003	0.302	0.409	0.179	0.146
Lithuania	1995	0.547	0.386	0.336	0.259	2004	0.330	0.503	0.164	0.165
Luxembourg	1997	0.360	0.365	0.229	0.167	1998	0.358	0.364	0.228	0.166

(continued)

TABLE 4A.7
Employees Only, Country Duncan Values for Industrial Employment Based on ISIC90 (continued)

Country	Early year	Duncan	Percentage of women in labor force	Percentage of women to change	Percentage of labor force to change	Late year	Duncan	Percentage of women in labor force	Percentage of women to change	Percentage of labor force to change
Macedonia, FYR	2001	0.278	0.409	0.164	0.134	2003	0.310	0.430	0.177	0.152
Malta	2000	0.267	0.323	0.181	0.117	2004	0.254	0.329	0.170	0.112
Netherlands	1995	0.342	0.414	0.200	0.151	2002	0.314	0.447	0.174	0.179
Norway	1996	0.354	0.473	0.187	0.177	2004	0.369	0.488	0.189	0.184
Poland	1995	0.349	0.465	0.186	0.173	2004	0.353	0.468	0.188	0.176
Portugal	1993	0.300	0.444	0.167	0.148	2003	0.340	0.465	0.182	0.169
Romania	1994	0.314	0.411	0.185	0.152	2004	0.294	0.457	0.159	0.146
Russian Fed.	2000	0.330	0.485	0.170	0.165	2004	0.344	0.496	0.173	0.172
San Marino	1995	0.319	0.398	0.192	0.153	2004	0.311	0.415	0.182	0.151
Slovenia	1993	0.262	0.485	0.135	0.131	2004	0.294	0.472	0.155	0.147
Spain	1993	0.357	0.339	0.236	0.160	2004	0.379	0.409	0.224	0.183
Switzerland	1991	0.300	0.436	0.169	0.148	2004	0.298	0.449	0.164	0.148
Turkey	2000	0.282	0.195	0.227	0.089	2004	0.277	0.204	0.220	0.090
Ukraine	2002	0.293	0.515	0.142	0.146	2004	0.322	0.528	0.152	0.161
United Kingdom	1993	0.305	0.503	0.151	0.152	2004	0.279	0.492	0.142	0.140

Source: Annex 4B.

Note: See note to annex table 4A.2.

TABLE 4A.8
Relative (Female-to-Male) Wages by Country

Country	Year	Relative wage	Year	Relative wage	Change (percent)	Type	Remarks
OCEANIA							
Australia	1969	0.647	2004	0.864	0.8	Hourly	B
Fr. Polynesia	1995	0.873	2003	0.893	0.3	Hourly	A
New Caledonia	—	—	1999	0.813	—	Hourly	A
New Zealand	1974	0.718	2004	0.859	0.6	Hourly	C
EUROPE							
Austria	2000	0.536	2001	0.534	−0.4	Monthly	A
Belarus	1995	0.790	2003	0.796	0.1	Monthly	A
Belgium	1999	0.833	2003	0.828	−0.1	Monthly	B
Bulgaria	1996	0.689	2003	0.812	2.4	Monthly	A
Croatia	—	—	2003	0.895	—	Monthly	A
Denmark	1995	0.829	2003	0.857	0.4	Hourly	B
Finland	1999	0.794	2003	0.804	0.3	Monthly	B
France	1999	0.736	2002	0.744	0.3	Monthly	A
Gibraltar	1980	0.659	2003	0.678	0.1	Weekly	B
Hungary	1992	0.808	2003	0.877	0.7	Monthly	A
Iceland	1998	0.825	2004	0.814	−0.2	Monthly	B
Ireland	1999	0.638	2003	0.662	0.9	Weekly	D
Isle of Man	1995	0.629	2004	0.676	0.8	Hourly	A
Latvia	1994	0.770	2004	0.846	0.9	Monthly	A
Lithuania	1994	0.696	1999	0.819	3.3	Monthly	A
Luxembourg	1980	0.497	1996	0.640	1.6	Monthly	A
Malta	2000	0.870	2004	1.000	3.5	Hourly	A
Netherlands	1994	0.776	2004	0.817	0.5	Monthly	A
Norway	1997	0.854	2002	0.853	0.0	Monthly	B
Portugal	1997	0.706	1998	0.728	3.1	Monthly	B
Romania	—	—	2003	0.812	—	Monthly	A
Sweden	1993	0.862	2004	0.883	0.2	Hourly	A
Switzerland	1994	0.730	2002	0.755	0.4	Monthly	B
Turkey	1988	0.858	2001	0.983	1.1	Daily	A
Ukraine	1993	0.617	2004	0.686	1.0	Monthly	A

(continued)

TABLE 4A.8
Relative (Female-to-Male) Wages by Country (continued)

Country	Year	Relative wage	Year	Relative wage	Change (percent)	Type	Remarks
United Kingdom	1995	0.701	2004	0.744	0.7	Weekly	A
ASIA							
Bahrain	1987	1.386	2004	1.095	−1.4	Monthly	A
Cyprus	1988	0.681	2004	0.731	0.4	Monthly	A
Georgia	1999	0.521	2003	0.526	0.2	Monthly	A
Hong Kong, China	1987	0.763	2004	0.912	1.1	Monthly	B
Japan	1969	0.485	2003	0.668	0.9	Monthly	B
Jordan	1980	0.836	1999	0.885	0.3	Daily	B
Kazakhstan	1998	0.758	2004	0.619	−3.3	Monthly	A
Korea, Rep. of	1976	0.470	2002	0.639	1.2	Monthly	B
Mongolia	2000	0.924	2004	0.895	−0.8	Monthly	A
Philippines	1993	0.928	1999	0.934	0.1	Monthly	A
Qatar	—	—	2001	0.994	—	Monthly	A
Singapore	1989	0.697	1997	0.760	1.1		B
Sri Lanka	1975	0.792	2004	0.916	0.5	Daily	B
Thailand	2000	0.863	2001	0.852	−1.3	Monthly	A
West Bank and Gaza	1996	0.832	2004	0.833	0.0	Daily	A
AMERICAS							
Brazil	1988	0.695	1997	0.754	0.9	Monthly	B
Colombia	2002	0.842	2004	0.753	−5.4	Monthly	A
Costa Rica	1987	0.821	2004	0.911	0.6	Monthly	A
El Salvador	1998	0.771	2003	0.774	0.1	Monthly	A
Guadeloupe	1998	0.891	2001	0.903	0.4	Hourly	A
Mexico	1991	0.728	2004	0.842	1.1	Monthly	A
Netherlands Antilles	1983	0.723	1986	0.646	−3.7	Monthly	B
Panama	1998	0.979	1998	0.980		Monthly	A
Paraguay	2000	0.674	2003	0.689	0.7	Monthly	A
Peru	—	—	1995	0.570	—	Weekly	B
Virgin Islands	—	—	1994	0.849	—	Hourly	A

TABLE 4A.8
Relative (Female-to-Male) Wages by Country (continued)

Country	Year	Relative wage	Year	Relative wage	Change (percent)	Type	Remarks
AFRICA							
Botswana	1998	0.971	2003	0.798	−3.8	Monthly	A
Egypt, Arab Rep. of	1969	0.750	1978	0.889	1.9	Monthly	B
Eritrea	—	—	1996	0.585	—	Monthly	B
Eritrea	—	—	1996	0.815	—	Monthly	E
Eritrea	—	—	1996	0.490	—	Monthly	F
Eritrea	—	—	1996	0.858	—	Monthly	G
Kenya	1977	0.935	1997	0.847	−0.5	Monthly	B
St. Helena	1994	0.744	2002	0.874	2.0	Monthly	A
Swaziland	1972	0.303	1997	0.926	4.6	Monthly	H
Swaziland	1977	0.705	1997	0.913	1.3	Monthly	I
Tanzania	1972	0.963	1981	0.917	−0.5	Monthly	B

Source: ILO.

Note: — = Not available.

A = Total.

B = Excluding agriculture and fishing.

C = Excluding agriculture, fishing, private households with employed persons, and extraterritorial organizations and bodies.

D = Only mining, quarrying, manufacturing, electricity, gas, and water supply.

E = Only construction, electricity, gas, and water supply.

F = Trade, hotels, and restaurants.

G = Education, social work, health, and community work.

H = Total: skilled labor.

I = Total: unskilled labor.

TABLE 4A.9
Three Scenarios of Simulated Changes in Female and Male Wages and GDP under Conditions of Equality

Country	Year	Actual data[a]				If the wage gap increased[b]				If female employment increased[c]			
		Change in female wages	Change in male wages	Change in GDP	Required reallocations of the labor force	Change in female wages	Change in male wages	Change in GDP	Required reallocations of the labor force	Change in female wages	Change in male wages	Change in GDP	Required reallocations of the labor force
Australia	2004	9	−4	1	17	17	−6	3	26	8	−4	1	17
Belgium	2003	18	−4	2	18	29	−4	4	23	18	−4	2	19
Brazil	2002	23	−5	4	24	33	−5	6	30	22	−5	4	25
Bulgaria	2003	16	−6	4	28	25	−8	6	37	15	−7	4	29
Costa Rica	2004	11	−2	2	14	20	−4	3	21	11	−3	2	15
Croatia	2003	12	−5	2	21	21	−6	4	30	12	−5	2	22
Cyprus	2004	28	−6	6	33	39	−6	8	38	27	−6	6	35
Denmark	2003	9	−4	1	17	16	−6	3	25	9	−5	1	17
Finland	2003	15	−6	3	27	24	−7	6	35	15	−6	3	28
France	2002	21	−6	4	30	32	−7	7	36	21	−6	4	31
Georgia	2003	30	−5	6	33	42	−5	8	38	30	−5	6	34
Gibraltar	2003	18	−5	3	28	28	−6	5	31	17	−5	3	26
Ireland	2003	39	−4	5	26	53	−4	7	28	39	−5	5	27
Japan	2003	48	−5	7	31	62	−5	10	33	47	−5	8	33
Kazakhstan	2004	32	−6	7	30	45	−6	10	36	32	−7	7	31
Korea, Rep. of	2002	45	−6	9	35	59	−6	11	37	44	−6	9	37

Latvia	2004	12	-4	2	20	20	-6	4	28	12	-5	3	20
Lithuania	1999	11	-5	2	20	18	-6	4	28	10	-5	2	20
Mexico	2004	19	-3	3	19	29	-4	5	25	18	-3	3	20
Netherlands	2003	19	-6	4	28	30	-6	6	34	19	-6	4	29
New Zealand	2004	16	-6	3	27	25	-7	6	35	15	-6	4	27
Norway	2002	9	-4	1	18	17	-6	3	27	9	-5	1	18
Portugal	1998	24	-5	4	28	35	-6	7	33	23	-6	5	29
Singapore	2003	36	-6	7	33	49	-7	10	37	35	-7	7	35
Sweden	2004	4	-2	0	8	9	-4	1	17	4	-3	0	9
Switzerland	2002	20	-7	4	29	29	-7	7	36	19	-7	4	30
Taiwan, China	2002	22	-6	4	29	33	-7	6	35	21	-6	4	30
United Kingdom	2003	25	-7	6	33	36	-7	8	39	25	-7	6	35
Ukraine	2004	21	-7	5	28	31	-7	7	35	20	-7	5	29

Source: Annex 4B.

a. Actual employment and wage data.

b. Wage gap increased by 10 percent, assuming actual employment levels.

c. Female employment increased by 10 percent, assuming actual wage levels.

Annex 4B: Data Description

The empirical analysis in this report uses data extracted from the International Labour Organization (ILO) database[19] on employment by industry and occupation and on earnings by industry.

Employment by industry is derived from both Labor Force Surveys and Establishment Surveys. The workers are grouped according to the ISIC revised in 1968 (ISIC68) and in 1990 (ISIC90). The former distinguishes between 10 economic activities compared with 18 in the latter. A comparison between the two classifications is shown in table 4B.1.

The occupational data are derived from Labor Force Surveys and other official estimates. Occupations are defined by ISCO revised in 1968 (ISCO68) and 1987 (ISCO88). The different categories are described in table 4B.2.

The data on industrial earnings by sex are derived from Establishment Surveys and Social Insurance Records. The latter provide figures on the earnings of insured individuals in employment. Earnings in this case include (as defined by ILO) wages, salaries, compensation for time not worked, bonuses, and housing and family allowances paid by the employer directly to the employee.

TABLE 4B.1
ISIC Categorization of Economic Activities

ISIC68		ISIC90	
Categories	*Coding*	*Categories*	*Coding*
agriculture, hunting, forestry, and fishing	1	agriculture, hunting, and forestry fishing	1 2
mining and quarrying	2	mining and quarrying	3
manufacturing	3	manufacturing	4
electricity, gas, and water	4	electricity, gas, and water supply	5
construction	5	construction	6
wholesale and retail trade, restaurants, and hotels	6	wholesale and retail trade; repair of motor vehicle, motorcycles, and personal and household goods	7
		hotels and restaurants	8
transport, storage, and communication	7	transport, storage, and communications	9
financing, insurance, real estate, and business services	8	financial intermediation	10
		real estate, renting, and business activities	11

TABLE 4B.1
ISIC Categorization of Economic Activities (continued)

ISIC68		ISIC90	
Categories	*Coding*	*Categories*	*Coding*
community, social, and personal services	9	public administration and defense; compulsory social security	12
		education	13
		health and social work	14
		other community, social, and personal service activities	15
		private households with employed persons	16
		extraterritorial organizations and bodies	17
activities not adequately defined	0	activities not adequately defined	0

Source: ILO.

TABLE 4B.2
Occupational Categories

ISCO68		ISCO88	
Categories	*Coding*	*Categories*	*Coding*
professional, technical and related workers	1	professionals	2
		technicians and associate professionals	3
administrative and managerial workers	2	legislator, senior officials, and managers	1
clerical and related workers	3	clerks	4
sales workers	4	service workers, shop and market sales workers	5
service workers	5		
agriculture, animal husbandry, and forestry workers; fishermen and hunters	6	skilled agricultural and fishery workers	6
production and related workers, transport equipment operators and laborers	7/8/9	craft and related trade workers	7
		plant and machine operators and assemblers	8
		elementary occupations	9
workers not classified by occupations	0	armed forces	0

Source: ILO.

Annex 4C: Gender Differences in School Enrollment Rates

FIGURE 4C.1
Gender Parity in Secondary and Tertiary Education

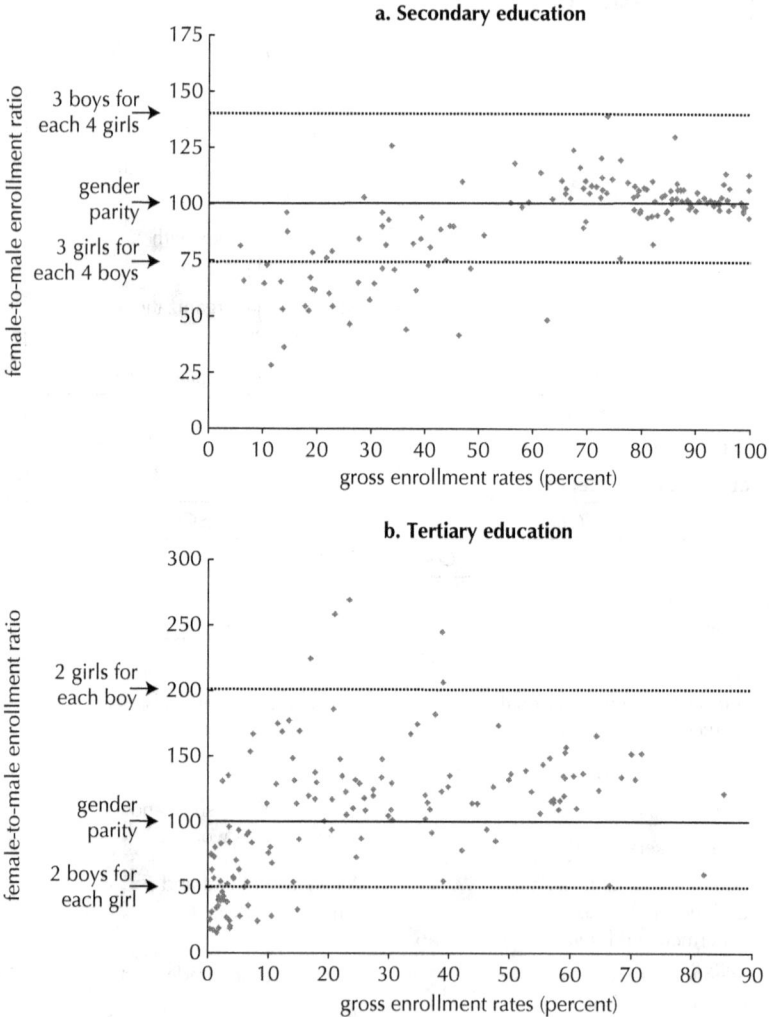

Source: World Bank 2004.

FIGURE 4C.2
Female-to-Male Ratio, Gross Enrollment Rates in Education:
Middle East and North Africa (regional unweighted average)

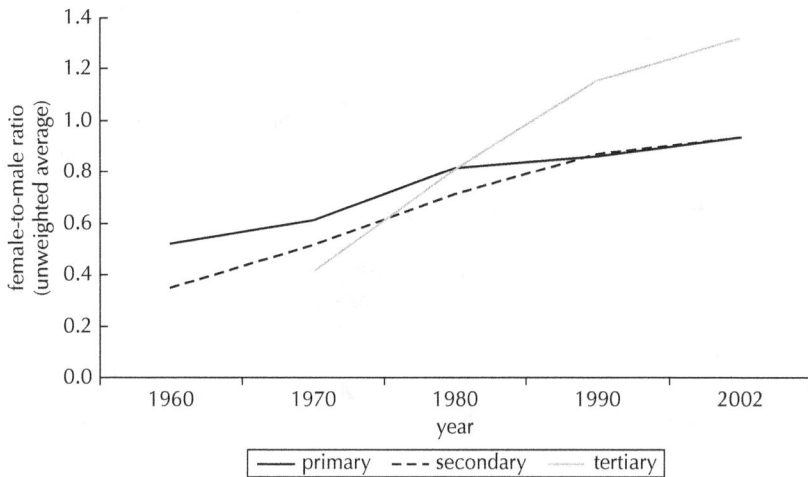

Source: World Bank 2007.

Notes

The chapter benefited from comments by Elena Bardasi, Lucia Fort, A. Waafas Ofosu-Amaah, Andy Morrison, Hiska Reyes, Mirja Sjöblom, and Eric Swanson, as well as able research assistance by Wael Mansour.

1. Naturally, the value of the Duncan index is sensitive to the number of categories (International Standard Industrial Classification [ISIC] "digits") adopted and the classifications used. Therefore, choices about how many industrial classification digits to consider and which classification to adopt are affecting comparisons both over time and across countries. This is why the chapter splits the time period in two (corresponding to a change in the industrial and occupational classification) and separately compares the initial and end points of the first and the second period.

2. The term "all workers" includes family workers, self-employed workers, and workers in wage employment.

3. Note, however, that the Duncan index is affected both by shares of workers in different sectors as well as by the size of the sectors. Changes in the value of the index over time can therefore reflect genuine changes in the sectoral shares of workers but also structural effects arising from the different growth rates of different sectors (for example, a decline in the share of agriculture and an increase in the share of services). Thus, the resilience of the value of the Duncan index for all workers may be affected by changes from both, for example, a change in the share of the self-employed in the total labor force and changes in

the share of women and men in self-employment. It is unclear to what extent these two elements can compensate for each other.

4. See annex 4B for a description of the various industrial and occupational classifications. The ISIC68 and ISCO68 are earlier classifications and cover the period 1979–96 in the sample, whereas the ISIC90 and ISCO88 typically cover the period 1996–2003.

5. As an example, using the industrial classification of 1968 (ISIC68), the value of the index for Sweden was 0.42 in 1969 and had fallen to 0.27 by 1994. However, using the more recent industrial classification (ISIC90) the value of the index was 0.40 in the same final year (1994) and was reduced only to 0.39 by 2004 (see annex table 4A.2).

6. Horizontal segregation exists when women and men are employed in different occupational groups, such as management and the professional and technical vocations. Vertical segregation exists when men and women work in the same occupational group, such as teachers, but men do the more skilled, more responsible, and better-paid activities, whereas women perform complementary activities; for example, within the teaching profession the majority of headmasters are men; within health-care fields the majority of women are nurses. Though this distinction is followed in much of the literature on segregation, treating vertical and horizontal segregation as separable, that is, as mathematical concepts suggesting two unrelated dimensions, is not always appropriate, for often the same social processes lead to both vertical and horizontal segregation.

7. The chapter uses the relevant ILO database that provides usable information for 55 countries at two times (annex table 4A.9).

8. The correlation coefficient between changes in female relative wages and number of years to which these changes relate is positive and significant (0.20) suggesting that, indeed, female relative wages tend to increase in the longer run.

9. A method to evaluate the wage and output effects under conditions of discrimination was proposed in the context of racial segregation (Bergmann 1971). This method can be extended to apply in a gender context (Tzannatos 1988).

10. For a more detailed presentation see Bergmann (1971) and Tzannatos (1988).

11. The unweighted average for the sample countries examined in this section comes to a 21 percent increase in female wages against a 5 percent reduction in male wages and an output gain of 4 percent. The portion of the labor force (women and men) that would have to change employment to achieve these hypothetical effects comes to 25 percent, not a small number, especially in the short run.

12. Inter-Agency and Expert Group on MDG Indicators, 6th Gender Indicators Subgroup meeting, New York, September, 26 2005. Chapter 2 in this volume notes that such an indicator is data intensive and will therefore be complex.

13. An empirical economic analysis of gender outcomes in six countries over time showed that, despite increases in segregation, women's earnings still increased in five of these countries relative to men (Tzannatos 1995).

14. Another area where information is largely lacking relates to the extent of women's involvement in providing "social services" within the household (in tasks related to teaching and nursing the children, health care, and caring for the old).

15. In Asia, for example, the rural nonfarm economy accounts for 20 percent to 50 percent of total rural employment and 30 percent to 60 percent of total rural income.
16. Additional noise in the data comes from the fact that some countries report average wages for all paid workers, but others report wages only for some subgroups.
17. Of course, the fact that women work fewer hours is an important issue in itself. The way this fact can be interpreted varies, however. It may mean that women are not as fully engaged in paid employment as men because of other "forced" commitments, or women combine work and other activities in a "voluntary" way.
18. Labor earnings, if broadly defined (as they should be), present additional problems for international comparisons because they include cash payments as well as in-kind benefits and are also affected by gender differences in hours worked (in addition to the effect arising from different wage rates).
19. The figures can be found at www.laborsta.ilo.org.

References and Other Resources

Bergmann, B. 1971. "The Effect on White Incomes of Discrimination in Employment." *Journal of Political Economy* 79 (2): 294–313.

Berik, G. 1987. *Women Carpet Weavers in Rural Turkey: Patterns of Employment, Earnings and Status.* Geneva: ILO.

Buviníc, M., M. Lycette, and W. P. McGreevy. 1983. *Women and Poverty in the Third World.* Baltimore: Johns Hopkins University Press.

Carlsson, H., and C. Valdivieso. 2003. "Gender Equality and the Millennium Development Goals." Unpublished, World Bank, Washington, DC.

De Medina, R. D. 2005. "Towards a More Comprehensive Model of Change for the Informal Economy: An ILO Perspective." Paper presented at the "Seminar on Labour Market Institutions and Employment in Developing Countries," Geneva, November 24–25.

Duncan, G. M., and D. E. Duncan. 1955. "A Methodological Analysis of Segregation Indices." *American Sociological Review* 20 (2): 210–17.

ILO (International Labour Organization). http://laborsta.ilo.org/.

———. 1990. *Yearbook of Labour Statistics: Retrospective Edition on Population Censuses 1945–1989.* Geneva: ILO.

———. 1994. *Equality for Women in Employment.* Geneva: ILO.

Maloney, W. F. 2004. "Informality Revisited." *World Development* 32 (7): 1159–78.

Nyberg, A. 1993. "The Social Construction of Married Women's Labor Force Participation." Paper presented at the conference "Out of the Margin: Feminist Perspectives of Economic Theory." Amsterdam, June 2–5.

Presser, H. B., and S. Kishor. 1991. "Economic Development and Occupational Sex Segregation in Puerto Rico, 1950–80." *Population and Development Review* 17 (1): 53–85.

Sayed, H., and Z. Tzannatos. 1998. "Gender Segregation." In *Encyclopedia of Third World Women,* ed. Nelly Stromquist. New York: Garland Publishing.

Tzannatos, Z. 1988. "The Long Run Effects of the Sex Integration of the British Labour Market." *Journal of Economic Studies* 15 (1): 1–18.

———. 1995. "Growth, Adjustment and the Labor Market: Effects on Women Workers." Paper presented at the IV Annual Meeting of the International Association for Feminist Economics, Tours, France, July 3–5.

———. 1998. "Women's Labor Incomes." In *Encyclopedia of Third World Women*, ed. Nelly Stromquist. New York: Garland Publishing.

———. 1999. "Women and Labor Market Changes in the Global Economy: Growth Helps, Inequalities Hurt and Public Policy Matters." *World Development* 27 (3): 551–69.

UN (United Nations). 2005. Inter-Agency and Expert Group on MDG Indicators, 6th Gender Indicators Sub-group meeting, New York, September 26, 2005.

UNDP (United Nations Development Programme). 2003. "Millennium Development Goals: National Reports A Look Through A Gender Lens." UNDP, New York.

UN Millennium Project Task Force on Education and Gender Equality. 2005. *Taking Action: Achieving Gender Equality and the Empowerment of Women*. New York: UN.

World Bank. 2004. *World Development Report 2004: Making Services Work for Poor People*. Washington, DC: World Bank.

———. 2005. "Agriculture and Achieving the Millennium Development Goals." A joint report by the Agriculture and Rural Development Department of the World Bank and the International Food Policy Research Institute, Washington, DC.

———. 2007. *The Road Not Traveled: Education Reform in the Middle East and North Africa*. Washington, DC: World Bank.

5

The Financial Requirements of Achieving Gender Equality and Women's Empowerment

Caren Grown, Chandrika Bahadur, Jessie Handbury, and Diane Elson

In September 2000, world leaders committed to achieving by 2015 the Millennium Development Goals (MDGs)—a set of interrelated development objectives that together define the basic minimum conditions for a decent life. The MDGs include halving poverty and hunger, ensuring universal primary schooling, reducing child and maternal mortality and infectious diseases, improving environmental sustainability, and achieving gender equality and women's empowerment. In 2006, progress toward the goals was mixed. While many countries have made strides toward some of the MDGs, there is great variation between and within countries in the pace and level of change. The goals of reducing maternal mortality and achieving gender equality and women's empowerment face the greatest challenges across all countries.

Although the MDGs have been reaffirmed in global forums, they have not been incorporated into operational planning within governments or international organizations. The weak link between policies and the corresponding investments needed for implementation is one barrier to progress. Achieving the MDGs requires long-term planning, as well as short-term expenditure and policy formulation. Within countries a range of actions are essential, including identifying appropriate strategies, reforming policies and institutions, and investing sufficient resources in a coordinated manner to build local capacity to deliver and scale up interventions. An assessment of the resources required is a critical first step in formulating, implementing, and monitoring the progress of strategies to achieve the MDGs.

The need for such an assessment is especially true for policies to promote gender equality and empower women. A particular challenge for national governments and the international community is how to accelerate implementation of Millennium Development Goal 3 (MDG3) at the country level. As the UN Millennium Project Task Force on Education and Gender Equality pointed out, sufficient knowledge exists about policies and interventions to eliminate many forms of gender inequality and empower women (UN Millennium Project 2005c). Yet, this knowledge has thus far not been systematically translated into comprehensive and large-scale change at the country level.

Too often, promising policy initiatives for gender equality and women's empowerment founder because insufficient resources are allocated to implement them. The shift of emphasis from women-specific projects to gender mainstreaming (see chapter 8 for an explanation of gender mainstreaming) is thought by many to have exacerbated this problem because mainstreaming has not been linked to flows of funding across all sectors (UN Millennium Project 2005c). The routines of government resource allocation have not generated information about financing requirements and funding gaps for the achievement of gender equality and women's empowerment.

The financial costs of efforts to reduce gender inequality are difficult to calculate because gender inequality is both multidimensional and multisectoral.[1] Apart from a recent effort piloted by the UN Millennium Project, there have been few comprehensive attempts nationally or globally to estimate the full range of these costs. Where they exist, most estimates calculate only the costs of achieving gender equality in education.

This chapter has two broad objectives. The first is to estimate, based on country-level analysis, the costs of interventions aimed at promoting gender equality and women's empowerment across multiple sectors. The intent is for this estimation to help identify the minimum resource envelope necessary to directly improve gender equality in low-income countries. The second objective is to estimate the share of all MDG investments that have the potential to improve outcomes for women and men, girls and boys. This exercise can help illustrate to what extent investments in other areas, if designed appropriately and accompanied by gender-mainstreaming interventions, can promote gender equality and women's empowerment.

The chapter extends the methodology developed by the UN Millennium Project (2005a) to estimate the costs of achieving the MDGs. From among the interventions that form the basis for the Millennium Project cost estimates, this chapter identifies those that promote gender equality and analyzes them to calculate the resources needed to achieve MDG3. The chapter derives the costs of these interventions in five low-income countries—Bangladesh,

Cambodia, Ghana, Tanzania, and Uganda. It then uses these estimates to calculate the costs of interventions to promote gender equality and women's empowerment in other low-income countries. Finally, the chapter projects the financing gap for gender-equality interventions, first for the five countries, and subsequently for all low-income countries.

Given data limitations, the calculations presented here are a rough approximation of the costs of financing gender equality. More important than the dollar figures, this chapter should be seen as providing a method that can be further revised and applied at the country level by governments, donors, and gender-equality advocates subsequent to the collection of more comprehensive data than was available initially. Ideally, the exercise within countries will be aligned with budget and Medium Term Expenditure Framework planning exercises and the Poverty Reduction Strategy Papers, contributing directly to expenditure planning in the different line ministries.

Achieving gender equality and women's empowerment requires a fundamental transformation in the way societies allocate gender roles and responsibilities. Most strategies to achieve gender equality require a mix of investments and changes in legislation, political and administrative rules, social attitudes, and norms. Resources alone will not achieve gender equality; they must be complemented by other changes in societies. Nonetheless, ensuring adequate resources for interventions aimed at gender equality and women's empowerment is an important first step toward broader social transformation.

The chapter is organized as follows. The first section following this introduction discusses how the concept of gender equality is operationalized. The second section reviews other exercises to estimate the cost of the MDGs and the evidence from previous attempts to estimate the costs of attaining gender equality in education and the costs of interventions to achieve reproductive health. The third section describes the method developed by the UN Millennium Project to estimate the costs of achieving the full set of MDGs. The fourth section explains how this chapter expands upon that methodology to estimate the costs of achieving MDG3 and gender equality within the other MDGs. The fifth and sixth sections present estimates of the costs of gender-equality interventions and the financing gap for such interventions in Bangladesh, Cambodia, Ghana, Tanzania, and Uganda. The seventh section scales up these results to an estimate of the costs of gender-equality interventions and the financing gap in all low-income countries while the eighth recommends establishing a fund specifically for achieving MDG3. The final section concludes with recommendations and next steps for donors, governments, and civil society advocates of gender equality.

Conceptualization of Gender Equality and Women's Empowerment

Most exercises that estimate the costs of the MDGs interpret MDG3 as the elimination of gender disparity in education. This is understandable because the time-bound target of MDG3 is to eliminate gender gaps in primary and secondary education. However, achieving gender equality and women's empowerment involves more than simply eliminating education gaps; it also requires equal economic opportunities, equal ownership and control over productive assets, freedom from drudgery, equal representation in decision-making bodies, and freedom from the threat of violence and coercion. Recognizing the broad spirit of the goal, the UN Millennium Project Task Force 3 on Education and Gender Equality adopted an operational framework for understanding gender equality in three dimensions:

- The *capabilities domain*, which refers to basic human abilities as reflected in education, health, and nutrition. These capabilities are fundamental to individual well-being and are the means through which individuals access other forms of well-being.
- The *access to resources and opportunities domain*, which refers primarily to equality in the opportunity to use or apply basic capabilities through access to economic assets (such as land, property, or infrastructure) and resources (such as income and employment), as well as political opportunity (such as representation in parliaments and other political bodies). Without access to resources and opportunities, both political and economic, women will be unable to employ their capabilities for their well-being and that of their families, communities, and societies.
- The *security domain*, which means reduced vulnerability to violence and conflict. Violence and conflict result in physical and psychological harm and lessen the ability of individuals, households, and communities to fulfill their potential. Violence directed specifically at women and girls often aims at keeping them in "their place" through fear.

The task force pointed out that these three domains are interrelated, and change in all three is critical to achieving MDG3 (UN Millennium Project 2005c). The attainment of capabilities increases the likelihood that women can access opportunities for employment or participate in political and legislative bodies, but does not guarantee it. Similarly, access to opportunity decreases the likelihood that women will experience violence (although in certain circumstances, it may temporarily increase that likelihood). Progress in any one domain to the exclusion of the others will be insufficient to meet the goal of gender equality. This conceptualization of gender equality implies that exercises to estimate the costs of interventions to achieve gender equality must consider interventions across all domains of gender equality, not in one domain alone.

Based on this conceptualization of gender equality, the task force identified seven strategic policy and intervention priorities for achieving MDG3 (see box 5.1).

The first two strategic priorities—strengthening opportunities for postprimary education for girls while meeting commitments to universal primary education and guaranteeing universal access to a broad range of sexual and reproductive health information and services—represent the priority for strengthening women's capabilities. The next four (investing in infrastructure to reduce women's time burdens, guaranteeing girls' and women's property and inheritance rights, eliminating gender inequality in employment, and increasing women's share of seats in national parliaments and local government bodies) reflect priorities for economic and political opportunity. The final strategic priority—significantly reducing violence against girls and women—addresses the security domain. The section titled Methodology for Costing Gender Equality and Women's Empowerment develops a list of interventions for each of these seven strategic priorities to achieve gender equality and women's empowerment.

Box 5.1
Seven Strategic Priorities for Action on MDG3

---

1. Strengthen opportunities for postprimary education for girls while meeting commitments to universal primary education
2. Guarantee sexual and reproductive health and rights
3. Invest in infrastructure to reduce women's and girls' time burdens
4. Guarantee women's and girls' property and inheritance rights
5. Eliminate gender inequality in employment by decreasing women's reliance on informal employment, closing gender gaps in earnings, and reducing occupational segregation
6. Increase women's share of seats in national parliaments and local government bodies
7. Significantly reduce violence against girls and women

Source: UN Millennium Project 2005c.

Estimating Country-Level Costs of Attaining All MDGs

There are several different approaches to developing cost estimates for achieving the full set of MDGs at the country level (see box 5.2). Each approach gives differing cost estimates, based on underlying assumptions and calculations.

Box 5.2
Costing the MDGs: An Overview of Different Approaches

Aggregate incremental capital output ratio (ICOR)–based cost estimates (for example, Devarajan, Miller, and Swanson 2002; Mbelle 2003; AfDB 2002) calculate overall aggregate estimates of investments needed to achieve the goal of halving income poverty. The method involves calculating the economic growth rate needed to halve poverty, based on assumed poverty-growth elasticities, typically estimated through cross-national regressions. The investment needed to achieve the required growth rate is then calculated using a simple growth model, typically of the following specifications:

$$g_y = I/Y \times 1/(ICOR - p),$$

where g_y is the per capita growth rate, p is the population growth rate, I is investment, Y is income, and $ICOR$ is the incremental capital output ratio, also calculated through growth regressions. Cost estimates based on the ICOR approach can be made at the national or global level. They are useful for providing a rough approximation of total investment needs but limited in their utility beyond such broad-brush estimates. For example, poverty elasticity estimates are poor guides for predicting the future relationship between growth and poverty because they are derived from marginal changes in income and poverty levels, and therefore cannot account for step increases in investment or the change in the composition of investments; they are poor predictors of ICOR rates for the same reasons. In addition, they are unable to account for those MDG-related investments that do not have a measurable impact on economic growth. While providing an overall magnitude of resources needed, such studies cannot provide guidance on budget programming, outlays, and planning.

Cost estimates based on input-outcome elasticities (Devarajan, Miller, and Swanson 2002; World Bank 2003) calculate the aggregate investment levels needed to achieve specific MDGs. The calculation is made by estimating a production function for specific goals, based on a range of inputs. As with aggregate ICOR studies, this method is useful in calculating overall resource needs. However, it raises several methodological issues, especially from a gender perspective. It can only model a small number of sectors in which production functions can be estimated based on historical elasticities. For the gender goal in particular, such production functions are difficult to model. As with ICOR studies, the elasticities are modeled on marginal changes, and cannot predict the input-outcome relationship with step increases in investments. Even for goals where production functions can be estimated, only a small number of variables can be modeled, often leaving out important MDG investments. Finally, such estimates do not guide budget planning and allocation.

Average unit cost–based estimates (Delamonica, Mehrotra, and Vandemoortele 2001; GWP 2000) calculate investment needs based on current expenditures and gaps in access or provision. Unit costs are derived by dividing current spending by the population covered and then applied to the population in need. This approach is based entirely on current expenditures; if the input mix changes, the unit costs will no longer be applicable for deriving total costs. Furthermore, typically, the population in need requires higher levels of investment (for example, excluded groups often need special interventions), which means that investment projections based on current expenditures tend to understate the overall needs.

Interventions-based needs assessments (Bruns, Mingat, and Rakatomalala 2003; United Nations and World Bank 2003, 2004; UN Millennium Project 2004) calculate bottom-up needs assessments based on identification of relevant interventions across multiple sectors. Such estimates provide detailed needs for financial resources, human resources, and infrastructure, and are useful for planning and budget programming purposes. However, they calculate the resource needs for different sectors separately and are not set up to account for synergies, which need to be estimated later and built into the sector analysis iteratively, making this a time-consuming and labor-intensive process. This approach offers guidance for planning and budget programming, but links to macroeconomic variables need to be modeled separately.

Source: UN Millennium Project 2004.

All long-term costing approaches described in box 5.2 are imperfect in their ability to calculate total needs accurately. First, it is difficult to predict what the costs of interventions will be 10 to 15 years from the baseline. It is also difficult to factor in the probability of shocks within the period. Second, most studies estimate only a small range of interventions necessary for achieving the MDGs, thereby limiting the scope of the financing strategy.

Another limitation of these aggregate or general costing exercises is that none have addressed the full range of gender-equality needs. Indeed, some of the existing costing estimates may even contain gender biases because they do not recognize the economic value of women's unpaid work. So, for instance, many of the HIV/AIDS-related costs may be underestimated because home-based care is seen to be less costly than institution-based care because women's labor is not counted or valued.

As noted above, estimating the resource needs for achieving MDG3 is especially difficult. Gender outcomes are not easily derived from production functions that can be parameterized. Moreover, economic growth does not automatically translate into reductions in gender inequalities or improvements in women's well-being (Seguino 2002). Actions to achieve gender equality cut across many different areas, raising the possibility of double counting. The approach described in the section Methodology for Costing Gender Equality and Women's Empowerment attempts to address each of these concerns.

Financing Interventions to Achieve Gender Equality in Education and to Provide Reproductive Health Services

Partly because of the difficulties described above, no approach has yet attempted to estimate a full set of comprehensive costs for interventions to promote gender equality and empower women. Previous exercises to estimate the financing requirements for gender-equality interventions only estimated the costs in certain sectors, such as health or education. The World Bank (2001), for instance, estimates that achieving gender equality in primary education through universal enrollment would require an increase of slightly more than 3 percent a year in public spending on primary education in South Asia and the Middle East and North Africa, but as much as 30 percent a year in Sub-Saharan Africa.[2] It further notes that ensuring equity in secondary education would add to these costs, but the total would still be affordable for the majority of countries that are currently off track for achieving that goal.

Devarajan, Miller, and Swanson (2002) estimate that meeting the 2005 MDG3 target of gender parity in secondary education would cost about $3 billion. In deriving this estimate, they assume constant average costs for enrollment and increasing the number of girls in school so that the ratio of girls to boys is 1:1 by 2005. Because the estimates refer to additional resource requirements and are based on average costs, the authors recognize their estimates likely understate the incremental costs of reaching the gender-equality target in education.

Other studies have attempted to estimate the costs of reproductive health. From a review of estimates of the financing necessary to achieve universal access to sexual and reproductive health services, the Alan Guttmacher Institute (AGI) and United Nations Population Fund (UNFPA) developed an interventions-based methodology and projected these costs at $11 billion a year (in 2003 dollars)—$7.1 billion to provide modern contraceptive services to current users and $3.9 billion to address unmet need. These estimates are higher than some others because they include labor, overhead, and capital, as well as contraceptive supplies (AGI/UNFPA 2004). Using new data, Vlassoff and Bernstein (2006) estimate the resource requirements for a basic package of sexual and reproductive health services in developing countries. They use detailed disaggregated direct service delivery cost estimates for family planning services, emergency obstetric care and neonatal survival interventions, sexually transmitted infection prevention and treatment interventions, and a broad range of HIV/AIDS services, and supplement them with overhead and systems improvement costs. They show that resource requirements for the basic sexual and reproductive health package will be significantly higher than estimated more than a decade ago. By 2015, the required annual costs will be about $36 billion, $14 billion more than originally anticipated. The costing exercise of Devarajan, Miller, and Swanson (2002) did not include reproductive health and did not provide separate estimates for the cost of meeting the maternal mortality goal. Instead, they assumed that the costs of achieving the maternal mortality goal would be of the same magnitude as the costs for meeting the under-five mortality goal.

The UN Millennium Project Needs Assessment Approach

The UN Millennium Project has developed an interventions-based, cross-sector assessment that aims to estimate the human, infrastructure, and financial needs of achieving the MDGs by 2015. The methodology, described in detail in UN Millennium Project (2004), comprises the following steps for each sector:

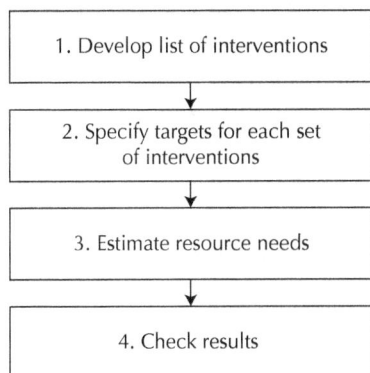

```
┌─────────────────────────────────────┐
│   1. Develop list of interventions  │
└─────────────────────────────────────┘
                  │
                  ▼
┌─────────────────────────────────────┐
│   2. Specify targets for each set   │
│          of interventions           │
└─────────────────────────────────────┘
                  │
                  ▼
┌─────────────────────────────────────┐
│      3. Estimate resource needs     │
└─────────────────────────────────────┘
                  │
                  ▼
┌─────────────────────────────────────┐
│          4. Check results           │
└─────────────────────────────────────┘
```

The identification of interventions used in UN Millennium Project (2005a) was based on the relevant priorities and plans articulated by governments and nongovernmental organizations within the countries, and on the recommendations from the UN Millennium Project Task Forces. The Millennium Project defines interventions as investments in goods, services, or infrastructure that directly contribute to the achievement of the MDGs; interventions are distinct from policies and institutions.

Sectors in this analysis refer to the different areas of investments for specific MDGs (with the exception of MDG3), and are termed "MDG sectors."[3] They include agriculture and rural development, education (covering primary and secondary education and adult literacy), health (including child and maternal health, malaria, HIV, tuberculosis, nutrition, and health systems), water and sanitation, energy and roads, and improving the lives of slum dwellers.[4] The analysis in this chapter does not include a gender sector because gender equality is not a stand-alone sector but a crosscutting issue. Rather, specific interventions required for the realization of MDG3 that have not been included in the other sectors are grouped together. In addition, the analysis identifies the specific gender-equality-related interventions in the other MDG sectors. This is explained in greater detail later in the chapter.

In each sector, targets are set based on the MDG targets and resource estimates are based on local or regional unit costs.[5] The results from all MDG sectors are then aggregated and revised to eliminate double counting and to account for synergies in provision and impact. The resource needs are based on total cost estimation (including capital and recurrent costs, covering both current and incremental costs), and estimated annually from 2006 through 2015.

This is a sensible way to calculate the costs of specific MDG sectors. However, from a gender perspective, there are some important caveats about this methodology. First, the needs assessment includes only some of the actions necessary to meet the goal of gender equality and empowerment of women. Although the intent was to develop an expansive list in the exercise below, it still likely excludes some interventions that may be important in particular country contexts. These would need to be identified through country-level planning exercises.

Second, and related to the first point, a gender needs assessment is possible only at the country level and meaningful only as part of a national poverty reduction strategy in which all stakeholders participate. To be credible, the analysis needs the inputs of all key stakeholders, including government officials at national, regional, and local levels; members of women's and other civil society organizations; and donors. The interventions to be costed need to be locally identified, based on nationally determined targets. Any assessment of needs has to be an iterative process, refined over time on the basis of experience.

Third, simply knowing the costs of interventions to achieve gender equality and women's empowerment is not sufficient to achieve gender equality. Leadership and political will are necessary to allocate the resources. To be successful, interventions may also require changes in legislation, political and administrative rules, social attitudes, and norms. The needs assessment, therefore, should be seen as a minimal but necessary set of actions to meet the goal of gender equality.

Even with these caveats, the UN Millennium Project needs assessment approach is more appropriate than the others described in box 5.2. This approach allows for a clear identification of interventions aimed specifically at improving outcomes for women within each sector, thus minimizing the possibility of double counting. It enables the estimation of the resource needs of a comprehensive set of interventions covering the multiple dimensions of gender equality. It can be extended to include different interventions (and costs) for different subgroups of the population. Like all long-term costing approaches, however, it is limited in its ability to accurately calculate total MDG needs, but the results can be revised iteratively as fresh data become available, making estimates more reliable. Its scope allows for necessary and bold financing strategies, and it is, therefore, preferred to the approaches discussed above.

At present, many countries are implementing gender-responsive budgeting initiatives, which seek to scrutinize the public budget from a gender-equality perspective. Unfortunately, actual budgeting and planning processes are not disaggregated along the lines discussed below. In country-level budgeting processes, this classification of the gender-equality interventions may need to be realigned within different line ministries. However, it is hoped that gender budget and other country-level planning processes will adapt the methodology developed here to illuminate what share of national budgets is being contributed to the achievement of gender equality.

Methodology for Costing Gender Equality and Women's Empowerment

The UN Millennium Project (2005a) developed a list of interventions for each sector and estimated the per unit capital and recurrent costs of implementing them. Each of those interventions is classified according to whether the main objective is to promote gender equality or whether the main objective is to promote another goal, such as reversing the spread of malaria. Based on this classification, the proportion of the cost of each intervention that can be attributed to promoting gender equality is calculated. The apportioned costs are then summed across interventions to obtain total costs attributable to promoting gender equality.

Classification of Interventions that Promote Gender Equality

Interventions that promote gender equality and women's empowerment are classified in two ways. Interventions in the first category explicitly aim to reduce gender inequality or empower women; these are referred to as GE (gender-equality) interventions. The second category of MDG interventions is designed primarily for the achievement of other MDGs, for instance, the construction of rural roads or health clinics, the provision of fertilizers or water services, and so forth. These interventions, henceforth referred to as NTGE (nontargeted gender-quality) interventions, can promote gender equality and may have the potential to help achieve MDG3, but that is not their primary purpose.

GE Interventions
There are two types of GE interventions. The first group covers those aimed at gender equality and women's empowerment that fall outside of the various other MDG sectors. These are denoted as MDG3-specific interventions. These interventions would be implemented through the ministry of women's affairs or a non-MDG sector ministry. (As a reminder, the MDG sectors are education, health, rural development, urban development and slum upgrading, water and sanitation, and energy.) For instance, interventions to reduce gender inequality in employment would be implemented through a ministry of labor. Interventions to reduce violence against women—such as mass media campaigns—might be implemented by the ministry of women's affairs. Box 5.3 gives examples of the various types of interventions in this category.

The second group of GE interventions includes interventions that are implemented within each MDG sector to help achieve gender equality and empower women in that sector. These are referred to as gender-mainstreaming interventions. The sectors of education, health, rural development, urban development, water and sanitation, and energy all include interventions that aim to promote gender equality. For example, in rural development,

Box 5.3
Interventions to Achieve MDG3 Not Included in an MDG Sector

Strategic Priority 2: Guarantee Sexual and Reproductive Health and Rights

- Increase awareness and provide education on sexual and reproductive health and rights through mass media and community-based programs
- Provide comprehensive sexuality education within schools and community programs

Strategic Priority 5: Reduce Gender Inequality in Employment

- Promote access to work through vocational training programs and school-to-work transition programs for adolescent girls
- Provide care services (for children, the elderly, the disabled, and the sick) to allow women to work

Strategic Priority 6: Increase Women's Political Representation

- Provide training to female candidates in elections at the local, regional, and national levels
- Provide training to female elected representatives at the local, regional, and national levels

Strategic Priority 7: Combat Violence against Women

- Prevent violence against women through awareness campaigns and education, hotlines, and neighborhood support groups
- Provide protection from violence through police and medical services, counseling, and emergency housing or short-term shelters to victims of violence
- Provide punishment for perpetrators of violence through legal redress

Capacity-Building Interventions

- Strengthen the capacity of governments to deliver the interventions identified above
- Strengthen ministries of women's affairs and gender focal points in other ministries
- Undertake institutional reforms through sensitization programs to train judges, bureaucrats, land registration officers, and police officers
- Invest in legal aid services to help women claim their rights and access the interventions identified above
- Improve registration systems for issuing identification documents to women (in those settings where applicable)
- Invest in data collection and monitoring activities to track gender outcomes

---

special efforts to recruit and train women extension workers can help ensure that the national extension service reaches female farmers to the same extent as it does male farmers. In education, increasing retention of girls in school may require special subsidies on the demand side, and special facilities, such as toilets for girls, on the supply side. Also included in gender-mainstreaming interventions are investments that strengthen the capacity of the sector (and the ministry) to achieve gender equality, for instance, the costs of gender focal points in each line ministry, the costs of gender training for line ministry staff, the costs of gender-disaggregated research, and so forth. Box 5.4 provides examples of gender-mainstreaming interventions in selected MDG sectors.

Box 5.4
Gender Mainstreaming Interventions

Education

Gender-sensitive hygienic facilities
Scholarships or subsidies for girls
Female teacher salaries
Male teacher salaries
Gender focal point unit in the ministry of education

Health

Community-based nutrition programs
Micronutrient supplementation programs for adolescent girls
Maternal health
Child health[a]
Mother-to-Child Transmission, Mother-to-Child Transmission Plus initiatives
Human resources for child and maternal health
Gender focal point unit in the health ministry

Rural Development

Female extension workers
Gender focal point unit in the ministry of agriculture

Slum Dwellers and Water and Sanitation

Gender focal point units in the ministries of housing or interior, water, and sanitation

a. Excludes public nutrition. The costs of child nutrition are attributed to gender equality because of the impact on a range of female empowerment outcomes (see Quisumbing and Maluccio [2000]; Haddad, Hoddinott, and Alderman [1997]).

The analysis in the next section reports the results separately for MDG3-specific and gender-mainstreaming interventions. It is important for donors, ministers of finance, and staff in in-line ministries to see the costs disaggregated in this way. In country-level planning exercises, disaggregating GE costs into MDG3-specific costs and gender-mainstreaming costs is encouraged.

NTGE Interventions
The second category of MDG interventions covers those designed for the achievement of other MDGs. As noted above, they can promote gender equality and have the potential to help empower women. NTGE interventions include micronutrient supplementation programs for underweight children; the provision of fertilizers, water services, energy infrastructure; and so forth. Further examples are provided in annex 5A to this chapter.[6]

Apportioning the Costs for Gender Equality

Gender-Equality Targeted Interventions (GE)
At the country level, the costs at time t of interventions specifically designed to promote MDG3-specific and gender-mainstreaming interventions, where there are p and q of each type intervention, can be expressed formally as

$$C_{GE} = \sum_{t=2005,}^{2015} \left[\sum_{i=1,}^{p} GE3_{i,t} + \sum_{j=1}^{q} GEM_{j,t} \right], \qquad (5.1)$$

where $GE3_{i,t}$ is the cost of an MDG3-specific intervention i at time t and $GEM_{j,t}$ is the cost of a gender-mainstreaming intervention j at time t.

Nontargeted Interventions that Promote Gender Equality (NTGE)
To estimate the financial resources that contribute to promoting gender equality through interventions that do not specifically aim at gender equality, the analysis needs to estimate that share of the cost of the intervention that goes toward reducing the gender gap and maintaining female access to that service. The relevant gender gap in the education, health, and rural development sectors is in use of services. For instance, use in education can be captured by sex-disaggregated enrollment rates; use of rural credit programs can be captured by sex-disaggregated borrower rates, and so forth. Annex 5A lists the relevant gender gaps for interventions in each sector that

have sex-disaggregated data and provides the formulas for calculating the proportion of these intervention costs that can be attributed to promoting gender equality. These formulas are based on the assumption that changes in the provision of services in these sectors will reduce the gap if it results in greater increases in women's use of the service than in men's.

Infrastructure interventions, such as water, sanitation, and energy services, benefit all members of the households that receive them (men, women, and children), but they also address an important gender gap— the gap in time spent collecting water and fuel.[7] For infrastructure, public or private sector provisioning is replacing household provisioning, thus reducing the unpaid labor of those household members (typically women and girls) who fetch the water and gather the firewood. Annex 5A also lists the ways that gender gaps are measured for water and sanitation and energy interventions and provides the formulas for calculating the share of costs of these interventions that can be attributed to promoting gender equality.

The total cost of NTGE interventions can be calculated in the following way. $NTGE_{k,t}$ is the cost at time t of nontargeted sector interventions that have a gender-equality benefit, where there are s nontargeted interventions. Let $\alpha_{k,t}$ be the proportion of the costs of these interventions that can be attributed to promoting gender equality at time t. The total cost of nontargeted interventions that can be attributed to promoting gender equality is therefore

$$C_{NTGE} = \sum_{t=2005}^{2015} \sum_{k=1}^{s} \alpha_{k,t} NTGE_{k,t}, \qquad (5.2)$$

where $\alpha_{k,t}$ is estimated separately for each intervention as described in annex 5A.

Total Cost of Gender Equality
The total estimated cost of interventions to promote gender equality is the sum of all gender-equality-promoting interventions and the share of the costs of nontargeted sectoral interventions that can be attributed to the promotion of gender equality. This is expressed formally as

$$C = \sum_{t=2005}^{2015} \left[\sum_{i=1}^{p} GE3_{i,t} + \sum_{j=1}^{q} GEM_{j,t} + \sum_{k=1}^{s} \alpha_{k,t} NTGE_{l,t} \right]. \qquad (5.3)$$

Country-Level Results

Table 5.1 reports the estimates of the average annual per capita costs of achieving gender equality in the five countries: $37.24 in Bangladesh, $46.71 in Cambodia, $51.91 in Ghana, $56.89 in Tanzania, and $52.01 in Uganda. These figures represent between 35 and 49 percent of total MDG

TABLE 5.1
Average Annual Per Capita Costs of Achieving Gender Equality (2003 $)

	Bangladesh	Cambodia	Ghana	Tanzania	Uganda
MDG3 specific interventions	3.80	3.46	3.14	3.90	3.18
Costs of mainstreaming gender interventions in MDG sectors					
Education	0.23	0.22	3.31	1.50	1.84
Energy	0.03	0.02	0.01	0.07	0.05
Health	6.77	8.31	6.87	7.22	10.54
Rural development	0.03	0.02	0.25	0.25	0.19
Slum dwellers	0.03	0.02	0.02	0.07	0.05
Water and sanitation	0.03	0.02	0.04	0.07	0.05
Total	7.12	8.61	10.50	9.18	12.72
Costs apportioned to promoting gender equality in MDG sectors					
Education	6.05	8.86	11.06	6.61	7.55
Energy	8.00	13.57	8.12	11.69	8.88
Health	7.59	7.97	11.59	17.97	14.20
Rural development	—	—	1.92	1.96	2.01
Slum dwellers	1.36	1.35	0.97	1.51	1.07
Water and sanitation	3.32	2.89	4.61	4.07	2.40
Total	26.32	34.64	30.27	43.81	36.11
Total cost of achieving gender equality	37.24	46.71	51.91	56.89	52.01
Total costs of achieving the MDGs	106.48	107.35	100.37	118.84	106.50
Gender costs as a percentage of the total cost of achieving the MDGs	35	43	52	48	49
Per capita GDP in 2003	395.38	313.37	275.86	308.70	276.54
Gender costs as a percentage of GDP in 2003	9	15	19	18	19

Source: UN Millennium Project 2005a.

costs in Bangladesh, Cambodia, Tanzania, and Uganda and slightly more than half of total MDG costs in Ghana.[8] They represent about 9 percent of 2003 GDP per capita in Bangladesh, 15 percent in Cambodia, 18 percent in Tanzania, and 19 percent in Ghana and Uganda.

The costs apportioned to gender equality in each MDG sector represent the largest share of costs, ranging from 67 to 74 percent in Bangladesh, Cambodia, and Ghana to 76 percent in Uganda and Tanzania. The costs of gender-mainstreaming interventions are more modest, representing about 19 percent of total costs to achieve gender equality in Bangladesh, 18 percent in Cambodia, 20 percent in Ghana, 16 percent in Tanzania, and 24 percent in Uganda.

Finally, the MDG3-specific interventions represent the smallest share of the total costs of interventions to achieve gender equality, ranging from 6 to 10 percent. Although the amounts seem small, it is important to remember that this category only comprises interventions that are not accounted for in other sectors and are critical to achieving gender equality in those sectors and in countries as a whole. Investment in MDG3-specific interventions and in gender mainstreaming provides a basis for the assumptions made in apportioning the costs of the interventions not targeted to gender equality. The portions are likely to be lower in the absence of spending on specific interventions and gender mainstreaming because the latter ensures that interventions are designed to meet women's needs as well as men's needs, and to make them as accessible to women as to men.

Table 5.2 shows the total annual costs of all three categories of interventions to promote gender equality in each of the five countries during 2005–15. The total costs for the period range from $6.5 billion in Cambodia to $50.3 billion in Bangladesh, with Ghana, Tanzania, and Uganda in the middle range.[9]

Detailed information for the cost categories in each country is presented in annex 5C.

Estimating the Financing Gap for GE Interventions

The analysis in the previous section found that between 35 and 52 percent of the total costs (or between $37 and $57 per capita per year) of the MDGs can be directly attributed to the achievement of gender-equality objectives. This is a crucial estimate for understanding the importance of multisector, gender-sensitive interventions. However, this percentage cannot be used to calculate the gender portion of the country-level

TABLE 5.2
Annual Costs of Mainstreamed Gender-Equality-Promoting Interventions (million 2003 $)

Country	2006	2007	2008	2009	2010	2011	2012	2013	2014	2015	Total
Bangladesh											
Cost of MDG3-specific interventions	228	261	277	307	358	441	583	827	1,251	1,980	6,513
Cost of mainstreaming gender interventions in other sectors	796	894	988	1,080	1,141	1,226	1,310	1,393	1,477	1,535	11,840
Costs apportioned to gender equality in other sectors	2,666	2,906	3,137	3,385	3,653	3,918	4,202	4,520	4,858	5,166	38,411
Bangladesh total	3,690	4,061	4,402	4,772	5,152	5,585	6,095	6,740	7,586	8,681	56,764
Cambodia											
Cost of MDG3-specific interventions	26	30	32	35	40	46	56	73	101	147	587
Cost of mainstreaming gender Interventions in other sectors	93	105	117	129	137	148	158	169	179	185	1,420
Costs apportioned to gender equality in other sectors	345	379	412	448	482	519	556	595	637	673	5,045
Cambodia total	464	514	561	612	659	713	770	837	917	1,005	7,052
Ghana											
Cost of MDG3-specific interventions	36	41	44	48	53	61	74	94	130	188	768
Cost of mainstreaming gender interventions in other sectors	259	287	317	347	369	402	435	471	511	546	3,945
Costs apportioned to gender equality in other sectors	932	1,013	1,155	1,204	1,286	1,385	1,482	1,588	1,710	1,869	13,624
Ghana total	1,227	1,341	1,516	1,599	1,708	1,848	1,991	2,153	2,351	2,603	18,337

(continued)

TABLE 5.2
Annual Costs of Mainstreamed Gender-Equality-Promoting Interventions (million 2003 $) (continued)

Country	2006	2007	2008	2009	2010	2011	2012	2013	2014	2015	Total
Tanzania											
Cost of MDG3-specific interventions	59	68	72	79	91	111	145	207	320	526	1,678
Cost of mainstreaming gender	448	482	519	558	589	634	684	740	804	864	6,321
Costs apportioned to gender equality in other sectors	1,695	1,847	2,075	2,215	2,391	2,583	2,771	2,966	3,188	3,553	25,284
Tanzania total	2,202	2,397	2,666	2,852	3,071	3,328	3,600	3,913	4,312	4,943	33,283
Uganda											
Cost of MDG3-specific interventions	45	52	56	61	69	82	102	135	194	295	1,090
Cost of mainstreaming gender interventions in other sectors	571	614	659	707	747	803	865	935	1,014	1,089	8,003
Costs apportioned to gender equality in other sectors	1,858	2,049	2,265	2,499	2,744	2,997	3,262	3,545	3,848	4,182	29,248
Uganda total	2,474	2,715	2,980	3,267	3,560	3,882	4,229	4,615	5,056	5,566	38,341

Source: Authors' calculations.

financing gap. Between 67 and 76 percent of the gender costs comprise the apportioned "gender-equality" costs in MDG sectors. These apportioned costs should not be counted as part of the gender-equality financing gap because the sector interventions will already have been covered by general MDG financing mechanisms. As noted earlier, the sector costs have been apportioned in this way to demonstrate the potential impact that resources in these sectors can have on gender equality.[10] Thus, this analysis calculates the financing gap based on direct gender-equality interventions across all MDG sectors only.

To determine the financing gap for the five countries, the analysis follows the UN Millennium Project methodology (UN Millennium Project 2005a). There are three broad sources of financing in this approach: household contributions, government resource mobilization, and external financial resources. The resources that can be raised within the country (through household contributions and increased government spending) are estimated first, leaving the residual as the "gap" that will need to be financed by donors (see UN Millennium Project [2005a] for more detail on the estimation procedure).

Household contributions are determined based on ability to pay. The UN Millennium Project divides the population into three categories: The first category includes the proportion of the population below the poverty line that is assumed to make no contributions to payments for MDG interventions. The second category includes people between the poverty line and two times the poverty line (corresponding broadly in this set of countries with the third and fourth income quintiles). This section of the population is expected to pay a portion of the MDG costs. This portion is calculated separately for each sector and includes interventions for which there is either a proven case of partial payments improving efficient delivery (water, energy, rural development) or where there is a demonstrated ability to pay for certain services (specific interventions in secondary education). For primary education, health care, and MDG3-specific interventions, no contributions are estimated. The third category includes the top quintile of the population; it is assumed that the population in this category will pay for all MDG services. Aggregating across these three categories of the population, and across different sectors, shows that household contributions in these five countries account for $10–$13 per capita.

Government resources for the MDG investments are based on projected increases in the share of MDG spending in countries as well as the overall increase in domestic revenue mobilization. The UN Millennium

Project assumes that governments can mobilize an additional 4 percentage points of GDP toward spending on the MDGs. For the five countries included in this analysis, this implies an increase from about 4–7 percent to about 8–11 percent of GDP for spending on the MDGs. Government contributions estimated in this way account for between 30 and 40 percent of total MDG needs.

Thus, between 40 and 47 percent of all MDG needs are estimated to be raised domestically. This still leaves a substantial financing gap of about half of the total—the MDG financing gap, which translates to between $60 and $73 per capita per year.

The Millennium Project assumptions for apportioning costs by source of financing are assumed to remain relevant for the analysis of the gender portion of the financing gap because household contributions and government resources are calculated independently of the composition of MDG needs.[11]

The costs of gender-equality-promoting interventions in all MDG sectors comprise between 23 and 31 percent of the total requirements for promoting gender equality in the five countries (see table 5.3). This translates into 18–27 percent of the total MDG financing gap. Though rarely included in national planning or budgeting processes and never fully covered by external assistance, MDG3-specific and gender-mainstreaming costs are a critical part of an overall financing strategy to achieve all the MDGs. Donors should pay particular attention to this portion of the financing gap.

At the same time, it is important to caution that funding MDG3-specific and gender-mainstreaming interventions alone should not be seen as a shortcut to achieving gender equality or the MDGs. Donors need to commit funding to cover the full financing gap for all the MDGs. Subsidies for female students will only be effective if female students have classrooms, teachers, and books. Interventions to achieve gender equality are interdependent, and this analysis reinforces that conclusion.

Estimating the MDG3 Financing Gap for Low-Income Countries

As noted above, this analysis used the financing gap estimates derived by the UN Millennium Project (2005a) in its estimation of the MDG3 financing gap for low-income countries. The total MDG financing gap is the difference between total MDG investment needs and domestic resource mobilization, assuming both a rise in government expenditures of up to 4 percent of GDP

TABLE 5.3
Average Annual per Capita MDG Costs and Financing Gaps (2003 $)

	Bangladesh	Cambodia	Ghana	Tanzania	Uganda
MDG3-specific costs per capita	3.80	3.46	3.14	3.90	3.18
MDG-mainstreamed costs per capita	7.12	8.59	10.49	9.17	12.71
Costs apportioned to promoting gender equality per capita	26.32	34.64	38.27	43.81	36.12
Annual gender needs per capita	37.24	46.71	51.91	56.89	52.01
Annual cost of gender interventions as % of total gender equality needs	29	26	26	23	31
Annual MDG needs per capita	106.48	107.35	100.37	118.84	106.50
Annual gender needs as % of MDG needs	35	44	52	48	49
Annual household contributions per capita	10.97	13.18	11.30	11.90	10.08
Annual government contributions per capita	35.36	31.58	28.57	34.05	36.85
Annual financing gap per capita	60.15	62.59	60.50	72.89	59.57
Annual financing gap as % of MDG needs	56	58	60	61	56
MDG3-specific costs as % of financing gap	6	6	5	5	5
Gender-mainstreamed costs as % of financing gap	12	14	17	13	21
MDG3+-gender-mainstreamed costs as % of financing gap	18	19	23	18	27

Source: Authors' calculations.

between 2005 and 2015 and household contributions based on ability to pay.[12] The MDG financing gap for low-income countries is $73 billion in 2006, rising to $160 billion by 2015.[13] Using these estimates, this analysis projects the cost of interventions to achieve gender equality and empower women in low-income countries.

To obtain the cost of achieving gender equality in low-income countries, the analysis first averages the proportion of MDG3-specific investment needs and gender-mainstreaming investment needs over the five countries for each year 2006–15 (table 5.4). These averages are then applied to the total MDG investment needs in low-income countries and three scenarios are developed for projecting how these MDG3 costs might be financed.

Scenario 1 assumes that gender-equality interventions are not financed by domestic resource mobilization. In its review of the evidence, the UN Millennium Project Task Force found that sufficient funds are rarely allocated for gender-equality interventions (UN Millennium Project 2005c). Moreover, gender budget initiatives around the world have highlighted that most interventions for gender equality are financed off-budget, primarily from contributions from bilateral and multilateral donors (Elson 2006). Scenario 1 assumes that this trend will continue, and all of the gender-equality interventions will be financed through external resources.

Scenario 2 assumes that government resources will partially support gender-equality interventions. Empirical research shows that in countries where such allocations are made, this proportion is generally small. On average, most gender budget initiatives have found that governments commit between 1 and 3 percent to two categories of interventions: women-specific programs and equal opportunity programs (Budlender et al. 2002; UNIFEM 2002). Given this information, the analysis assumes that in 2006 governments commit 1 percent of public expenditure (the latter is assumed to be about 13.1 percent of GDP in low-income countries, net of debt repayments[14]) to gender-equality interventions, and this is scaled up to 3 percent by 2015.

Scenario 3 assumes that the share of government resources spent on gender-equality interventions is proportionate to the share of the

TABLE 5.4

Gender Costs as a Percentage of Total MDG Costs Averaged across Bangladesh, Cambodia, Ghana, Tanzania, and Uganda

	2006	2010	2015
MDG3-specific needs as % of MDG investment needs	2	2	6
Mainstreaming needs as % of MDG investment needs	10	9	8
MDG3-specific and mainstreaming needs as % of MDG investment needs	12	11	15

Source: Authors' calculations.

gender-equality intervention costs in total MDG costs, which is the assumption made by the UN Millennium Project analysis (UN Millennium Project 2005a). Consequently, the financing gap for gender in scenario 3 reflects the share of gender-equality costs in total MDG costs.

Table 5.5 shows that scenarios 1 and 2 produce similar financing gap estimates for gender-equality interventions in 2006, between $28 billion and $30 billion. The financing gap under scenario 3 for gender-equality interventions is much lower in 2006, at $8.6 billion. However, the financing gap changes substantially in 2015 under scenarios 1 and 2. Under scenario 1, the financing gap grows at the same rate as MDG costs, to $83 billion, but under scenario 2, the financing gap decreases to $73 billion because governments contribute $10 billion from own-source revenues to gender-equality interventions. Under scenario 3, if governments commit domestic resources to gender-equality interventions in the same proportion as their contributions to overall MDG interventions, the financing gap shrinks to just $23.8 billion.

The assumptions used in scenario 2 reflect the proportion of domestic resources currently allotted by governments to gender-equality interventions. Experience from gender budget initiatives around the world suggests that even if governments assume an increasing share of the costs over time, they continue to rely on donor assistance for many gender-equality-promoting interventions. This is not a viable scenario in the long term; countries must assume greater responsibility for mobilizing domestic resources for gender-equality interventions. Scenario 3 thus assumes a more active role for governments in mobilizing resources for gender equality; this is the scenario encouraged for governments and donors to strive to attain in the long term.

Domestic resources are particularly important for gender equality. First, they signal that a country is committed to achieving gender equality through investments of their own resources. They indicate that governments have taken ownership of the problem and intend to solve it. Second, only domestic resources can ensure longer-term sustainability for those interventions and activities that are needed to create the fundamental transformation in the way that societies conceive of and organize men's and women's roles and responsibilities.

Although domestic resources are key to supporting gender-equality interventions in the long term, external resources are important in the short term to jump-start the allocation of domestic resources for gender-equality interventions in low-income countries. Yet evidence suggests that donor

TABLE 5.5
Total Gender Costs and Source of Financing for Low-Income Countries
(billion 2003 $)

	Scenario 1		Scenario 2		Scenario 3	
	2006	2015	2006	2015	2006	2015
Achieving the MDGs						
Investment needs	251.7	560.1	251.7	560.1	251.7	560.1
Domestic resource mobilization	178.9	399.9	178.9	399.9	178.9	399.9
Financing gap	72.8	160.2	72.8	160.2	72.8	160.2
MDG3 specific						
Investment needs	5.3	35.9	5.3	35.9	5.3	35.9
Domestic resource mobilization	0	0	0.5	2.5	3.8	25.6
Financing gap	5.3	35.9	4.8	33.4	1.5	10.3
Mainstreaming costs						
Investment needs	24.4	47.3	24.4	47.3	24.4	47.3
Domestic resource mobilization	0	0	1.5	7.5	17.3	33.8
Financing gap	24.4	47.3	22.9	39.8	7.1	13.5
MDG3 specific + mainstreaming costs						
Investment needs	29.7	83.2	29.7	83.2	29.7	83.2
Domestic resource mobilization	0	0	1.9	10.1	21.1	59.4
Financing gap	29.7	83.2	27.7	73.2	8.6	23.8
Financing gap (per capita 2003 US$)	11	27	10	23	3	8

Source: Authors' calculations.

financing is not currently sufficient to cover the full costs of gender-equality interventions (UN Millennium Project 2005c).[15] There is thus a financing gap created by the inadequacy of both domestic financing and external resources for interventions to promote gender equality and women's empowerment.

A Fund for Gender-Equality Interventions

If gender equality and women's empowerment are to be realized, financial support for the interventions described in this chapter needs to be commensurate with country needs. The UN Millennium Project estimates that in most low-income countries the costs of achieving all the MDGs will require substantial external resources, especially in the short to medium term, despite increases in domestic resource mobilization. This chapter has illustrated that achieving gender equality requires investments in all the MDGs. At the same time, empirical evidence shows that gender-equality investments are typically accorded low priority within budget allocations. This lack of attention means that special focus is needed to make sure that both MDG3-specific and gender-mainstreaming interventions are systematically included in scaling up strategies to achieve the MDGs.

Based on this analysis, this chapter recommends that donors create a special fund to support MDG3-specific and gender-mainstreaming interventions in low-income countries. Averaging the estimates derived under scenario 3, the analysis calculates that about $13 billion per year is needed for the next five years to accelerate implementation of these interventions in all low-income countries.[16] This translates into $4.44 per capita annually. For their part, countries will need to ramp up their financing to $34 billion per year for the next five years, which translates into $11 per capita, on average. Based on progress made, the resource estimates should be revised in 2011 to reflect current and emerging country needs.

The investment needs for gender-equality interventions is small compared with overall commitments to official development assistance (ODA) and even total MDG needs. If the Organisation for Economic Co-operation and Development (OECD) countries make good on their commitments to allocate 0.7 percent of their gross domestic product (GDP) to ODA, it would result in $200 billion per year in ODA. MDG3-specific and gender-mainstreaming costs represent just 6.5 percent of this amount. This is an investment that is well worth the cost.

Conclusion

This chapter illustrates, through a quantitative assessment, that investments that directly and indirectly promote gender equality and women's empowerment represent a significant share of total investments for the Millennium Development Goals. Any serious effort to promote gender equality and women's empowerment should cost money—a fact often ignored by governments in both rich and poor countries. At the same time, the chapter's results show that these investments are affordable, given existing commitments made by donor governments of increasing ODA to 0.7 percent of GDP by 2015, and more recent commitments, such as doubling aid to Africa by 2010.

This analysis of nontargeted gender-equality (NTGE) interventions shows that investments in other MDG sectors also have important payoffs for gender equality and women's empowerment but especially if designed and implemented appropriately. In particular, investments in education, health, and infrastructure are crucial to improving the lives of poor women; for the five countries analyzed, between 31 and 74 percent of the investments in these areas could be directly attributed to improving gender-equality outcomes. The policy implications of this analysis are clear: the multidimensional nature of gender implies that investments in a range of sectors and activities are needed concurrently to achieve MDG3.

This analysis has also attempted to operationalize gender mainstreaming and link it to budgeting needs and flows of funding. It shows that the costs of gender-mainstreaming interventions represent 7–13 percent of total MDG needs. Gender mainstreaming requires specific resource allocation within sector investment plans, a fact often overlooked in the current discourse on gender mainstreaming. The gender-mainstreaming interventions identified in this chapter are critical for making the sector interventions successful.

However, gender mainstreaming alone may have limited impact in achieving gender equality and women's empowerment. Successful strategies combine gender mainstreaming with specific, targeted actions to promote MDG3. Investing for MDG3 is crucial for achieving all the other MDGs. Because more than 90 percent of the investments to achieve gender equality are, in fact, implemented through other MDG sectors, governments cannot hope to achieve any of the MDGs without paying adequate attention to the specific interventions and actions (and the accompanying investments) needed to reach underserved women in the population.

Greater allocation of domestic resources toward promoting gender equality and women's empowerment is encouraged. However, external financing can be important to jump-start an increase in domestic allocation. Based on scenario 3 above, it is recommended that donors commit resources in the range of $13 billion annually between 2006 and 2011 to finance MDG3-specific and gender-mainstreaming interventions in low-income countries, and that this amount be readjusted thereafter based on domestic resource commitments to these interventions.

Gender-equality interventions should be part of a broader, comprehensive effort by national governments to achieve the MDGs. The input of key stakeholders, including government officials at national, regional, and local levels; members of women's and other civil society organizations; and donors, are critical to the success of the process. The interventions to be costed need to be locally identified based on nationally determined targets and refined over time on the basis of experience.

Finally, we must reiterate a point made at the beginning of this chapter. While adequate resources alone will not achieve gender equality, knowing both the specific interventions and their costs creates the conditions for the fundamental transformation required to achieve gender equality. Transformation of social norms and patriarchal structures can begin through policies, interventions, and projects that have adequate funding. Thus, the gender needs assessment and associated financing gap analyses should be seen as critical tools for generating resources—and perhaps even leadership and political will—for gender equality and women's empowerment.

Annex 5A: NTGE Interventions

This following sections explain how this chapter calculates the gender-equality-promoting share of NGTE interventions in education, health, rural development, and infrastructure.

Education Interventions

The relevant gender gap in the education sector is enrollment. For sufficient progress toward the MDGs in any given year, the education sector needs continued expenditure on the existing education system, as well as new capital and recurrent expenditures on the construction of new schools and the provision of new staff, new materials, and so forth. For simplicity, this analysis uses incremental[17] enrollment to estimate the proportion of capital costs that can be attributed to females and to males, and current enrollment to estimate the proportion of the recurrent costs that go toward females and males.

If fewer girls than boys are in school, the gender-equality-promoting share of the capital costs of education sector interventions is the incremental enrollment of girls as a share of total incremental enrollment. This can be expressed mathematically as follows:

$C_{c,e,t}$ = capital cost, per new pupil[18] of an education intervention, where c is capital cost, and e is an educational intervention in year t;

$C_{c,e,t} \delta M_{e,t}$ = capital cost of additional male pupils, where δ is the difference operator, and $M_{e,t}$ is the number of males enrolled in year t;

$Cc,e,t\ \delta F_{e,t}$ = capital cost of additional female pupils, where δ is the difference operator, and $F_{e,t}$ is the number of females enrolled in year t; and
$C_{c,e,t}(\delta M_{e,t} + \delta F_{e,t})$ = total capital cost in year t.

The proportion of total capital costs in year t that are attributable to promoting gender equality is

$$\alpha_{c,t} = \frac{\delta F_{e,t}}{\delta M_{e,t} + \delta F_{e,t}}.$$

The proportion of the total recurrent cost in year t that is attributable to maintaining girls' enrollment can be expressed mathematically as follows:

$C_{r,e,t}$ = recurrent cost, r, per pupil of an education intervention, e, in year t;

$C_{r,e,t}(M_{e,t})$ = recurrent cost of all male pupils enrolled in year t;

$C_{r,e,}(F_{e,t})$ = recurrent cost of all female pupils enrolled in year t;

$C_{r,e,t}(M_{e,t} + F_{e,t})$ = total recurrent cost in year t; and

$C_{r,e,t}(F_{e,t})$ = total recurrent cost of maintaining girls' enrollment in year t.

The proportion of the total recurrent cost in year t of maintaining girls' enrollment at its level in year t is

$$\alpha_{r,e,t} = \frac{F_{e,t}}{M_{e,t} + F_{e,t}}.$$

Female Teachers: A Special Case

Because research has shown that the presence of female teachers can attract more girls to school when fewer girls are enrolled than boys (UN Millennium Project 2005c), this chapter has apportioned the costs associated with female teacher training and employment differently than those of other education interventions. Female teacher training and employment interventions are classified as NTGE interventions, but a proportion of their costs are treated like GE (mainstreaming) interventions. Because the role that female teachers play in boosting girls' enrollment decreases as the gender gap in enrollment decreases, this proportion is estimated to be the distance of the girls' share of enrollment from 0.5. All of this proportion of the female teacher costs is attributed to gender equality. The remaining proportion of female teacher costs is treated in the same manner as other recurrent education costs. This can be expressed mathematically as follows:

$C_{ft,e,t}$ = total cost associated with the hiring and training of a female teacher;

$$\varepsilon_t = 0.5 - \frac{F_{e,t}}{M_{e,t} + F_{e,t}}, \text{ and}$$

$$\alpha_{r,e,t} = \frac{F_{e,t}}{M_{e,t} + F_{e,t}},$$

where ε_t is the proportion of the female teacher costs associated with boosting girls' enrollment in year t, $\alpha_{r,e,t}$ is the proportion of recurrent hiring and training costs attributed to gender equality, and $M_{e,t}$ and $F_{e,t}$ are the number of boys and girls, respectively, enrolled in school in year t.

The proportion of the female teacher costs in year t attributed to the promotion of gender equality is

$$\alpha_{ft,e,t} = \varepsilon_t + (1 - \varepsilon_t)\, \alpha_{r,e,t}.$$

Health Interventions

The health sector includes a range of NTGE interventions.[19]

Nutrition

Utilization data are not available, so prevalence is used as a proxy. The costs of nutrition interventions targeting children under age five are apportioned according to the ratio of female prevalence of malnutrition to the total prevalence of malnutrition:

$$\alpha_n = \frac{P_{n,f}}{P_{n,m} + P_{n,f}}.$$

The analysis assumes that women and men benefit equally from population-wide nutrition interventions and, therefore, apportions half of their cost to this estimate.[20]

Infectious Diseases: HIV/AIDS, Tuberculosis, and Malaria

Utilization data are not available, so prevalence is used as a proxy. The ratio of female prevalence to total prevalence of each disease is used to apportion the cost of prevention and treatment interventions that can be attributed to gender equality. Because utilization rates for these services are not available, the analysis assumes that they reach women and men suffering from the disease equally and apportions their costs as follows:

$$\alpha_d = \frac{P_{d,f}}{P_{d,m} + P_{d,f}},$$

where α_d is the proportion of the cost of prevention and treatment that promotes gender equality and $P_{d,f}$ and $P_{d,m}$ are the prevalence rates of the disease among females and males, respectively. For each disease, the latest available gender-disaggregated prevalence data are used and the analysis assumes that the ratio of female to male prevalence does not change over time.[21]

Health Systems

Half the cost of the human resources requirements and infrastructure in the health sector (with the exception of resources dedicated to maternal and child health) are apportioned to gender equality. In other words,

$$\alpha_{hr,t} = 0.5.$$

Rural Development Interventions

The relevant gender gap in the rural development sector occurs in access to inputs and services that improve the productivity of farmers. Both recurrent and capital costs of rural development interventions are apportioned by estimating the ratio of average use of inputs or services by female smallholder farmers relative to male smallholder farmers, multiplied by the female share of smallholder farmers. For example, the analysis uses gender-disaggregated fertilizer usage data from Malawi (Mukhopadhyay and Pieri 1999) as the proxy for current farm input and nonextension agricultural service use in time t in Ghana, Tanzania, and Uganda.

The analysis makes the reasonable assumption that average female smallholder fertilizer use is influenced by women's access to female extension workers and will rise as the proportion of female extension workers increases. The analysis assumes that when the ratio of female extension workers to male extension workers is equal to the ratio of female farmers to male farmers, average female fertilizer use will equal average male fertilizer use. Thus, farm input and nonextension services costs are apportioned according to the following formula

$$\alpha_{a,t} = \frac{A_{ft}}{A_{mt}} \times \frac{E_f}{E_m + E_f},$$

where $\alpha_{a,t}$ is the proportion of the cost of agricultural inputs and nonextension services that contributes to gender equality; $A_{f,t}$ and $A_{m,t}$ are average female and male utilization of fertilizer or other relevant inputs in year t; and $(E_f/E_m + E_f)$ is the ratio of female agricultural employment to total agricultural employment.[22]

Infrastructure Interventions

The method for determining what portion of the costs of infrastructure promotes gender equality is analytically similar to the above examples, but the measurement of the gender gap is different.[23] The initial gap is not differences in the numbers of males and females using the intervention but in male and female time spent in providing the service, in the absence of the infrastructure. The provision of infrastructure saves time, and thereby narrows the gender gap in time spent in unpaid work.

This is illustrated with the example of water:

$F_{w,t-1}, M_{w,t-1}$ = hours females and males, respectively, spend at time $t-1$ collecting water;

$F_{w,t}, M_{w,t}$ = hours females and males, respectively, spend collecting water at time t, after the provision of a water tap to the household;

$\delta F_{w,t}$ = female time saved by the intervention, where δ is the difference operator;

$\delta M_{w,t}$ = male time saved by the intervention, where δ is the difference operator; and

$\delta F_{w,t} + \delta M_{w,t}$ = total time saved by the intervention.

The proportion of the total cost of water intervention w that is attributable to reducing the gender gap in year t is

$$\alpha_{w,t} = \frac{\delta F_{w,t}}{\delta F_{w,t} + \delta M_{w,t}}.$$

More generally, the proportion of the total cost of an infrastructure intervention, i, that is attributable to reducing the gender gap in year t is

$$\alpha_{i,t} = \frac{\delta F_{i,t}}{\delta F_{i,t} + \delta M_{i,t}},$$

where $\delta F_{i,t}$ and $\delta M_{i,t}$ are the amounts of time that females and males, respectively, except when the infrastructure intervention, i, is introduced at time t.

TABLE 5A.1
Average Alphas from 2006 through 2015 for Each MDG Sector

	Bangladesh	Cambodia	Ghana	Tanzania	Uganda
Primary education					
Capital costs	0.85	0.64	0.56	0.72	0.59
Recurrent costs	0.48	0.48	0.48	0.48	0.48
Female teachers' salaries	0.49	0.49	0.49	0.49	0.49
Secondary education					
Capital costs	0.51	0.53	0.43	0.58	0.64
Recurrent costs	0.49	0.48	0.47	0.47	0.43
Female teachers' salaries	0.48	0.51	0.49	0.49	0.47
Adult literacy	0.58	0.68	0.65	0.67	0.66
Nutrition					
Infant	—	—	0.48	0.51	0.46
Child	—	—	0.49	0.49	0.49
Adult	—	—	0.50	0.50	0.50
Infectious diseases					
HIV/AIDS	0.17	0.30	0.56	0.60	0.56
Tuberculosis	0.24	0.29	0.31	0.31	0.36
Malaria	0.45	0.30	0.50	0.50	0.50
Health systems	0.50	0.50	0.50	0.50	0.50
Rural development	—	—	0.59	0.39	0.67
Infrastructure					
Water					
Rural	0.55	0.50	0.57	0.74	0.74
Urban	0.56	0.50	0.52	0.71	0.71
Sanitation	0.50	0.50	0.50	0.50	0.50
Energy					
Rural	0.42	0.92	0.57	0.74	0.79
Urban	0.42	0.92	0.46	0.74	0.83

Source: Authors' calculations.
Note: — = data not available.

For energy interventions, the amount of time women and men spend collecting firewood is used as a proxy for time saved, and for both water and sanitation interventions, the amount of time women and men spend collecting water is used as a proxy for time saved.

The Value of Alpha

Table 5A.1 provides the average value of alpha (α) for interventions in each MDG sector from 2006 through 2015.

Annex 5B: Assumptions Underlying the Coverage Targets and Cost Calculations

The UN Millennium Project (2004) provides a detailed explanation of the assumptions underlying the resource estimates to achieve the MDGs in the five countries. Additional assumptions or changes relevant to the gender costing are explained in this annex.

Throughout, the analysis uses the OECD-DAC deflator to rebase estimates to 2003 U.S. dollars.

MDG3-Specific Interventions

The MDG3-specific interventions costed in this chapter follow:

- *Community-based awareness campaigns for women's reproductive rights.* Coverage target is 100 percent of the country's female population by 2015. Average costs of the program correspond to the costs of a program that can potentially reach up to 35,000 people.
- *School-based awareness programs for reproductive health and rights.* Coverage target is 100 percent of primary and secondary school students by 2015.
- *Sensitization programs for public officials.* Coverage target is 100 percent of public officials (bureaucrats, judges, and police force) by 2015.
- *Vocational training for female secondary school students.* Coverage target is 25 percent of the adolescent female population by 2015, except for Tanzania, where it is 40 percent.
- *Training for women candidates standing for election.* Coverage target is 100 percent of electoral seats.
- *Interventions to address violence against women* are based on domestic violence prevalence rates.
  - Mass media campaigns (assumed to run twice per year)
  - Counseling services, with a coverage target of 50 percent of women who have experienced abuse by 2015
  - Shelters, with a coverage target of 10 percent of women who have experienced abuse by 2015
- Strengthening women's ministries. The analysis assumes an average per capita cost of $1.56. This number is based on the costs of the Ministry of

Women's Affairs in Cambodia in 2004, which has been adjusted for the other four countries. Another method for obtaining unit costs of other countries would have been to calculate the budget of a similar ministry in those countries as a proportion of the total budget, but such data are both difficult to obtain and vary enormously. This chapter has adapted the costs of a reasonably well-funded ministry as the benchmark for the other countries.

Other important interventions identified by Task Force 3 that have not been costed in this exercise are sex-disaggregated data collection; monitoring and evaluation activities; school-to-work programs; minimum income guarantee schemes; public employment schemes; support to women's organizations; support to women elected representatives; legal, mediation, and rehabilitation services for violence against women; and improved enforcement of antidiscrimination laws.

Gender-Equality Mainstreaming Interventions

Education. The analysis assumes that females will constitute 50 percent of primary and secondary school teachers by 2015. Scholarships for girls are assumed to reach 50 percent of the female primary and secondary school population by 2015. It is assumed that there is one female toilet in every classroom catering to about 40 females by 2015, except for Tanzania where it is 20 females by 2015. Also included in this category are the costs of a gender focal point unit in the ministry of education. On average, the analysis assumes the unit has a professional staff 0.5 percent of the current civil service size (covering both central and provincial levels) with salaries based on middle-senior management scales within the civil service in each country. The costs of activities (for example, training programs), supplies (for example, vehicles), administrative personnel, and other materials that are needed for a gender focal point unit to function effectively are not included, so total gender-mainstreaming costs are likely to be underestimated.

Energy. The energy needs assessment targets households as the coverage population; therefore, there are no other specific interventions for gender mainstreaming other than the cost of a gender focal point unit (as per the education paragraph above) within the energy ministry.

Health. As noted in box 5.4, all maternal and child health costs are assumed to be "mainstreaming" costs. Child and maternal health interventions include the Integrated Management of Childhood Illness package, immunizations, the neonatal package, antenatal care, skilled birth attendants and clean delivery, emergency obstetric care, contraception and family planning services, and safe abortions and care of complications. The analysis assumes universal coverage of essential health services by 2015.

Rural development. The primary gender-mainstreaming intervention is female extension workers, which are scaled up to the proportion of female smallholders in the smallholder farmer population by 2015. Each extension worker is assumed to service 205 households by visiting them at least twice in one year. Mainstreaming costs also include a gender focal point unit (as in the education paragraph above) in the ministry of agriculture.

Slum dwellers. The slum dwellers needs assessment targets households as the coverage population; therefore, there are no other specific interventions for gender mainstreaming other than the cost of a gender focal point unit (as in the education paragraph above) within the housing or interior ministry.

Water and sanitation. The water and sanitation needs assessment targets households as the coverage population; therefore, there are no other specific interventions for gender mainstreaming other than the cost of a gender focal point unit within the water and sanitation ministry (as in the education paragraph above).

Other MDG Sectors

Education. Interventions for building classrooms, developing curricula, and providing the operational costs of running a school system are included in the overall education needs assessment. Needs are based on enrollment rates in these countries and aim for 100 percent completion in primary education by 2015 and a transition rate of 80 percent for secondary education by 2015, except for Tanzania, where the target transition rate is 60 percent by 2015.

Energy. Interventions include rural and urban electrification, rural and urban off-grid energy devices, and clean cooking fuels.

Rural development. Interventions include chemical fertilizers, fertilizer trees, green manure, improved seeds, shallow wells, gravity irrigation, wells, storage tanks, and pumps.

Health. Interventions for treatment of infectious diseases include antiretroviral treatment therapy and the basic UNAIDS HIV prevention and care package; for malaria, Artemisinin combination treatment, insecticide-treated bed nets, and indoor residual spraying; and for tuberculosis,

Directly Observed Treatment–Short Course, and Directly Observed Treatment–Short Course Plus.

Water and sanitation. Specific interventions for water and sanitation fall into four broad categories: extension, rehabilitation, and operation of water supply and treatment infrastructure; extension, rehabilitation, and operation of sanitation and wastewater treatment infrastructure; promotion of hygienic behavior by households and proper use of water and sanitation facilities through hygiene education and behavior change programs; and extension of infrastructure for water storage and transport coupled with Integrated Water Resources Management to ensure adequate supply of water for domestic, agricultural, and industrial use, as well as ecosystem functioning.

Annex 5C: Country Data and Figures

TABLE 5C.1
Bangladesh: Per Capita Costs of Achieving Gender Equality (2003 $)

	2006	2007	2008	2009	2010	2011	2012	2013	2014	2015	Annual average
Costs of MDG3-specific interventions	1.49	1.67	1.75	1.91	2.18	2.64	3.43	4.78	7.10	11.06	3.80
Costs of mainstreaming gender intervention in MDG sectorss											
Education	0.13	0.15	0.16	0.18	0.20	0.23	0.26	0.29	0.33	0.38	0.23
Energy	0.03	0.03	0.03	0.03	0.03	0.03	0.03	0.03	0.03	0.03	0.03
Health	4.98	5.49	6.00	6.43	6.67	7.03	7.37	7.68	7.98	8.12	6.77
Rural development	0.03	0.03	0.03	0.03	0.03	0.03	0.03	0.03	0.03	0.03	0.03
Slum dwellers	0.03	0.03	0.03	0.03	0.03	0.03	0.03	0.03	0.03	0.03	0.03
Water and sanitation	0.03	0.03	0.03	0.03	0.03	0.03	0.03	0.03	0.03	0.03	0.03
Total	5.23	5.76	6.28	6.73	6.99	7.38	7.75	8.09	8.43	8.62	7.12
Costs apportioned to gender equality in MDG sectors											
Education	3.81	4.15	4.52	4.96	5.40	5.93	6.55	7.37	8.29	9.54	6.05
Energy	7.80	7.93	7.99	7.98	8.11	8.09	8.11	8.10	8.15	7.74	8.00
Health	4.84	5.51	6.23	6.90	7.47	8.05	8.59	9.06	9.46	9.75	7.59
Slum dwellers	0.97	1.04	1.12	1.20	1.29	1.38	1.48	1.59	1.71	1.83	1.36
Water and sanitation	2.31	2.38	2.47	2.54	2.61	2.70	2.80	2.99	3.79	8.61	3.32
Total	19.73	21.01	22.33	23.58	24.88	26.15	27.53	29.11	31.40	37.47	26.32
Total costs of achieving gender equality	26.45	28.44	30.36	32.22	34.05	36.17	38.71	41.98	46.93	57.15	37.24

Source: Authors' calculations.

FIGURE 5C.1
Bangladesh: Cost of Gender-Equality-Promoting Interventions as a Portion of Total Costs of Achieving the MDGs, 2006–15

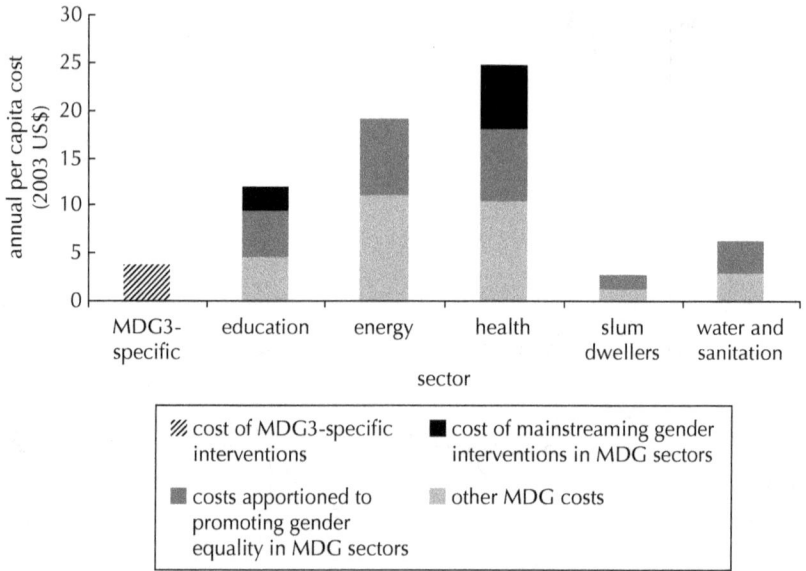

Source: Authors' calculations.

TABLE 5C.2
Cambodia: Per Capita Costs of Achieving Gender Equality (2003 $)

	2006	2007	2008	2009	2010	2011	2012	2013	2014	2015	Annual average
Costs of MDG3-specific interventions	1.74	1.96	2.07	2.23	2.45	2.80	3.32	4.20	5.72	8.10	3.46
Costs of mainstreaming gender intervention in MDG sectors											
Education	0.15	0.17	0.18	0.19	0.21	0.23	0.24	0.26	0.28	0.30	0.22
Energy	0.02	0.02	0.02	0.02	0.02	0.02	0.02	0.02	0.01	0.01	0.02
Health	6.11	6.72	7.35	7.89	8.15	8.64	9.04	9.46	9.79	9.91	8.31
Rural development	0.02	0.02	0.02	0.02	0.02	0.02	0.02	0.02	0.01	0.01	0.02
Slum dwellers	0.02	0.02	0.02	0.02	0.02	0.02	0.02	0.02	0.01	0.01	0.02
Water and sanitation	0.02	0.02	0.02	0.02	0.02	0.02	0.02	0.02	0.01	0.01	0.02
Total	6.34	6.97	7.61	8.16	8.44	8.95	9.36	9.80	10.11	10.25	8.61
Costs apportioned to gender equality in MDG sectors											
Education	7.02	7.28	7.57	7.95	8.29	8.77	9.26	9.89	10.69	11.91	8.86
Energy	11.07	11.73	12.41	12.96	13.49	14.05	14.51	14.99	15.36	15.08	13.57
Health	5.20	5.91	6.59	7.24	7.78	8.42	8.95	9.49	9.91	10.21	7.97
Slum dwellers	0.99	1.05	1.13	1.20	1.28	1.37	1.46	1.57	1.68	1.79	1.35
Water and sanitation	1.58	1.72	1.88	2.05	2.24	2.48	2.74	3.11	3.88	7.23	2.89
Total	25.86	27.69	29.58	31.40	33.08	35.09	36.92	39.05	41.52	46.22	34.64
Total costs of achieving gender equality	33.94	36.62	39.23	41.79	43.97	46.84	49.60	53.05	57.35	64.57	46.71

Source: Authors' calculations.

FIGURE 5C.2
Cambodia: Cost of Gender-Equality-Promoting Interventions as a Portion of Total Costs of Achieving the MDGs, 2006–15

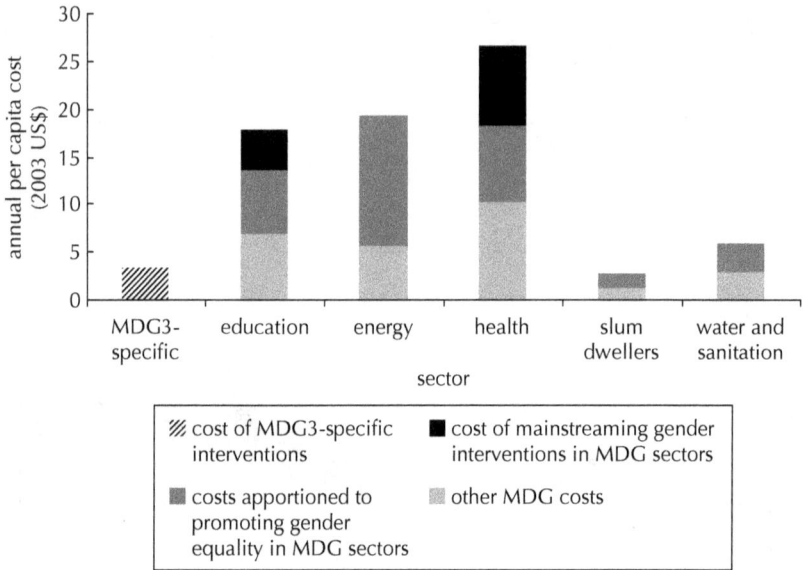

Source: Authors' calculations.

TABLE 5C.3
Ghana: Per Capita Costs of Achieving Gender Equality (2003 $)

	2006	2007	2008	2009	2010	2011	2012	2013	2014	2015	Annual average
Costs of MDG3-specific interventions	1.64	1.83	1.92	2.05	2.24	2.53	3.00	3.77	5.11	7.28	3.14
Costs of mainstreaming gender intervention in MDG sectors											
Education	1.79	1.98	2.22	2.50	2.83	3.24	3.70	4.26	4.91	5.68	3.31
Energy	0.01	0.01	0.01	0.01	0.01	0.01	0.01	0.01	0.01	0.01	0.01
Health	5.55	5.95	6.34	6.66	6.73	7.03	7.28	7.54	7.76	7.82	6.87
Rural development	0.22	0.22	0.22	0.22	0.23	0.24	0.25	0.28	0.32	0.37	0.25
Slum dwellers	0.02	0.02	0.02	0.02	0.02	0.02	0.02	0.02	0.02	0.02	0.02
Water and sanitation	0.04	0.04	0.04	0.04	0.04	0.04	0.04	0.04	0.03	0.03	0.04
Total	7.63	8.22	8.85	9.45	9.86	10.58	11.30	12.15	13.05	13.93	10.50
Costs apportioned to gender equality in MDG sectors											
Education	9.45	9.51	12.29	10.69	10.67	11.05	11.21	11.58	11.83	12.32	11.06
Energy	6.88	7.17	7.49	7.76	8.02	8.31	8.55	8.81	9.18	9.03	8.12
Health	8.12	9.00	9.90	10.75	11.46	12.24	12.88	13.47	13.90	14.21	11.59
Rural development	0.76	0.86	0.99	1.16	1.37	1.69	2.08	2.64	3.33	4.33	1.92
Slum dwellers	0.70	0.75	0.80	0.85	0.91	0.98	1.05	1.13	1.21	1.30	0.97
Water and sanitation	3.06	3.15	3.26	3.37	3.50	3.68	3.86	4.20	5.40	12.59	4.61
Total	28.97	30.44	34.73	34.58	35.93	37.95	39.63	41.83	44.85	53.78	38.27
Total costs of achieving gender equality	38.24	40.49	45.50	46.08	48.03	51.06	53.93	57.75	63.01	74.99	51.91

Source: Authors' calculations.

FIGURE 5C.3

Ghana: Cost of Gender-Equality-Promoting Interventions as a Portion of Total Costs of Achieving the MDGs, 2006–15

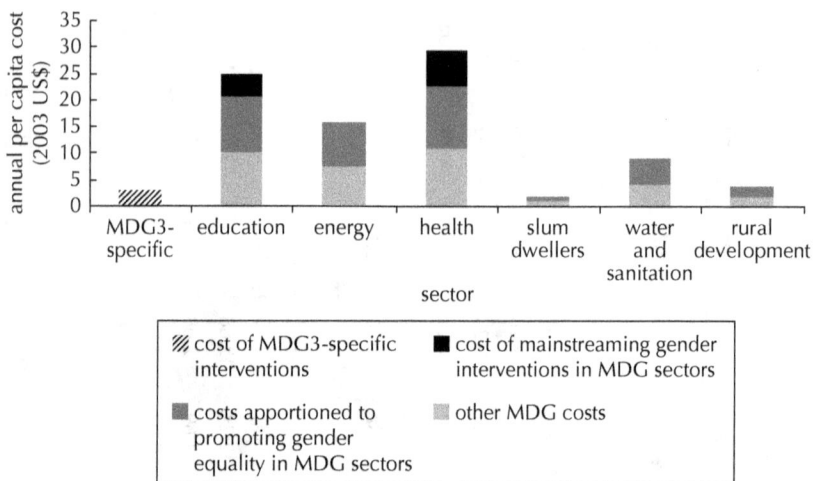

Source: Authors' calculations.

TABLE 5C.4

Tanzania: Per Capita Costs of Achieving Gender Equality (2003 $)

	2006	2007	2008	2009	2010	2011	2012	2013	2014	2015	Annual average
Costs of MDG3-specific interventions	1.55	1.73	1.81	1.96	2.21	2.64	3.40	4.76	7.24	11.65	3.90
Costs of mainstreaming gender intervention in MDG sectors											
Education	0.58	0.70	0.85	1.02	1.22	1.46	1.74	2.07	2.45	2.89	1.50
Energy	0.07	0.07	0.07	0.07	0.07	0.06	0.06	0.06	0.06	0.06	0.06
Health	6.56	6.75	6.93	7.11	7.13	7.29	7.44	7.58	7.72	7.68	7.22
Rural development	0.13	0.14	0.16	0.17	0.20	0.23	0.27	0.33	0.40	0.49	0.25
Slum dwellers	0.07	0.07	0.07	0.07	0.07	0.06	0.06	0.06	0.06	0.06	0.06
Water and sanitation	0.07	0.07	0.07	0.07	0.07	0.06	0.06	0.06	0.06	0.06	0.06
Total	7.48	7.80	8.15	8.51	8.76	9.16	9.63	10.16	10.75	11.24	9.15
Costs apportioned to gender equality in MDG sectors											
Education	5.33	5.55	5.79	6.08	6.39	6.71	6.98	7.34	7.70	8.18	6.61
Energy	10.16	10.56	10.94	11.31	11.65	11.98	12.26	12.52	12.76	12.78	11.69
Health	11.40	12.83	14.53	16.26	17.86	19.37	20.64	21.65	22.38	22.77	17.97
Rural development	0.80	0.91	1.07	1.24	1.49	1.77	2.18	2.65	3.32	4.20	1.96
Slum dwellers	1.08	1.16	1.24	1.33	1.43	1.53	1.64	1.76	1.89	2.03	1.51
Water and sanitation	2.76	2.89	3.05	3.24	3.47	3.73	4.13	4.71	5.62	7.16	4.07
Total	31.53	33.90	36.62	39.46	42.29	45.09	47.83	50.63	53.67	57.12	43.81
Total costs of achieving gender equality	40.56	43.43	46.58	49.93	53.26	56.89	60.86	65.55	71.66	80.01	56.86

Source: Authors' calculations.

FIGURE 5C.4

Tanzania: Cost of Gender-Equality-Promoting Interventions as a Portion of Total Costs of Achieving the MDGs, 2006–15

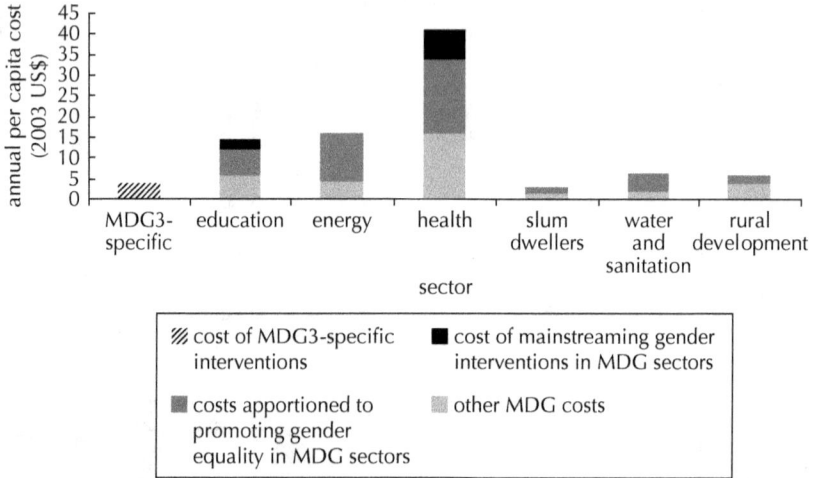

Source: Authors' calculations.

TABLE 5C.5
Uganda: Per Capita Costs of Achieving Gender Equality (2003 $)

	2006	2007	2008	2009	2010	2011	2012	2013	2014	2015	Annual average
Costs of MDG3-specific interventions	1.62	1.80	1.88	2.00	2.19	2.48	2.97	3.81	5.28	7.75	3.18
Costs of mainstreaming gender intervention in MDG sectors											
Education	0.74	0.90	1.09	1.30	1.54	1.82	2.14	2.52	2.95	3.44	1.84
Energy	0.05	0.05	0.05	0.05	0.05	0.05	0.04	0.04	0.04	0.04	0.05
Health	9.42	9.75	10.08	10.35	10.42	10.66	10.89	11.11	11.31	11.37	10.54
Rural development	0.08	0.09	0.10	0.11	0.13	0.15	0.19	0.25	0.33	0.46	0.19
Slum dwellers	0.05	0.05	0.05	0.05	0.05	0.05	0.04	0.04	0.04	0.04	0.05
Water and sanitation	0.05	0.05	0.05	0.05	0.05	0.05	0.04	0.04	0.04	0.04	0.05
Total	10.39	10.89	11.42	11.91	12.24	12.78	13.34	14.00	14.71	15.39	12.72
Costs apportioned to gender equality in MDG sectors											
Education	6.11	6.32	6.55	6.85	7.22	7.54	7.92	8.44	8.92	9.60	7.55
Energy	6.44	7.07	7.68	8.25	8.79	9.28	9.75	10.20	10.60	10.77	8.88
Health	9.94	10.79	11.83	12.89	13.87	14.86	15.79	16.65	17.39	18.00	14.20
Rural development	0.98	1.08	1.24	1.40	1.62	1.87	2.21	2.64	3.18	3.87	2.01
Slum dwellers	0.84	0.88	0.93	0.98	1.03	1.09	1.15	1.21	1.28	1.35	1.07
Water and sanitation	1.37	1.47	1.59	1.73	1.91	2.14	2.44	2.86	3.51	4.98	2.40
Total	25.68	27.61	29.82	32.10	34.44	36.78	39.26	42.00	44.88	48.57	36.11
Total costs of achieving gender equality	37.69	40.30	43.12	46.01	48.87	52.04	55.57	59.81	64.87	71.71	52.01

Source: Authors' calculations.

FIGURE 5C.5
Uganda: Cost of Gender-Equality-Promoting Interventions as a Portion of Total Costs of Achieving the MDGs, 2006–15

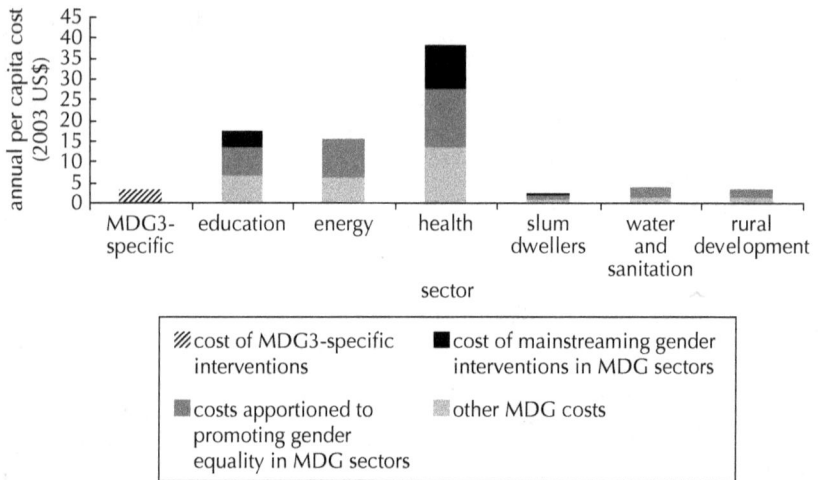

Source: Authors' calculations.

Notes

The authors gratefully acknowledge the assistance of Jessica Dixon and Emily Bosch in the preparation of this chapter. Thanks also are due to the following individuals for assistance with data collection: Kristin Haffert, National Democratic Institute; Alice Weimers, Guido Schmidt-Traub, Gonzalo Pizarro, Brian Lutz, and Joanna Rubinstein, UN Millennium Project; and Ky Tu Lam, Denyse Morin, and Helene Carlsson, World Bank. The authors appreciate the constructive suggestions of Shanta Devarajan, Eric Swanson, Andrew Morrison, Ian Gillson, and the members of the Gender Unit at the World Bank during a presentation of an initial draft of this paper in November 2005. Task Force 3 of the UN Millennium Project provided the intellectual framework for the gender analysis, and the UN Millennium Project Secretariat developed the analytical framework and the estimates of MDG costs used in this chapter.

1. Another reason for underfunding is that expenditures for gender equality are perceived to be additional to the core investment and achieve only a marginal return when, in fact, they are essential for maximizing the return on the core investment (UN Millennium Project 2005c).

2. Using data on GNP, share of GNP spent on education, and the share of primary education in public education, the study first computes initial public spending on primary education. Then it calculates the necessary increase in public spending to achieve universal primary education. The calculation takes into account the price elasticity of demand for education for girls and boys and the price cut needed to increase demand, and it factors in the estimated decline in private spending from reduced prices. Finally, it includes a 9 percent increase in program costs.

3. MDG sectors may cover the activities of various line ministries. For example, agriculture and rural development could include activities implemented by ministries of agriculture, water, energy and power, roads, sanitation, labor, science and research, and women's affairs. The objective of this classification is to streamline all of the actions that contribute to a specific MDG, recognizing that many of these activities overlap and can be reclassified in different ways.

4. Some MDG sectors, such as roads, science and technology, environment, and large-scale infrastructure, such as dams, are not included in the analysis in this chapter because needs assessment numbers were not available or the allocation is particularly difficult to undertake. Moreover, many sector interventions are not aimed at any particular population or address multiple goals simultaneously (often through integrated interventions), so it is difficult to isolate accurately the gender component of their cost.

5. For a listing of MDG targets, see UN Millennium Project (2005a).

6. This chapter only estimates these costs in the ministries of education, health, rural development, water and sanitation, energy, and housing. Given the current lack of information on specific costs (for example, gender training for ministry staff, data collection and research, support services, and so forth) the mainstreaming costs are likely to be an underestimate.

7. Glick, Saha, and Younger (2004, iv) state that "Household access to publicly provided water supply is not the appropriate indicator to capture gender

specific impacts. These impacts come in the form of time savings. For a descriptive benefit incidence analysis, one can make the assumption that the benefit is the reduction in the individual's time spent in water collection made possible by the service."

8. Annex 5B explains the assumptions used in the costing analysis.

9. Overall costs are estimated to grow exponentially, based on the assumption that countries will scale up more slowly in initial years. This assumption takes account of current trends in revenue generation in these countries between 2006 and 2009. In future exercises to estimate gender-equality costs at the country level, scale-up functions will differ by interventions, based on sector-specific constraints to scaling up.

10. We stress that the general sectoral interventions will only promote gender equality to the extent that they are complemented by the gender-mainstreaming and MDG3-specific interventions.

11. Although it was not included in the UN Millennium Project financing analysis, we analyzed the impact of funding for rural development on gender equality because it is such an important sector for women farmers, the majority of whom are poor.

12. Appendix 3 of UN Millennium Project (2005a) explains how aggregate MDG investment needs across low-income countries were calculated. The project first calculated the unadjusted investment need in each country and then adjusted those estimates for the relative price level in each country.

13. We follow the World Bank World Development Indicators classification of low income for grouping countries.

14. Based on the average, weighted by population, of government final consumption expenditure as a percentage of GDP in low-income countries in 2003 (World Bank 2005b).

15. A recent analysis by the OECD-DAC (2005) of the percentage of foreign assistance that promotes gender equality shows that between 1999 and 2003, donors gave approximately 18 percent (or $3.1 billion) of total foreign assistance to programs and projects that had gender equality as a principal or significant purpose. (Principal refers to projects that would not have been undertaken without a gender-equality objective; significant means that gender equality is an important but secondary objective of the activity). However, these numbers cannot be strictly compared with the analysis in this chapter because we do not have information on the external financing gap. However, the OECD-DAC data are the only available data on donor support for gender-equality programs relative to total foreign assistance.

16. To rectify the historic underfunding of gender-equality interventions, and to increase the probability of success, we believe that funds should be front-loaded. We therefore use the annual average of the financing gap estimates of scenario 3 for our recommendation.

17. Incremental refers to current year minus past year.

18. Capital costs are accounted for in the year in which the students use the new facilities. For simplicity, we assume that unit costs are the same for girls and for boys. Although there may be an argument for differential unit costs, this

methodology takes into account the main differences by identifying the specific interventions needed to reach females. We therefore assume that all other nontargeted interventions have the same unit costs.

19. This methodology does not apply to maternal health interventions.
20. This assumption may need to be modified in countries where male food consumption is greater than female food consumption.
21. This assumption may need to be modified in future work if sex-disaggregated utilization data can be located.
22. We make the simplifying assumption that this ratio does not change over time, although in future work this could be modified.
23. Sanitation is an exception. We treat sanitation like health systems, apportioning half of the cost of sanitation requirements to gender equality.

References and Other Resources

AfDB (African Development Bank). 2002. "Achieving the Millennium Development Goals in Africa: Progress, Prospect, and Policy Implications." AfDB, Abidjan.

AGI/UNFPA (Alan Guttmacher Institute/UN Population Fund). 2004. "Adding It Up: The Benefits of Investing in Sexual and Reproductive Health Care." AGI/UNFPA, New York.

ASEAN Secretariat (Association of South East Asian Nations Secretariat). 2006. "Compendium of Information on Selected ASEAN Civil Service Exams." Association of Southeast Asian Nations, Jakarta.

Bruns, B., A. Mingat, and R. Rakotomalala. 2003. "Achieving Universal Primary Education by 2015: A Chance for Every Child." World Bank, Washington, DC.

Budlender, D., D. Elson, G. Hewitt, and T. Mukhopadhyay, eds. 2002. *Gender Budgets Make Cents: Understanding Gender Responsive Budgets.* London: Commonwealth Secretariat.

Council for Administrative Reform (CAR). 2003. "The Remuneration System of Cambodian Civil Service." Royal Government of Cambodia, Phnom Penh.

Elson, D. 2006. *Budgeting for Women's Rights: Monitoring Government Budgets for Compliance with CEDAW.* New York: Kumarian.

Delamonica, E., S. Mehrotra, and J. Vandemoortele. 2001. "Is EFA Affordable? Estimating the Global Minimum Cost of 'Education for All.' " Innocenti Working Paper No. 87, UNICEF, Innocenti Research Center, Florence.

Devarajan, S., M. J. Miller, and E. V. Swanson. 2002. "Goals for Development: History, Prospects, and Costs." Policy Research Working Paper No. 2819, World Bank, Washington, DC.

Glick, P., R. Saha, and S. Younger. 2004. "Integrating Gender into Benefit Incidence and Demand Analysis." Report, Cornell University, Food and Nutrition Policy Program, Ithaca, NY.

GWP (Global Water Partnership). 2000. "Towards Water Security: A Framework for Action." Paper prepared for the Second World Water Forum, The Hague, March 17–22.

Haddad, L., J. Hoddinott, and H. Alderman. 1997. *Intrahousehold Resource Allocation in Developing Countries: Methods, Models, and Policy.* Baltimore: Johns Hopkins University Press.

Mbelle, A. 2003. "The Cost of Achieving Millennium Development Goals and Evaluation of Their Financing: Tanzania's Experience." Presentation at the Forum on the Millennium Development Goals (MDGs), Dakar, Senegal, February 26–28.

Mukhopadhyay, M., and C. Pieri. 1999. "Integration of Women in Sustainable Land and Crop Management in Sub-Saharan Africa." World Bank, Washington, DC.

National Democratic Institute (NDI). 2005a. "Estimated Training Costs for NDI Women's Programming in Mali." NDI, Washington, DC.

——. 2005b. "Estimated Training Costs for NDI Women's Programming in Morocco." NDI, Washington, DC.

——. 2005c. "Programming for Women by Donor: Independent Grants for Women's Program." NDI, Washington, DC.

OECD-DAC. 2005. *Creditor Reporting System on Aid Activities: Aid Activities in Support of Gender Equality 1999–2003 Volume 2005 Issue 6.* Paris: OECD-DAC.

Quisumbing, A. 1995. "Gender Differences in Agricultural Productivity." Discussion Paper No. 5, IFPRI, Food Consumption and Nutrition Division, Washington, DC.

Quisumbing, A. R., and J. Maluccio. 2000. "Intrahousehold Allocation and Gender Relations: New Empirical Evidence from Four Developing Countries." FCND Discussion Paper No. 84, IFPRI, Washington, DC.

Saito, K., and D. Spurling. 1992. "Developing Agricultural Extension for Women Farmers." Discussion Paper No. 156, World Bank, Washington, DC.

Seguino, S. 2002. "Gender, Quality of Life, and Growth in Asia 1970–1990." *Pacific Review* 15 (2): 245–77.

Seguino, S., and C. Grown. 2003. "Feminist-Kaleckian Macroeconomic Policy for Developing Countries." University of Vermont, Brattleboro, and the ICRW, Washington, DC.

UNIFEM (United Nations Development Fund for Women). 2002. *Gender Budget Initiatives: Strategies, Concepts and Experiences. Papers from a High Level International Conference "Strengthening Economic and Financial Governance through Gender Responsive Budgeting."* Hosted by the government of Belgium to launch A Global Vision to Strengthen Economic and Financial Governance, Brussels, October 16–18.

United Nations. 2004. "United Republic of Tanzania: Public Administration Country Profile." Department of Economic and Social Affairs, United Nations, New York, NY.

United Nations and World Bank. 2003. "Joint Needs Assessment for Iraq." United Nations and World Bank, Washington, DC.

——. 2004. "Joint Needs Assessment for National Transitional Government of Liberia." United Nations and World Bank, Washington, DC.

UN Millennium Project. 2004. "Millennium Development Goals Needs Assessments for Ghana, Tanzania, and Uganda." Background paper, UN Millennium Project, New York.

————. 2005a. *Investing in Development: A Practical Plan to Achieve the Millennium Development Goals.* Report to the UN Secretary General. London and Virginia: UNDP, Earthscan.

————. 2005b. "Preparing National Strategies to Achieve the Millennium Development Goals: A Handbook." UNDP, Washington, DC.

————. 2005c. *Taking Action: Achieving Gender Equality and Empowering Women.* Report prepared by the Taskforce on Education and Gender Equality. London and Virginia: UNDP, Earthscan.

Vlassoff, M., and S. Bernstein. 2006. "Resource Requirements for a Basic Package of Sexual and Reproductive Health Care and Population Data in Developing Countries: ICPD Costing Revisited." Background Paper for the UN Millennium Project, United Nations, New York.

World Bank. 2001. *Engendering Development through Gender Equality in Rights, Resources and Voice.* Policy Research Report. New York: Oxford University Press.

————. 2003. *World Development Report 2004: Making Services Work for Poor People.* Washington, DC: World Bank.

————. 2005a. "Public Sector Compensation and Employment Issues (Bangladesh)." World Bank Washington, DC.

————. 2005b. *World Development Indicators.* World Bank: Washington, DC.

World Bank and the Asian Development Bank. 2003. "Cambodia: Enhancing Service Delivery Through Improved Resource Allocation and Institutional Reform, Integrated Fiduciary Assessment and Public Expenditure Review." World Bank, Washington, DC.

6

What Money Can't Buy: Getting Implementation Right for MDG3 in South Asia

Maitreyi Bordia Das

The preceding chapter estimated the financial requirements for achieving the third Millennium Development Goal (MDG3). Adequate funding is necessary but not sufficient: policies must also be appropriate, and execution of these policies must be reasonably efficient. This chapter argues that inordinate focus on financing can detract from urgent institutional and policy reform issues. One key argument is that, while financing is important, institutional and implementation-related impediments constitute the real constraints to achieving MDG3 in South Asia and perhaps other low-income countries as well. Often, institutional change does not require large amounts of funding, but rather, strong commitment to implementation and monitoring based on political will.

The issue of financing is at best complex and at worst confounding. This chapter documents the fact that financing can have some rather unexpected correlates and impacts. In particular, the chapter has three main points:

- Funds allocated toward achieving MDG3 frequently remain unspent because of low capacity of implementation agencies and poor attention to bottlenecks.
- There are serious inefficiencies in expenditures and allocations related to mistargeting, corruption, and lack of monitoring, among other factors.
- Outcomes can vary considerably, and good outcomes do not necessarily result in countries with a high level of financing and vice versa. There are cases, as in Nepal most recently, where health and education outcomes have improved despite low and unchanged expenditures.

The chapter also points out that the level of economic development seems to have little relationship to progress in gender equality. Economies with low growth and low per capita income, such as the state of Kerala in

261

India, and Sri Lanka, succeeded in reducing infant mortality, furthering education for all, and charting the course of rapid fertility decline. This did not happen in other countries. The issue of policy reform, to start with, is difficult because of issues of design and political will, but even when good policies are in place, poor implementation can thwart positive impacts.

The major theme underpinning this chapter is that accountability to citizens and to women in particular is missing from the discourse on MDG3 and in countries where outcomes are poorest. The chapter suggests that such lack of accountability to women and to gender issues, accompanied by women's poor voice in decision-making processes, is at the core of the poor implementation of MDG3. The key pathways to change are to enhance women's voice through such measures as enforcement of property rights, physical security of women, and incentives that will change norms and behavior.

One of the greatest impediments to assessing the impact of public spending and, hence, of financing MDG3, is the fact that literature on the differential impact of financing, or indeed, of weak implementation, on males and females is not easy to find. Conversely, recent public expenditure reviews and other studies on the impact of spending on outcomes have measured the differential impacts of public spending on the poor and nonpoor. An unusual benefit incidence analysis of public expenditures conducted for the Pakistan Gender Assessment showed that the marginal impact of an increase in total expenditures was higher for boys' enrollment than for girls', indicating that boys tend to benefit more from public expenditure on education than girls at both the primary and secondary levels (World Bank 2003).

Conversely, it is difficult to say whether additional allocations in these sectors would positively affect women unless specific efforts are made at targeting and key demand-side issues are taken into account. For the most part, all the countries in question have policies that expressly address the needs of women and girls, at least on paper. Education enrollment, for instance, specifically addresses the problem of lower enrollment among girls, and health policies also take into account the culture of discrimination that leaves girls behind in access to basic health care. But as this chapter will show later, even allocations that are made remain unspent, and neither allocations nor the policy focus on women and girls in the health and education sectors have led to much progress (except in Bangladesh recently). What will change the focus away from the rhetoric contained in policy documents and the attendant allocations made in these sectors and toward implementation and innovations in enhancing demand where it is currently low? This chapter discusses some of the pathways to change.

The Human Development MDGs

This section is based on the argument that meeting MDG3 in health and education is a subset of general outcomes in these sectors. When health and educational systems perform badly, both females and males are affected. For the most part, the poorest women and girls tend to bear the disproportionate burden of poor public services because of their different needs and abilities to access systems. Therefore, reform of dysfunctional and inefficient education and health systems will positively affect all populations, and within them, women and girls.

Health

The MDGs use issues of child and maternal mortality as key indicators of gender equality in health, but in most countries in South Asia, primary health care is seriously constrained for everyone, especially for rural populations and those from the poorest families. Within these constraints, women tend to fare worse because of their special needs during their reproductive years and their differential ability to access services. This section shows that while public health expenditures in the region are low as a proportion of GDP, even the allocated funds are poorly used and outcomes vary substantially across the region, often showing no connection with allocations or expenditures.

Health expenditures per capita vary across the region. India, with historically large public health programs that address everything from immunization and communicable diseases to reproductive and child health, spends about $27 on health per capita per year, while Bangladesh, Nepal, and Pakistan each spend less than half that—between $12 and $13 (table 6.1). However, most of these expenditures are private; public health expenditures count for no more than 1 percent of GDP in any of these countries. Bangladesh has the highest share of public expenditures as a proportion of total health expenditures.

There are Large-scale Inefficiencies in Health Spending

Filmer and Pritchett (1997) found that cross-national higher public spending on health as a share of GDP was only tenuously related to improved child health status. The observed efficacy of public spending was several orders of magnitude lower than the apparent potential. This lack of efficacy was seen to be linked to three possible reform options—increasing the cost effectiveness of public spending, increasing the net impact of additional public supply, and enhancing public sector efficacy—none of them easy and

TABLE 6.1
South Asia: Expenditures on Health, 2003

Country	Health expenditure per capita (current $)	Health expenditure, total (% of GDP)	Health expenditure, public (% of GDP)	Health expenditure, public (% of total health expenditure)
Bangladesh	13	3	1	28
India	27	5	1	17
Nepal	13	6	1	24
Pakistan	12	2	0	18

Source: World Bank Development Indicators Database 2007.

each politically intractable. However, only countries that have taken a tough stand on these issues have succeeded in lowering their mortality levels. Other public expenditure reviews across the region show similar inefficiencies, especially with regard to the mistargeting of subsidies and benefits of the public health system flowing to the nonpoor rather than the poor. Thus, Mahal et al. (2001) show that while in general public health care is skewed toward the rich in India, some states do manage to make their spending more pro-poor, pointing again to the importance of institutional change and policy focus. This chapter draws on these studies as examples of analyses that show the inefficiency of public health spending but, unfortunately, have little information on the impact of spending by gender.

While public health expenditures are low, institutions do not seem to absorb these limited public sector allocations and money often remains unspent. "Surrender" of funds—a commonly used administrative term—by districts to subnational treasuries toward the end of fiscal years is common in India. In particular, funds earmarked for the "soft" side of health, for instance, capacity-building initiatives, awareness drives, and demand creation initiatives, such as setting up mothers' groups, are poorly used. In some areas even allocations made for buildings and hardware are not spent.

These low levels of utilization are not just true of India. In most of the years in the period 1999–2004, Nepal spent only about three-fourths of its allocations in health. Table 6.2 shows that the relatively high expenditure of more than 86 percent during 2003–04 was driven largely by high "regular" expenditure, which is a term used for salaries and other recurrent costs. "Development" expenditures (which indicates investments other

TABLE 6.2
Nepal: Proportion of Health Allocations by Expenditure Category

Fiscal year	Regular expenditure as a proportion of allocation (primarily salaries and other recurrent costs) %	Development expenditure as a proportion of allocation (including donor funds) %	Spending as a proportion of total allocations (regular + development) %
1999–2000	85.79	72.32	77.18
2000–01	93.10	65.40	75.48
2001–02	88.86	66.48	76.16
2002–03	94.18	57.79	74.00
2003–04	97.40	62.38	86.45

Source: HMGN, Ministry of Health 2004.

than salaries and overhead) as a proportion of allocations are relatively smaller, at about 62 percent of allocations. In fact, the gap between regular and development expenditures as a proportion of allocation widened over the five-year period from 1999–2000 to 2003–04.

Low spending as a proportion of allocation results from a combination of poor program design, rigidity of spending norms, low public awareness that restrains demand for services, capacity constraints of implementation agencies, and low levels of accountability of service providers. Indian states with the poorest health indicators also have the weakest institutional capacity and are unable to spend the allocated funds.

A recent performance audit of a sample of 12 districts in Uttar Pradesh by the highest office of the Comptroller and Auditor General of India (CAG) found that only 64 to 78 percent of the funds allocated for the Reproductive and Child Health Program had been used during 2000–05. In absolute terms, the unspent balance actually increased in the five-year period under review. The report also identifies a number of institutional and implementation constraints that led to the poor use of funds (CAG 2006). Similar reports from the Planning Commission indicate that funds in the lowest performing states remain unspent despite hefty allocations in recent years. Corruption is another major issue in all sectors and this, too, becomes a particular problem in areas with the weakest governance and transparency levels and where state and service-provider accountability are poor.

Outcomes Vary Considerably, Seemingly Having Little Connection with Allocations or Expenditures

Although India spends twice as much per capita as Bangladesh on health care, it has worse outcomes in every health indicator except maternal mortality. Infant mortality rates range from 61 per 1,000 in Bangladesh to 75 per 1,000 in Pakistan. The decline in infant mortality in Bangladesh has been more dramatic than in any of the other countries. Both Nepal and Bangladesh had high infant mortality rates in the 1950s but have brought their infant mortality rates equal to (Nepal) or below (Bangladesh) those of India (table 6.3). Gender differences in infant mortality are similarly uneven. Bangladesh's infant mortality rate for girls is now lower than that for boys, while India continues to have higher mortality for infant girls. Sex ratios in India are declining, favoring boys, while Bangladesh is close to reaching parity in sex ratios. Pakistan has fared most poorly in bringing down its infant mortality rate for both boys and girls.

Immunization rates are similarly puzzling. On the one hand, despite large donor and nationally funded programs for immunization, Indian immunization rates are the lowest in the region and in some states, seem to actually be declining as the Reproductive and Child Health Surveys show (Government of India 2005). On the other hand, Nepal enhanced its immunization coverage despite the Maoist insurgency in the early years of the present millennium. This led to an immunization-driven decline in infant mortality in Nepal. Bangladesh lowered early childhood mortality from vaccine-preventable diseases through the dogged implementation of its national immunization program. These facts point to the salience of factors other than financing.

TABLE 6.3
Pace of Decline in Infant Mortality over Half a Century

	Male		Female	
	1950–55	*2000–05*	*1950–55*	*2000–05*
Bangladesh	199.6	63.0	201.4	59.5
India	166.1	60.9	165.2	64.2
Nepal	211.7	64.5	210.0	64.4
Pakistan	168.1	73.4	169.1	77.5

Source: United Nations 2007.

Note: Infant deaths per 1,000 live births based on medium variant 1950–2005.

Often Even Well-Intended and Well-Funded Interventions Do Not Work

One intervention, India's Reproductive and Child Health (RCH) Program, serves as an instructive example. The objective of this large national program was to enhance reproductive and child health. The program has been a challenge to implement and maternal mortality remains stubbornly high. Phase I of the program identified the lack of money for transportation as one of the bottlenecks to getting pregnant women to health facilities. The program's response was to set aside money for transportation to be administered by the *panchayat,* the local government with the *sarpanch* at its head. However, when the program was reviewed, evaluators found that most of this money was left untouched partly because the *panchayat* did not know that the funds should be used for this purpose. Moreover, getting pregnant women to hospitals or centers for safe delivery is not a community priority, so the head of the local government never considered spending the money to be a priority, either. Absenteeism among medical personnel is so common that the auxiliary nurse midwife often does not live in the village and, hence, is not available to coordinate the transportation of a pregnant woman to a health center for delivery.

Even when money is available and accessible, frequently no transportation is available to take a woman to the health center. In still other cases the health center is so far and road conditions so difficult that women make local arrangements for birthing, however unsatisfactory these are. Even in the few cases where both the allowance and the transportation are available, there is no guarantee that a doctor would be available at the health center (see figure 6.1).

Setting aside money for transportation was a laudable intervention, but it just did not work well. This example serves to illustrate how well-intended and well-funded interventions are not implemented because of either lack of flexibility and information, or poor demand for and supply of services. The next phase of the program (RCH II) tried to address some of these difficulties by creating greater flexibility and increasing awareness. However, the program is still struggling in many states with low institutional capacity and poor implementation and monitoring systems. A recent audit of RCH II in Uttar Pradesh found that none of the money released for this referral transport was accounted for through "utilization certificates," thus stymieing the release of the next tranche (CAG 2006). The CAG's report also highlights the importance of human resources management and the availability of medical personnel in remote areas.

FIGURE 6.1
India: Doctor Absence at Public Health Facilities by State and Reason, 2003

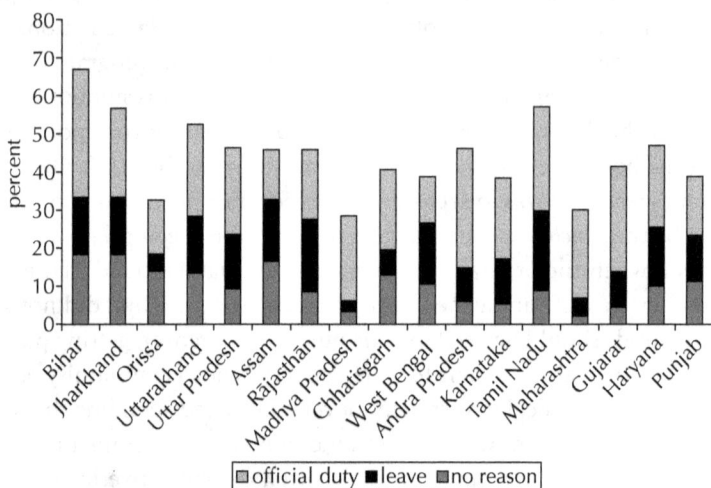

Source: Hammer, Samji, and Aiyar 2006.

Education

As with health, the relationship between spending and outcomes in education does not yield the expected results. Annex table 6A.1 shows that a country's income level has little bearing on girls' education outcomes. Also, table 6.4 shows that even spending on education overall does not seem to matter much. Per capita spending on education in Bangladesh is much lower than that in India, or even in Nepal for primary education, but progression to secondary school for girls in Bangladesh is much higher. Bangladesh also spends a lower proportion of its GDP on education than India. Income level similarly has little correlation with girls' schooling. Compared with other low-income countries, Bangladesh stands out as a success story in female secondary education, along with some ex-socialist countries and Vietnam. In Bangladesh, moreover, targeted expenditures to girls have succeeded in improving outcomes at the secondary level. Therefore, quality of spending as well as design of programs is important, in addition to implementation.

Bangladesh, Sri Lanka, and Kerala state in India demonstrate what policy and its tenacious implementation could do for girls' education. Though not as dramatic as Bangladesh, Nepal shows that despite the Maoist insurgency

TABLE 6.4
South Asia: Select Education Expenditures and Outcomes, 2003

	Public spending on education, total (% of GDP)	Public spending on education, total (% of government expenditure)	Expenditure per student, primary (% of GDP per capita)	Expenditure per student, secondary (% of GDP per capita)	Progression to secondary school, female (%)	Progression to secondary school, male (%)
Bangladesh	2	15	8	13	92	86
India	4	11	11	20	82	87
Nepal	3	15	12	10	74	79
Pakistan	2	9	6	11	74	74

Source: World Bank Development Indicators Database 2007.

and continuing low expenditures in education, it is rapidly catching up with India in girls' secondary school enrollment. Both supply and demand for girls' schooling rose dramatically in the late 1990s and early 2000s. In India, learning outcomes are improving very slowly despite higher expenditures and larger education programs. Improvements in education outcomes have been stymied by serious implementation constraints and imperfect setting of priorities. For instance, governments tend to be preoccupied with enrollment targets without addressing quality of education and dropout rates. Teacher absenteeism, poor teaching quality, and lack of accountability are other issues that are not addressed that lead to poor outcomes.

Figure 6.2 is based on a nationwide survey using unannounced visits to schools in India, and indicates that fewer than half of teachers were both present and engaged in classroom activities at the time of the visit. Another recent analysis for India found that the correlation between public spending on elementary education and enrollment rates was not strong. However, when efficiency and demand-side factors were controlled for, public spending was positively correlated with enrollment and with quality of education as measured by teacher-pupil ratio (Pradhan and Singh 2000). Fixing control factors, such as efficiency, and enhancing demand for services are at the heart of institutional reform and building trust between providers and their clients.

FIGURE 6.2
India: Teacher Engagement by State

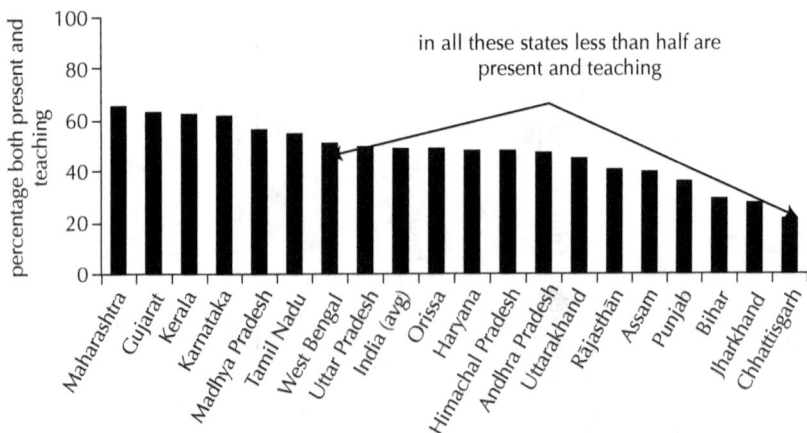

Source: World Bank (2006) based on Kremer et al. (2005).

Some groups and areas are more disadvantaged than others and face the brunt of a poorly functioning public education system. Overall enrollment rates in India are driven down by extremely low educational enrollment for girls from the Scheduled Castes and, more so, the Scheduled Tribes. In Orissa, one of India's poorest states, the overall literacy rate (denoted by ability to write one's name) in the 2001 census was 63 percent, but for Scheduled Tribes it was 37.3 percent. This was an increase from 22.3 percent in 1991, but it is scant comfort that even today the literacy rate for Scheduled Tribe women is only slightly higher than 23 percent (for men it is 51.5 percent); fewer than 10 percent of working age women from the Scheduled Tribes have postprimary education according to estimates based on the National Sample Survey 2004–05 (Das 2006b). Central government allocations to Orissa are high and special programs for Scheduled Tribes exist, funded by both the state and central governments.

The greatest institutional constraints are also in states like Orissa, which find it very difficult to implement policy. Allotted positions remain vacant for years because health and education professionals are even less willing to live in tribal areas where social infrastructure, such as roads, transport, and schools for the children are unavailable. Higher levels of government also find it difficult to monitor these areas for similar reasons. Perhaps at the heart of the problem is the fact that the tribal areas do not have the same priority as coastal areas, home to the majority of the political elite who exercise the greatest voice over political and administrative decision makers. Tribal disempowerment is not merely a result of low levels of infrastructure and services but also the ambivalent rights over the forests in which the tribes live. This situation is not peculiar to Orissa—most of India's tribal populations living in so-called Scheduled Areas have identical issues. As figure 6.3 shows, tribal women in Orissa fare the worst in educational outcomes. This is also true of their health and livelihood outcomes.

In many areas cultural practices combined with structural impediments constitute real barriers to progress. The Pakistan Gender Assessment points out that the practice of restricted female mobility plays a large role in perpetuating gender gaps in school enrollment (World Bank 2005). In Pakistan, school attendance for girls is very sensitive to school proximity, and girls are much less likely to attend school if one is not available within the settlement. This sensitivity to school proximity worsens as girls grow into adolescence. Qualitative studies suggest that concerns over safety and norms of female seclusion are the primary factors behind the precipitous drop in enrollment beyond age 12. This concern is also evident in the rising expenditure on transportation to school reported for older girls.

FIGURE 6.3

Orissa: Change in Postprimary Education by Caste and Gender, 1983–2004/05

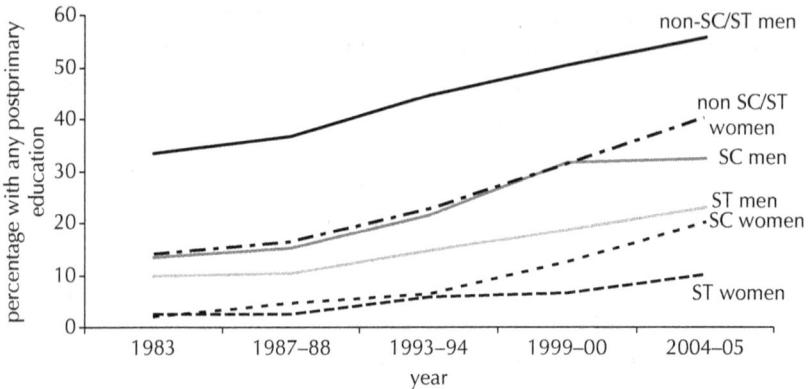

Source: Author's calculation based on National Sample Survey for working-age population.

Note: SC = Scheduled Caste; ST = Scheduled Tribe.

Decreasing the physical cost of attending school for girls is thus likely to pay big dividends. How can this be achieved? Because large parts of rural Pakistan are underserved or lack schools for girls, school construction will continue to be important. Where feasible, construction of schools is likely to face another important constraint: there simply are not enough educated women in many Pakistani (or Afghani) villages to staff schools for girls. Government schools and most private schools for girls require female teachers, but insecurity and significant barriers to female mobility prevent educated women from relocating or commuting to areas with teaching jobs. Hiring and retaining female teachers will continue to be a problem, and this problem will be worse in precisely those areas that are poorly served at present (World Bank 2005).

Bangladesh shows that with national vision, the right policy mix, dogged imple-mentation, and high demand, outcomes can change dramatically. Bangladesh's success in female secondary school enrollment is especially commendable because this growth took place within a democratic regime and started from a low base. A clearly articulated national vision for girls' education, and implementation of deliberate policy, propelled Bangladesh's success. In the 1980s, primary school enrollment rose rapidly after the introduction of a food-for-education program for poor children. Following the introduction of a national scholarship program for secondary schools in 1994, female enrollment exceeded male enrollment in rural areas, and urban-rural differences in girls' education diminished and even reversed. Nongovernmental organizations (NGOs) have also played a large part in improving access to education. For instance, the Bangladesh Rural Advancement Committee initiated a nonformal education program that grew to 35,000 schools covering material for the first three years of primary school. However, there is still work to be done, as indicated in box 6.1.

Institutions have an important role in education and health outcomes. Areas in South Asia with strong implementation mechanisms, discretion at the local level to spend money according to need, strong civil society movements, and efficient administrations have fared the best in education and health outcomes. While Bangladesh, Kerala state in India, and Sri Lanka are the best known cases, others include the states of Tamil Nadu, Karnataka, and Maharashtra. Conversely, poorly administered areas with a high degree of social fragmentation, weak movements to demand accountability, opaque state systems, and poor implementation machinery have fared the worst. Mahal et al. (2001) showed that although the majority of Indian states indicate little difference in the share of inpatient bed days between men and women, this was not the case in Bihar, the North East states,

---

Box 6.1
Bangladesh through the Eyes of Youth: Improving Educational Outcomes Further

---

While Bangladesh is a success story in girls' education, challenges relating to boys' enrollment, urban enrollment, education for the poorest children, and overall quality of education remain. The World Bank study "Whispers to Voices" conducted detailed focus group discussions in 2006 with adolescent boys and girls to identify gaps in the education system. Almost every focus group lamented the quality of their teachers. Young women, particularly those still in school and aspiring to higher education, outlined the need for gender-segregated facilities. For instance, schoolgirls in Satkhira said, "There is no college in our area—we want a college to be established here." In Sunamgonj, an area known for its conservatism and yet with very high demand for education among adolescent girls, schoolgirls aspiring to higher education said, "We would like a separate library for girls and more girls' hostels." If appropriate facilities and opportunities are provided, the gap between girls and boys at the higher secondary and college levels can be bridged.

Source: World Bank 2008.

and Uttar Pradesh. In Bihar, for example, the share of men and women below the poverty line is similar (53 percent of women and 52 percent of men), but a smaller share of inpatient bed days was used by poor women (12 percent compared to the 20 percent used by men). All of these states have weak institutions to hold the state accountable and poor implementation of several development programs.

Some ethnic groups seem to fare worse. Women are a heterogeneous category and those belonging to minority ethnic groups and living in remote areas fare worse than men and other women. Figure 6.3 shows the change in secondary school education over time in Orissa for different groups of men and women. A clear hierarchy of who benefits seems to emerge with upper caste (or non-Scheduled Caste and non-Scheduled Tribe) men at the top, followed by upper caste (non-Scheduled Caste and non-Schedule Tribe) women, and then Scheduled Caste men. Scheduled Tribe women are the bottom of the heap in access to education and this pattern is replicated in access to health.

Similarly, in Nepal, access to and use of a range of health and family planning services for rural women is lowest among the Dalit (lowest caste) and Tarai Middle Caste women. Knowledge levels of Dalit women are also very low compared with the dominant caste Newar, Brahman, and Chhetri and also the Hill Janajati. Contraceptive use among married rural women is lowest for Dalits and Muslims (World Bank and DFID 2006).

Employment and Labor Force Participation

While one of the MDG3 indicators is the share of women in wage employment in the nonagricultural sector, the fact is that nonfarm wage employment is a very small proportion of all employment in many countries, whether for men or for women. In India, for instance, only 15 percent of women and 42 percent of men were in any type of wage work in the late 1990s; of this, the major part was casual agricultural work. In Bangladesh, only 10 percent of employed women and 22 percent of men ages 20–55 received any cash wages in 2003/2004[1] (Das 2006a; World Bank 2008). Most low-income countries are predominantly agricultural and enhancing nonfarm employment is a development goal in itself, so to speak about women's participation in this arena as a marker of gender inequality seems unrealistic and detracts from issues as such barriers to entry into the labor force, unequal wages, and work conditions.

Nevertheless, many countries set up large public employment or safety-net programs for the poor; these programs are typically public works programs in the nonagricultural sector. India's new National Employment Guarantee Scheme (NREGS), with its rights-based approach to livelihood and its avowed objective of "guaranteeing" women avenues for wage employment and "empowerment," is a very recent example, although it has precursors in earlier similar programs. However, despite its focus on enhancing the participation of women, the results are uneven across Indian states. Table 6.5 shows that whereas the uptake of the employment guarantee is high in Rājasthān, Assam, Madhya Pradesh, and the North Eastern states, women's participation in the program exceeds 50 percent only in Rājasthān. Only Tamil Nadu ranks higher than Rājasthān in women's participation, but the overall uptake of work through NREGS (table 6.5, column 1) is so low that the absolute impact of the program for women is limited.

Voice and public action can change outcomes. Why is the participation of women in NREGS in the top-performing states lower than in Rājasthān, a state otherwise known for its poor indicators of gender equality, its feudal culture, and restrictions on the mobility of women? States like Madhya Pradesh and Gujarat, where rural poverty and tribal populations are high—both factors that would pull women into the scheme—do not do as well as Rājasthān. It can be argued that Rājasthān's performance is a function of voice and public action. The state has had a long history of struggle against irregular payment of wages in public employment programs. In fact, the movement for equal wages for women workers has its origins in the Women's Development Program (WDP) in the 1980s. The WDP took up the issue of wages to women in public employment programs, where contractors would take thumb-impressions of uneducated women on receipts but pay them lower wages than were due (see Das [1992]). Subsequent movements and programs built upon the WDP's momentum. The Mazdoor Kisan Shakti Sangathan (MKSS), for example, is perhaps the most vocal and influential network today, and has taken it upon itself to ensure that the NREGS succeeds in Rājasthān. The MKSS voluntarily and tenaciously monitors the program, demanding government accountability. As a result of its efforts, public officials and government institutions in Rājasthān are much more responsive and alert to problems in NREGS.

In many cases women are "discouraged workers" because of hiring practices or wage discrimination. Oaxaca-Blinder decompositions conducted for wages of male and female casual workers in India and Bangladesh found that unobserved factors accounted for more than 70 percent of the difference in wages (Das 2006a; World Bank 2008). Of these unobserved factors, a large proportion is likely to be discrimination. In Nepal as well, both agricultural wages and unskilled nonagricultural wages for women are lower than for men.

TABLE 6.5
India: Performance of the National Rural Employment Guarantee Scheme, 2007

	Person-days of NREGS employment per rural household	Share of women in NREGS employment (%)
Rājasthān	77	67
Assam	70	32
Madhya Pradesh	56	43
North East	45	49
Chhattisgarh	34	40
Orissa	21	36
Himachal Pradesh	20	12
Uttarakhand	20	30
Karnataka	17	51
Jharkhand	14	28
Jammu and Kashmir	13	4
Uttar Pradesh	11	17
Andra Pradesh	10	55
Haryana	9	31
Tamil Nadu	9	81
Bihar	8	17
Gujarat	7	50
Punjab	7	38
West Bengal	6	18
Maharashtra	4	37
Kerala	3	66
INDIA	17	40

Source: Drèze and Oldiges 2007 Table 2.

Note: Unskilled labor only. North East states excludes Assam (approximate figures, based on incomplete data). All figures pertain to the districts where NREGA came into force on February 2, 2006. This table is based on figures up to and including February 2007.

Even if equal wages are mandated by law, enforcement is weak. A social audit conducted by an NGO working with the NREGS in a village in Orissa showed that women were actually paid a lower wage, despite equal wages being set for both men and women under the program. This was because the prevailing agricultural wages for men were higher than the wages set under NREGS and men refused to work on NREGS unless their wages were raised. Instead of allowing men to leave the program, their wages were raised and women ended up being paid wages lower than the mandated wage (AID Rural Technology Center 2007). However, when governments are serious about ensuring equal pay for equal work by putting in place enforcement mechanisms, it is worthwhile for women to enter the labor force, as happens in Organisation for Economic Co-operation and Development (OECD) countries.

The issue of wage employment for women with some skills and better human capital endowments is not in the policy discourse. South Asia ranks second only to Middle Eastern and North African countries in having the lowest women's labor force participation rates. Evidence from India and Pakistan shows that education lowers the probability of women participating in the labor force (Das and Desai 2003; Das 2006a; Sathar and Desai 2000) and that returns to education are low for women in India (Kingdon and Unni 1997). With increasing levels of education across South Asia, women with even low levels of education will not accept manual work and will stay out of the labor market if there is another earning household member (see Das 2006a). Both cultural and structural factors have been implicated in these patterns.

Increases in female labor force participation can result from policy changes, although this may not be the expressed policy goal. Most countries in the region have had policies in place to "protect" women and guard their "morality," and it is often difficult to overturn these policies unless the right opportunities appear. The Indian Shops and Establishments Act 1953 is one example, in that it prevented night work for women in a paternalistic bid to protect women and safeguard public morality. Amending the act so that the information technology (IT) industry was exempt from restrictive provisions regarding night work for women led to the large-scale entry of young educated women into this growing sector. Amendments enabled IT companies to employ women between 8 p.m. and 6 a.m., provided the companies make special arrangements for security, employ women in groups with a minimum of 10 female employees, ensure toilet and rest facilities, and have at least 50 employees in a given shift. Although the amendments to the act were prompted more by the need to tap into a larger supply of skilled labor for the burgeoning IT industry, it opened up that job market for women. While women employed in the IT sector represent a small proportion of all women workers, there is widespread recognition that the visibility of young women in the IT workforce is changing social mores about what is acceptable female employment. Thus, a small amendment can lead to a transformation of cultural norms that are perceived to be restrictive.

Growth in specific sectors resulted in a dramatic increase in female labor force participation rates in Bangladesh. Female labor force participation rates increased from 9 to 26 percent from the early 1990s to 2003 (World Bank [2008], based on Bangladesh Labor Force Survey). Two factors explain the increase in female labor force participation. The first is growth in the garment sector resulting from Bangladesh's advantage through the Multi-Fiber Trade Agreement. The second is growth in the teaching and health care sectors. These two factors meant that women entered the manufacturing and the social services sectors in larger numbers. West Bengal, similar to Bangladesh in cultural norms governing women's work and mobility, actually has lower female labor force participation rates than Bangladesh and this has changed little over time (World Bank [2008] based on Indian National Sample Survey 1999–2000).

Policies that control migration of women similarly show that policy can have unexpected consequences. In a bid to eliminate cross-border trafficking and exploitation of women, several countries have age restrictions and other safeguards in place that require women to produce documentation to show that they will be legitimately employed and their interests in the receiving country will be protected. However, migration policies that seek to protect women have been double-edged swords—responding to genuine threats, but also preventing women from responding to demand for female labor in other countries in the process. The Indian Emigration Act was amended to prevent women under age 30 from migrating as housemaids and caregivers. NGOs are concerned that this will lead to illegal and undocumented migration of younger women and prevent them from accessing any benefits they may be entitled to in the receiving country. Other countries also have age limits for women migrants, but whether this contributes to women's welfare or increases vulnerability is unclear (Manchanda 2007).

Cross-Cutting Issues and Ways Forward

The discussion in the previous section shows that institutional failures, and women's lack of voice and limited decision-making powers are at the heart of poor progress toward MDG3 in most countries in South Asia. This section will examine cross-cutting issues and focus on what is needed to advance the achievement of MDG3.

Women's Poor Voice and Lack of Decision-Making Power

The MDG indicator "proportion of women in national parliaments" is viewed as an indicator of women's voice in decision making. As noted in chapter 3, this indicator has several weaknesses. It ignores not only women's roles in local-level decision making, but also the fact that national parliaments have only limited power in seeing how polices are implemented. What appears to be more important in the achievement of the MDGs for gender equality is the fact that women lack voice and power at the local level to hold service providers and governments accountable. They are, moreover, not perceived as clients in their own right or decision makers for themselves, either in the public or the private domains. Central to the ability to exercise voice are issues of information, institutions, groups, and rules that place the onus on providers to be accountable to all, and to women in particular. Issues linked to accountability and decision-making power will be discussed in this section.

Many countries have reserved seats in local governments for women. Bangladesh, Pakistan, and India have reserved one-third of the seats in local governments for women. However, no comprehensive evaluation has been made of the impact this has had on women and women's issues, especially on the progress toward achieving MDG3. There are two levels at which such impacts are important. At the level of developing women's leadership, the demonstration effect of having more women in the public domain is instructive for society as a whole and can change perceptions about women's voice. At another level is the question of whether women's presence as decision makers changes outcomes for other women and for gender equality. So, do women take up issues that are important to women? The evidence is thin and it is mixed. Some studies find that women leaders tend to invest more in areas that are a priority for women (figure 6.4). For instance, women leaders in West Bengal are shown to invest more in water and road projects and less in nonformal education, while in Rājasthān women leaders invest more in water and less in roads (Duflo and Topalova 2004 and Bardhan et al. 2005 cited in Ban and Rao 2007). Others find that reservation of government seats for women does not increase accountability to women.

Microcredit groups also have huge empowerment potential. Women's ability to form successful groups is an indication of their voice. Women's solidarity groups have been shown to have a salutary effect on women's ability to seek and access services and markets. In South Asia the impact of microcredit groups on poverty reduction and employment generation is contested, but it is fairly well established that microcredit groups empower women in many different ways. In addition, the general welfare benefits to the household are undeniable (improved child nutrition, immunization coverage, and higher contraceptive use) and the individual benefits for poor women are widely acknowledged. These include a greater role in household

FIGURE 6.4
India: Elected Women Members in Local Governments Enhance Women's Voice

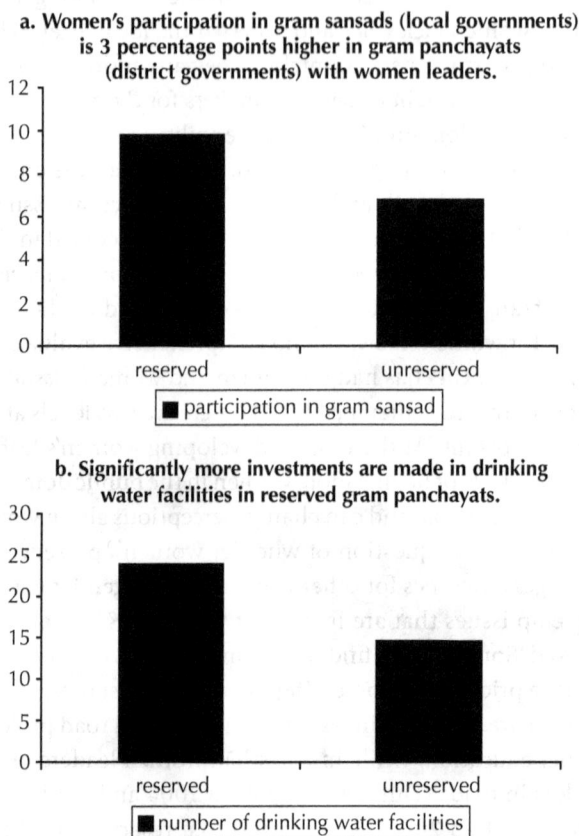

a. Women's participation in gram sansads (local governments) is 3 percentage points higher in gram panchayats (district governments) with women leaders.

■ participation in gram sansad

b. Significantly more investments are made in drinking water facilities in reserved gram panchayats.

■ number of drinking water facilities

Source: World Bank 2006 based on Chattopadhyaya and Duflo 2004.

Note: Reserved indicates those constituencies where the position of the head of the local government was reserved for women.

decision making, mobility, access to services, enhanced self-esteem, and greater public participation (World Bank 2008).

In Bangladesh, the delivery of microcredit through informal groups has helped to nurture a functional space in an institutional environment in which not only formal rules and regulations were very exclusionary for the poor but more specifically exclusionary for women (Rahman 2006). Thus, the informal microcredit group emerged as a separate space for poor women that allowed them to recognize their weaknesses and consolidate their own strengths, and provided the launching pad for women to enter the public space of entrepreneurship. Within this space they were able to learn the "rules of the game," how to handle household-based microenterprises while negotiating intrahousehold power dynamics, and to effectively operate larger group enterprises (land lease, water selling, and pond fishery, for example) within broader societal power dynamics (Rahman 2006; World Bank 2008).

A similar debate is under way in India with the massive number of self-help groups that were initially formed with state backing and that also draw on traditional women's groups, or *mahila mandals*. A recent study on moving out of poverty finds that the existence of women's self-help groups enhances the overall development performance of a village and the welfare of individual members. Perhaps what these groups succeed in doing most effectively is to provide collective voice for women's issues (Narayan, Prennushi, and Kapoor 2007). The role of these groups as an antialcohol lobby in Andhra Pradesh is legendary. These groups serve also as training grounds for women leaders. Newspaper reports have pointed to large numbers of women who belonged to self-help groups and contested the recent local elections in Bihar and won.

Policy and government programs, such as India's Development of Women and Children in Rural Areas (DWCRA) in the 1980s (which was the precursor of other policies that built upon it), as well as nongovernmental initiatives, such as Bangladesh's Grameen Bank, have aided the formation of these groups. DWCRA started as a component to a standard integrated rural development program but later received central bank backing. Public sector banks, which constituted in the late 1980s and early 1990s the majority of the banking sector, were mandated to lend a certain share to self-help groups. This was monitored most effectively by the National Bank for Agriculture and Rural Development. Simultaneously, state governments put in place their own programs to develop self-help groups.

Therefore, while many microcredit or savings and thrift groups may start out as state-sponsored and supply-driven groups, over time they appear to evolve into viable solidarity groups, provided some conditions exist (Sanyal 2007). However, there are also areas where such movements have not taken off; for instance, in remote tribal areas in India and Bangladesh these groups are either very weak or nonexistent. Other factors may impede their strength—in Bangladesh microcredit does not reach the poorest because women who access microcredit need some collateral.

Access to Assets and Property

That ownership of property, especially of land, matters greatly has long been recognized. This fact has been established empirically through a study of domestic violence in India that finds that ownership of land more than any other factor protects women against violence, thus enhancing their esteem and worth in the household and the community (Panda and Agarwal 2005). Ownership, of course, is not the same as control, but it is a starting point to enhance voice. Although formal property rights in South Asia do not exclude women and some legislation even emphasizes women's rights of inheritance, cultural pressures often force women to give up their inheritance.

Unfortunately, information on ownership of assets by women and men is not collected in regular surveys. Special surveys and tabulations from censuses show, however, that women tend not to be owners of assets. Less than one-fourth of women in Pakistan in a recent survey managed to inherit and retain their parental property (World Bank 2006). In Bangladesh, while the practice of giving up parental property is declining, approximately 25 percent of women who were eligible to inherit property gave it up, and less than 20 percent of older women (who have greater say in household decisions) had their names on rental agreements or title deeds. According to the Bangladesh agricultural census of 1996, out of 17.8 million agricultural holdings only 3.5 percent were female owned (World Bank 2008). In Nepal, according to the 2001 census, only 17 percent of households had at least one female member who owned land, housing, or livestock, and less than 1 percent of households reported female ownership of all three types of assets. Although 84 percent of all households in Nepal own land, just 11 percent of women do so, and whereas more than 90 percent of Nepali households own their home, just 6 percent of women do so (World Bank and DFID 2006).

Demand and Ability to Access Markets and Services

Related to women's voice and accountability of service providers, elected representatives, and government functionaries to women is the issue of whether women are able to access services and markets. Intrinsic to women's access to education, health, and labor markets is their ability to leave the home and seek these services and markets. Ability refers to both the absence of restrictions and the financial wherewithal to seek these opportunities. These have been written about at length, usually based on the questions from the Demographic and Health Surveys (DHS). While much is made of constraints on mobility, the DHS show that the main reason women did not seek antenatal care in Bangladesh was because they did not find it necessary to do so. Thus, demand for maternal health care is severely constrained even if the supply is good. But issues of demand and supply are too mutually intertwined to be easily separated. For example, maternal care facilities may be available, but if women do not like the quality of service, they would suppress demand for the service. Lack of awareness and information come through as key constraints to demand (see World Bank [2008] for Bangladesh).

Women's limited voice in the household and community restricts their access to services. Women's influence in household decision making is typically confined to aspects of household functioning (figure 6.5). In particular,

FIGURE 6.5

Bangladeshi and Pakistani Women Are Usually Consulted in Matters Related to the Home but Not Necessarily in Decisions about Their Own Lives

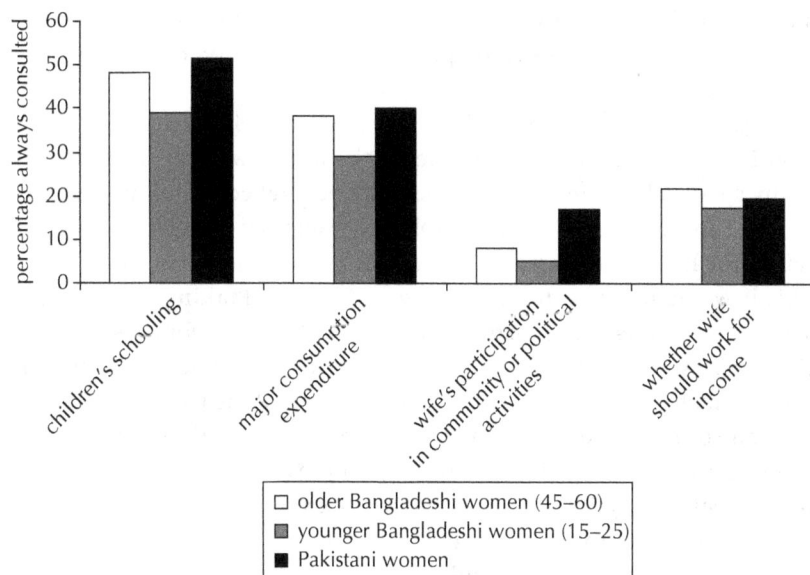

Sources: World Bank 2006, 2008.

women are consulted in areas that have to do with children. Even so, only half of all women surveyed in Bangladesh were regularly consulted in such matters as discipline of children, decisions regarding a sick child's treatment, and children's schooling (World Bank 2008). In addition, in areas dealing with their own relationship with their external environment, women's influence shrinks considerably. This lack of influence has ramifications on their voice in the community as well. In Bangladesh, for instance, women are usually not invited to be mediators in alternative dispute resolution systems (*shalish*), and only some of them can even approach these informal conflict resolution systems (World Bank 2008). In the wake of low access to the formal judiciary for all Bangladeshis in rural areas, such mechanisms are the primary channels through which community-level influence is exercised.

Lack of safety in public spaces can seriously hamper demand for markets and services. Even when demand for services, such as education, exists, factors other than the supply of that service play a major role in constraining access. One such factor is safety and security in public spaces. Figure 6.6 indicates that fewer than half of married women surveyed in Pakistan or Bangladesh feel safe moving alone outside their village or settlement, even during the day (World Bank 2006, 2008). This is a strong reflection of the state of public safety for women. Even the perception of lack of safety can have seriously deleterious consequences on their ability to access markets and services.

Cultural norms are also correlated with perceptions of insecurity by families of girls and women. Permission to leave the home, which is measured in many surveys like the DHS, may actually be a reflection of more than a cultural norm of seclusion or control being exercised by elders. It may also reflect the hazards to personal security in public spaces that women face. This is where policy can make a huge difference. Making public spaces safe for women is a major step forward in enhancing women's access to these spaces. Anecdotal evidence about the pressure on local administrations in such cities as Bangalore, Hyderabad, and Pune (India), where the new outsourcing industry employs young women working shifts, indicates that governmental response to such pressure is important. Moreover, issues of security in general and women's security in particular have been taken up by India's National Association of Software and Service Companies. Backing by such influential lobbies is important in ensuring that security concerns are addressed, but in rural areas, women seldom have lobbies that articulate this demand.

FIGURE 6.6
Perceptions of Safety among Pakistani and Bangladeshi Women

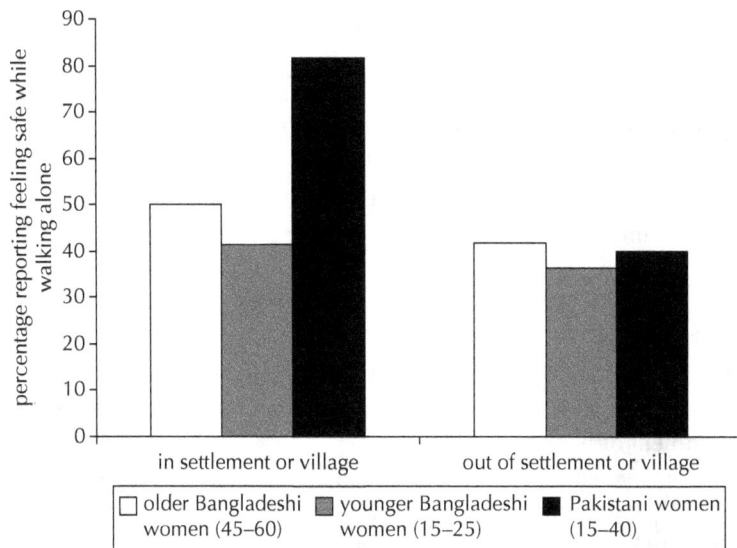

Sources: World Bank 2006, 2008.

Policy and Gender-Equality Outcomes

Policy and national vision have clear roles in achieving gender equality and meeting MDG3. Although women's empowerment is often not central to the design of key policies, in some instances it has been an unintended consequence. Not every good outcome for women needs to necessarily be the result of a formal policy, but the recognition that many policies have different impacts on men and women is an important step and draws from the overarching national framework.

Integrating women's empowerment and gender-equality goals into the design of national policy yields good results. Outcomes for women toward gender equality have usually resulted from a central policy directive, attendant rules, and good monitoring based on a national or subnational vision. The experiences in Bangladesh and Sri Lanka show that a clear national vision that includes women's education and health as priorities has helped shape all policies, not just those that target women. In OECD countries, tax laws that reward employed women while also encouraging fertility have been central in high levels of women's labor force participation. In India, central bank guidelines that mandate public sector banks to lend to women's credit groups or self-help groups have helped to catalyze a movement of savings and credit groups across the country by placing the onus equally on banks and state governments.

Each of these initiatives first defined an objective of gender equality or women's empowerment, in these cases, facilitating women's entry into the labor force or fostering women's credit groups, and then looked at which macro-level policy needed to be "gendered." These initiatives give the term "mainstreaming gender into macroeconomic policy" a different meaning. Rather than trying to include a gender flag in every policy, which sometimes leads to a "checking the box" approach, this strategy makes gender equality a key national goal. The Bangladesh Poverty Reduction Strategy Paper, for instance, has one of the most forward-looking chapters on gender and sees progress on gender equality as a key remaining national development issue (Government of Bangladesh 2005).

Policy pronouncements by themselves often do not lead to a real impact on processes and outcomes. Most countries have constitutional provisions, gender-equality policies, and laws that forbid discrimination. The policy and legal landscape sometimes seems littered with well-meaning pronouncements. These seldom translate into good enforcement. In extreme cases, seemingly retrogressive policies may be announced, but even these may not have the intended consequence. Bangladesh's progressive National Policy for the Advancement of Women was overturned in 2004 because of political considerations, and several conservative clauses were introduced surreptitiously. This generated widespread criticism and protests from activists in the women's movement and other members of civil society. From 2004 to 2007, there have been no indications that these changes have spearheaded more conservative policies in other areas. Therefore, the mere enactment of policies or laws is not enough. Unless marked by implementation and monitoring within a clear national goal, the effects will at best be patchy.

A strong civil society movement that safeguards women's rights and progress toward gender equality is indispensable for good outcomes. This chapter has reviewed several examples of citizen monitoring and public action as the propellant for good outcomes. Pressure from grassroots movements and increased awareness about gender inequalities in the public domain help to pressure policy makers and implementing agencies. The role of NGOs in Bangladesh not only in direct provision of services, but also in carrying out innovations and in representing the interests of poor rural women has been well documented. In India, NGOs take up specific issues, as examples from NREGS in this chapter have shown. The women's movement in South Asian countries is typically an amorphous entity comprising both men and women from academia, NGOs, governments, and political parties. In some countries, its voice and influence is larger than in others. Efforts that can enable these organizations to network successfully to create "movements out of initiatives" are one of the ways in which external aid can help. Governments can help by creating the enabling environment for such organizations to thrive and by building components of third-party monitoring into their programs.

Conclusion

This chapter argues that to achieve MDG3 in South Asia, and perhaps in other low-income countries, we have to think beyond resources and funding. In fact, this chapter shows that pushing money at the problem will not make it go away. As it points out, the issue of financing is at best complex and at worst confounding. Policy reform is difficult because of issues of design and political will; even when good policies are in place, poor implementation can thwart positive impacts. The major theme underpinning this chapter is that despite similar levels of allocation as a proportion of overall spending, outcomes vary considerably across countries. Moreover, even funds allocated to specific programs that should benefit the MDG3 indicators often remain unspent. Finally, the quality of the spending is often poor.

The missing element is accountability to citizens and particularly to women. This issue is even more intractable in areas with poor institutions to start with—not only are outcomes for women worse in such areas, but women have lower voice than in other places. Minority women and women residing in geographically far-flung and inaccessible locales are at even greater risk of not benefiting from policies implemented to meet MDG3. Strengthening the voice of women requires strong social movements and public action, as well as strong national vision that puts in place conditions for women to participate effectively. These include enforcement of property rights, equal wages, child care arrangements, physical security, and incentives that will change norms and behavior.

Annex 6A

TABLE 6A.1
Female Secondary Education in Low-Income Countries, 2000

Country	Female gross secondary school enrollment (%)	Per capita GDP at constant prices ($)
Angola	15	715
Bangladesh	47	360
Benin	15	362
Burkina Faso	8	231
Cambodia	13	282
Chad	5	177
Congo, Rep. of	28	934
Eritrea	22	155
Ethiopia	14	102
Gambia, The	28	321
Ghana	32	254
India	40	450
Kenya	29	347
Kyrgyz Republic	87	279
Lao PDR	31	324
Lesotho	36	493
Malawi	28	166
Mauritania	19	355
Moldova	72	301
Mongolia	77	395
Mozambique	9	208
Nepal	33	238
Nicaragua	58	779
Niger	5	167
Pakistan	19	531
Papua New Guinea	20	695
Rwanda	14	235
Senegal	14	459
Sierra Leone	22	126
Sudan	30	388

(continued)

TABLE 6A.1
Female Secondary Education in Low-Income Countries, 2000 (*continued*)

Country	Female gross secondary school enrollment (%)	Per capita GDP at constant prices ($)
Tajikistan	71	160
Uganda	7	253
Vietnam	64	397
Yemen, Rep. of	27	538
Zambia	21	328
Zimbabwe	40	570

Source: World Bank Development Indicators Database.

Notes

Comments from Dan Biller, Shanta Devarajan, Andrew Morrison, and Tara Vishwanath are gratefully acknowledged.

1. Current weekly status for those not attending school.

References and Other Resources

AID (Association for India's Development) Rural Technology Resource Center. 2007. "Audit of NREGA Work in Gosani Block of Gajapati District in Orissa." Orissa.

Bardhan, Pranab, Mookherjee Dilip, and Monica Parra-Torrado. 2005. "Impact of Reservations of Panchayat Presidents on Targeting in West Bengal." BREAD Working Paper No. 104, November 2005. http://ipl.econ.duke.edu/bread/papers/working/104.pdf.

Ban, Radu, and Vijayendra Rao. 2007. "Local Accountability in South Asia: A Brief Review of the Survey Evidence." Unpublished, World Bank, Washington, DC.

Berg, Andy, and Zia Qureshi. 2005. "The MDGs: Building Momentum." *Finance and Development* 42 (3): 21–23.

CAG (Comptroller and Auditor General of India). 2006. *Audit Report (Civil), Uttar Pradesh for the Year 2005–2006.* New Delhi: Comptroller and Auditor General of India.

Chattopadhyaya, Raghabendra, and Esther Duflo. 2004. "Women as Policy Makers: Evidence from a Randomized Policy Experiment in India." *Econometrica* 72 (5): 1409–43.

Das, Maitreyi. 1992. "The Women's Development Program in Rajasthan: A Case Study in Group Formation for Women's Development." Policy Research Working Paper No. 913, Population and Human Resources Department, World Bank, Washington, DC.

Das, Maitreyi Bordia. 2006a. "Do Traditional Axes of Exclusion Affect Labor Market Outcomes in India?" South Asia Social Development Discussion Paper No. 3, World Bank, Washington, DC.

———. 2006b. "Orissa: Social Inclusion During a Period of Anticipated Growth." Background Paper for the Orissa Growth Report. World Bank, Washington, DC.

Das, Maitreyi Bordia, and Sonalde Desai. 2003. "Why Are Educated Women Less Likely To Be Employed in India? Testing Competing Hypotheses." Social Protection Discussion Paper No. 313, World Bank, Washington, DC.

Das Gupta, Monica. 1995. "Life Course Perspectives on Women's Autonomy and Health Outcomes." *American Anthropologist* 97 (3): 481–91.

Drêze, Jean, and Christian Oldiges. 2007. "How is NREGA Doing?" Unpublished. www.ansiss.org/doc/seminar2007July20-22/jean_dreze.doc.

Duflo, Esther, and Petia Topalova. 2004. "Unappreciated Service: Performance, Perceptions, and Women Leaders in India." Unpublished, Massachusetts Institute of Technology Department of Economics. http://econ-www.mit.edu/files/793.

Filmer, Deon, Jeffrey S. Hammer, and Lant H. Pritchett. 2000. "Weak Links in the Chain: A Diagnosis of Health Policy in Poor Countries." *World Bank Research Observer* 15 (2): 199–224.

Filmer, Deon, and Lant Pritchett. 1997. "Child Mortality and Public Spending on Health: How Much Does Money Matter?" Policy Research Working Paper No. 1864, World Bank, Washington, DC.

Government of Bangladesh, General Economics Division, Planning Commission. 2005. "Unlocking the Potential: National Strategy for Accelerated Poverty Reduction." Planning Commission, Dhaka, Bangladesh.

Government of India. 2005. *Ministry of Health and Family Welfare. Reproductive and Child Health Survey.* New Delhi: MOHFW.

Hammer, Jeffrey S., Salimah Samji, and Yamini Aiyar. 2006. "Bottom's Up: To the Role of Panchayati Raj Institutions in Health and Health Services." Social Development Papers, South Asia Series, Paper No. 98, World Bank, Washington, DC.

HMGN (His Majesty's Government of Nepal), Ministry of Health. 2004. Budget Performance, Kathmandu.

Jaumotte, Florence. 2003. "Labour Force Participation of Women: Empirical Evidence on the Role of Policy and other Determinants in OECD Countries." *OECD Economic Studies* 37 (2003/2): 52–108. http://www.oecd.org/dataoecd/12/39/34562935.pdf.

Kingdon, Geeta Gandhi, and Jeemol Unni. 1997. "How Much Does Education Affect Women's Labor Market Outcomes in India? An Analysis Using NSS Household Data." Working Paper No. 92, Gujarat Institute of Development Research, Ahmedabad.

Kremer, Michael, Nazmul Chaudhury, F. Halsey Rogers, Karthik Muralidharan, and Jeffrey Hammer. 2005. "Teacher Absence in India: A Snapshot." *Journal of the European Economic Association*, April/May 2005, 3 (2–3): 658–67.

Mahal, Ajay, Abdo S. Yazbeck, David H. Peters, and G. N. V. Ramana. 2001. *The Poor and Health Service Use in India.* HNP Discussion Paper. Washington, DC: World Bank.

Mahmud, Simeen. 2006. "Economic Participation of Women in Bangladesh." Background Paper for the Bangladesh Gender Assessment, World Bank, Dhaka.

Manchanda, Rita. 2007. "Grounded Till Thirty." India Together Web site. http://www.indiatogether.org/2007/aug/wom-migrant.htm.

Narayan, Deepa, Giovanna Prennushi, and Soumya Kapoor. 2007. "People's Organizations and Moving out of Poverty: Rural Andhra Pradesh." Unpublished, World Bank, Washington, DC.

Panda, Pradeep, and Bina Agarwal. 2005. "Marital Violence, Human Development and Women's Property Status in India." *World Development* 33 (5): 823–50.

Pradhan, Basanta K., and Shalabh Kumar Singh. 2000. "Policy Reforms and Financing of Elementary Education in India: A Study of the Quality of Service and Outcome." National Council of Applied Economic Research, New Delhi.

Pritchett, Lant, and Varad Pande. *Making Primary Education Work for India's Rural Poor: A Proposal for Effective Decentralization.* Social Development Paper No. 95, World Bank, Washington, DC.

Rahman, Rushidan Islam. 2006. "Gender and Labour Market: Trends and Determinants." Background paper for the Bangladesh Gender Assessment, World Bank, Dhaka.

Sanyal, Paromita. 2007. "From Credit to Collective Action: Microfinance, Women's Group-Based Mobilizations and Implications for Social Capital." Unpublished, Department of Sociology, Harvard University, Cambridge, MA.

Sathar, Zeba, and Sonalde Desai. 2000. "Class and Gender in Rural Pakistan: Differentials in Economic Activity." In *Women, Poverty and Demographic Change,* ed. Brigida Garcia. Oxford: Oxford University Press.

United Nations. 2004. *World Urbanization Prospects: The 2005 Revision.* New York: UN Population Division.

———. 2007. *World Population Prospects: The 2006 Revision.* New York: UN Population Division.

World Bank. 2003. "Bridging the Gap: Opportunities and Challenges." Pakistan Gender Assessment Concept Note, World Bank, Washington, DC.

———. 2005. "Pakistan: Country Gender Assessment—Bridging The Gender Gap: Opportunities and Challenges." World Bank, Washington, DC.

———. 2006. "India: Inclusive Growth and Service Delivery: Building on India's Success." Development Policy Review, World Bank, Washington, DC.

———. 2008. "Whispers to Voices: Gender and Social Transformation in Bangladesh." World Bank, Dhaka.

World Bank and DFID (Department for International Development). 2006. *Unequal Citizens: Gender, Caste and Ethnic Exclusion in Nepal.* Kathmandu: World Bank and DFID.

7

Policy Interventions to Meet the MDG3 Challenge in Developing Countries: Experiences from Mexico

Miguel Székely

The main feature of the third Millennium Development Goal (MDG) of "promoting gender equality and empowering women" is that it challenges cultural norms and traditions and requires deep changes in day-to-day individual behavior and practices, which are normally regarded as a "private matter." This feature is also the main challenge for implementation.

The other seven MDGs have at least three common features. The first is wide agreement that achieving them has direct benefits for specific families and individuals. Second, they generate positive externalities to the rest of the population. Third, well-identified public policies can contribute to the achievement of the goals. These three features help to build consensus around these goals and contribute to generating a perception of their desirability for society as a whole.

Take, for instance, the second MDG. Few would doubt that improving schooling levels through universal coverage of primary education has a positive impact at the household level through higher income-earning capacity. Furthermore, human capital accumulation is regarded as one of the engines of higher productivity and greater aggregate economic growth. Finally, there is clear scope for public intervention, either by expanding and improving the quality of services, or by supporting households so that the demand for education can be strengthened. Similar arguments can be made for the remaining six MDGs, which deal with poverty; reducing child mortality; improving maternal health; combating HIV/AIDS, malaria, and other diseases; ensuring environmental sustainability; and developing a partnership for development.

The three features are not usually universally shared by MDG3, and this imposes additional challenges for building consensus around it. On the one hand, changing the role of women and empowering them modifies household arrangements substantially, and in many cases this is not regarded as a desirable change for specific family members. On the other hand, identifying effective public policies for promoting gender equality is especially difficult in the context of deeply entrenched traditions and cultural patterns (although, as shown later in this chapter, some interesting experiences may be a useful point of reference). Moreover, the enactment of specific policies may generate intense resistance from different sectors of society.

As for the second feature, basic economic and social analysis indicates that promoting gender equality and empowering women could have important positive externalities for society as a whole (for more details, see chapter 1). However, it cannot be said that this is widely recognized and accepted in developing countries yet.

These features illustrate the difficulties in implementing MDG3 in developing countries, as opposed to the other Millennium Development Goals. The additional difficulty calls for more analysis and for the identification of promising country experiences that can enlighten the discussion and suggest ways for moving forward. This chapter contributes on this front by presenting the experience of implementing and following up on the MDGs in Mexico. The chapter highlights and provides information about the main obstacles found in a country in which cultural patterns and traditions usually favor and promote male predominance, and discusses some of the policy responses that have been able to confront these obstacles, to some extent.

The main argument is that the primary challenge for implementing MDG3 is to focus on the underlying mechanisms generating gender differences and not only on the outcomes observed. If the *laws and mechanisms* by which society operates and the underlying *cultural patterns* are not modified, policy will be swimming against the tide, making it difficult to identify efficient policy interventions to address gender disparities.

The chapter is organized as follows: The next section briefly discusses a scheme to classify different policy interventions according to their impact on specific elements of the gender inequality process. It is followed by a section focusing on changing market outcomes. The subsequent two sections discuss interventions that can change the rules by which society operates, and focus on cultural patterns. The final section presents conclusions.

Identifying the Scope for Government Intervention

Gender disparities are the outcome of at least three underlying elements. The first, and most important, are the cultural norms by which women are relegated to fulfilling certain roles within the household and in society, and through which they are excluded from a variety of activities and opportunities for human development. These norms are reproduced generation after generation and become part of the "normal" operation of societies. They are many times reinforced by religion, tradition, and education, and are manifested openly in different types of discrimination against women.

The second element has to do with the rules of society. For instance, legislation may explicitly exclude women from or limit their access to certain activities—labor laws and hiring and firing rules are usually the mechanisms by which this is done. Market and public institutions may openly treat women differently and restrict their opportunities through written or unwritten rules under arguments of lower productivity, lower capabilities, or different objectives and needs, and even government programs may discriminate against women implicitly through program design and eligibility requirements. Although these practices are mostly a consequence and reflection of the first element, the difference is that, strictly speaking, they can be modified independently of—and most of the time, in spite of—cultural norms and traditions.

The third element includes the mechanisms through which final outcomes are determined. Perhaps the best example is income. Even in societies in which cultural norms provide equal opportunities for women and the "rules of the game" do not explicitly inhibit women's development, there may still be market mechanisms, such as the low returns to specific types of labor, including housework and other activities predominantly performed by women, that undermine their development potential. Of course, this element is also intimately related to the first two, and can even be regarded as one of their consequences, but the main differences are that, they can be modified independently, and that they also respond to other factors, such as market supply and demand.[1]

In extreme cases, these three elements reinforce each other and produce a vicious circle in which women play a passive secondary role in a variety of dimensions; they are restricted from development opportunities, which, in turn, undermines their capacity to participate and contribute to society, and this strengthens traditional cultural norms, and so on. That is, gender inequalities may reproduce gender inequalities.[2]

This scheme is useful for analyzing the implementation challenges of MDG3 because it helps clarify the scope and potential of different government interventions. For example, a public action focused only on modifying outcomes, say, by providing income allowances to women (for instance, to single mothers), might, in fact, close the gender income gap temporarily. However, if the rules of the game and cultural patterns remain in place, the risk is that when the income support is eliminated, gender gaps will reappear. Most important, the change in income may not produce the desired effect, for example, if it triggers new behavior, such as household violence—to appropriate the income benefit—with a negative net effect for women's well-being.

Similarly, changing just the rules may generate some positive effects on the gender gap but these effects may be modest if market outcomes and cultural norms remain unaffected. Take, for instance, labor legislation. Even if laws are modified to guarantee equal access to opportunities for women, if traditions and norms exclude women from education, or labor markets tend to reward low-skilled jobs poorly because of supply and demand conditions, the effect on women's welfare may be lower than expected.

The implications of changes in culture and tradition are quite different because they depend on the time frame under analysis. In the short run, changes in these factors may not modify gender gaps in such dimensions as income, health, and education if the rules and market mechanisms remain unaltered, but eventually they trigger processes that also have an impact the other two elements.

In sum, a comprehensive policy approach for promoting gender equality and empowering women ideally should aim at modifying each of these three elements simultaneously in such a way that they generate a virtuous circle by positively reinforcing each other.

Changing Market Outcomes

Perhaps the most straightforward way of modifying the gender gap through policy is by changing market outcomes directly, that is, focusing on the last of the links of the gender inequality circle. One possibility, already discussed, would be to provide women with income allowances to close the income gap. Another option would be to expand access to education and health services by actively seeking women's enrollment. Other possibilities include establishing hiring quotas for the private and public sector to increase women's employment, establishing a differential minimum wage by gender (with higher incomes for women), or at least mandating an equal wage for men and women for equivalent jobs.

As mentioned, although these types of interventions can modify outcomes, they do so at the risk of having only short-run, temporary effects, and most worrying, they may not generate the desired impact on permanent well-being if they trigger unexpected side effects, or they are nullified by rules or cultural patterns. For instance, expanding female education in a context in which labor laws and cultural norms hinder the hiring of women is likely to have relatively low effects on welfare in the future. Establishing a differential minimum wage may also discourage the hiring of women, with an ultimate negative effect on their employment level.

There are many similar examples of why just changing market outcomes may have very a limited impact on MDG3 in the long run. Even though changes to market outcomes may appear to be the easiest solution, such changes may undermine other more powerful interventions, and shift the focus away from the need for more fundamental and permanent changes.

Interventions for Modifying Day-to-Day Rules

Common policy interventions for promoting gender equality and empowering women are those that change the way in which certain government programs, labor market practices, and other parts of the economic system operate. As opposed to modifying market outcomes, which can be achieved while maintaining underlying mechanisms and cultural norms, these interventions alter the way in which socioeconomic systems function because they affect the rules of day-to-day behavior and operation.

At least three important areas for government intervention emerge in this case. One area, which usually implies a structural change, is to modify legislation to change the rules of the game by which society works. Another option is to alter the way in which public programs are implemented and designed or to modify other less formal rules that are not backed up by law. A third possibility, which is perhaps the most commonly pursued, precisely because it does not require structural changes or drastic modifications of rules, is to tailor government benefits, goods, services, and interventions to women's needs. The chapter discusses each of these in what follows.

Modifying Legislation

One option for reducing gender disparities through changing or imposing new rules in society is the introduction and enforcement of legislation against discrimination. Several developed countries have made significant progress in this regard, with important positive results, and one of the keys for success has been that the introduction of new rules has gone hand in hand with strict enforcement.

The experience is much more limited in developing countries, few of which have introduced gender discrimination laws, and those that have have not been able to consolidate them as mechanisms for changing the operation of the socioeconomic system. One example is Mexico, where a discrimination law (including gender issues) was introduced in 2003, although with very limited enforcement, and therefore, limited effects on real opportunities and better conditions for women.

Thus, there is still wide scope for introducing and enforcing such legislation in developing countries. The experience of developed countries shows that antidiscrimination legislation is an effective way of modifying final outcomes in a permanent way.

Other less obvious but equally important areas of existing legislation also promote and generate deep gender inequalities and low empowerment for women. Perhaps the best example is labor legislation. In developing countries, the final outcome of labor legislation is usually very low labor market participation by women, low wages, and lack of or very limited social protection and benefits for women.

In Latin America, the main reason behind such outcomes is that traditional mechanisms for protecting labor were designed by men, for men. Their objective was to generate formal employment with benefits and with guarantees for stable jobs. But this implicitly induces discrimination against women, on the one hand, because such laws impose higher implicit costs for hiring women (because of maternity leave and allowances), and on the other hand, because restricting employment to full time and limiting flexibility in hours makes it a prohibitive venture for many women. These efforts at protection have resulted, in reality, in much lower participation rates, especially among poor, uneducated women.[3]

The main alternative to facing up to this reality is to promote reforms to labor legislation that introduce greater flexibility into contracting conditions to allow for part-time or temporary workers who have to deal with household tasks as well as labor market activities. But this must be accompanied by the corresponding (but proportional) benefits enjoyed by full-time workers. This legislative reform can be complemented with unemployment protection mechanisms to stabilize workers' incomes if they temporarily exit the labor market voluntarily or involuntarily and socialization of the direct (and even perhaps the indirect) maternity costs in the formal sector of the economy. If, rather than charging these costs to employers, they are financed through fiscal revenue, the incentives to hire women would improve, and with this, their opportunities.

Changing the Way Social Programs Operate

It is common to find that the ways in which governments deliver public services and provide support through social programs implicitly reproduce, and are even a source of, gender inequalities. In developing countries, until recently, government interventions targeted males as the counterpart, and public programs were designed using the assumption that males were the subject of policy interventions as the head of the household. Even in programs designed for women, including, for instance, health interventions, males played a predominant role by being empowered to authorize (or not) the receipt of the benefit by women family members.

However, some recent examples show that designing policies not only *for* women, but also for their operation *by* women can significantly reduce the gender gap and enhance women's empowerment. Perhaps the best known are the Conditional Cash Transfer (CCT) programs that have proliferated in Latin America and the Caribbean, including Bolivia, Brazil, Chile, Colombia, the Dominican Republic, Ecuador, Honduras, Jamaica, Mexico, Peru, and Nicaragua, and are extending to countries in other regions, such as South Asia. These programs provide a series of benefits to selected households, conditional on compliance with certain obligations. One of the main features of these types of programs is precisely the predominant role played by women.[4]

Figure 7.1 illustrates a prototype of what would be the most comprehensive version of a Latin American CCT. The first step in the implementation of these programs is geographical targeting. The second step consists of identifying through means testing the households in the selected areas that fall below a certain predefined standard.

The third step in targeting introduces a significant innovation in the role played by women. It consists of defining the female head of the household as the counterpart entitled to receive the cash transfer. This rather subtle change in program design has had a huge impact on women's empowerment, and it has proved to yield important results in the use of the cash support obtained by the household. Several rigorous impact evaluations show significant changes in consumption among beneficiary households of the Oportunidades program in Mexico, with a 7.1 percent increase in

FIGURE 7.1
Gender-Targeted Conditional Cash Transfer Program

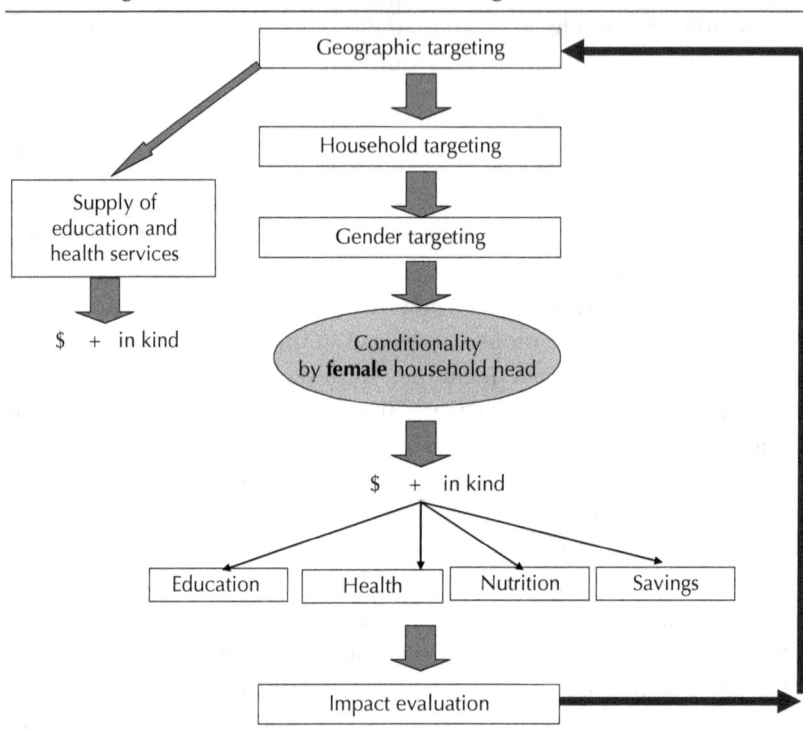

Source: Author's compilation.

caloric intake by family members resulting from improved food selection; of Familias en Acción in Colombia, where food consumption increased in beneficiary households by 19.5 and 9.3 percent in rural and urban areas, respectively; and in the Red de Protección Social in Nicaragua, where expenditures increased particularly in nutrient-rich food and in health care, education, footwear, and clothing for children. Presumably, most of these changes are to a large extent a result of the selection of the female head as the family counterpart for the program.[5]

The changes in consumption patterns, combined with greater access to health services, have strong implications for nutrition. For instance, in the first phase of implementation of Oportunidades, the height of children between 12 and 26 months of age increased by approximately 16 percent, which yields an increase in lifetime earnings through productivity of 2.9 percent per year when children reach working age. The height of

12-month-old boys who participated in Familias en Acción was on average approximately 0.5 centimeters greater than for those who were not part of the program, while the Red de Protección Social registered a 5 percent decline in child stunting—a rate of decline that is 1.5 times higher than the improvement observed at the national level.

The fourth step in the operation of CCT programs is the introduction of conditionality. Conditionality shifts the scope of cash transfer programs from social assistance to social investment because it induces changes in family behavior that entail the accumulation of income-earning assets with permanent effects. Transfers for education are conditional on regular school attendance; transfers for health are linked to the use of health services; nutrition and food support requires monitoring the height and weight of children at health clinics and also on attendance at training workshops by the female head of the household.[6]

A second innovation is that female household heads are the main partners in registering and complying with conditionality (at the center of figure 7.1), which has proved to have important additional effects on both women's empowerment and their capabilities and development potential.

A third innovation introduced by some CCT programs, such as Oportunidades in Mexico, is the use of differential cash transfers by gender. Because female school attendance rates were traditionally lower, and dropout rates were higher, than those for males, cash transfers were established at higher levels for girls. The effect was a dramatic reduction in educational disparities, to the extent that after about three years of operation, the schooling gender gap was reversed—one of the major contributions to the fulfillment of MDG3 in Mexico (Secretaría de Desarrollo Social, Mexico, and UNDP 2004).

In sum, experience with CCT programs is showing that social policies for and by women can contribute to reversing gender disparities through changing the rules of the game in government programs and providing incentives that modify household dynamics. These innovations have been able to improve outcomes significantly and seem to be cost-efficient interventions for achieving MDG3.

Tailoring Programs and Benefits to Women's and Girls' Needs

In many cases, introducing legislation, or even implementing programs, that change the rules of the game in the short run is not possible. In these contexts, one option to move forward has been to tailor program design and delivery to women's needs, such that women are guaranteed equal or better access.

Female labor market participation illustrates different possibilities in this regard. Even under current legislation, access to employment opportunities can be improved through the provision of basic social infrastructure and services that lower the cost of household chores and free some time for women. For instance, child care and health services can be enhanced and expanded to create a network of support for women who wish to engage in the labor market but who do not because of the restrictions imposed by household tasks. Child care and health services can either be subsidized by the state, or they can be promoted through appropriate tax schemes or other incentives for private firms.

Another option for economic activity that has been relied upon in many developing countries is the design of social programs that favor women's engagement. One of the best known initiatives with these characteristics is the Grameen Bank in Bangladesh, which provides microcredit to women, tailored to their specific requirements and situations. The scheme has proliferated and has created a wide range of development possibilities that allow women to engage in economic activity while fulfilling other roles at the same time.

An alternative approach is to design government programs such that they meet girls' and women's needs specifically. Health programs are perhaps the most common of these types of interventions, but there are several other policies, including programs that offer nutritional supplements for different stages of the life cycle—including supplements for girls, pregnant women, and nursing mothers—training programs, and the like, all of which are designed to address specific problems or restrictions faced by women.

Policies for Addressing the Challenge of Cultural Norms and Traditions

Cultural norms and traditions are usually at the core of gender disparities and of low women's empowerment in developing countries. However, because of the difficulty of addressing norms and traditions, specific policies aimed at modifying them are much less common than either modifying legislation or tailoring programs to women's needs.

One of the reasons policies aimed at modifying norms are less common is that they take much more time than the other two alternatives to generate visible changes in final outcomes. Changing cultural norms and traditions may take generations, while it is possible to modify outcomes directly and change the rules of the game rather quickly. Another difficulty is that when men are the policy makers, there tend to be fewer incentives to engage in long-term processes that challenge the status quo. Building consensus around the desirability of MDG3 may be difficult even with those responsible for policy implementation. Still another obstacle is that (as with most fundamental change) not only policy makers but other interest groups, too, may openly oppose these initiatives and gain enough political support to stop them.

Three types of government policies can contribute to forward progress despite these problems. The first is to generate information about the magnitude of discrimination against women. The second is to generate information on the value of women's contributions to society. The third is to invest in increasing the productivity of activities predominantly performed by women to empower them and enhance their economic potential.

How Much Discrimination Is There?

There is a saying that "one cannot solve a problem that cannot be quantified or measured." At first sight, this seems not to be an issue for gender disparities and women's empowerment because considerable research and widely disseminated information document these phenomena. However, as already argued, gender disparity and lack of empowerment are outcomes of much more complex processes. When it comes to the underlying causes that generate gender disparities, information is more limited. Information is particularly sparse about the magnitude of the discrimination against women inherent in the cultural norms and traditions confining them to certain activities and restricting their development potential.

One of the few data sources systematically producing such information is the Latinobarómetro Survey, carried out every year throughout Latin America with the main objective of measuring political perceptions, but that also includes two specific questions on attitudes toward women.[7] The first of these questions asks if there is agreement or disagreement with the statement that "it is better for women to concentrate on domestic chores and for men to concentrate on work." On average, about 48 percent of Latin Americans fully agree with this statement, and the results range from 67 percent in Honduras to 17 percent in Mexico. Of interest, on average, almost 55 percent agree with the statement that "women get in trouble if they earn more money than men," with results varying from 63 percent in the Dominican Republic to 31 percent in Uruguay.

These results reveal still deeply entrenched male-dominated societies, where there seems to be agreement that women should only play certain roles or that they should play alternative roles as long as they do not do so to the extent that they overcome men's predominance.

Little more information of this type is available for Latin America. Therefore, there is wide scope for governments in this region to contribute to MDG3 by generating or promoting the generation of information on discriminatory practices in specific countries, to help uncover the underlying causes of gender differences.

One recent example of this option is the recently disseminated National Discrimination Survey by the government of Mexico, which includes information on the extent of gender discrimination in the country.[8] The survey includes modules that reveal discrimination attitudes of the population; it also incorporates a series of modules that show the extent to which certain population subgroups (including women, the elderly, the indigenous, and so forth) feel discriminated against. The results provide a surprising image of a society in which women's opportunities and human development are severely restricted by cultural norms and traditions that are entrenched in labor markets, the education system, and most important, within the household itself.[9]

A first look at responses by male adults in the survey reveals that

- about 90 percent think that denying a job opportunity to a pregnant woman is a violation of her human rights,
- 83 percent say that they would be willing to pay maternity benefits to protect women's rights, and
- almost 100 percent think that there is no justification for domestic violence against women.

However, discriminatory practices and attitudes against women are still clearly apparent among average Mexican males:

- One out of every five thinks that it is completely natural to prohibit women, rather than men, from performing certain activities.
- Almost 40 percent agree that women should be confined to "women's" jobs.
- Almost one out of every three thinks that men should earn more than women when performing the same job.
- Twenty-one percent believe that women have fewer abilities to handle high-pressure jobs.
- Almost one out of every four believes that women are to blame when they are raped because they seduce men.

- Fifteen percent think that it is not worth investing in the education of their daughters, because they will get married and someone else will provide for them.
- One out of every four would ask for a pregnancy test before hiring a woman.

On the other hand, responses by women show that

- nine out of every ten think that there is discrimination against them because of their gender;
- for four out of every ten, discrimination is expressed through not respecting their human rights;
- the rights that are most frequently violated are well-remunerated jobs, equal access to justice, and domestic violence; and
- the two main obstacles that they perceive for their development are discrimination because of pregnancy and access to jobs.

But perhaps the most revealing information is that

- the two places where discrimination is more intense and apparent are the labor market and the household;
- for one out of every four women, the space where they suffer discrimination the most is their own household;
- within the household, discrimination is expressed through assigning specific "women's" roles and through the exclusion from development opportunities; and
- one out of every five women thinks that women themselves are responsible for the discrimination against them by remaining passive while they are discriminated against.

The effect of the presentation of these results in Mexico was to reveal an image that Mexicans had not seen so explicitly drawn. The results reflect a society with intense exclusion and discrimination practices against women that limit their opportunities, freedom, and development possibilities. Perhaps most worrying, the results reveal that discrimination is deeply entrenched in cultural norms and traditions that are still considered normal for large sectors of society and that are reproduced within the household.

However, on the positive side, the survey results generated an unprecedented debate on discrimination, and in particular, gender discrimination in the country. The discussion was fueled by the media, which played a key role in the dissemination of the results of the survey, as well as in the analysis and debate. This process is a good example of how the media can have enormous influence in changing perceptions about the appropriate roles for women in society and within the household and of how the media may contribute to disseminating and generating analysis of valuable information.

The debate had many effects, the most important of which were a congressional initiative for reforming labor laws (along the lines discussed in this chapter), an initiative for reforming the 2003 antidiscrimination law to create enforcement mechanisms, and a discussion of the possibilities of changing educational content in public schools to increase awareness of gender discrimination. Perhaps the survey's most important contribution has been to make explicit how strongly policy has to "swim against the tide" to guarantee equal treatment and opportunities by gender.

The Economic Contribution of Women

Another area in which governments can contribute to the empowerment of women through the generation of information is by making an accounting of economic contribution by gender.

Even though women in many developing countries tend to devote most of their productive time to household activities with high value added, these activities are neither registered nor valued economically. One of the best illustrations of this fact arises commonly in the process of conducting household surveys, where interviewers face women that are holding one or more children while performing household chores, feeding domestic animals, and answering the survey at the same time. When the interviewer asks, "do you work," the typical answer is "no." This reveals that women themselves do not value these activities or regard them as "productive" and that society as a whole tends to neglect this contribution.

Another fact that reveals the low value attributed to the activities performed by women is that National Accounts do not register household work as an economic activity, nor do they account for its contribution. This is another area in which governments can take the lead in the generation of information to empower women.

In providing information on discrimination, Mexico serves as an example. In 2005, the Ministry of Social Development set forth an initiative to formally quantify and acknowledge the economic contribution of activities typically performed by women, by presenting estimates of the "true" value of women's work. As was the case in the discrimination survey, the results generated intensive discussion, as well as an initiative (that, unfortunately, did not move forward) for formally estimating the economic value of women's activity in the system of National Income and Products Accounts.

Estimates were made possible by the data from a specific module on time use in the National Income and Expenditure Household Survey by the National Statistical Institute for 2004. This information revealed that Mexican women work 62 hours a week on average, of which 37 correspond to labor market activities and 25 to nonremunerated housework. In contrast, the average male works 55 hours a week, most of which time is dedicated to the labor market, and typically remunerated. From these data the conclusion would be that women contribute to about 30 percent of total gross domestic product (GDP) in Mexico, while men account for the remaining 70 percent.

However, conservative estimations of the economic value of women's nonremunerated activities show that the invisible, unacknowledged economic contribution is at least an additional 17 percent of GDP.[10] Not accounting for and not registering this contribution is an explicit way of neglecting women and of introducing obstacles to their empowerment. In essence, it is the expression of deeply rooted cultural norms.

Women's Productivity

Another area of policy intervention with the potential to reduce gender disparities and empower women by challenging culture and tradition is the provision of and access to private infrastructure and assets. Access to such assets could change family dynamics and free up and enhance the value of women's time by increasing the productivity of labor within the household.

For instance, the same time use module in the Mexican household survey shows that household infrastructure and appliances can reduce the time and effort expended on household work considerably. Having access to potable water, a gas stove, a refrigerator, and a microwave oven may free almost half an hour a day each—equivalent to about 3.5 hours per week—which implies time savings of around two hours per day altogether. This additional time can be devoted to a series of market and nonmarket activities that provide more freedom and economic potential to empower women.[11]

Although there are public interventions aimed at providing or facilitating access to these types of assets by households, they are normally not aimed explicitly at improving household dynamics for women. There is definitely scope for enhancing such programs in the hope that they will contribute to cultural change leading to recognition of the value of women's real contributions.

Concluding Remarks

The central argument of this chapter is that the major challenge to implementing MDG3 in many developing countries is the cultural norms and traditions that tend to undermine and underestimate women's contributions to society, that relegate them to nonpredominant roles, and that severely restrict their development potential. If policy addresses this fact explicitly, government interventions will be more effective and are likely to have long-lasting effects.

There are three broad policy areas that can contribute to the achievement of MDG3 in this context. The first includes policies that directly aim at modifying outcomes—such as low income, low education, and low health—by introducing allowances for women in vulnerable situations or by expanding the coverage of services by guaranteeing women access to them.

The second, which seems to be the most common in policy-making efforts, attempts to change some of the rules of the game in government programs and social interactions. Three specific ways of doing so are to reform legislation, to change program design and rules of access, and to provide goods and services tailored to women's specific needs. A good example of the introduction of legislation is the antidiscrimination law in Mexico, although the priority area for legislation reform across Latin America is labor laws, which tend to restrict opportunities for women. For improvements in program design, the CCT program Oportunidades in Mexico is a relevant reference point. Oportunidades has proved to empower women and includes a series of mechanisms through which women are guaranteed greater opportunities. Similar programs have been introduced in other Latin American countries and other regions of the world.

The third broad area, the least common in practice but the most ambitious and probably the most effective, is to aim at modifying the underlying cultural norms and traditions prolonging gender inequalities. Three ways of doing so have already proved to have some positive effects. One is to generate information on the extent of discrimination practices so that society can take a look in the mirror and acknowledge the problem. The recent National Discrimination Survey for Mexico is a good example of how such information can unveil entrenched cultural practices and by doing so contribute to generating high-level debate and legislative initiatives to address the problem.

A second is to generate information on the value of women's contributions to economic activity, an issue commonly neglected in National Accounts and by statistics institutes. Estimating the economic contribution of women's work in Mexico, which accounts for about one-half of total GDP after correcting for the underestimation of its value, also fueled a productive debate as well as greater awareness about the importance of this issue.

A third possibility is investment in and provision of private assets that increase women's productivity in the household and free up time to modify household dynamics and contribute to valuing women's contribution adequately. Data from Mexico help illustrate the importance of the issue. Estimates show that access to household appliances can help women free up about two hours per day, time that could be devoted to economically remunerated or other activities.

Each of these areas can contribute to reducing gender inequalities, and if applied simultaneously, can generate a powerful virtuous circle of empowerment and development for women in developing countries. Perhaps the main challenge for having simultaneous action on all fronts is to face the feature that makes MDG3 different from the rest of the Millennium Development Goals, which is that still, in the 21st century, a large part of society in developing countries believes that the role women are confined to play is largely a private matter, in which public policy should not become involved.

Notes

The author thanks participants at the World Bank's High-Level Consultation on "Promoting the Gender Equality MDG: The Implementation Challenge," as well as two anonymous referees for useful comments and suggestions.

1. One example that illustrates this quite clearly is the case of domestic work, an occupation predominantly held by women in developing countries. The income generated by this activity is evidently influenced by cultural patterns and by the rules of the game, but it may change significantly depending on supply and demand factors. These demand and supply factors are what we regard as some of the important mechanisms that determine final outcomes.
2. Another source of gender disparities, not discussed here, is the presence of biological differences between men and women. This is a controversial issue that is beyond the scope of this paper.
3. This argument is supported by solid empirical evidence presented in Inter-American Development Bank (IDB) (1998).

4. For a detailed description of these programs, see Székely (2006) and Fonseca (2006).
5. These and other evaluation results are summarized in Székely (2006).
6. Apart from cash transfers, several programs provide in-kind benefits, such as nutritional supplements. In some countries, support for families is combined with mechanisms to strengthen the supply of education and health services, including allowances for teachers, infrastructure provision, or incentives for performance. In all these cases, women also play a predominant role.
7. A summary of survey results can be found at http://www.latinobarometro.org.
8. The original name of the survey is the Encuesta Nacional Sobre Discriminación en México. The survey, which was commissioned by the Ministry of Social Development, includes 1,200 observations, and it is representative at the national level and for rural and urban areas.
9. The Latinobarómetro results suggest that Mexico is an interesting case in the context of Latin America because it was found to be the country where fewer people agree with the statement that "it is better for women to concentrate on domestic chores...," while at the same time it was found to present the second highest share agreeing that "women get in trouble if...." This reveals a society where the role of women is far from being accepted as "equal" to that of men for a large part of society.
10. Estimates were obtained by two different methods, which yielded very similar results. The first method used standard regression analysis for predicting the opportunity cost of not participating in the labor market by estimating the income women of a certain profile would obtain if, instead of performing housework, they participated in the labor market. The second method consisted of obtaining the market value of a large range of activities (including housework) and then imputing incomes for women who perform such activities without remuneration, according to the time spent at each activity (this information is provided by the time use module). The productivity in each case depends on the remuneration to each particular activity.
11. This example is presented as an illustration for the particular case of Mexico, and it might not necessarily be relevant in other contexts. Obviously, the positive effect of access to these assets depends on the availability of electricity and other factors, and they may not be viable in many settings.

References

Fonseca, A. 2006. "Programas de Transferencia de Ingresos en una Perspectiva Internacional: Características y Desafíos." Unpublished, UNDP, Sao Paulo, Brazil.

IDB (Inter-American Development Bank). 1998. *Facing Up to Inequality in Latin America*. Economic and Social Progress Report. Washington, DC: Johns Hopkins University Press.

Secretaría de Desarrollo Social, Mexico, and UNDP (United Nations Development Programme). 2004. "Más Allá de las Metas del Milenio." México DF.

Székely, M. 2006. "Pro-Growth Social Policies for Latin America." In *Economic Growth with Equity: Challenges for Latin America*, ed. Ricardo French-Davis and Jose Luis Machinea, 126–52. New York: Palgrave Macmillan.

8

Gender Mainstreaming: Making It Happen

Rekha Mehra and Geeta Rao Gupta

Gender mainstreaming is now at a critical crossroads. Many early supporters are disillusioned with the way it has worked so far and are beginning to feel that it has failed.[1] This chapter argues that it may be too soon to pass judgment because, from the perspective of a development agency, the most critical element of mainstreaming—mainstreaming in operations—has not yet been seriously attempted. Implementation has focused solely on internal organizational dimensions, such as staffing, policies, developing indicators, and staff training, which are often interpreted as preconditions or precursors to interventions at the operational level.[2] This chapter asserts that although mainstreaming gender in operations requires some of those organizational elements, it does not have to wait for all those changes to be implemented. It can begin in an entrepreneurial and strategic way and show success in small measures to gain credibility.

Achieving progress is especially important now because the United Nations (UN) Millennium Development Goals (MDGs), especially MDG3 on gender equality and the empowerment of women, offer an invaluable opportunity to reinvigorate efforts to achieve positive development outcomes. In addition, since the first World Conference on Women, held in Mexico City in 1975, a vast amount of experience and knowledge has been acquired and become available on what works and what does not in development interventions across different sectors. This information can be applied to make more rapid progress on mainstreaming gender into operations. As results emerge and development effectiveness improves from mainstreaming gender in operations, success and growing experience will generate additional interest, learning, and enthusiasm, and the process will gather momentum. Changes at the operations level will also improve the lives of women and men—the purpose for which gender mainstreaming was adopted. Concrete results in increased development effectiveness constitute a way forward in the current impasse with gender mainstreaming and will make important and growing contributions toward achieving the wider institutional goals of empowerment and equality for low-income and disenfranchised people that are not currently being met.

Background

Gender mainstreaming was adopted as a major strategy for promoting gender equality at the Fourth World Conference on Women in 1995. That conference called for mainstreaming gender in all Critical Areas of Concern, including poverty, human rights, economy, violence against women, and armed conflict. In addition, the Beijing Platform of Action established that gender analysis should be undertaken on the respective situations and contributions of both women and men before undertaking development policies and programs.

The inclusion of a goal on gender equality and the empowerment of women in the MDGs reestablished the commitment voiced in Beijing. In addition, in outlining the way forward toward achieving that goal, the report of the Task Force on Education and Gender Equality of the UN Millennium Project reinforced the importance of investing in gender mainstreaming as a tool and reiterated the need to expedite mainstreaming responses and actions and put in place the systems to hold institutions accountable.

In the decade since gender mainstreaming was endorsed and adopted by countries and institutions, however, it has yet to be fully implemented anywhere. It is not surprising then that the world fell behind on a key target set for MDG3—eliminating gender disparity in primary and secondary education by 2005. Over the years, the attempt to mainstream gender in a wide range of development agencies has, however, elicited important lessons, insights, and some evidence. These lessons can now be used to model future success and to achieve the target set for 2015 for MDG3—to eliminate gender disparity in primary, secondary, and tertiary education—and to improve development effectiveness overall.

This critique examines what it will take to effectively implement gender mainstreaming. The chapter is restricted to implementation issues within development agencies, although in discussing those issues, it draws on the experience of countries that have sought to mainstream gender into their policies and programs to better address the development challenges they face.

Definition

The commonly accepted and most widely used definition of gender mainstreaming is the one adopted by the UN Economic and Social Council:

> Mainstreaming a gender perspective is the process of assessing the implications for women and men of any planned action, including legislation, policies or programmes, in all areas and at all levels. It is a strategy for making women's as well as men's concerns and experiences an integral dimension of the design, implementation, monitoring and evaluation of policies and programs in all political, economic and societal spheres so that women and men benefit equally and inequality is not perpetuated. The ultimate goal is to achieve gender equality. (UN ECOSOC 1997)

Gender mainstreaming was adopted mainly to address the perceived failure of previous strategies, such as women-specific projects, to bring about significant changes in women's status. There was widespread consensus that the failure of women-specific projects in the 1970s and 1980s was due to the marginalization of those projects. Gender mainstreaming was designed to overcome this marginalization and to bring gender-equality issues into the core of development activities.

Interpretations, Applications, and Results of Gender Mainstreaming

As currently understood, gender mainstreaming encompasses all aspects of planning, implementing, and monitoring any social, political, or economic action. A common understanding is that implementation involves changes in both "internal" organizational and "external" operational procedures. The former refers to changes needed within organizations to embrace the goals and values of gender mainstreaming and to alter systems and procedures to meet these goals. Changes may include staffing and personnel policies, such as hiring more women or appointing a particular percentage to leadership positions, or more structural elements, such as changing the culture of the organization through gender-equality mandates to make the workplace more egalitarian. The external dimension generally pertains to the steps needed to mainstream gender into development operations such as design, implementation, and evaluation. These steps may include influencing goals, strategies, and resource allocations at the start and providing specialized gender technical input, such as gender analysis, and technical assistance for the design, implementation, and evaluation phases.

In a somewhat different framework, Rao and Kelleher (2002) suggest three dimensions in which changes are needed—in gender infrastructure, within organizations, and in institutions. Gender infrastructure involves putting in place gender policies, gender units, increased female staff and managers, and additional resources for women's programs. Organizational changes, similar to the internal formulation, pertain to "deep structure," such as improving the work-family balance and equalizing power relations within organizations. Institutional changes refer to broader societal shifts needed to change embedded power relationships and gender roles and relationships throughout the social structure in families, communities, markets, and the state. In Rao and Kelleher's view, gender mainstreaming involves the development and implementation of processes, capacities, and techniques, as well as shifts in structural and normative dimensions, such as beliefs, norms, and power. Although it is true that achieving gender equality in society requires all these changes, this formulation is missing a discrete focus on development operations, the more immediate concern of development organizations.

In response to the call for gender mainstreaming, many development organizations, private donors, and nongovernmental organizations (NGOs) took steps to implement mainstreaming policies. They set up gender units, hired gender specialists, and adopted gender training. Some organizations also made budget allocations. On the operational side they required gender analysis at various stages of development assistance and some started working with other organizations, such as civil society or country governments and other donors (Hannan 2004; NMFA 2002; UNESCAP 2003).

At the country level, governments established national women's machineries (ministries, departments, or offices), charging them with responsibility for gender mainstreaming throughout government institutions and operations. In practice, women's machineries played multiple roles as policy coordinating units, knowledge and support providers, and advocates and catalysts (CIDA 2000). Like development organizations, they also appointed gender specialists and focal points and launched training programs for all staff. A few countries also established accountability mechanisms to assess progress.

The early and necessary steps to put structures and systems in place to begin to implement mainstreaming policies soon became the focus of gender mainstreaming. In the decade following Beijing, a great deal of energy and resources went into getting the organizational culture right.

Organizations launched extensive transformation processes to restructure internal systems and procedures and to change attitudes and values, especially male bias, primarily through gender training. Some international development agencies, such as Oxfam GB and NOVIB, also involved their developing country partners in these efforts. Other developing country organizations, such as BRAC, embraced these ideas themselves and started their own programs (Dawson 2005; Rao and Kelleher 2002; NMFA 2002; Van Dueren 2001). Most organizations met significant resistance and faced a steep learning curve about what it takes to change people's attitudes and values (Dawson 2005; Sandler 2002; Van Dueren 2001). As the realization grew that they were involved in a lengthy process, some organizations extended their time schedules and intensified their efforts. Others abandoned them.

During the decade of focus on internal organizational change, a new understanding began to emerge that gender mainstreaming required organizations to first demonstrate their own commitment to gender-equality goals and values and that this had to be done through significant internal organizational change. This understanding solidified into a stronger implicit assumption that internal organizational changes were a precondition for mainstreaming gender in operations. As Oxfam staff put it, "Could we realistically expect to achieve at the programme-level what we could not achieve in our own workplace?" (Moser and Moser [2005] from Oxfam [2003, 4]). Moser and Moser report that organizational culture was mentioned as a constraint to successful gender mainstreaming by international NGOs and their developing country partners, and by the United Nations Development Programme (UNDP) and U.K. Department for International Development (DFID). The end result of these understandings was an absence of focus on gender in operations and the loss of a decade of opportunity to acquire experience and learning and to show impact on development on the ground.

Recent reviews and evaluations show a huge gap between policy commitments made at Beijing and actual implementation (Hannan 2004; Moser and Moser 2005). In fact, evaluators assert that policy commitments to gender mainstreaming "evaporated" or became "invisible" in planning and implementation (Macdonald 2003). Other assessments describe implementation as "patchy" and "embryonic." The gap is most pronounced in mainstreaming gender into operations (Aasen 2006; Norad 2005; UNDP 2006; Tornqvist 2006). A review of UN agencies found that many had not even taken the first step of using gender analysis to inform policies and programs

(Hannan 2004). Moser and Moser (2005) studied 14 international development agencies representing a mix of bilateral and multilateral donors, UN agencies, and NGOs and also found that gender was not reflected in country and strategy documents. Because these documents form the basis for developing sector programs and interventions, this shortcoming at the start of the process is reflected throughout planning, design, implementation, and monitoring and evaluation processes. Perhaps reflecting the imbalance between internal organizational focus and programming, an Organisation for Economic Co-operation and Development (OECD) Assistance Committee review found that evaluations also focused exclusively on organizational mainstreaming processes and not on results (Watkins 2004), even though the goal of gender mainstreaming is precisely to have an impact and to show results—to demonstrate development effectiveness.

A second widespread understanding that limits gender mainstreaming is that all staff should be responsible for its success. A potentially contrary outcome of this understanding is that when mainstreaming is everyone's task, it can become nobody's responsibility. This was the experience of the Dutch government in attempting to mainstream gender throughout the policy-making process. An immediate consequence of the policy's adoption was closure of all gender-equality offices at the local level—nobody assumed specific responsibility, procedures did not change, and as a result, gender-equality policies totally disappeared from local government (Verloo 2001). There is a real danger that gender-equality goals can be swept away by the mainstream, instead of changing it. Worse still, it can provide an easy "out" for not addressing gender in an effective and coherent manner (NMFA 2002).

Evidence from experience shows that most staff do not assume, let alone fulfill, gender-mainstreaming responsibilities. In most cases the task falls upon key individuals who are willing or appointed to take on the responsibility. Many factors are behind this lack of commitment to assume gender mainstreaming responsibilities. Staff may be reluctant to take on additional work or they may think they lack the knowledge and skills for it. Also important, they may lack motivation because they may not see a connection between incorporating gender considerations and the success of their own work goals and plans (Khan 2003; NMFA 2002; UNDP 2006; UNESCAP 2003).

Along with the requirement for all staff to be responsible for gender mainstreaming comes the expectation that they should be gender aware and responsive, conversant with gender issues, and knowledgeable about them. Often they do not have this knowledge and may state that this is a personal obstacle in addressing gender issues. Oxfam GB's country-based staff, for example, stated that their work on gender was "not up to level" because they lacked training and would welcome an opportunity to obtain it (Zuckerman 2002a). Acknowledging the difficulty, organizations attempted to address it in various ways, the most important being through training and by the appointment of gender focal points. Neither has worked well so far.

The role of gender focal points is to act as resource persons, complementing and supplementing the work of gender specialists, thereby extending more widely the outreach of a gender unit within an organization. In many cases, however, gender focal points have not been successful. They often get marginalized. They tend not to be gender experts themselves, are often young and inexperienced, and lack clout and influence. They take on, or are assigned, focal point duties in addition to their routine responsibilities, and can experience difficulty managing their competing time demands and responsibilities. It is an issue that cuts across development agencies (NMFA 2002). Rao Gupta (2004) found this to be the case in the World Health Organization as did Tornqvist (2006) among most agencies in a review that included 11 multilateral and bilateral organizations.[3]

The experience with gender training has generally been less than satisfactory. Staff pushed to perform quickly demand training, as reflected in Zuckerman (2002a), cited above. Organizations responded by investing heavily in time and resources in all types of training, such as gender sensitization, gender concepts and analysis, and, much less so, specialized sector- or project-based training. Except for raising awareness, the response to a decade of training has been dissatisfaction reflected in negative attitudes toward gender issues and continuing lack of understanding about basic concepts. Training participants claim they are unable to see the relevance of the training and that they do not acquire the skills they need to apply it to their own work. The dissatisfaction ends up being identified as a "need" for more and better training at all levels (Moser and Moser 2005). It does not translate, as it should and, as argued below, as a need for a completely different type of technical and hands-on, sector-specific and project-specific training that builds capacity to integrate gender into specific types of operational work.

Thus, a decade after Beijing, gender mainstreaming is in crisis. There is a sense among some proponents that it has fallen off the agenda of international organizations and countries and, in some cases, has been displaced by attention to the MDGs (Watkins 2004). They are, therefore, discouraged. They believe that little has been accomplished and less has changed (Macdonald 2003; NMFA 2002; UNDP 2006; World Bank 2005; Watkins 2004). However, these conclusions may be hasty and the disillusionment premature. As this chapter shows, gender mainstreaming has not been pursued fully or systematically enough to support definitive conclusions about its success or failure. In most cases the process is incomplete or not properly implemented, and in some cases it has been abandoned midstream. Most important, especially in the context of multilateral and bilateral development organizations, the process of gender mainstreaming has stopped short of operations—the very dimension that has an impact on development and can show results of development effectiveness.

However, the few organizations that have been successful in mainstreaming gender into their operations offer important initial lessons for speeding up the process of gender mainstreaming where it really counts—in improving development effectiveness and the lives of people, both women and men. The next section takes a look at case study evidence on successes in gender mainstreaming in operations to determine what works and to discover commonalities that might point the way forward.

What Works

In determining what works in mainstreaming gender into operations, there is very limited information to draw upon because, as noted, this has not been the focus of gender mainstreaming activities so far. Nevertheless, the little information available enables us to begin to draw out common factors and to test a new approach. The three cases presented below are a violence prevention initiative for Latin America and the Caribbean at the Inter-American Development Bank (IDB); five NGO-implemented, community-based, poverty-eradication programs in Africa; and an infrastructure development project at the Asian Development Bank (ADB).

In 1996 the IDB launched a major initiative to address violence, in response to demand from countries in Latin America and the Caribbean to address a serious and growing problem in the region. Between 1998 and 2004 the IDB approved loans worth $123 million for violence prevention in Chile, Colombia, Honduras, Jamaica, and Uruguay and leveraged substantial counterpart funds for this purpose in all five countries. The IDB mainstreamed the reduction of domestic violence against women into this broader initiative to enhance citizen security. Gender-based activities took different forms in each country and included, in Colombia, data collection on domestic violence and police training to handle cases of domestic violence; in Jamaica, training for judges and probation officers on intrafamily violence; and in Honduras and Uruguay, components to prevent domestic violence and treat its victims. Buvinić (2004) identifies six key elements that contributed to success and can form the basis for replication: relevance, leadership, grant financing, expertise, research, and innovation. They are shown in box 8.1.

The second example is of five NGO affiliates of InterAction: CARE/Niger, Catholic Relief Services (CRS)/Kenya, Heifer/Zambia, Lutheran World Relief (LWR)/Kenya, and World Vision/Ghana, each of which systematically took measures to integrate gender into their programs. In the relatively short time frame of a year or two, they were able to demonstrate both development effectiveness and reductions in poverty in the poor rural communities in which they worked (James-Sebro 2005). Three of the five organizations,

---

Box 8.1
Factors Contributing to Effective Gender Mainstreaming in a
Violence Prevention Initiative at the Inter-American Development Bank

---

- *Relevance.* A high priority issue for citizens because Latin America and the Caribbean is the second most violent region in the world and there was growing awareness of the victimization of women.
- *Leadership.* The IDB president launched the initiative and, most important, assigned resources to it.
- *Grant financing.* The IDB and the Nordic Trust Fund awarded modest but critical grant funding to the initiative.
- *Availability of expertise.* The IDB tapped into local expertise in the region on domestic violence, which facilitated research and project interventions.
- *Research.* Research showed both the intrinsic and instrumental value of mainstreaming attention to domestic violence and made a sound economic case for investments to reduce it.
- *Openness to innovation.* The opportunity for mainstreaming arose in the launch of a new set of operations—citizen security lending. Gender could be mainstreamed from the start and increased the likelihood that it would be incorporated in future designs.

Source: Buvinić (2004) in UN Millennium Project (2005).

CRS, World Vision, and CARE were engaged in multisectoral work in such activities as health, HIV/AIDS, livelihood security, agriculture, microfinance, and education. LWR's focus was on improving smallholder farming, while the Heifer projects were in livestock development and farming.

All five organizations embraced aspects of InterAction's gender-mainstreaming framework, which is rooted in four key dimensions to promote change—political will, technical capacity, accountability, and organizational culture. The framework encompasses both organizational and operational elements. The NGOs embraced both dimensions but focused on making a difference in their operations. World Vision/Ghana, for example, devoted 2 percent of its budget to gender mainstreaming throughout its operations. Heifer/Zambia challenged prevailing taboos by giving animals to women and training the women in their upkeep and care. By changing its selection criteria, LWR in Kenya increased women's participation in agriculture training programs. Organizational change actions included increasing the number of women staff, setting up gender task forces, and reviewing personnel policies and practices in light of their impact on women.

Significant benefits resulted from these concerted efforts, both for the African communities and for the organizations themselves. The economic and social benefits to communities included greater agricultural production, better sanitation, improved health and nutrition indicators, and improved primary school enrollment rates, particularly for girls. There were also significant changes in cultural attitudes toward the division of labor in the household and field. Factors contributing to these successes are shown in box 8.2. Some of them mirror those contributing to success in the IDB's violence-prevention initiative.

In Bangladesh, the ADB was successful in mainstreaming gender in a rural infrastructure development project called TRIDP. The project objectives were to accelerate agricultural and nonfarm economic and social development in 13 districts by improving roads, bridges, and culverts; tree planting; construction of local government complexes; and improvements to rural markets and construction of women's sections in them. Mainstreaming gender enabled more than 2,000 women to obtain steady employment and wages for the duration of the project; increased business skills and opportunities for women in retail; enhanced women's mobility and self-confidence; and improved household living standards, nutrition, and education for children (Thomas, Lateef ,and Sultana 2005; Pulley, Lateef, and Begum 2004). Upfront institutional dimensions that

Box 8.2
Factors Contributing to Effective Gender Mainstreaming in NGOs and Projects in Africa

- *Poverty eradication linked to program quality,* which was important for acceptance by project staff and the community.
- *Clearly articulated gender policy* and action plans; all organizations had gender equality in their social justice missions.
- *Support from top leadership* in the organization, who understood and acted upon the link between gender equality and poverty alleviation and encouraged greater participation by women internally and in project communities.
- *Gender embraced in its fullest application to both sexes,* not just to women or men as targets or obstacles but rather as partners; proactively hired women for senior-level positions, hired young women, and supported nontraditional roles for women.
- *Political will* in organizational headquarters passed on to the field by senior leadership and backed by policies and directives.
- *Multifaceted strategies* for gender mainstreaming that came out of organizational self-assessments.
- *Technical capacity built* among organizational and project staff and, in some cases, beneficiaries, through training and development of gender-analysis tools.
- *Gender technical expertise enhanced* because all organizations hired a gender specialist or gender coordinator

Source: James-Sebro 2005.

contributed to success were the ADB's adoption of a clear gender policy, operational guidelines, and support from leadership. Mandating a country gender assessment helped to identify key issues and strategic possibilities for action while external pressure from donors helped to maintain momentum on mainstreaming, as did their additional financial support. In implementation, Gender Action Plans (GAP) provided focus and accountability, and gender experts provided ongoing technical support. Other contributing factors were project- and sector-specific training for project implementers and community members and careful monitoring and fine-tuning of activities during implementation. Key lessons learned about how a GAP contributes to project success are summarized in box 8.3.

Box 8.3
How a Gender Action Plan Can Deliver Gender-Equality Results: Lessons from the Asian Development Bank's Loan Operations

- *Design* that is linked to the main project components, is based on detailed gender analysis of each component, and offers a strong rationale to support gender mainstreaming.
- *Realistic targets* that can be achieved through step-by-step progress closely linked to project objectives.
- *Step-by-step actions* spelled out to accomplish each gender-related target, flexible implementation, and a learn-as-you go approach to address unanticipated constraints.
- *Structured training* opportunities for project team members and other stakeholders to promote ownership and commitment to the GAP.
- *Sufficient skills and resources* developed in the project team to ensure GAP targets can be met.
- *A participatory approach* to designing the GAP to ensure all team members understand why resources are allocated to specific measures to ensure that women benefit.
- *Leadership and good management* from senior management in the country's executing agency to overcome challenges and resistance during implementation.
- *Consistent monitoring of indicators* suitable to assessing progress across all gender activities.
- *Gender expertise* of a local gender specialist to ensure country-specific sustained input and consultations with women beneficiaries and civil society networks.

Source: Thomas, Lateef, and Sultana 2005.

These three operational case studies and the results of assessments of gender mainstreaming in other organizations have a number of features in common. These common features are highlighted below with a view to determining a pattern for success that can be replicated more widely by other organizations.

The adoption of a gender policy was deemed important in the case of the ADB and one of the five NGOs. The value lay in spelling out organizational commitment as a reference point for action. However, lack of a policy in three of the five NGOs did not impede mainstreaming. Based on this evidence, it is not clear whether a gender policy is necessary to move forward. In fact, most multilateral and bilateral development organizations now have gender policies and some also have operational guidelines. However, the evidence does show that having a policy does not guarantee success. A mandate without backing lacks "teeth." By itself it is not enough to ensure action or implementation. The policy mandate must be accompanied by leadership, financial support, and technical expertise.

Leadership was critical for success in each case. At the organizational level, leadership from the top proved necessary to get the ball rolling. At the IDB, the president himself took the initiative to launch the violence-prevention program. In the NGOs, top leaders provided the impetus for mainstreaming. Once launched, leadership was needed to keep the ball in motion. Although it was important for leaders to express will and commitment, it was even more important for them to demonstrate it by allocating resources. The IDB president backed up his commitment to violence prevention and the gendered elements of it by allocating resources. The ADB showed that leadership was also important at the operational level—the project director's support, openness to learning, and personal attention proved invaluable to successfully mainstream gender. Some recent evaluations (2003–06) of bilateral and multilateral institutions show support for gender mainstreaming at high levels but inconsistent support or lack of it at senior management levels (Tornqvist 2006).

In all cases mainstreaming worked best when its relevance was clear. The relevance and civic support for the violence-prevention initiative in Latin America and the Caribbean derived from the fact that the region is the second most violent in the world, with rates increasing since the mid-1980s and high rates of violence against women. Awareness of the need to mitigate violence, especially against women, was growing and violence reduction was an important priority for people. Related to relevance is the crucial issue of making the links with gender through research and analysis, whether in violence prevention or poverty reduction or any other issue. Research at the IDB made the case that violence was mostly a learned behavior and that one of the earliest opportunities for learning violence was in the home. Therefore, domestic violence deserved attention in its own right and as a key to preventing the intergenerational transmission of violence. Additional studies of the costs of violence made the case for the value of investing in prevention. At the ADB, gender analysis revealed how women and men used infrastructure in different ways and where the potential opportunities lay for engaging low-income women and changing their life options. Assessing and documenting project implementation and results made an important contribution to filling the prevailing gaps in knowledge about how to mainstream gender into operations.

Also related to relevance is the extent to which mainstreaming contributes to program quality and development effectiveness. In Africa, James-Sebro (2005, 124) found that mainstreaming was most successful when it was "directly and clearly linked to the improvement of program quality and, specifically, to the eradication of poverty." The links between gender and poverty were especially compelling to the intervention communities and local staff, and facilitated adoption of gender-based goals and activities. Similarly, in the World Food Programme the gender policy was clear to staff, 90 percent of which is field-based. They understood that 7 out of 10 of the world's hungry are women and girls, they are in charge of households, and food in their control promotes food security and reduces hunger and poverty (Women's Commission 2006).

The technical skills of gender experts were employed in all cases and proved invaluable. Each of the NGOs in Africa hired a gender expert to function as an internal resource. The local gender expert in the ADB's Bangladesh resident mission played a critical role in the initial process of mainstreaming. Later, with additional support from the International Fund for Agricultural Development, the project hired a dedicated gender specialist (Thomas, Lateef, and Sultana 2005). In fact, the ADB regards the hiring of local gender experts at resident missions as being the main driver for gender mainstreaming in country projects (S. Lateef personal communication). In another context, Zuckerman (2002a, 2002b) suggests that the relative success in integrating gender concerns into Rwanda's Poverty Reduction Strategy Paper, as compared with other countries that did not, was mainly the result of the use of a gender expert.

Another critical role for gender experts during implementation is to provide technical assistance to implementing staff. In Bangladesh, gender experts played a vital role in monitoring project implementation and in recommending midcourse corrections. Expertise was also used to determine the kind of information and skills project staff needed to implement gender-specific activities. In this case, the ADB offered extensive and specialized training tailored to meeting mainstreaming goals in the project context. The training generated its own momentum and, in the end, proved most effective when it triggered peer-to-peer exchange (T. Pulley, personal communication). In other cases, specialized training may be needed on related issues, such as addressing religious concerns about potential changes in gender roles and relations. CARE/Niger, for example, found that it had to involve local religious leaders to address gender concerns in its programs (James-Sebro 2005). Training appears to be most valuable when it is context specific and tailored to operational goals.

Finally, the need for accountability is widely mentioned in the literature (Hannan 2004; NMFA 2002; Norad 2005; World Bank 2005). Accountability is one of the four key steps needed for mainstreaming in InterAction's framework, and James-Sebro's (2005) assessment identifies lack of accountability mechanisms as a shortcoming of the NGO programs. In the ADB context, accountability was systematically integrated into project implementation via the GAP that included a monitoring and evaluation framework. The monitoring and evaluation effort was effectively used to keep on track and to determine results and impact. At the organizational level, at the ADB, mainstreaming was greatly helped by a subtle but powerful accountability mechanism—board member attention and queries about gender in loan projects and Country Strategies and Programs. At DFID, integration of gender targets into the performance management framework helped institutionalize gender mainstreaming in primary and secondary education and maternal health. These sectors also regularly tracked and reported results (DFID 2006).

Logically, accountability would appear to be necessary. Its value in facilitating project-level implementation and demonstrating results is clear. However, its worth is impeded by a lack of attention to broader (nongender) project outcomes and effects in many organizations. Evaluation of gender results, more specifically, is constrained by the ongoing shortage of gender-disaggregated data and also, perhaps, by the lack of agreed-on gender-equality indicators. The role of accountability at the highest organizational level is also clear; it is one of the elements that gives a policy mandate teeth. More broadly, this analysis suggests that accountability for gender mainstreaming may not need to be as diffuse as generally believed. Rather, the need may be concentrated at the very top and at the implementation level. This makes the task of designing accountability mechanisms more manageable. It also suggests that such mechanisms should be strategic and carefully targeted. Finally, it argues for doing a better job at building accountability into project operations because this can enhance overall effectiveness.

Because this discussion focuses on operations, it abstracts somewhat from one broader critical dimension that must underpin development activities, namely, country cooperation. Razavi and Miller (1995) found that the work of mainstreaming was much harder when a country had not bought into the process. However, in such countries as Cambodia, Rwanda, and South Africa, which have demonstrated commitment to gender equality by writing it into their constitutions and by making legal and other reforms, mainstreaming is accepted (UN Millennium Project 2005). In these countries, it may be relatively easy to collaborate and build on local support. Of interest, the countries adopted gender-equality and mainstreaming goals in the context of civil strife, genocide (Rwanda), and rapid changes. These conditions may have created an open atmosphere favorable to the new perspectives and creativity required for mainstreaming gender. But these examples should not be taken to mean that equality and mainstreaming cannot be pursued under more ordinary circumstances.

It is quite possible through information, education, and advocacy to build awareness and demand. Civil society groups can often serve as helpful partners in this process and so can women's groups, especially those already involved in raising gender and development awareness. In the 1990s the ADB worked fairly successfully with governments and civil society organizations in a number of Asian countries to further awareness of the role of gender in development (ADB 1999). These activities, in some cases, paved the way for later mainstreaming. DFID's (2006) gender evaluation found that lobbying by a team of civil society organizations and donors worked well in integrating gender concerns into Poverty Reduction Strategies whereas a gender-blind process did not. Support for women's organizations can contribute to raising demand for better development and for holding institutions accountable for progress. Such support is likely to become even more important as donors realign their programs in keeping with country-led priorities agreed on in the Paris Declaration on Aid Effectiveness (2005). Australia has already incorporated support for women's organizations as part of its gender-equality strategy (AusAID 2007).

Besides building country support and ownership for mainstreaming and development, nurturing women's and civil society groups and movements and soliciting their participation are intrinsically valuable exercises because they enable women and men to build capacity and confidence in democratic processes. For women, specifically, these groups provide opportunities for visibility and for them to begin to change cultural perceptions about women's roles and place in society.

An Alternate Approach

Refocusing gender mainstreaming on operations, based on the experiences cited above, requires adopting a quite different approach from the one used so far. It means questioning some of the common understandings described above. It requires new perspectives and the generation of new information and knowledge. Perhaps a more difficult task, it also requires new and different ways of looking at and employing current methods for the purpose of improving operations. The following describes an alternate approach supportive of mainstreaming in development operations, which is grounded in these fundamental ideas:

- Gender mainstreaming in operations is possible and necessary, and under certain circumstances it can occur fairly rapidly.
- It is important to get results on the ground because such success is motivating and helps to lower organizational resistance.
- Success based on demonstrable results contributes to learning and serves as a model for replication.
- All the organizational pieces do not have to be in place for gender mainstreaming at the operational level to succeed. It is possible to get results by adopting a pragmatic approach that responds to strategic operational opportunities.
- Once an opportunity for gender mainstreaming in operations has been identified, it is important to have a systematic and sustained approach, to allocate sufficient financial resources, to employ gender expertise, and to show results.
- An instrumental approach that focuses on operations can yield intrinsic benefits for women.

The alternate approach based on the above principles is driven by the need to improve development effectiveness. It is entrepreneurial, results oriented, and has impact. It delivers concrete benefits to women and low-income communities. It offers the opportunity to model success that can be replicated and can build momentum.

The explanation of the alternate approach begins by clarifying that the term "gender mainstreaming" refers to both a process and the goal to be achieved. As a process, it is important not to expect gender mainstreaming to instantly deliver the bigger institutional changes in norms and values—those needed to change people's hearts and minds. Rather, it is important to focus on what *can* be accomplished in practical terms, especially in meeting the immediate and urgent needs of low-income people and improving their lives. The gradual accretion of such changes over time is much more likely to result in the bigger goals of cultural and social change and empowerment and equality. By contrast, failing to attempt the practical changes by neglecting operational opportunities is not likely to result in achievement of the bigger goals.

Therefore, contrary to the dictum that a gender perspective needs to be incorporated into all policies and programs, the alternate approach requires being *strategic* at all stages of the development process. Initially, it requires being strategic in selecting the development issue on which to work. It requires identifying and acting on strategic opportunities that are likely to yield tangible results to people on the ground. It implies working on high priority development issues, such as poverty reduction or violence prevention. A significant advantage of this approach is that the issue already has *relevance*. It does not have to be proved. It requires less effort to convince nonbelievers of its importance. Another advantage of a strategic approach of this type is that it helps order priorities for gender-based input and intervention all along the development process or operation to achieve the broader development goals.

However, it may still, and often does, require demonstrating the gender link. This can be done through *research and analysis*. To the extent that research can demonstrate the costs of not investing in gender or the value added of doing so, the case is strengthened. These are tasks for gender specialists.

After the issue has been selected, *gender expertise* is needed to lay out a course of action.[4] Once again, it is not necessary to do everything or to act on all levels. Nor is it necessary for everyone involved in the project to have gender-based knowledge and skills, just as it is not necessary for sector-specific technical experts to be knowledgeable about each others' expertise. However, it is helpful for gender experts also to have specialized sector- or issue-based knowledge. Such sector-specific expertise can help the gender expert gain credibility with sector specialists and determine a strategic and practical course of action or set of actions likely to yield the desired results. Succeeding also requires selecting the appropriate levels on which to act, not necessarily acting on all levels. Thus, it may be necessary and possible to obtain the support and increase the understanding of the project director or task manager to mainstream gender but not as necessary at other levels. The important point is that who is to be influenced and what tasks have to be accomplished for successful mainstreaming will have to be empirical and context specific. This greatly, and helpfully, narrows down the tasks.

When a course of action has been determined in line with the broader operational goals, gender expertise is needed to provide *hands-on technical assistance* on the "how to" of mainstreaming to project staff. Gender experts are also needed to design monitoring and evaluation systems and to document outcomes. Monitoring is important for ensuring that mainstreaming and project implementation are on track and for troubleshooting and, if implementation is not on track, offering solutions for midcourse corrections. Following project completion, gender expertise is needed for documenting results, effectiveness, and strategy. This documentation is vital for filling the current gap in knowledge about gender mainstreaming in operations. It is also important for building a body of knowledge in this area.

Contrary to popular belief that additional resources are not needed for gender mainstreaming, the allocation of appropriate *financial resources* is actually critical for success (see chapter 5 for more details). As with any other project component, financing is needed to ensure that the necessary technical "backstopping" described above occurs. More important, financing is needed to ensure that resources are available to fund activities and components deemed vital to the success of mainstreaming. For example, ensuring that women have the opportunity to obtain training on an agricultural extension project may require holding additional sessions. The need may arise because of a cultural taboo against women participating in coeducational sessions or to accommodate the time constraints posed by women's household duties. In any case, financial resources would be needed to add sessions. Financial resources are also needed to ensure that the required gender expertise is available. As gender mainstreaming becomes more successful in an organization and shows results, the demand for gender specialists can be expected to grow, not diminish.

Accountability is vital to this approach. Accountability is the means for determining whether mainstreaming has happened. Only by examining outcomes and results and assessing them relative to expectations (or baseline conditions) will it be possible to determine the extent to which gender and development goals have been met. Accountability requires setting up a *monitoring and evaluation system,* preferably right at the start of a project. It also requires adopting indicators, and both process and outcome indicators are necessary. Process indicators can help determine whether project implementation, including gender goals and activities, are on track and can help diagnose and fix problems. Indicators are also important for assessing, if relevant, the extent of community and women's participation on the project. Outcome indicators are needed for assessing results—whether project goals were met and the extent to which the economic and social conditions and the well-being of target populations improved. Most important, if intended goals and improvements did not occur, or were partially achieved, accountability would require determining the causes, learning from them, and fixing them.

Understanding gender outcomes, and hence, the success of gender mainstreaming on a project, would require the adoption of *gender-specific indicators*. For instance, in a rural poverty reduction program it would be important to know not only whether economic opportunities and incomes increased overall but also if opportunities for women improved, if their incomes were higher, and if they had control over their earnings. Admittedly, in an improving economic environment, women's incomes could improve without particular attention to gender. This would be a fortunate and happy outcome. Equally, women's economic situations could worsen, even with improvements in the overall economy; this would signal a need for gender analysis to understand the reasons and to remedy the process.

However, accountability for gender mainstreaming may be difficult to implement because overall project accountability mechanisms tend to be weak in many organizations. Conversely, the need to determine accountability for mainstreaming offers one among many reasons for strengthening project accountability mechanisms. Development effectiveness overall would benefit from doing so.

Finally, undertaking something new, like gender mainstreaming, in organizations with established ways of doing things, and garnering the resources needed, requires *leadership*. Not only does the leadership have to have will and commitment, it has to be open to innovation and, of great importance, be willing to allocate resources and to expect results. While the support of top leadership is invaluable, leadership may be needed from other levels as well and would have to be determined contextually for each project.

The approach described here diverges from current frameworks in that it focuses mainstreaming around the particular development issue being addressed operationally. In a sense, gender mainstreaming is "driven" by the issue and the practical problems involved in solving it rather than by the need to implement a generalized process. It thus offers a way to make it meaningful to those involved in implementation while simultaneously helping to structure gender-based responses tailored to the development issue at hand. It requires picking only those actions that are likely to help bring about results—not doing everything. It also requires selecting the appropriate levels on which to act. It may, therefore, help in addressing the details needed for successful mainstreaming—the selection of implementing variables to act upon, and a way to determine the right mix, level, and type of actions required to accomplish a selected development operation, meet its goals effectively, and make a difference in the lives of both women and men.

Moving Forward

Even with a new approach, moving forward on gender mainstreaming to achieve MDG3 goals and targets will require a sense of urgency, renewed commitment, and most important, financial resources. Moving forward will require focusing on poverty reduction and economic development—issues that must be at the heart of development work in a world in which a billion people still live on less than a dollar a day (Chen and Ravallion 2004). It will require creativity and innovation in identifying problems, devising solutions, and testing interventions. It will need technical gender expertise in multiple sectors, especially economic development and poverty reduction, research and analysis, project implementation, and monitoring and evaluation. Regional or country-specific technical expertise will also be needed. The strength of this technical work will depend on the availability of gender-disaggregated data, a continuing gap, although one that is beginning to be met.

Many countries have taken actions to move forward on the MDGs in a focused way by, for example, concentrating their poverty reduction strategies on the MDGs. Meanwhile, donors have begun to coordinate their efforts, especially on poverty reduction and on HIV/AIDS prevention, care, and treatment. In the latter, for example, donors have adopted the "three ones" approach of having in a country a common national strategy, a single coordinating body, and one monitoring and evaluation framework. A gap still remains, however, in addressing the gender dimensions of HIV/AIDS, as it does in poverty reduction.

It is important also to caution that the new aid modalities involving harmonization and general budget support pose significant new challenges and, in practice, have diverted attention away from gender equality and mainstreaming (Aasen 2006; DFID 2006; Norad 2005). However, these new modalities also offer important new opportunities and avenues for gender mainstreaming, especially in country-level policy and dialogue and in preparation of Joint Country Assistance Strategies and Sector Wide Approaches. Every effort should be made to put gender into these agendas and integrate key gender indicators into results-monitoring frameworks associated with them. Influencing these processes will require gender representation not only in donor gender coordination forums but, critically, also in sectoral forums.

With renewed commitments fueling demand in countries and greater cooperation among donors, now is a good time to help countries success- fully meet their obligations on the MDGs, especially MDG3. It is also an opportune moment to launch the new approach to gender mainstreaming and to enhance the focus on operations. It is a time to seek out innovations, test new ways of gender mainstreaming, and have a greater impact. Doing so will require greater and more strategic financial investments in innova- tive mainstreaming and development efforts and in technical expertise to make them work. The payoff will be in reducing poverty and improving the lives of low-income women and men.

Conclusion

This chapter argues that although gender mainstreaming is a complex and lengthy process, it can be done. Gender mainstreaming offers a vision of the future—a vision that was articulated eloquently in the report of the UN Millennium Project Task Force on Education and Gender Equality as "a world in which women and men work together as equal partners to build better lives for themselves and their families... where women and men share equally in the enjoyment of basic capabilities, economic assets, voice, and freedom from fear and violence... where women and men share the care of children, the elderly, and the sick; the responsibil- ity of paid employment, and the joys of leisure" (UN Millennium Project 2005, 20).

Development organizations are already attempting to implement gen- der mainstreaming with varying degrees of success. Most important, such attempts have elicited useful lessons that must be used to move ahead to ensure that the next decade of gender mainstreaming is more successful. The MDGs, by setting time-bound targets, force us to expedite the process of learning and implementation to accomplish MDG3: gender equality and the empowerment of women. All that remains is the doing.

Notes

The authors would like to thank Mayra Buviníc, World Bank, for her constructive suggestions and comments; Aslihan Kes, program associate, ICRW, for research assistance; and Elvira S. Bustamante, executive assistant to the president, ICRW, for administrative support.
  1. See, for example, Aasen (2006) who reviewed nine evaluations of bilateral and multilateral institutions between 2002 and 2006 and found that they all pointed to the conclusion that gender mainstreaming had been unsuccessful.

2. The term "operations" is used here to describe all activities related to development projects or interventions designed to have a beneficial impact on low-income people.
3. Institutions were the Australian Aid Agency (AusAID), Finland's Ministry of Foreign Affairs, Ireland, New Zealand, the Norwegian Agency for International Development Cooperation (Norad), the Swedish International Development Cooperation Agency (Sida), DFID, the International Labor Organization (ILO), UNDP, UN-Habitat, and the World Food Program.
4. Recent evaluations of gender mainstreaming by the UNDP (2006), Sida (2002a, 2002b), the World Bank (2005), and the ILO (2005) also emphasize the importance of gender expertise centrally located at head offices and at country offices (cited in Aasen 2006).

References

Aasen, Berit. 2006. "Lessons from Evaluations of Women and Gender Equality in Development Cooperation." Norad Synthesis Report No. 2006/1, Norwegian Institute for Urban and Regional Research (NIBR), Oslo.

ADB (Asian Development Bank). 1999. "Gender and Development: Weaving a Balanced Tapestry." ADB, Manila.

AusAID. 2007. *Gender Equality in Australia's Aid Program—Why and How.* Canberra: AusAID.

Buviníc, Mayra. 2004. "Mainstreaming Attention to Domestic Violence in Lending Operations: Six Elements of Inter-American Development Bank Success." Inter-American Development Bank, Washington, DC.

CIDA (Canadian International Development Agency). 2000. "Accelerating Change: Resources for Gender Mainstreaming." CIDA, Quebec.

Chen, Shaohua, and Martin Ravallion. 2004. "How Have the World's Poorest Fared Since the Early 1980s?" Policy Research Paper No. 3341, World Bank, Washington, DC.

Dawson, Elsa. 2005. "Strategic Gender Mainstreaming in Oxfam GB." *Gender and Development* 13 (2): 80–9.

DFID (Department for International Development, UK). 2006. "Evaluation of DFID's Policy and Practice in Support of Gender Equality and Women's Empowerment," vol. 1, Synthesis Report. Evaluation Report EV669, DFID, London.

Hannan, Carolyn. 2004. "Gender Mainstreaming: A Key Strategy for Promoting Gender Equality at National Level." Paper presented at "UN-ESCAP High-Level Intergovernmental Meeting to Review Regional Implementation of the Beijing Platform for Action and Its Regional and Global Outcomes," Bangkok, Thailand, September 7–10.

International Labour Office (ILO). 2005. "Thematic Evaluation Report: Gender Issues in Technical Cooperation." Geneva.

James-Sebro, Meryl. 2005. "Revealing the Power of Gender Mainstreaming: Enhancing Development Effectiveness of Non-Governmental Organizations in Africa." Interaction, Washington, DC.

Khan, Zohra. 2003. "Closing the Gap: Putting EU and UK Gender Policy into Practice: South Africa, Nicaragua, and Bangladesh." One World Action, London.

Macdonald, Mandy. 2003. "Gender Equality and Mainstreaming in the Policy and Practice of the UK Department for International Development." Womankind, London.

Moser, Caroline, and Annalise Moser. 2005. "Gender Mainstreaming Since Beijing: A Review of Successes and Limitations in International Institutions." *Gender and Development* 13 (2): 11–22.

NMFA (Norwegian Ministry of Foreign Affairs). 2002. "Strategies for Gender Equality: Is Mainstreaming a Dead End?" Report from Informal Consultation of Gender Focal Points in Multilateral Development Organizations, NMFA, Oslo.

Norad (Norwegian Agency for Development Cooperation). 2005. "Evaluation of the 'Strategy for Women and Gender Equality in Development Cooperation (1997–2005).'" Norad Evaluation Report 5/2005. Oslo. http://norad.no/default. asp?FILE=items/1651/108/Evaluering20av20kvinnestrategien.pdf.

Keating, Maree. 2003. "Taking a Lead on Gender Equality." *Links*. Oxfam. May.

Pulley, Tulin, Shireen Lateef, and Ferdousi Sultana Begum. 2004. "Making Infrastructure Work for Women in Bangladesh." In *Gender Mainstreaming in Action: Successful Innovations from Asia and the Pacific*. Washington, DC: InterAction's Commission on the Advancement of Women.

Rao, Aruna, and David Kelleher. 2002. "Unraveling Institutionalized Gender Inequality." Occasional Paper Series No. 8, Association for Women's Rights in Development, Toronto.

Rao Gupta, Geeta. 2004. "The Devil Is in the Details: Mainstreaming Gender in WHO." International Center for Research on Women (ICRW), Washington, DC.

Razavi, Shahra, and Carol Miller. 1995. "Gender Mainstreaming: A Study of Efforts by the UNDP, the World Bank, and the ILO to Institutionalize Gender Issues." UNRISD Occasional Paper No. 4, United Nations Research Institute for Social Development, Geneva.

Sandler, Joanne. 2002. "Strategies for Gender Equality: Is Mainstreaming a Dead End?" Speech by deputy executive director of UNIFEM. http://www.unifem. org/news_events/story_detail.php?StoryID=159.

Sida (Swedish International Development Cooperation Authority). 2002a. "Mainstreaming Gender Equality: Sida's Support for the Promotion of Gender Equality in Partner Countries." Evaluation Report 02/01, Sida, Stockholm. http:// www.sida.se/shared/jsp/download.jsp?f=Utv02-01HRejoms.pdf&a=2357.

———. 2002b. "Sweden's and Holland's Strategies for the Promotion of Gender Equality in Bolivia." Evaluation Report 02/09, Sida, Stockholm.

Thomas, Helen T., Shireen Lateef, and Ferdousi Sultana. 2005. "Gender Equality Results in ADB Projects: Bangladesh Country Report." Asian Development Bank, Manila.

Tornqvist, Annika. 2006. "Gender Mainstreaming Evaluations: An Assessment." Unpublished, World Bank, Washington, DC.

UNDP (United Nations Development Programme). 2006. "Evaluation of Gender Mainstreaming in UNDP." Evaluation Office, UNDP, New York.

UN ECOSOC (United Nations Economic and Social Council). *Agreed Conclusions 1997/2*, July 18, 1997. 1997/2. Online. UNHCR Refworld. http://www.unhcr .org/refworld/docid/4652c9fc2.html [accessed June 16, 2008].

UNESCAP (UN Economic and Social Commission for Asia and the Pacific). 2003. *Putting Gender Mainstreaming into Practice.* New York: United Nations.

UN Millennium Project. 2005. "Taking Action: Achieving Gender Equality and Empowering Women." Task Force on Education and Gender Equality, New York.

Van Dueren, Irma. 2001. "More Power, Less Poverty, Novib's Gender Policy Until 2000." E-Conference on Gender and Institutional Change, March.

Verloo, Mieke. 2001. "Another Velvet Revolution? Gender Mainstreaming and the Politics of Implementation." IWM Working Paper No. 5/2001, Vienna.

Watkins, Francis. 2004. "Evaluation of DFID Development Assistance: Gender Equality and Women's Empowerment. DFID's Experience of Gender Mainstreaming: 1995 to 2004." DFID, London.

Women's Commission for Refugee Women and Children. 2006. "Moving up the Food Chain: Lessons from Gender Mainstreaming at the World Food Programme." Women's Commission for Refugee Women and Children, New York.

World Bank. 2005. "Evaluating a Decade of World Bank Gender Policy: 1990–99." Operations Evaluation Department (OED), World Bank, Washington, DC.

Zuckerman, Elaine. 2002a. "Evaluation of Gender Mainstreaming in Advocacy Work on Poverty Reduction Strategy Papers (PRSPs)." Gender Action, Washington, DC.

———. 2002b. "A Primer on Poverty Reduction Strategy Papers and Gender." Gender Action, Washington, DC.

Index

ECO-AUDIT
Environmental Benefits Statement

The World Bank is committed to preserving endangered forests and natural resources. The Office of the Publisher has chosen to print *Equality for Women* on recycled paper with 30 percent postconsumer fiber in accordance with the recommended standards for paper usage set by the Green Press Initiative, a nonprofit program supporting publishers in using fiber that is not sourced from endangered forests. For more information, visit www.greenpressinitiative.org.

Saved:
- 8 trees saved
- 6 million BTUs
- 696 lbs. of CO_2 equivalent
- 2,888 gallons of wastewater
- 371 lbs. of solid waste

green press
INITIATIVE

www.ingramcontent.com/pod-product-compliance
Lightning Source LLC
Chambersburg PA
CBHW070544270326
41926CB00013B/2198